Foundations of Education

Also Available from Bloomsbury

Education for Social Change, Douglas Bourn
Global Citizenship Education, Edda Sant, Karen Pashby, and Lynette Shultz
Civic Contestation in Global Education, edited by Meira Levinson, Ellis Reid, Sara O'Brien, and Tatiana Geron
Educational Equity in a Global Context, edited by Meira Levinson, Tatiana Geron, Sara O'Brien, and Ellis Reid
Comparative and International Education: An Introduction, Esther E. Gottlieb, Radhika Iyengar, and Matthew A. Witenstein
Comparative and International Education, David Phillips and Michele Schweisfurth
Education and International Development, edited by Tristan McCowan and Elaine Unterhalter

Foundations of Education

American Schools and the Common Good

Maike Ingrid Philipsen and Hillary Parkhouse

BLOOMSBURY ACADEMIC
LONDON • NEW YORK • OXFORD • NEW DELHI • SYDNEY

BLOOMSBURY ACADEMIC
Bloomsbury Publishing Plc, 50 Bedford Square, London, WC1B 3DP, UK
Bloomsbury Publishing Inc, 1359 Broadway, New York, NY 10018, USA
Bloomsbury Publishing Ireland, 29 Earlsfort Terrace, Dublin 2, D02 AY28, Ireland

BLOOMSBURY, BLOOMSBURY ACADEMIC and the Diana logo are trademarks of Bloomsbury Publishing Plc

First published in the United States of America 2011

This edition published 2026

Cover design by Chris Bromley
Cover image: Tony via Adobe Stock

A catalogue record for this book is available from the British Library.

A catalog record for this book is available from the Library of Congress.

ISBN: HB: 978-1-350-44200-9
PB: 978-1-350-44202-3
ePDF: 978-1-350-44206-1
eBook: 978-1-350-44204-7

Typeset by Integra Software Services Pvt. Ltd.
Printed and bound in Great Britain

For product safety related questions contact productsafety@bloomsbury.com.

We dedicate this book to Nathan, Tobias, Letizia, and David Haller; Felix and Elise Parkhouse; and August Wergin, along with all children, who deserve good schools and qualified, caring teachers.

Contents

Figures

Tables

Preface

In writing this book, we had our own students in mind. They are typically at the beginning of their journey into educational careers. Some of them are uncertain about what or whom to teach or whether to teach at all, while others can hardly wait to enter the classroom. Still others may decide to become school counselors, administrators, or librarians, or to serve students in other ways.

This book was written as a foundation for understanding important issues that transcend grade levels, disciplines, and specific job descriptions, for these issues are central to all educators' professional preparation. They are enduring rather than faddish, big rather than small, and they affect each and every one of us insofar as they shape the context in which we practice our professions as educators.

Our intention is to provide thoughtful analysis that will allow both critical reflection and the construction of an interpretive framework giving structure to professional practice. The book is an outgrowth of our deep conviction that, no matter what specific challenge educators face during these times of political contentiousness and economic upheaval, they must still understand that professional work is more than a job with a prescribed set of activities. Teachers are and always have been professionals, and in order to act as such they must understand relationships between school and society. This includes not only relationships in classrooms, playgrounds, or school hallways but those in the larger political, economic, and social frameworks that impact the places where education occurs.

Good professional teaching necessitates reflective decision-making that depends on a thorough understanding of the historical and contemporary nature of the issues that influence professional practice. Prospective educators need familiarity with existing scholarship that sheds light on what shapes education. They need to see beyond their own immediate experience and situate their practice within the wealth of knowledge accumulated over time by scholars and fellow practitioners.

The book is organized by chapters focusing on issues that continue to play significant roles in schooling. These issues include teaching as a profession and school governance and control. They involve race, ethnicity, social class, gender, and disability, all connected with the quest for equal educational opportunities. They also touch on ideas of freedom of thought and belief, which roils contemporary education no less than the contemporary world of politics and diplomacy. Our analytic approach is a multidisciplinary one in which, rather than devoting one chapter to "the history of education," another to "the philosophy of education," and still another to "the sociology of education," and so on, these disciplinary lenses are used where appropriate for a richer treatment. Each chapter draws on relevant historical, philosophical, and sociological research of sufficient breadth and depth to ground prospective educators for subsequent professional studies.

The book is organized into seven chapters. Chapter 1 (Teaching as a Profession) introduces readers to the profession they are about to enter. It provides historical and philosophical background on how the role of teachers evolved over time, and it explores the struggle to be recognized as a profession and the efforts to find a more unified voice at the present time. Readers are presented with daily realities teachers face, selected ethical aspects of teaching, and an analysis of how the teaching profession serves the common good. Chapter 2 (School Governance and Control) includes the evolution of school governance and how schools are currently controlled, encompassing the role of school funding and the interplay of different stakeholders, reform efforts, and legislation.

Chapters 3 through 7 focus on specific aspects of schooling for the common good: social class, race and ethnicity, immigration and language, gender, and disabilities. Each chapter examines how its particular topic is engaged in the struggle for equal educational opportunity, and how that engagement has shaped educational theory and practice. The chapters also address ideas and conditions that illuminate both the successes and the continuing impediments to the provision of a strong education for all, with description and analysis of various policy initiatives and reform proposals aimed at change.

Chapter 3 (Social Class and Education) concerns how social class connects, historically and currently, with school funding, tracking, ability grouping, and school choice. Chapter 4 (Race, Ethnicity, and Education) examines the impact of race on American education in terms of racial socialization, social stratification, segregation/desegregation, and ethnic studies and culturally relevant education. Chapter 5 (Immigration, Language, and Education) addresses the history of the unity-diversity tension in American society and education, including the education of Native Americans and selected immigrant groups (Polish, Italian, Chinese, Central Americans, and undocumented immigrants) as well as controversies surrounding bilingual education and contemporary conditions for students learning English as a new language. Next, Chapter 6 (Gender, Sexuality, and Education) delves into gendered approaches to schooling, thinking and knowing, and learning and achievement, as well as how students of all genders fare in today's schools. Chapter 7 (Education of People with Disabilities) examines the development of leading theories and practices within special education, including mainstreaming and inclusion.

The style of the book is meant to be clear and informative, with a concerted effort to avoid jargon but without overly simplistic prose or pages overloaded with graphics. The text is designed to provide foundational preparation for readers about to embark on what the authors hope will be fulfilling professional lives as teachers and other education professionals. Such students need material that avoids sugarcoating contentious issues, but they also need analysis that offers a sense of possibility for those who want to journey into the nation's classrooms and schools.

To aid reading and study, each chapter begins with objectives and a list of questions to prepare readers for what is to come. Brief tables and text boxes are used throughout to provide details to textual content. In addition, strategically placed notes are provided with questions for class discussion, suggestions for relating text material to personal experiences, and activities for further investigation and reflection. Key terms are bolded throughout the text, with an appropriate and alphabetized vocabulary list provided at the end of each chapter.

All in all, the book is an invitation to think, discuss, and engage in debates with members of the readers' communities of discourse and practice, be they classmates, faculty, or colleagues. The goal is to stimulate increased awareness of the complex nature of contemporary education. Indeed, as in so many other spheres of life, absolute certainty is scarce in education, while differences of opinion are plentiful.

The conditions in which contemporary education exists seem to breed contention, but they also appear to generate suggested solutions. The authors hope the text will encourage readers to become intellectually involved, and those who truly want to be educators are invited to join the efforts to better understand the world of education, and to add their own voices to those trying to make sense of it all.

Acknowledgments

First and foremost, we acknowledge the crucial role of Dr. Samuel M. Craver. He was the first author of the first edition of this book, and especially the historical sections of each chapter continue to reflect his writing. We gratefully acknowledge the scholarly advice and feedback we received from unknown reviewers and the following colleagues: Serra de Arment, Kurt Stemhagen, and Kevin Sutherland of Virginia Commonwealth University and Thomas Gumpel of Hebrew University of Jerusalem. Their insights were invaluable. Many thanks also to the countless students with whom much of this material was field-tested over the years. They informed our understanding of the type of learning material students need. In addition, we want to thank Mark Richardson and Elissa Burns at Bloomsbury Publishing for their professional consideration, courtesy, and support throughout this process. Finally, we are grateful for the support of our partners in life, Jon Wergin and Thomas Loeber.

1

Teaching as a Profession

Chapter contents

Chapter objectives

- To sketch the history of the teaching profession.
- To develop appreciation of teachers' struggles for professional status and control over time.
- To increase understanding of what it means to be a "professional."
- To describe contemporary changes in the working conditions of teachers, including increases in accountability and standardization.
- To present recent efforts to strengthen the teaching profession and teacher workforce.
- To increase understanding of teachers' professional societies and unions.

Opening questions

1. What were the historical challenges teachers faced in becoming established and recognized as professionals?

2. What is the meaning of "profession," and does the term best capture the status of teachers?
3. How have working conditions and the work of teachers changed over the last few decades?
4. What efforts are in place to strengthen the teaching profession and diversify the workforce?
5. What are the ethical obligations of teachers?
6. How are teachers organized, and what are the debates surrounding these organizations?

The issue

Is teaching truly a **profession**, is it a mere job, or is it a "calling"?[1] While teachers are perceived as crucial to societal well-being, they lack the extrinsic rewards enjoyed by professions such as engineering or medicine. Teachers often face contradictory public perceptions: They are praised for their efforts to educate the young but also pitied for their lack of recognition or reward. Curiously, while teaching is seen as demanding, the old saying persists that "anyone can teach." Proponents insist that the teaching profession can transform society, while critics deplore teaching as a job for drudges unqualified for the lucrative professions. In other words, the teaching profession faces a significant **status discrepancy**. Teaching has high status if measured by public admiration, low status if measured by professional autonomy and salary.

What is effective teaching, and who defines "effective"? Much current debate focuses on high-stakes testing and teacher accountability, but there is a human component to good teaching. Those hoping to become effective teachers need subject-matter preparation, foundation understandings, teaching methods, and classroom management skills, but they also need compassion, egalitarianism, a sense of humor, and the ability to work with diverse people, to name a few.[2]

In short, debate surrounds what characterizes the teaching profession. Some critics declare that teaching should not be considered a true profession at all but a "quasi-" or "managed" profession. Others call the entire debate superfluous and argue that teachers should focus on the valuable things they do rather than argumentative definitions. The point of departure taken here is that teaching is, indeed, a genuine profession, but some unique characteristics as well as contentious points of view swirl around its status.

Historical background

Teaching has traditions going back across the centuries. Of course, gifted teachers develop their own effective approaches, but much of what we do in education comes not from creativity so much as from social and cultural traditions. In fact, many of our ideas about education are like mother tongues not consciously chosen but handed down.

> **Suggested Activity:** Compose an "educational biography." How were you taught throughout your educational journey? What teacher(s) left the deepest impressions, both positively and negatively? What have you learned from these role models, and how might your experience shape the way you will treat your own students?

European heritage

Key elements of the European educational tradition come from ancient Greece and Rome. For the Greeks, language and literature as well as philosophical and mathematical studies were central to their concept of a proper education. Roman educators used this tradition to develop an education based on what came to be called the **liberal arts**. The concept of **liberal education** is derived from the Greco-Roman **classical tradition**, that is, an education that "liberates" the mind through the study of important branches of knowledge. By the Middle Ages, the curriculum was formalized into the "seven liberal arts" (arithmetic, geometry, music, astronomy, grammar, rhetoric, and logic or dialectic), but it also became heavily supplemented by Christian doctrines that emphasized education for the salvation of the soul. The study of classical languages, particularly Latin, retained supremacy in formal education, even as the **vernacular** (or native) languages of Europe expanded. This was because Latin was the official language of the Roman Catholic Church, the chief provider of formal education in medieval Europe, but also because Latin continued to be used in such pursuits as scholarly writing and international diplomacy.[3]

Originating in Italy probably in the late fourteenth century, the Renaissance eventually swept across Europe and invigorated intellectual curiosity. "*Renaissance*" means "rebirth," but for education it was not solely a rebirth of classical studies. It helped to revive the liberal arts, with its emphasis on the humanities, and spurred new interest in astronomy, mathematics, and knowledge of the natural world. Liberal education became imbued with the goal of producing well-rounded individuals pursuing excellence in a wide range of artistic, intellectual, and cultural endeavors. The present-day view of liberal education encompasses the liberal arts, human cultures, and scientific and mathematical studies, sometimes collectively referred to as the **arts** (or **humanities) and sciences.**[4]

> **For Further Reflection:** Consider your own college experience with course requirements that were supposed to broaden your horizons. Does liberal education truly "liberate" the person, or does it put a greater premium on loyalty to the past and to cultural traditions and old ways of thinking? Or is the purpose of liberal education different from either? Relatedly, should higher education seek to broaden prospective teachers' minds generally, or should it train them for the job market?

As the Renaissance gained headway, Europe also experienced the Protestant Reformation and the Catholic Counter-Reformation. Among other things each movement emphasized, the Protestants advocated widespread literacy to enable as many as possible to read the Bible, while the Catholics renewed secondary and higher education to strengthen their institutions and adherents. Such emphases, along with the invention of the printing press and other developments, stimulated the growth of elementary education in the vernacular languages, with classical and vernacular studies boosted in secondary and higher education. Although Protestantism was dominant in the English colonies of North America, Catholic educational ideals would exert a degree of influence on later American education.[5]

> **For Further Reflection:** How do you see the purpose of literacy? Conduct some historical research to answer the following questions: Did literacy for common people become important only after religious leaders connected reading with salvation, or did it have other sources as well? Is there any difference between literacy for religious salvation and literacy for individual and social well-being?

Thus, many educational ideas were brought from Europe that shaped American education. Teaching in the United States did not start with a blank slate but with traditions from across the centuries. Americans built on these traditions and made their own educational contributions in the process. In addition, educational practices had been present, of course, among Native Americans before European colonizers ever arrived, and were at times starkly different from European practices. While there was a great deal of diversity among various native cultures, generally they differed from Europeans, for example, in terms of their approach to discipline. Corporal punishment was not used as frequently as it was among people of European descent.[6]

American education

In the English colonies in North America, at least three levels of schooling developed, each with its own kind of teachers: elementary **"petty" schools**, secondary "grammar" schools, and colleges. Various schemes were tried, but perhaps the most notable departure came in Massachusetts with a 1647 law that helped foster petty schools in its requirement that every township of at least fifty households should appoint someone "to teach all such children as shall resort to him to write and read." Once a town increased to 100 households, it should "set up a grammar school" to educate youth to be "fitted for the university." The law was followed in some jurisdictions and virtually ignored in others, but it set a pattern used throughout New England by the end of the colonial period.[7] Indeed, most colonies had at least a few petty and grammar schools, although not on the scale of New England.

Colonial teachers

Background preparation of petty school teachers was varied; some had suitable background while others were barely adequate. One form of petty school was the "dame school," usually conducted in a household by a literate woman, sometimes a mother who took in a few children along with her own to provide rudimentary instruction (and perhaps a small income). Other petty schools were more formal. The manner in which petty schools were financed differed: Some were given public support by towns, some charged tuition fees, and some were "charity" schools, free of charge to poor children and financed by endowments from benefactors. Some petty schools might only teach reading, others might offer both reading and writing, and still others might have a more complex curriculum. Despite variability, petty school teachers taught a relatively common curriculum in the sense that students were started on simple hornbooks of the ABCs, then moved to spelling, psalters, and catechisms, and then possibly to more advanced reading, writing, arithmetic, and religion.

Suggested Activity: Use the internet to locate definitions, descriptions, and illustrations of historic educational terms, such as hornbooks, psalters, and primers.

A famous colonial textbook was the ***New England Primer***, used for reading, vocabulary development, and moral and religious instruction. For example, the 1737 edition of the *Primer* began with letters of the alphabet, each followed by a verse or moral dictum and an illustration to drive home the meaning: On the left of the page was the letter "*A*," with a small drawing of a man and woman contemplating an apple, accompanied on the right with the verse, "In Adam's Fall, We Sinned all." Next came the letter "*B*," with a small image of an open book fortified by "Thy Life to mend, This Book attend." For the letter "*C*," with an illustration of a cat playing with a mouse, the admonition read, "The Cat doth play, And after slay." The *Primer* proceeded all the way through the alphabet, then to syllabic pronunciation tables, stories, and other material.[8]

Grammar (or secondary) school teachers were expected to have more advanced academic preparation than petty school teachers. Preparation for secondary teachers grew out of the European university tradition. It was composed of undergraduate study in the **liberal arts** (leading to the bachelor of arts degree) and graduate study in liberal arts (leading to the master of arts degree) as well as professional studies in law, medicine, or theology. Although there were no specific courses on how to teach, universities contributed to secondary teacher preparation by providing the liberal arts background that was expected and the bachelor of arts degree that was highly desired.

For Further Reflection: Early in American educational history, teachers relied on textbooks such as the *New England Primer*. Schools continue to rely on textbooks. What are the advantages and potential disadvantages of textbook usage? How should reading materials be diversified?

This tradition was reflected in what secondary teachers were expected to know: They should be able to speak and write Latin, understand some Greek and perhaps some Hebrew, and have capacity in English usage as well. They also needed general knowledge of history, mathematics, and perhaps a bit of science.[9] There were expectations concerning teachers' religious qualifications, too, as reflected by Massachusetts in a 1654 law that prohibited anyone from teaching school children or college youth if the applicant demonstrated unsound belief, scandalous behavior, or "'not giving due satisfaction according to the rules of Christ,'"[10] presumably meaning untrustworthy performance. Both the depth of preparation and the performance of teachers were uneven; consequently, colonial schools experienced frequent **teacher turnover**, not only because well-qualified grammar school teachers were difficult to find and retain but also because of a persistent labor shortage during the time, with many teachers moving on as more promising job prospects became available.

> **For Further Reflection:** Topics of great relevance today, such as teacher turnover and variation in teacher preparedness, obviously have a long history. How should we attract and retain qualified teachers today?

In the eighteenth century, petty schools continued as before, but grammar schools actually declined. One reason was a decrease in value placed on classical learning. Another was the growth of town-supported "writing schools" that emphasized more advanced instruction in English, arithmetic (or "ciphering"), and accounting, all subjects that had greater practical application. As the colonial economy expanded, private "vocational" schools arose that taught such subjects as geometry, trigonometry, navigation, surveying, double-entry bookkeeping, foreign languages, and foreign currency exchange, all of which found practical application in the growth of American business, industry, and shipping and trade.[11]

Teachers for the new nation

In hindsight, it may appear that after the American Revolution the success of the United States was a foregone conclusion, but its existence was actually precarious. Numerous efforts were made to remedy this, not only with the adoption of the Constitution in 1789 but also with pleas for greater educational opportunity as one of the surest ways to strengthen the new republic. For example, Noah Webster called on education to develop a national unity around "the American tongue," while Benjamin Rush advocated an education to "convert men into republican machines" to bind the country together.[12] However, questions about the preparation of teachers did not receive similar examination.

Suggested Activity: Apply the ideas of Webster and Rush to contemporary contexts and discuss to what extent modern schools perceive their mission as being to prepare students to develop national unity around "the American tongue," and to "convert men to republican machines" to bind the country together. While the language is certainly dated, Anglo-centric, and exclusionary, do these ideas still hold relevance today? Why or why not?

As the nineteenth century dawned, the belief was that a good grounding in reading, writing, arithmetic, some religion, and a smattering of history and geography was sufficient preparation for most elementary teachers. For secondary teachers, a liberal arts education seemed adequate to provide all the moral, social, psychological, and academic knowledge needed. Educational theory and teaching methodology, if studied at all, were to be gained from personal study and on-the-job experience.[13]

For Further Reflection: What do teachers need to know and experience in order to be competent professionals?

With the passage of time, teaching came under increased scrutiny. One reason was the growing awareness that for the new republic to succeed, as many citizens as possible should be educated as far as practicable. This led to the establishment of statewide systems of public schools, a significant phase of which was the **common school movement**, a widespread development of public elementary schools from the 1830s up to about 1860. A second phase was the spread of public high schools after the Civil War, a movement that lasted well into the twentieth century. An essential need was a sufficient supply of properly educated teachers to make the public schools successful, which also spurred the growth of teacher education institutions.

Why did the United States move from a mixed bag of sectarian schools, private schools, charity schools, and municipal public schools inherited from the colonial period toward the eventual founding of statewide systems of locally controlled public schools? A simple answer is that by the 1830s, there was public demand for more widely available educational opportunities, with emphasis not so much on producing refined scholars as on forming virtuous and morally upstanding citizens. A more complex answer is that more people came to believe that a truly educated person must not only be literate but possess culture and character as well, however defined. The goal was as much social and cultural as it was literary and intellectual, views that also spilled over into the preparation of teachers. Thus, the push became to prepare teachers not only to develop the mental capacities of their students, but also to serve as proper role models for them and to maintain discipline while implanting desired character traits in them.[14]

> **For Further Reflection:** To what extent do we still expect teachers to be ethical role models who adhere to higher moral standards than citizens working in other professions? Should this be the case? Why or why not?

Women enter teaching

In earlier times, teaching was mainly a male occupation. It was believed that men were more suitable because they were better educated, more intellectually capable, and made of the stern temperament and physical strength needed to quell unruly pupils and demand achievement. Such beliefs would undergo change as growing numbers of women became teachers in the nineteenth century.[15]

Educational opportunities remained limited for females when the United States was young. As far as white people were concerned, wealthier parents had long secured private tutors for their daughters, and there were a limited number of "finishing schools" that polished the social graces of young women and provided a veneer of intellectual training. But a more rigorous academic preparation became the rallying point for reformers who believed that females were as intellectually capable as males.[16] People of color, male and female, were largely excluded from schooling until after the Civil War.

As the public school movement gained momentum during the nineteenth century, women increasingly entered the teaching profession. Although denied access to most professions at the time, it is arguable that their entry into teaching helped women also enter other professions later on, a trend that held true for white women as well as, ultimately, women of color.

There were also strong economic reasons for women becoming teachers: When the public common schools appeared in the nineteenth century, the Industrial Revolution was a growing force. Developments such as the electric telegraph, the steam engine, and the mass production of goods rapidly changed social and economic life. Consider textile production as an example: Old-fashioned spinning wheels and hand-operated looms disappeared from the home as mechanized factories mass-produced high-quality cloth that consumers could buy more cheaply than make at home. Where teaching once attracted the likes of John Adams, young men were now attracted to more lucrative jobs in an expanding industrial economy. With industries producing affordable household goods, more women became available for jobs outside the home and family, a trend that was at least true for white women as women of color had always worked outside of the home. Connect these factors with the growth of the common schools and the need for more teachers, and connect public opposition to higher taxes with the fact that women were paid less than men, and it is a small step to see one reason women teachers gained acceptance—they were cheaper. As reformer Alonzo Potter dryly noted at the time, local school districts wanted the best teachers possible—as long as they were the cheapest.[17]

There was also the growing belief that, contrary to tradition, women were actually suited by temperament to teach. Just as men were better suited for action in the outside world by virtue of their traditional roles as warriors and hunters (the thinking went), women were more understanding and sympathetic to children because of their softer temperaments and natural capacities as mothers. At a time when people were questioning the extensive use of corporal punishment in schools, there was increasing acceptance that most women preferred moral suasion over physical force; therefore, they were desirable additions to the teaching profession. In many respects, this change was due to the intellectual movement called the Enlightenment, which swept Europe and America from the late seventeenth through the early nineteenth centuries and produced philosophers such as John Locke (seventeenth century), social critics including Jean-Jacques Rousseau (eighteenth century), and educators like Johann Pestalozzi (early nineteenth century). These thinkers promoted such ideas as children being educated according to the natural developmental processes of childhood, with their natural traits recognized, their manners and morals sympathetically nurtured, and their characters shaped through rational, humane instruction rather than physical force.[18]

For Further Reflection: Do men and women truly differ in their natural, inborn capacities to teach? If so, in what ways? Have you personally encountered beliefs and attitudes that portray women as nurturers and men as disciplinarians? What is your reaction to such views? Interrogate and complexify this type of thinking when you consider non-binary approaches to gender identities.

Teacher preparation

As the school-age population grew, there were never enough qualified teachers to fill the demand in the schools. It had long been the expectation that secondary school teachers should have, if not a full academic degree, at least some higher education preparation. As many educational reformers saw it, elementary teachers needed more extensive preparation too. It was not until the appearance of the **normal school** that an institution dedicated to elementary teacher preparation appeared in the United States.

Normal schools

Why the term "*normal*" for a teacher-training institution? The idea for such a school probably originated with the Prussian "teacher seminaries" of the mid-eighteenth century, but the specific term *normal school* apparently was derived from the French, the first being the *École Normale Supérieure,* founded in 1794 during the French Revolution to serve as the model for other such schools across France. In the United States, the Model School of Philadelphia opened in 1818 to train teachers in that city; in 1823, a private teacher-training institution was opened in Concord, Vermont; and in 1826, two others were opened, one in New Harmony, Indiana, and the other in Lancaster, Massachusetts. But the term *normal school* did not gain common American usage until the founding of the state-supported Lexington Normal School in Lexington, Massachusetts, in 1839.[19] The growth of the public common schools and their demand for greater numbers of teachers subsequently spurred the opening of many normal schools throughout the remainder of the nineteenth century.

Most normal schools followed a four-point plan of study: a review of the branches of knowledge, the study of pedagogy (the art or science of teaching), some training in classroom/school management, and practice teaching. At first, normal schools used the secondary school curriculum, along with some pedagogical applications, to train teachers for the elementary common schools, but as public high schools increased, many normal schools added the training of high school teachers and school administrators as well. Over time, some normal schools took on collegiate functions, particularly where there was little or no postsecondary education available within reasonable geographic proximity.[20] In some cases, this expansion of mission weakened normal schools because it detracted from their original objectives.

> **For Further Reflection:** Educational hierarchies have a long history, and the status of elementary school teachers has suffered in comparison to secondary teachers. Turn this type of thinking upside down and construct a rationale for why young children might need teachers whose preparation is even more sophisticated than that of teachers of older students.

By the beginning of the twentieth century, normal schools were fairly common. In 1860, there were only 11 nationwide, but by 1898 there were 166 public and 165 private normal schools, with a combined graduation total of 11,255 students in that year. Between 1870 and 1900, normal school enrollments grew from 10,000 to 70,000 students, but normal schools never provided more than about half the teachers actually needed in most states. Consequently, many poorer school districts, particularly rural ones, had to employ teachers with no more preparation than an elementary school background. Even in Massachusetts, with its reputation for educational innovation, more than 60 percent of teachers had no pedagogical training at all. By 1900, the normal schools faced stiff competition from the growing number of state colleges and universities, many of which claimed teacher preparation as one of their missions. As colleges and universities increasingly took over the preparation of teachers, normal schools closed, merged with existing higher-education institutions, or became four-year **state teachers colleges** themselves.[21]

State colleges and universities

Traditionally, colleges and universities prepared secondary school teachers as a byproduct of their regular liberal education programs, but not with any special emphasis on pedagogy per se. By the twentieth century, most state colleges and universities assumed the primary responsibility of preparing both elementary and secondary teachers. This involved establishing departments and schools of education to deliver courses in the foundations of education, curriculum, teaching methods, student teaching, school administration, school counseling, and other specialized studies.

At those state teachers colleges that had developed out of normal schools, there was usually a strong carryover of commitment to teacher education. Commitment was also present in some new, general-purpose state colleges and universities, but not in all. It was probably strongest in those institutions where the presidents had backgrounds as school teachers and administrators or were graduates of departments or schools of education. Such presidents often stayed in their posts for years, and where there were good relationships between top administrators and schools or departments of education, the latter enjoyed greater support and stability.[22]

However, teacher education did not fare so well in those institutions accepting it reluctantly. As public school enrollment grew, state governments often assigned teacher preparation to their public colleges and universities as a duty to taxpayers, whether or not those institutions were willing. Thus, tying teacher education to a reluctant institution was not always successful. For one thing, some liberal arts professors saw teacher education as tainted by its inferior normal school origins, and they scorned it as a result. For another, teaching did not wield the economic clout of other professions such as law or medicine, and it suffered in comparison. Also, some aspects of teacher education lacked the scholarly research base of the traditional professions, and this reinforced biases that teacher education lacked intellectual substance. Indeed, there were teacher education faculty more interested in how-to techniques than intellectual substance and, in turn, some of them dismissed their academic critics as impractical and out-of-touch intellectuals. Where there were failures on the part of both academic and teacher education faculties to cultivate common interests, teacher preparation and the public interest were probably not well served.

Suggested Activity: On your own campus, examine the relationship between the teacher preparation program and other degree programs and disciplines. Does your institution have its roots in a normal school or teachers college, and what difference does this make for the current status of teacher education? How do your observations compare with the accounts given in this book?

Professionalism and professionalization

There was an additional factor at work, too, and this was the drive to "professionalize" public education. According to Jurgen Herbst, there are two essential distinctions one can make—**professionalism** and **professionalization**. Teacher *professionalism* is something to be valued: Among other things, it involves the teacher's fundamental duty to be well-prepared in both subject matter and teaching skills in order to provide competent educational service to students, and to exercise responsible professional judgment in regard to teaching, curriculum, and evaluation of student progress.

This view borrows heavily from traditions in the historic **learned professions** trained in the universities (ministers, lawyers, physicians, and college and university professors), whose professional status grew from their extended preparation that allowed them to exercise judgment and a high degree of autonomy in professional practice. In this view, professionals collectively determine admission criteria and the ethical standards of good practice. Properly trained members of the profession should be allowed to carry out their duties, as guided by expertise and professional ethical standards, taking responsibility for results without intrusive external supervision. Such a strong tradition was not established when pedagogical training was transferred from normal schools to colleges and universities. For a long time, teacher preparation remained at the undergraduate rather than the graduate level where other learned professions were taught. Efforts to achieve greater depth in professional preparation, which might have boosted teacher claims to professional autonomy and judgment, were restricted rather than enlarged.

> **Suggested Activity:** Use your imagination and rewrite history. What path would the teaching profession have had to take in order to achieve similar status as other professions?

At that time, what enjoyed far greater success was the *professionalization* of school administrators and specialists. Such factors as graduate training, workplace autonomy, peer evaluation, and accountability to society—all recognized traits of the learned professions—became common features for administrators and educational specialists but not classroom teachers. The policy makers who controlled the schools established a hierarchical, bureaucratic form of corporate organization in which teachers were defined as employees who carried out directives, not professionals who exercised judgment or autonomy in their work.

Incentives for teachers to pursue greater professionalism were curtailed if not eliminated outright. As the twentieth century advanced, teacher education did in many states move at least temporarily toward the graduate level, but by then a pervasive pattern of administrative control was firmly entrenched. For teachers

Figure 1.1 The Grandview Parent Teacher Association (PTA) meeting on May 15, 1918.

to get "promoted" to "full" professional status, they had to leave the classroom and enter the ranks of administrators and specialists.[23]

Teachers organize

Soon after the advent of public school systems in the nineteenth century, teachers, administrators, reformers, and education-minded citizens began forming educational associations, which arose from the need to seek workable solutions to problems, share successful ideas, and influence public policy on education. Some of the participants, including many teachers, also believed there was a need to promote the interests of the teaching profession itself, including better pay, improved working conditions, and the protection of professional autonomy.

National Education Association

Today's largest teacher organization traces its origins to 1857 and the founding of the National Teachers Association. In 1870, this group merged with the National Association of School Superintendents and the American Normal School Association to form the **National Education Association (NEA)**.

The NEA supported public and private schooling at all levels, but it was mainly devoted to the goals of reformers, school superintendents, and college presidents, not classroom teachers. In 1917, the NEA reorganized itself into a tri-level organization of local, state, and national divisions. Teachers gained some influence through the "classroom teachers' associations" formed at the local and state levels, but traditional interests maintained organizational dominance at the national level.[24]

> **Suggested Activity:** Compare the NEA to other professional organizations and unions. To what extent do leaders of professional organizations perceive themselves as the avant-garde rather than the representatives of the membership? Is there often a disconnect between leaders and ordinary members?

Teachers and bureaucratic controls

One issue that generated teacher unrest was the controversy over "merit rating," one of the practices superintendents instituted to get more "efficiency" out of classroom teachers. As school bureaucracies grew, additional layers of administration exercised control over teachers. In some school systems, teachers might be rated by four or more layers, from the building principal to grade or subject supervisor to assistant superintendent to superintendent. In some systems, the rating criteria were kept secret, with teachers not knowing what they were rated on or how results were decided. Needless to say, this created teacher distrust.[25]

The NEA made some efforts to improve relations, but tensions remained. During the Great Depression, the NEA conducted a national salary study in 1935. Findings revealed pay discrepancies between elementary and secondary teachers, male and female teachers, and Black and white teachers. The NEA recommended salary equity for the elementary-secondary and male-female discrepancies, but the issue of race-based salaries was deferred to the prerogatives of local education authorities.[26]

The NEA would later change many of its positions and become a stalwart defender of teacher interests. Such changes occurred not only because of conditions but also because of agitation from dissatisfied members and from outside competition.

Margaret Haley, a Chicago classroom teacher-advocate

Margaret Haley was an elementary school teacher from the tough "stockyards" district of Chicago and also a longtime member of the National Education Association (NEA). Goaded by underfunded schools and cynical city policies, she and other elementary teachers formed the first union for teachers, the Chicago Teachers Federation (CTF) in 1897. In 1901, Haley became the first elementary teacher (and also the first woman) to speak from the floor during a general session of the NEA. The featured speaker was William T. Harris, a former superintendent of the St. Louis schools and then US commissioner of education. When Harris argued that the most important thing for schools was to strengthen their ties with the business community, Haley rose to challenge him, saying that, on the contrary, the top priority should be higher salaries for teachers. Harris retorted that delegates should not listen to the speaker, obviously a "grade teacher…worn out, tired, and hysterical," words that probably only strengthened Haley's resolve. Under her leadership, the CTF grew rapidly and affiliated with the Chicago Federation of Labor in 1902. Haley delivered a formal speech at the NEA convention of 1904, calling on the delegates to address the poor working conditions and "wholly inadequate" salaries of teachers. She also criticized the corporate model of school organization, charging that it produced factory-like mechanical processes in schools and unthinking minds in students.[a]

[a]Sources: "Margaret Haley becomes the first woman and first teacher to speak at the NEA," http://fcis.oise.utoronto.ca/~dschugurensky/assignment1/1901haley.html (accessed on September 23, 2010); and Margaret Haley, "Why Teachers Should Organize [1904]," *Woman's True Profession: Voices from the History of Teaching*, Nancy Hoffman, ed. (Old Westbury, NY: The Feminist Press, 1981), 289–95.

American Federation of Teachers

From its beginnings, the **American Federation of Teachers (AFT)** identified with the labor movement, and it took strong positions on better pay and working conditions for teachers. The first successful effort at forming a union for classroom teachers started in Chicago where poorly supplied classrooms, inadequate facilities, meager salaries, ineffective administration, and politically motivated board policies led to the founding of the Chicago Teachers Federation (CTF) in 1897. When the CTF sued the Chicago Board of Education for reneging on a promised pay raise for teachers, the board claimed a lack of funds. After it was discovered that the board allowed some Chicago corporations to escape paying their lawful city taxes, the court ordered the corporations to pay up and the board to deliver its promised pay raise. CTF membership grew rapidly and, on April 15, 1916, the organization joined with the Chicago Federation of Men Teachers, the Chicago Federation of Women High School Teachers, and the Teachers Federation of Gary, Indiana, to form the American Federation of Teachers (AFT). Joined by other locals in New York City, Oklahoma, Pennsylvania, and Washington, D.C., the AFT was admitted into the American Federation of Labor on May 19, 1916.[27]

Some boards of education fired teachers who joined the AFT, but it still projected an image of teachers as upstanding citizens rather than servants. It also advocated popular election of school boards, free textbooks for school pupils, job tenure for teachers with meritorious service, and adequate pensions for teachers.[28]

The salary issue and union status

Despite their differences, at first both the NEA and the AFT rejected the use of "withdrawal of professional service" (or **strikes**) to get improvements in salaries, working conditions, or resources for school children. Indeed, the AFT had a no-strike policy for many years. However, due to Depression-era cutbacks in the 1930s and war-related cutbacks from 1941 to 1945, American schools were in poor straits. During the 1950s, school enrollments climbed dramatically from the Second World War "baby boom," and when state and local authorities proved reluctant to increase funding to meet conditions, the AFT decided to resort to strikes and **collective bargaining**.

Suggested Activity: Extreme discrepancies in pay existed between white and Black teachers in the past, particularly during the times prior to the Supreme Court decision of *Brown v. Board of Education of Topeka* (1954). Civil rights lawyer Charles Hamilton Houston documented race-based pay scales and other such discrepancies in building his legal argument that "separate is not equal." What was his role in ending legally sanctioned school segregation? Find out more by researching Charles Hamilton Houston's work on school desegregation. Compare also with Chapter 4: Race, Ethnicity and Education pp. 165–220

For Further Reflection: Should teachers strike, or are strikes anathema to professionalism? Justify your position.

The influx of "baby boomers" into the schools in the 1950s and 1960s meant overcrowding, poor working conditions, low teacher morale, and increased public criticism of schools. In 1953, there were almost 60,000 one-room schools still in existence, and in 1957, the nation had an estimated shortage of around 247,000 classrooms. By 1958, there were 47,564 school districts with 42.4 million students and 1,644,000 teachers. Under these conditions, the idea of strikes gained popularity among members, particularly after the 1960 formation of the United Federation of Teachers (UFT), a new AFT local in New York City. Over the next several years, successful UFT strikes brought the AFT to national prominence as never before.[29]

Meanwhile, in lieu of strikes, the NEA recommended "sanctions" (issuing a warning about substandard conditions in a school system and advising teachers against accepting employment there) and "professional negotiations" (negotiating contracts with local school systems without resorting to strikes). In actual practice, both tactics made the NEA appear weak because, in the absence of strikes, there was no incentive for school boards to negotiate in good faith or make the changes necessary to lift NEA sanctions. The NEA finally decided that to negotiate successful contracts it had to change, and in 1973, it adopted a new constitution that made it a union.[30]

Several attempts were made by the AFT to merge the two organizations, but each time it fell through. Sticking points included NEA members who refused to affiliate with the AFT's parent organization, the American Federation of Labor and the Congress of Industrial Organizations (AFL-CIO). In addition, the NEA favored secret ballots and term limits for union presidents, while the AFT did not. While both organizations signed a "NEAFT partnership agreement" in 2001, whether an actual merger will occur remains to be seen.[31]

Professionalization and teacher education reforms

After the Second World War, the United States experienced domestic and international tensions from the Cold War that fed increased criticisms of teachers and schools. The relative stability that teacher education programs once received in many colleges and universities gave way to instability. Several times over the years, powerful economic and political interests launched reforms of both school curricula and teacher education that created new uncertainties.

Teacher preparation after 1950

During the 1950s, both teacher education and the teaching profession were pummeled by harsh criticisms from political ideologists, business interests, tax-cut lobbyists, national defense advocates, and academic critics. Teachers and schools were accused of weakening scholastic standards and failing to teach the "basics" in the curriculum. Accusations from the political right that American youth were being endangered by subversive left-wing forces in education only increased the public's fears. This was the era of high-pressure political tactics called "**McCarthyism**" (named after US senator Joseph McCarthy of Wisconsin, who claimed that communists had infiltrated important American institutions). Fears led to greater emphasis on patriotic symbols and increased censorship of textbooks, curriculum materials, and school library holdings. In some jurisdictions, schoolteachers were required to sign loyalty oaths in order to keep their jobs.[32]

> **Suggested Activity:** Research McCarthyism and how it affected society in general and educators in particular. Taking into account contemporary political developments, what is the debate today about the relationship between citizens' rights and perceived threats to national security, both internal and external?

In little more than a decade, however, teachers had to face strong political criticisms from another direction, this time from the left. During the Vietnam War era (roughly, the mid-1960s to the mid-1970s), there was a rising level of criticism directed at traditional society, including condemnations of teachers and schools as insensitive tools of the "power establishment." Teachers were admonished to become more attentive to student needs, to provide "soft" teaching styles and curricular programs that recognized different interests, and to be more critical of the status quo.[33]

By the 1980s, conservative politics returned with renewed vigor, and teachers and schools were once again castigated for pampering students, weakening academic standards, and failing to teach the basics. In 1983, during Ronald Reagan's first term as President of the United States, the US Department of Education released a critical national report, ***A Nation at Risk***, that claimed "the educational foundations of our society are presently being eroded by a rising tide of mediocrity that threatens our very future as a Nation and a people."[34]

This was followed by other reports, such as those released by the Education Commission of the States, various private foundations, and other interest groups. In the calls for reform, a term emerged that became a mantra for many reformers—***teacher accountability***. By the 1990s, state-mandated high-stakes testing programs were widely implemented as ways to hold teachers and schools accountable for how students were taught and what students retained. Teacher education programs were once again forced, not only by political pressure but also by state and federal laws, to revise certification and graduation standards, irrespective of whether the imposed changes had adequate research behind them. Efforts increased to move teacher preparation programs to the graduate level, although the economic remuneration and professional status of teachers in the educational hierarchy did not noticeably improve as a result.[35]

> **For Further Reflection:** Based on the historical evidence, it seems obvious that the preparation of teachers is directly connected to political developments outside education. Discuss the implications for educators.

Among the criticisms of teaching that arose in the 1980s and 1990s was the claim that, when compared to other learned professions, teaching simply does not measure up. Another was that too many teacher education students lack the intellectual background of students in other professional programs. Still another was that education research only produces "soft" knowledge, and few if any causal claims can be drawn from it. Of course, this could be said about research in the social and behavioral sciences generally, as opposed to the more predictable, "hard" knowledge of the physical sciences. Indeed, education research mostly deals with human factors that tend to be unpredictable and difficult to control; hence, an extensive body of stable professional knowledge has been difficult to produce. But there may be issues beyond intellectual substance or stable professional knowledge that impact teaching's status more than in other professions: Most teachers come from working- or lower-middle-class backgrounds, and the majority of them are women; therefore, social class and gender biases may exert more adverse effects on the status of teaching than on other professions.[36]

During the last decades of the twentieth century, several groups sought to elevate teaching through professionalization reforms. Three of the more significant are the **Holmes Partnership**, the **Carnegie Corporation**, and the **National Board for Professional Teaching Standards (NBPTS)**.

> **Suggested Activity:** Conduct an informal poll in your college/university asking faculty and students who are not involved in teacher preparation about how they view the quality of teacher education programs. Analyze and discuss the results.

Holmes Partnership

Launched by a consortium of schools of education in leading research universities in 1986, the Holmes Partnership began as the Holmes Group, a major advocate of teacher professionalization that gained wide attention with its 1989 publication titled *Tomorrow's Teachers.* Attempting to reform both teacher education and the teaching profession, the Holmes Group sought to improve teacher preparation by toughening entry standards, increasing candidates' command of academic subjects and teaching practices, cultivating stronger cooperation between the public schools and the teacher preparation programs in the colleges and universities, and encouraging more research and its dissemination. It also pushed the identification of "professional development schools" in cooperating school systems where student teachers, experienced teachers, and university professors could work together to solve "real world" teaching and learning problems. In 1996, the Holmes Group changed its name to the "Holmes Partnership," but it continued to promote high-quality professional preparation, strong partnerships among public schools and teacher preparation institutions, and more research and its dissemination.[37]

The Holmes Partnership was dissolved in 2010; however, the **Holmes Scholars Program,** which had been established by the Holmes Group in 1991, lived on under the umbrella of the **American Association of Colleges for Teacher Education (AACTE).** The Holmes Scholars Program aims to foster equity, diversity, and cultural competence in higher education as well as PK-12 education and enrich the academic preparation of graduate students of color.[38]

Carnegie Corporation

An influential 1986 publication that heightened interest in the professionalization of teaching was *A Nation Prepared: Teachers for the 21st Century*. Issued by the Carnegie Corporation's Forum on Education and the Economy, the report proposed that teacher preparation should include both a bachelor degree in the arts or sciences and a master of teaching degree based on a new graduate curriculum in both the arts and sciences and in teacher education. Although the report's focus was on the economic aspects of education, and although it proposed more centralization of teaching and more accountability for student progress, it also pushed for greater decision-making power for teachers, increased resources and technology to enhance teacher productivity, and major improvements in teachers' salaries and career opportunities on par with other professions.

National Board for Professional Teaching Standards

One of the important results flowing from teacher education reform initiatives was the creation of the National Board for Professional Teaching Standards (NBPTS) in 1987. NBPTS established a voluntary program through which a number of teachers have since pursued studies leading to **National Board Certification (NBC)**. The program aims to improve K-12 teacher preparation, retention, and recognition leading to school improvement across the nation. Teachers may obtain board certification in twenty-five certificate areas, including art, **career and technical education**, health education, library media, literacy, mathematics, music, school counseling, and more. One of the prerequisites to become certified is that teachers have to provide standards-based evidence of their positive effects on student learning. As of this writing, over 133,000 teachers in the United States have been board certified.[39]

> **For Further Reflection:** Are such efforts as those made by the Holmes Group to enhance the status of teaching a promising development? Is the Carnegie-backed National Board Certification idea a good thing? Justify your position. What other possibilities can you suggest to achieve the goals of improving and strengthening the teaching profession?

Impact of professionalization

The 1980s and 1990s witnessed a flurry of reports that questioned the effectiveness of schools and teachers and put forward various reform proposals. An obvious question is, how much actually changed as a result of late twentieth-century professionalization reforms?

In a 1999 study, two-thirds of the teachers interviewed indicated that some aspects of the various reforms had been incorporated into practice, a trend reflected at the national level as well. Although most resulting reforms were imposed by policy makers, the study found that reforms incorporating active teacher involvement were more successfully implemented than those pushed from the top down. However, little has been done to remove major obstacles to teacher involvement, including the rigid structure of the workday that severely restricts teacher participation in professional planning or collaboration, lack of resources committed to high-quality faculty development, reluctance to establish genuine peer evaluation (where teachers systematically evaluate one another), and unwillingness to allow teachers to exercise any significant control over their own professional practice. Most participants doubted that any substantial increase in teacher power would take place, and some felt that what actually occurred was only a slight increase in their advisory role. Many crucial decisions on budget, curriculum, and personnel continue to be made at the district and state levels rather than the individual school level.[40]

Cross-reference: For a discussion of school governance and decision making, see Chapter 2: School Governance and Control, pp. 61–112.

Contemporary conditions

Teaching continues to be one of the largest and most important occupations in the United States. Teachers influence not only the individual lives of their students, but also the social, political, and economic health of the nation. About 8 percent of the college-educated labor force are K12 teachers.[41] This size imposes an upper limit to the degree of selectivity teacher preparation programs and schools can exercise in deciding whom to admit to the profession. Because prestige is tied to selectivity, the occupation continues to struggle to achieve the status it arguably deserves based on the complexity and importance of the work.

Compounding this problem, the working conditions of teachers have worsened over the last few decades, leading fewer teachers to remain in the profession and fewer people to pursue the career in the first place. Shortages have become particularly pronounced in special education, **STEM** fields (science, technology, engineering, and mathematics), career and technical education (CTE), bilingual education, and English as a Second Language. The COVID-19 pandemic exacerbated many factors that were already driving people away from the profession: low wages, high costs of teacher preparation, and poor working conditions. Some of the $122 billion provided to states and school districts through American Rescue Plan Elementary and Secondary School

Emergency Relief (ARP ESSER) funds were used to address teacher shortages, while other funds were used to safely reopen schools and address the emotional and academic needs of students. Although this funding did help bring staffing numbers back up to their pre-pandemic levels, teacher shortages continue to impact high-poverty neighborhoods, students with disabilities, and English learners.[42]

A 2024 study found that the state of the profession is at its lowest level in fifty years, as measured by four indicators: occupational prestige, interest in the profession, number of people in teacher preparation programs, and job satisfaction of current teachers.[43] Nevertheless, thousands of people do continue to find satisfaction and fulfillment in the job. And if the prestige and conditions are to improve, it will require members of the profession to continue advocating and drawing attention to the important and impactful work teachers do.

There are also many efforts underway to strengthen the profession. Pay is increasing in many parts of the country and policy makers are directing attention to recruiting and retaining high-quality teachers from a variety of backgrounds.

Portrayal of teaching in popular culture

Popular media tend to idealize good teachers, portraying them as heroes and saviors, a limited understanding at best. The image of the heroic teacher usually projects an entrepreneurial, independent individual who works in isolation from others, which is not necessarily typical of how most teachers work, including the most capable and effective ones. Heroic teachers also are often portrayed as maverick outsiders with little or no formal professional preparation.[a]

One example is the classic movie "*Stand and Deliver.*"[b] The main character is Jaime Escalante (played by Edward James Olmos), a computer expert seeking to become a teacher. He lands a job in a barrio in Los Angeles, teaching a group of underprivileged, underachieving students who always seem to live down to the low expectations of their teachers. His colleagues argue that high expectations only set up the students for failure. The students doubt themselves as well, and they challenge Escalante's authority as they contend with the crushing weight of family and community problems. Escalante rejects low expectations and challenges the students to take calculus and prove themselves on national exams. In the end, the students do rise to their teacher's challenge and gain a sense of accomplishment, and Escalante prevails after devoting all of his energy to the task, even suffering a stress-induced heart attack in the process. Overall, throughout the film, Escalante is portrayed as a heroic, highly successful teacher who, after defying colleagues and the entrenched educational bureaucracy, helps a group of marginalized students learn that they can succeed. And he accomplishes all this without any formal teacher preparation or attention to educational theory and methodology. Once again comes the message that formal teacher preparation is superfluous, that what teachers really need to know is the "common sense" they presumably learn on the job.

Have you encountered similar portrayals of teaching in popular culture? What are your reactions?

[a]Sari Knopp Biklen, *School Work: Gender and the Cultural Construction of Teaching* (New York: Teachers College Press, 1995),1–6.

[b]"*Stand and Deliver,*" American Playhouse, Warner Brothers Pictures, 1988.

Working conditions for teachers

Many people choose careers in teaching because they enjoy working with young people, want to make a difference, or were inspired by a former teacher.[44] Yet for others, these benefits of the profession are outweighed by concerns about working conditions such as salary, lack of autonomy, inadequate support, and the realities of teaching in our current accountability regime.

Salary and pay gap

Low teacher salary is the top reason most say they are not interested in teaching careers.[45] A majority of parents also said they would not want their children to become teachers, citing low pay as a major factor, according to a 2018 poll. This was the first time since the annual poll began, fifty years earlier, that over half of respondents answered this way. At the same time, most agreed that the low pay should be addressed: 73 percent of respondents said they would support their local teachers going on strike for more pay.[46] The majority (61 percent) also said they had trust and confidence in public school teachers, though this rate was the lowest since the question was first asked in 2010.

Trends in public perception of teacher pay mirror actual changes in salaries over the years, relative to other careers requiring similar levels of education. In 1996, teachers earned 6.1 percent on average less per week than their college-educated non-teacher peers. However, by 2021, that number had ballooned to 23.5 percent. This gap varies greatly by state, but teachers are paid less than their peers in every state, even when accounting for benefits, teachers' shorter work year, and cost-of-living differences across regions. In the majority of states, teachers are paid less than 80 cents for every dollar earned by their similarly educated peers.

This reflects a broader pattern of less spending on education. In 2015, twenty-nine states were spending less per pupil, adjusted for inflation, than they did before the Great Recession of 2008. Many teachers view this divestment as part of a decades-long, bipartisan attack on public schools.[47] The wage gap shrank slightly in 2019 after a series of teacher walkouts in several states led to pay raises, but these gains did not last.[48]

However, teacher pay in many regions was increased through COVID-era ESSER funds. Although these were one-time funds, many states and districts found new funding sources to sustain those salary increases beyond the end of ESSER.[49] In 2023, US Secretary of Education Miguel Cardona called for states and the Department of Education to address the teacher shortage by increasing salaries. Congress also introduced the *American Teacher Act* and the *Pay Teachers Act* to increase federal support for raises.

Suggested Activity: Research various aspects of teacher salaries, for example how they compare across states. How is your state doing? What do you think might be some reasons for your state's ranking in teacher pay?

See "Gains in Teacher Pay May Not Be Enough to Ease Shortages" in *NEA Today* (April 30, 2024) https://www.nea.org/nea-today/all-news-articles/gains-teacher-pay-may-not-be-enough-ease-shortages

Moral rewards, standardization, and high-stakes accountability

Many decide to pursue careers in teaching despite the lower pay because of the **moral rewards** teaching offers. Moral rewards have been defined as the fulfillment teachers experience when they feel they are "doing what is right in terms of their students, the profession, and themselves." Trends over the last few decades have made these rewards less and less available to teachers.[50] These trends have been called the **standards, assessment, and accountability movement,** often associated with the passage of the **No Child Left Behind Act** of 2002.[51] The curriculum has become more standardized and prescriptive, and teachers' success is increasingly measured through narrow metrics such as students' scores on high-stakes tests. Teachers have thus faced increased pressures to prioritize preparing students for tests over development of knowledge, skills, and lifelong love of learning. These pressures are most severe in schools serving high-poverty neighborhoods, resulting in a narrowing of the curriculum that serves to further marginalize the already marginalized.[52]

> **For Further Reflection**: Teaching has been referred to as a "labor of love." What is your response to this statement?

In some cases, concern over test scores has led districts and schools to adopt **scripted curriculum**. Scripted curricula are typically commercially prepared and require teachers to read directly from a script, limiting teachers' ability to tailor lessons to their students' interests, allow spontaneous discussion prompted by student questions, and apply their expertise to improve the materials. Although the intent behind scripted curriculum is to ensure quality and consistency in student instruction, researchers have demonstrated that such curriculum stifles teachers' creativity and autonomy, inhibits responsiveness to cultural and individual student differences, and signals to teachers that their professional judgment is not trusted.[53]

Also referred to as "teacher-proof" curricula, these are often viewed as attempts to **deskill** the work of teaching. Others have argued that scripted curriculum threatens democracy insofar as it suppresses "students' intellectual freedom and hence their capacity to grow into autonomous citizens especially when accompanied by standardized assessments and accountability measures."[54]

Scholars also point to the special interests at play, given the high profits these curricula garner for publishers, often through district purchases which are funded through taxpayer dollars. Schools in high-poverty communities are more likely to use scripted curricula, which leads to less teacher autonomy, responsiveness, and flexibility in the classrooms that arguably most need these. Studies comparing the effectiveness of scripted to non-scripted curricula have yielded mixed results.[55]

When considering the high-stakes testing movement, it is important to remember **Campbell's Law**. Named for Donald T. Campbell, an American social scientist, Campbell's Law states that the more a society relies on a specific numerical measure to make important decisions, the more likely that measure will end up distorting the very processes it was originally intended to assess. For example, if standardized test scores are meant to assess students' content knowledge, but teachers then devote extra time to test-taking skills, those test scores will become a better measure of students' test-taking skills than their actual content knowledge.

> **For Further Reflection:** Overall, do you think the movement toward more assessment and accountability has affected the moral rewards of teaching? Why or why not?

Teacher evaluation systems and merit pay

Throughout most of the history of public school systems in the United States, teacher evaluation systems were determined at the local level—either at the district or school level. Teacher efficacy was generally assessed through observations by a principal or other administrator. As accountability-focused policy makers implemented systems for measuring student performance through high-stakes standardized tests, they began looking toward those same tests to measure the performance of teachers. President Obama's 2009 Race to the Top (RTTT) program provided states with competitive funding based on a range of criteria, one of which was that they develop teacher evaluation policies that incorporated student test score data. At the same time, laws were introduced to limit teacher unions' capacities to collectively bargain for particular evaluation systems. Among the states, there was bipartisan enthusiasm for this idea as well as significant funding from both the federal government and philanthropic organizations like the Bill & Melinda Gates Foundation.

Critics have argued that teaching and learning are so complex that it is difficult, if not impossible, to design evaluation systems that capture the "outputs" of an individual teacher within the network of support a student receives. However, proponents of test-based teacher evaluation pointed to a relatively new statistical approach called ***value-added modeling (VAM)*** as a means of estimating the contributions of a single teacher to a student's academic achievement. VAM uses past test scores of a given student to estimate the growth expected of that student in the upcoming year. In doing so, VAM was purported to account for the effects of external-to-teacher factors, like student socioeconomic status and prior achievement. However, researchers found many challenges in reliably and accurately applying this model. For one, VAM in a content area such as reading could influence VAM in another teacher's class, such as science or mathematics. Researchers also found that the model was statistically biased toward students with higher prior achievement, even though VAM was intended to address that very issue. Cautionary statements were released by several prominent education organizations, and support for test-based teacher evaluation systems rapidly declined. By 2015, the federal government abandoned this approach to measuring teacher quality, though some states kept test scores as one component of their evaluation systems.[56]

Another component of the standards, assessment, and accountability reforms has been an increased focus on incentivizing teachers through means such as **merit pay,** also called *pay for performance.* Merit pay is typically defined as temporary or permanent salary increases based on effectiveness. Since 2006, the federal government has awarded billions of dollars in grants to fund merit pay systems across the country. Merit pay is generally tied to students' performance on standardized tests, which poses challenges described in the paragraph above. Moreover, linking pay to test scores can incentivize teachers merely to teach to the test—or worse—cheat. Teachers may also be disincentivized to teach in schools with high truancy, or high rates of students with disabilities or language learning needs. Other critics point out that merit pay sets up a system of competition rather than cooperation, when the latter is what is most needed in schools.[57] As with scripted curriculum, the research has yielded mixed results with regard to the effectiveness of merit pay for increasing student performance, in part because merit pay plans differ so greatly from one another.[58]

Suggested Activity: Research current debates about merit pay. What are valid arguments for and against this practice?

Many have argued that the emphasis on high-stakes testing, prescriptive curriculum, and **teacher accountability** systems is missing the mark. Instead of schools as organizations where success depends on top-down tinkering with administrative structures, technological tools, and teacher accountability measures, work environments in schools ought to be seen as professional communities where reflective professional practice, collegial collaboration, and mutual responsibility in educating students are the norms. Relationships among teachers, students, and subject matter constitute the "stuff of schooling," and these things all occur within a professional community that plays a large role in whether teachers succeed or get burned out. Hence, **reflective professional communities** must be nurtured to encourage critical inquiry, focus on solving classroom problems, and support professional growth and change. Teachers tend to thrive in supportive environments of this kind, as opposed to those characterized by a lack of intellectual stimulation, overly individualistic norms of privacy, lack of collegial interaction and feedback, and lack of exposure to new ideas.[59]

> **Suggested Activity:** Research the teacher evaluation system in your state. Does your state include student test scores as one component of a teacher's evaluation? What other measures are included? Overall, how well do you think your state's evaluation system can accurately capture the effectiveness of teachers?

COVID-19, partisan polarization, and teaching sensitive topics

The convergence of the COVID-19 pandemic of 2020 and growing partisan polarization (which predated that event but has only since increased) has placed teachers in the crosshairs of political battles. COVID-related school closures affected an estimated 94 percent of the global population. Within the United States, much instruction shifted to a remote format, often through video conferencing. The early months of virtual instruction saw an outpouring of parental appreciation for the difficult work teachers do, spurred by parents' direct observations of the instruction now happening on computers in their homes.[60]

However, this appreciation was short-lived. When many teachers called for schooling to remain virtual to minimize COVID exposure risk for both students and staff, teacher unions became vilified and blamed for prolonged school closures.[61] "Parents matter" emerged as a campaign slogan that increased support for conservative politicians and decreased support for teachers and public schools. Conservative politicians capitalized on and expanded this anti-teacher sentiment by renewing old culture war attacks on public schools as bastions of left-wing ideological indoctrination.[62] This charge against teachers came behind the Black Lives Matter protests following the murder of George Floyd by police officers on May 25, 2020. Many schools and districts across the country responded to this movement by increasing their equity and inclusion efforts in various ways such as creating equity offices, providing training on racial awareness, and initiating other related programs. In response, conservative politicians and media figures began a coordinated effort to dismantle these changes.[63]

Across the country, states and localities implemented policies restricting how teachers could discuss race, gender, and diversity. Educational researchers have called this movement the **conflict campaign**, referring to the exploitation of divisions over how to teach race and inclusion in our society in order to win political campaigns. Though these divisions are indeed real, they have been magnified by political strategists disseminating model legislation across the country.[64]

Between September 2020 and September 2024, a total of 861 bills, executive orders, and other measures were introduced across the United States that would restrict teaching on race and gender.[65] Eighteen states enacted bans through legislation or other avenues, with most of these being Southern or Central states. Most of these bans prohibit the teaching of what has been labeled "divisive concepts," which originates from a September 2020 executive order issued by then-President Trump. That order, which was later rescinded by President Biden, banned trainings that included such ideas as that people of a certain race have unconscious bias, that any individual should feel discomfort or guilt on account of their race or sex, and that the United States is fundamentally racist or sexist. Proponents of these types of bans have intentionally mislabeled this set of ideas "critical race theory" (for more on critical race theory, see Chapter 4).[66] Christopher Rufo, a conservative activist and one of the architects of the conflict campaign, explained his reason for this intentional mislabeling in his post on Twitter/X:

> We will eventually turn Critical Race Theory toxic, as we put all of the various cultural insanities under that brand category. The goal is to have the public reading something crazy in the newspaper and immediately think 'critical race theory.' We have decodified the term and will recodify it to annex the entire range of cultural constructions that are unpopular with Americans.[67]

Teachers and school leaders have reported confusion about what qualifies as a "divisive concept" or "critical race theory" and what they are still allowed to teach. This appears to be part of the intention behind the bills—to produce a chilling effect, meaning that teachers self-censor in an attempt to err on the side of caution. Research suggests teachers are indeed more afraid to discuss sensitive topics as a result of this campaign, even in states that have not been affected by bans. One study estimated that 35 percent of all K12 students in the United States have been impacted by local actions related to the conflict campaign, such as hostility at school board meetings.[68]

Another survey found that one in three teachers have changed or skipped topics because they feared backlash, despite the fact that three out of four educators agree on the importance of teaching students how to have respectful conversations with people they disagree with on important issues. The survey also found, however, that the vast majority of teachers who did continue to address controversial topics in their classrooms reported no negative consequences. The majority (63 percent) said no one noticed, while 21 percent reported that they received positive feedback about the approach they thought might be controversial.[69]

Another survey found that 66 percent of adults believe teachers should have "substantial say in what's taught in schools," which is more than those who say they would like local residents, school boards, or lawmakers to have this kind of influence.[70] Thus it seems that the laws are misleading teachers into thinking they are more at risk of repercussions than they actually are. In the midst of these fraught sociopolitical contexts, it is important for teachers to remember three things:

(1) Teachers have greater jurisdiction over their classrooms than they may think;
(2) Teachers can find and create safety and solidarity through professional organizations and local networks; and
(3) Teachers are positioned to carry on an impressive legacy of teaching for social justice and advocating for students' right to learn.[71]

Teachers must also remember that one of the (perhaps most important) roles of public education in a democracy is to equip students with the ability to engage in informed dissent and critical analysis of social problems. Thus, self-censorship may feel safer in the moment but ultimately fails to prepare students to sustain and strengthen democracy.[72]

Improving education through strengthening the teaching profession

These are both challenging and exciting times for the profession of teaching. The growing recognition of the problem that too few people (and particularly people of color) are entering and staying in the teaching profession has spurred numerous efforts to reimagine pathways into the career. These include new pathways within university-based teacher education programs as well as alternative pathways such as accelerated licensure programs and even online, for-profit credentialing companies. Many states, in attempts to address their teacher shortages, have opted to lower barriers to entry rather than improve salaries and working conditions for teachers.[73] Though that approach may help with recruitment of new teachers, it may actually be counterproductive in terms of retention. Research has found that teachers who complete a teacher preparation program including student teaching are three times more likely to remain in the profession after their first year than those who do not.[74]

Many of the reimagined pathways into the profession are attempting to address two problems at once: the lack of ethnic and racial diversity in the teacher workforce and the overall recruitment and retention issues.

Diversifying the teacher workforce

Over the past few decades, the share of teachers of color in the workforce has grown from 12 to 20 percent. However, this is still far below the rates of adults of color in the general population and students of color in the K12 population, which was 55 percent in the fall of 2024. There are many reasons to be concerned about this disparity. A few include:

- Studies have found that a racially and ethnically diverse workforce has academic, social, and emotional benefits for all students, particularly students of color.
- Students of color have fewer absences and suspensions when they have greater access to teachers of color, which may be due, at least in part, to the relationship building and classroom climate strategies employed by these teachers.
- Teachers of color often feel called to teach in low-income communities of color where positions are sometimes hard to fill. They also hold higher expectations of students of color.
- Having more teachers of color provides a support network for other teachers of color, resulting in higher retention rates and school stability.[75]

There are also fewer multilingual teachers than multilingual students. Over 20 percent of K12 students speak a language other than English at home; however, only 13 percent of K12 teachers do. Research finds that teachers who speak the same home language as their students and teachers with bilingual certificates are more effective at improving the achievement of English learners. Research also suggests that recruiting and retaining more teachers with disabilities would have a positive impact on students with diverse needs and abilities. Both school leaders and paraprofessionals tend to be more diverse than classroom teachers.[76]

Research has identified several promising practices for recruiting and retaining teachers of color. Many of these target the costs associated with teacher preparation, given this is one reason many people of color choose not to enter the profession. Promising practices include:

- Ensuring access to high-quality teacher preparation programs through means such as reducing tuition costs;
- Modifying state licensure requirements to allow for more authentic assessments of teaching performance than multiple-choice exams;
- Paying teacher candidates for the work they perform as interns, for example, through residency or apprenticeship programs (described below);
- Improving district hiring practices and mentorship of new teachers of color, and
- Improving teaching conditions including positive school cultures and ensuring administrative support is provided to teachers.[77]

During the Biden administration, the US Department of Education expanded its grant programs to diversify the teacher workforce through recruitment, preparation, and retention. From 2022 to 2023, they increased the number of grants from 165 to 263 and funding from $370 million to $450 million. Some of these efforts include reducing the financial debt burden of attending teacher preparation programs and ensuring high-quality pathways with strong clinical experiences, such as residencies, apprenticeships, and grow-your-own programs, described in the next sections.[78]

Suggested Activity: Research characteristics of public school teachers, such as gender, race/ethnicity, languages spoken, educational attainment across elementary and secondary schools. See "Characteristics of Public School Teachers," National Center for Education Statistics,

https://nces.ed.gov/programs/coe/indicator/clr/public-school-teachers and "America's Missing Bilingual Teachers," https://tcf.org/content/commentary/americas-missing-bilingual-teachers/#:~:text=Just%2013%20percent%20of%20U.S.,21%20percent%20of%20U.S.%20children.

Residency, apprenticeship, and Grow-Your-Own programs

Teacher residency programs are modeled after the medical residencies completed by people training to become doctors. Rather than spend twelve or fifteen weeks as a student teacher in one's final semester of coursework, teacher residents spend a full year co-teaching with a highly trained mentor teacher in a high-needs classroom. Residents typically take courses at the same time as their clinical experience, which allows them to immediately apply theories learned in their coursework to classroom practice. The first residency program began in 2001 in Chicago, and they have now spread to over sixty locations across twenty-six states.[79] Most residencies offer tuition support and stipends to offset living expenses during the year, in exchange for a commitment to work for a minimum number of years in the partnering district. Most residencies also offer support and mentoring for recent graduates of the program. Some also cluster their residents in particular schools so that the network of residents and alumni can support one another.[80]

Residency models are helping to diversify the teaching profession, increase teacher retention, and staff high-needs schools and subject areas. In 2023–4, 67 percent of residents identified as persons of color, compared to 21 percent of new teachers nationally.[81] Teachers who graduate from residency programs are much less likely to leave the profession in the first five years, even though most teach in Title I schools with higher teacher turnover. Part of the reason for this may be that these programs attract more mid-career switchers than traditional and alternative programs, which means residents have more life experiences. Graduates of residency programs also serve in more high-needs subject areas such as special education, STEM, and English as a Second Language.[82] Finally, surveys of principals have found that 94 percent report that graduates of residency programs are more effective than a typical first-year teacher.[83]

Registered apprenticeships similarly pay teacher candidates while they are learning on the job, with the main difference from residency programs being that apprentices are actually employees of their schools while they are learning. While the US Department of Labor has long funded apprenticeship programs in other industries, it was not until 2022 that the Department began funding apprenticeship programs in teaching. Through these funds, states can sponsor districts to hire apprentices and coordinate with educator preparation programs (EPPs) to provide apprentices with necessary training. Apprentices earn a livable wage and do not have to pay for tuition while they are learning to teach. In these ways, apprenticeship programs are designed to address shortages while also enhancing the quality of teacher preparation and diversifying the workforce.[84]

One final model that has shown promise for increasing teacher retention and diversity is **Grow-Your-Own (GYO) programs**. These are programs in which prospective teaching candidates are recruited from local communities—for instance, through outreach to paraprofessionals, graduating high school seniors, and career changers. Similar to apprenticeship programs, the model is that these local community members are paid while they earn their degree and license.[85] Research on this model is difficult to synthesize because programs vary widely across states and localities, making it challenging to compare them. However, a central idea of these models is that those from the community or already serving within the community may be more equipped and committed to culturally responsive, affirming, and language- and race-conscious approaches to instruction. Some preliminary research suggests that this focus on community solidarity and affirming practices does help recruit and retain teachers of color, especially in high-needs schools.[86]

What does it mean for teaching to be a profession?

As described in the historical background section of this chapter, educators have long argued that teachers should be treated as professionals, meaning that their profession is based on knowledge, training, ethical conduct, status, rewards, and a degree of autonomous control over the work. However, public school teachers have never been treated as professionals in the same way that, say, physicians, lawyers, and professors have.

Teaching as a traditional profession

Some observers maintain that teaching must claim its place among the traditional learned professions. For example, Lee Shulman argues that teachers are professionals because their work is guided by standards rather than mere rules. Their work requires them to make informed decisions when confronted with unpredictable situations and challenging teaching-learning conditions. Rather than following static guidelines, teachers must respond frequently to unexpected circumstances by using expertise derived from professional standards, something they share in common with other learned professions.[87]

Teachers as intellectuals

Some observers would like to see the teaching profession adopt a model of teachers as **transformative intellectuals**. Henry Giroux, a theorist of **critical pedagogy**, has long argued that teachers should be involved in debates about educational policy and school reform, and he has been highly critical of the model of teachers as technicians who simply follow other people's orders. He maintains that teachers perform *intellectual* labor rather than purely *technical* (or instrumental) labor. Furthermore, teachers play a distinctive political role because they are morally obligated to raise questions about the curriculum and about what and how they teach, rather than uncritically teaching everything handed to them. They also should not accept being relegated to "mere employee" status, but should link their preparation and professional knowledge to the goals of education for a more democratic society.

Schools are not isolated institutions immune to politics, because political power is so often used to control them; instead, they should be places where knowledge and values from the past and present are taught to rising generations to help them shape their own visions of the future, particularly when powerful interest groups try to dictate what is taught in schools and exert control over the minds of the young. This is apparent in curriculum controversies over such issues as school prayer, evolution, patriotism, and censorship of materials. Neutrality may be difficult, but rather than partisanship, teachers should be dedicated to preparing students for active roles as democratic citizens who try to understand issues, solve problems, and achieve a more just society. As Giroux sees it, this is the crucial transformative role of teachers.[88]

> **For Further Reflection:** Should teachers be transformative intellectuals, and if so, what does that mean in the specific context of the daily routines of schooling?

Teachers, technical expertise, and moral agency

Certainly, there is ample historical and contemporary evidence to show that technical expertise has helped accomplish advances in many areas of life. As Robert Welker points out, however, sometimes these accomplishments get mythologized into a belief that technical expertise ultimately will solve our problems. Such a viewpoint fails to recognize the realities faced by teachers in actual classrooms and schools. Clearly, teachers gain from acquiring better technical expertise, but they also face problems that do not simply reduce to technical solutions. For example, teaching a child to read is helped by a teacher's technical know-how, but bridging the gap between teaching a child to read and other, sometimes conflicting, societal expectations requires more than just technical skill.

Society's expectation that schools should build a strong sense of identity with the greater community may actually come into conflict with society's expectation that schools also should build a strong sense of individual freedom. Community identity and individual freedom do not have to be in conflict, but they often are. Again, it is one thing to teach a child to read (which may be difficult enough), but educating a child to accept a strong community identity while at the same time imbuing that child with an equally strong sense of individual freedom may be far more difficult and take longer to accomplish. "Community identity" and "individual freedom" are primarily moral goals, not technical ones. Their achievement depends not only on what teachers do but on society clarifying its moral and social expectations and achieving a better understanding of what schools may reasonably accomplish.

Complex educational goals are likely to call for complex solutions, and while technical efficiency helps, by itself it is not sufficient. The technical expertise model for the teaching profession remains strong, however, for if teachers are seen as technical experts (the thinking goes), then they will gain a place among the more exclusive professions whose technical proficiencies have brought them high status and credibility (such as the engineering profession).

A problem with such a view is that teaching is not the same as engineering, for no particular teaching technique has yet been devised that is as predictably successful as the mathematical precision of many engineering techniques. The language of technical expertise promises predictable, consistent success, but as experienced teachers well know, perseverance, patience, humor, and good will, which are moral and social qualities, play a vitally important role in good teaching. In sum, teaching is different from professions defined primarily by technical expertise; hence, we must recognize the moral basis of teaching, not in some sentimental sense, but in the larger sense of what kind of person or citizen we want to develop and what kind of individual and social life we want to cultivate, questions that are as fundamental now as when they were first raised centuries ago.[89]

Teaching as a unique profession

There are various ways of defining the term "*profession.*" It may mean doing something for pay, as in "professional athlete." It could connote objective detachment, disinterest, or technical excellence. It might indicate the results of prolonged and rigorous study of a particular field or simply a high level of competence at certain tasks. Such an array of definitions not only allows neurosurgeons to be considered professionals but also football players and car thieves. In other words, the term "*profession*" is a social construct, carrying particular meanings according to usage and context.

Despite these variations, however, there are characteristics most people associate with the term *"learned" profession,* that is, a profession based on knowledge, training, ethical conduct, status, rewards, and a degree of autonomous control of the work. By and large, to be a member of a learned profession has positive connotations as something desirable in both an individual and a social sense. Various professional groups, such as physicians, have invested much time, effort, and resources in pursuing public respect and protecting their professional status with both public relations and legal safeguards. Teachers are not very different, for while they may not enjoy as much status, remuneration, or legal protection as physicians, teachers have long claimed professional status and have sought to establish themselves as a full-fledged profession.[90]

The argument continues, however, that teachers err when attempting to emulate established professions such as medicine, because teachers are simply unable to replicate the same path that medicine took. Physicians once had to contend with a historic image that included incompetent quacks who sullied the medical profession's reputation to the detriment of its competent practitioners. Medicine's image improved significantly only after several major developments: scientific and technological advances that brought more predictable results to the practice of medicine and tougher entry requirements for medical school students and their more rigorous preparation in appropriate scientific and technical knowledge. These changes noticeably improved the services provided by physicians, and they also helped give the medical profession an authoritative image.

An outpouring of new educational science and technology that yields similar results for teaching seems unlikely in the foreseeable future. Teachers should bury the dream of becoming like physicians, mainly because comparing physicians and teachers is akin to comparing apples and oranges: They are not the same, either logically or practically. The recommendation is that teachers should drop such comparisons and focus instead on what is unique and applicable to teaching itself, such as its moral basis. Students are sent to school in compliance with compulsory attendance laws, and they are placed in the charge of teachers who may be virtual strangers to both the parents and the students. In turn, teachers are supposed to give competent, ethically committed instruction to all students equally, providing them with opportunities to grow intellectually and to develop their humanity. These particular traits are unique to the teaching profession and make teaching an inherently moral endeavor.[91]

This line of argument is bolstered by Gary D. Fenstermacher, who points to three significant factors that make the teaching profession fundamentally different from other learned professions. The first factor is the **mystification of knowledge** found in traditional learned professions such as medicine and law. For example, physicians and lawyers "mystify" knowledge when they embrace claims that only they know how to diagnose and treat illnesses or interpret and argue points of law. In education, however, teachers strive to give away their knowledge.

The second factor deals with **social distance**, something other professions maintain by typically avoiding involvement in the lives of clients/patients beyond specific conditions (i.e., a client's property rights, a patient's liver condition). Teachers, however, cannot ignore the life experiences of learners. The third factor is **reciprocity of effort**. Those in other learned professions usually want the client or patient to defer to their professional judgments without needing them to fully understand either the reasoning or the knowledge behind those judgments. In teaching, however, reciprocity of effort is central because success depends on the active involvement of students in learning the teacher's field of knowledge and becoming skillful in applying its concepts.[92]

Paulo Freire goes even further and argues that, not only must students actively participate in the learning process, but teachers also must be active learners concerning what and who they teach and how they and their students might grow from the process. In other words, both students and teachers must be involved in one another's intellectual growth.[93] Freire's 1970 book *Pedagogy of the Oppressed*, inspired by his work teaching literacy to impoverished villagers in Brazil, is a foundational text in the critical pedagogy movement. In the book, he argues that education serves either to produce conformity in the next generation or to liberate people to transform their world.[94]

> **Suggested Activity:** Interview three people at random about their definitions of "*professional*." Compare their responses and analyze what the differences and similarities mean.

Professional ethics

A long-recognized feature of any learned profession is to be guided by ethical standards. The relation of ethics to education is a very old concern, for just as people today encounter controversy over what proper education ought to be, so did people in ancient times. For example, in the fourth century BCE, Aristotle complained that there were "no generally accepted assumptions about what the young should learn" or whether education should be directed "at things useful in life, or at those conducive to virtue, or at exceptional accomplishments."[95] Today, debate continues to surround what should be taught, what the purpose of schools should be, and whether the chief result should be job preparation, intellectual achievement, virtuous moral character, or a combination of such ends.

Part of the debate concerns the preparation of professional educators themselves. Some observers argue that what teachers most need is practical "hands-on" experience in the "real" world of schools, not time spent on "theoretical" studies such as **professional ethics**. Others argue that while teachers need practical preparation, they also need the intellectual depth that comes from reading, debating, and reflecting on the ethical issues of their profession and the larger society. The position taken here is that members of the teaching profession need to know not only what to teach and how to teach it but also the ethical standards for good professional practice and how to apply them.

What is professional ethics?

Aristotle claimed that all human conduct aims at some notion of "the good," but the pursuit of a good (such as wealth, power, or respect) may be used for evil purposes. What we need is a better understanding of "the good" in the general sense, which for Aristotle was "the good of the human community or society." The way we define good in ordinary life is related to specific practical goods, such as health, success, and the enjoyment of life. For Aristotle, the pursuit of all goods should aim at one end, "happiness," by which he did not mean mere pleasure. He meant ways of living chosen for their inherent goodness. This involves avoiding the excesses of too much (overindulgence, compulsiveness) and too little (insufficient effort, shallowness). In other words, it means seeking the ethical "golden mean" between extremes and pursuing moderation in life situations by using rational thought and ethical principles to guide conduct and achieve happiness.[96]

Nel Noddings has articulated a contemporary view of Aristotelian happiness, with application to certain educational issues. She argues against the current emphasis on higher test scores as the ultimate aim and proposes instead an earnest debate on the aims of education. One central aim should be to help students work toward happiness, not as frivolous pleasure but as an essential life goal. In this sense, "happiness" is the avoidance of fatalism and the development of talents (such as learning to appreciate what is morally valuable and increasing knowledge of life and the world). All of us need to understand that, while we cannot solve every problem confronting us, we are not totally helpless and can work toward at least some improvements in personal and social life.

However, caught up in today's test-driven mentality (a singular focus on measurement and quantification), schools are often forced to ignore such moral aims. What the curriculum should reflect is helping students better understand, appreciate, and become more skillfully engaged in life in communities, civic responsibilities, friendships, and meaningful occupations. This does not mean weakening the curriculum with simplistic "how-to" courses, but—for example—using literature to help students explore life experiences reflecting both happiness and tragedy. Rather than test score mania, students should be taught a challenging academic curriculum that builds the kinds of understandings, appreciations, and skills needed in life.[97] When education is considered from the ethical standpoint of happiness as one of its ultimate aims, it leads to useful conceptions of value that far outweigh test scores.

> **For Further Reflection:** Do you think one of the aims of education should be happiness? How would you define happiness? How would schools pursue this aim?

The origin of the English word "ethics" is derived from the Greek word *ethos*, which originally meant the customs and usages of a society, including its views on character and disposition. Similarly, in Latin, the word for those concepts was *mores*, from which the English word "moral" is derived. The meanings of both terms cover ways of behaving that are approved by a society, and to act against the ethos (ethics) or mores (morals) of a society is to violate norms of "good" and "bad," "right" and "wrong."[98]

Today, ethics is still concerned with right or wrong and the good or bad of human conduct. It involves thinking critically about what we do and how we do it in order to make sound judgments and take good or right actions. Ethical thought and action involve both the "inner" life of individual reflection and the "outer" life of social relationships. Ethical life involves interactions with other people, especially how we should treat others and how we expect to be treated by them in turn. Factual knowledge about individual and societal conditions (or "what is") may help us make ethical judgments, but facts alone rarely solve ethical dilemmas. A condition long recognized by ethicists is that factual claims try to describe the world as it is, and they are true if the world is as described. Ethical claims, however, are different: They do not describe the world as it is, factually speaking, but how personal and social life should or ought to be lived. In short, factual claims *describe*, whereas ethical claims *prescribe* ways to help us reflect on how we should live. Therefore, we need to be informed by ethical traditions and customs, by great moral teachers and moral teachings, and by our own critical (or reflective) thought and experience.[99]

Professional ethics is the application of general ethical principles to professional conduct and to solving ethical dilemmas encountered in professional practice. Working for good and doing right may seem to be clear-cut things: We should simply choose the good and right and act accordingly. Of course, a clear path is not readily apparent. One good may conflict with another, or we may find ourselves facing only bad choices in which all the likely options we can devise seem seriously flawed. Most teachers need background preparation to help them understand ethical issues in professional practice and to develop better reasoning skills. Professional practice, as life itself, requires us to make ethical choices and decisions.

For Further Reflection: Are people born with an innate sense of right and wrong, or are these things learned from one's environment? Do teachers need specific preparation in professional ethics, or do they learn all they need to know about ethics and moral reasoning from ordinary life experiences? Consider arguments both for and against your own conclusions.

Ethical values and professional educators

There is a need to be wary of mere lists of values and virtues because they might lull us into assuming they contain all we need to solve any ethical dilemma. In fact, solving ethical dilemmas is hard work, and difficult ethical problems rarely have simplistic solutions. Reflecting on values never hurts, however, and the following list provides some well-known examples to consider in both professional and personal life:

- Honesty. Truthful conduct in professional interactions with students and others, including judgments on student progress and teaching the curriculum without intentionally distorting subject matter.

- Candor. Being forthright when a student thinks he or she is performing satisfactorily but is not. Candor should be provided in helpful, supportive ways that foster student growth, not in punitive ways that diminish the student.
- Competence. Competence is not a moral virtue per se, but an incompetent professional cannot deliver trustworthy professional service. Becoming more competent should be a constant goal.
- Diligence. Carrying out professional duties and obligations in timely manners, such as always being prepared for class and evaluating student work in a timely fashion.
- Discretion (or Confidentiality). Care of personal knowledge and opinions professionals gain of students as well as official school records. It is the educator's obligation to protect confidential information about students in accordance with law and school policy.
- Fairness. Treatment of an individual student or group of students in comparison with other individuals and groups of students. The educator's obligation to fairness stems from the principle of democratic equality.
- Loyalty. Working for the good of students but not in unethical ways (such as glowing but untruthful recommendations to a student's prospective employers). Ordinarily, the educator's foremost loyalty should be to the student, but this may sometimes conflict with obligations to third parties such as parents.

Sources: Adapted from Material in Michael D. Bayles, Professional Ethics, 2nd Edition, Belmond, CA.: Wadsworth, Inc., 1989, 79–99; and the National Education Association, *Code of Ethics for the Education Profession*, (adopted 1975), at http://www.nea.org/home/30442.htm (accessed on September 23, 2010).

Ethical obligations of the teaching profession

For teachers and other educators, the primary ethical obligation is the educational well-being and growth of students. A related obligation is met in serving student growth, because in doing so educators are serving society itself (including third parties such as parents, citizens, and taxpayers). Closely related are obligations to the employer and to the profession itself and how these impact students and third parties. In other words, professional ethical obligations serve to prescribe (or even to proscribe) certain professional actions or character traits of professionals.[100]

"Trust" refers to students' (and the public's) moral right to expect (or trust) that professional educators will work to promote the educational growth of each student. The teacher's overall ethical obligation is to provide professional services worthy of student and public trust. This obligation is sometimes called "beneficence," and it is a major reason why professional standing is granted by society through certification or licensure, which is supposed to signify that the holder is competent to deliver good professional service.[101]

Although a professional educator's primary obligations are to students, there are also obligations to third parties, such as parents, taxpayers, citizens, and prospective employers. This means that professional service ought to be delivered in ways that serve not only the good of students but also the public good (or the good of the wider society). In other words, ethical obligations to students must be reasonably balanced with obligations to others.[102]

Sometimes professionals provide services to other professionals, such as serving on committees that evaluate peers for awards, promotions, or other personnel-related tasks. One should protect confidential information about fellow employees, but one should be candid and truthful to the employer concerning relevant information about other employees encountered in legitimate personnel deliberations.[103]

Obligations to the profession include engaging in research and study for knowledge acquisition, skill development, and other improvements in one's competence and encouraging the same commitment among colleagues. A professional is also obligated to improve the status, working conditions, remuneration, and prestige of the profession because public respect enhances professional effectiveness; however, this should not be merely self-serving. Positive public opinion is extremely important for the teaching profession, because it cannot effectively provide professional services without ethical and competent members and without public respect and support.[104]

Suggested Activity: Interview an educator about the potential tensions between the ethical obligations and the reality of their daily experiences in their jobs.

Professional organizations and societies

Teachers have long come together in professional organizations or societies to learn from colleagues and researchers, and these organizations are important tools in extending professional knowledge and skills. They range in size, scope, and mission. Almost all of them are engaged in supporting and enhancing the professional work of teachers. For example, some organizations are devoted to broad teaching fields, such as the National Council for the Social Studies (history, geography, civics, or government), the American Council on the Teaching of Foreign Languages (French, Spanish, German, etc.), or the National Science

Teachers Association (biology, chemistry, physics, etc.). Others are dedicated to specific disciplines or subjects in the curriculum, such as the National Council for Teachers of English and the National Association of Biology Teachers. Some are national in focus while others are international, such as the Association for Childhood Education International or the International Reading Association. Some organizations focus on a specific age or school level while others concentrate on certain needs, such as the Council for Exceptional Children.

All of the major professional organizations have central goals of disseminating research, information, publications (reports, white papers, newsletters, journals). Almost all major organizations also have state and local chapters, so wherever teachers are located there will likely be chapters within reasonable geographical access that hold meetings and disseminate publications and other materials.

Suggested Activity: Visit the website of the professional organization that most closely represents your own professional interests. See what helpful information you can find.

Educators forming and joining professional societies organized around subjects, student ages or school levels, or other specific professional interests seems to generate little or no controversy. Such organizations appear to be clearly dedicated to the development of professional competencies or the extension of education to more people. Controversy tends to emerge only when educators join groups that speak out forcefully for advancing the economic interests of the profession.

For Further Reflection: Why does a teacher's right to organize in unions seem more controversial than other people's rights to do the same? What is your opinion about the issue, and why?

Should professionals belong to unions?

When the topic of teacher unions is raised, it is usually collective bargaining that comes to mind. To be fair, teacher unions do far more than advocate collective bargaining on economic issues, but the use of strikes is usually one of the features of being a union. In 2024, the NEA claimed over 3 million members and the AFT claimed 1.8 million.[105] As these numbers attest, many teachers apparently value

Figure 1.2 January 22, 2019. UTLA teachers rally downtown to celebrate the end of the strike.

unions, not only for their focus on research, publications, and teaching-learning issues, but also the benefits that may come from collective bargaining. Salary and fringe benefits are certainly important aspects of collective bargaining but so are issues such as educators being required to teach subjects for which they are not qualified, or situations where the health and safety of students and teachers are threatened by unsafe conditions, to name but two. Without collective bargaining, teachers individually would have to confront powerful forces and bear the full costs of legal fees and loss of personal time.

Teacher unions also have vociferous critics. For example, one critic calls teacher unions the "worms in the American Education Apple" and the NEA the "National Extortion Association."[106] One criticism is that unions lead to overpayment of public employees, and another is that unions protect bad teachers from being dismissed and reward seniority over merit. However, one study comparing human resource practices in school systems with collective bargaining versus without found (1) little difference and (2) that many of the criticized practices are likely the result of the bureaucracies of the large urban districts in which most of the studied unions operate, rather than of collective bargaining.[107]

Multiple studies have found a positive relationship between teachers unions and student achievement on standardized tests. Some studies suggest that the reason for this increased achievement is the higher salaries and greater autonomy secured by unions.[108] Unions also help attract and retain higher-quality teachers and boost morale through better working conditions. One study found the relationship between student achievement and collective bargaining was particularly strong for Black and Hispanic students.[109]

Summary and conclusions

How the teaching profession is viewed today is conditioned by centuries of traditions. The conditions encountered in establishing a new nation and subsequent efforts to build widespread public schools added some unique American innovations as well, including higher numbers of women admitted to the teaching profession. Along with the growth of schooling came an increased need for better teacher preparation and institutional frameworks to carry out the task. Normal schools played an important role, but teacher education was eventually assumed by colleges and universities.

Efforts to elevate the teaching profession by improving teacher knowledge and expertise (professionalism) helped strengthen teaching's ethical claims to professional autonomy. However, this was hindered by the bureaucratization of school systems in the late nineteenth and early twentieth centuries. The growth of educational hierarchies and the professionalization of administrators reduced teacher autonomy and made efforts to elevate teacher status more difficult. These developments encouraged many teachers to form organizations, but there was disagreement over whether professional societies or unions best served teacher interests.

Class and gender composition of the teaching profession continues to have implications for its professional status and remuneration. The relative racial homogeneity of the profession also poses questions about how to best serve an increasingly diverse society. Efforts toward professionalization in teaching may well depend on whether teachers truly see themselves as professionals. Some participants want to achieve status parity with other learned professions through more rigorous preparation programs and competitive career ladders, while others argue that teaching should stop comparing itself to other professions; instead, teaching should build on the particular professional and ethical characteristics that make it unique among the learned professions.

The debate over the teaching profession's status apparently has made an impact. Many teacher preparation programs moved, at least temporarily, to the graduate level to elevate their status, although the teacher shortages of the 2010s led many states to reduce their requirements for obtaining a license. Research also indicates that teachers feel more empowered when they participate in educational decision-making, and if such participation becomes the norm, it could strengthen the profession. However, many teachers continue to see themselves left out of decisions directly affecting their professional duties and obligations.

Today, there are numerous professional organizations striving to advance education and promote teachers' professional growth. Among them are those devoted to academic subject areas, pupil age levels, and other such specialized interests. Through them, opportunities to collaborate and share ideas within the profession are probably greater than ever before. Here, as with many other aspects of education, differences of opinion are encountered but also a high degree of commitment to common goals.

Teaching is a multifaceted profession central to any society. Its status problem is only part of the story, because there are those who continue their efforts to improve it, just as they also seek to understand more fully its future possibilities.

Vocabulary

American Association of Colleges for Teacher Education (AACTE)
American Federation of Teachers (AFT)
A Nation at Risk
arts (or humanities) and sciences
Campbell's Law
Carnegie Corporation
career and technical education (CTE)
classical tradition
collective bargaining
common school movement
critical pedagogy
deskill
Freire, Paulo
Grow-Your-Own (GYO) programs
Holmes Partnership
Holmes Scholars Program
learned professions
liberal arts

liberal education
McCarthyism
merit pay
moral rewards
mystification of knowledge
National Board Certification (NBC)
National Board for Professional Teaching Standards (NBPTS)
National Education Association (NEA)
New England Primer
No Child Left Behind Act
Noddings, Nel
normal school
petty schools
profession
professional ethics
professionalism
professionalization
reciprocity of effort
reflective professional communities
registered apprenticeships
scripted curriculum
social distance
standards, assessment, and accountability movement
status discrepancy
science, technology, engineering, and mathematics (STEM)
strikes
teacher accountability
teacher residency programs
teacher turnover
transformative intellectuals
value-added modeling (VAM)
vernacular

Notes

1 David T. Hansen, *The Call to Teach* (New York: Teachers College Press, 1995).
2 Jeffrey A. Kottler, Stanley J. Zehm, and Ellen Kottler, *On Being a Teacher: The Human Dimension*, 3rd edn (Thousand Oaks, CA: Corwin Press, 2005).

3 Gerald L. Gutek, *Historical and Philosophical Foundations of Education: A Biographical Approach* (Upper Saddle River, NJ: Pearson/Merrill, 2005); Christopher J. Lucas, *Our Western Educational Heritage* (New York: Macmillan, 1972); and James Mulhern, *A History of Education: A Social Interpretation* (New York: Ronald Press, 1959).

4 See also W. H. Stahl, *Martianus Capella and the Seven Liberal Arts*. Records of Civilization, No. 84 (New York: Columbia University Press, 1971); and William Harrison Woodward, *Desiderius Erasmus Concerning the Aim and Method of Education*. Classics in Education, No. 19 (New York: Teachers College Press, 1964).

5 Frederick Eby, *Early Protestant Educators: The Educational Writings of Martin Luther, John Calvin, and Other Leaders of Protestant Thought* (Chicago, IL: American Theological Library, 1962); and Neil G. McCluskey, S. J., ed., *Catholic Education in America: A Documentary History* (New York: Bureau of Publications, Teachers College, 1964).

6 Margaret Connell Szasz, *Indian Education in the American Colonies, 1607–1783* (Lincoln and London: University of Nebraska Press, 1988, 2007), 18.

7 Lawrence A. Cremin, *American Education: The Colonial Experience, 1607–1783* (New York: Harper Torchbooks, 1970), 176–84.

8 Ibid., 185; and Timothy J. Shannon, "Pages of the 1805 New England Primer," *History 341: Colonial America Homepage*, at http://www.gettysburg.edu/~tshannon/his341/nep1805contents.html (accessed on January 20, 2010).

9 Merle Borrowman, "Liberal Education and the Professional Preparation of Teachers," in *Teacher Education in America: A Documentary History*. Classics in Education, No. 24 (New York: Teachers College Press, 1965), vii.

10 Cremin, *American Education: The Colonial Experience, 1607–1783,* 187.

11 Jon Teaford, "The Transformation of Massachusetts Education, 1670–1780," in *The Social History of American Education*, B. Edward McClellan and William J. Reese, eds (Chicago: University of Illinois Press, 1988), 31–5.

12 Thomas Jefferson, *Notes on the State of Virginia*, William Peden, ed. (1787, reprint, New York: W. W. Norton, 1972), 146–9; Noah Webster, "The Call for a National Culture [1789]," in *The Educating of Americans: A Documentary History*, Daniel Calhoun, ed. (Boston, MA: Houghton Mifflin, 1969), 89, 94; and Benjamin Rush, "Of the Mode of Education Proper in a Republic [1798]," in *The Founders' Constitution*, vol. 1, Philip B. Kurland and Ralph Lerner, eds (Chicago, IL: University of Chicago Press, 1987), at http://press-pubs.uchicago.edu/founders/print_documents/v1ch18s30.html (accessed on January 20, 2010).

13 Borrowman, "Liberal Education and the Professional Preparation of Teachers," 2–4.

14 Paul H. Mattingly, *The Classless Profession: American Schoolmen in the Nineteenth Century* (New York: New York University Press, 1975), 45–7.

15 Donald H. Parkerson and Jo Ann Parkerson, *Transitions in American Education: A Social History of Teaching* (New York: Routledge Falmer, 2001), 63.

16 Willystine Goodsell, ed., *Pioneers of Women's Education in the United States: Emma Willard, Catherine Beecher, Mary Lyon* (1931, reprint, New York: AMS Press, 1970).

17 Parkerson and Parkerson, *Transitions in American Education,* 70–1.

18 Ibid., 129–31; and Robert Welker, *The Teacher as Expert: A Theoretical and Historical Examination* (Albany: State University of New York Press, 1992), 46–7.

19 Richard J. Altenbaugh and Kathleen Underwood, "The Evolution of Normal Schools," in *Places Where Teachers Are Taught,* John I. Goodlad et al., eds (San Francisco, CA: Jossey-Bass, Inc., Publishers, 1990), 137–8; and James W. Fraser, *Preparing America's Teachers: A History* (New York: Teachers College Press, 2007), 45–55.

20 Jurgen Herbst, *And Sadly Teach: Teacher Education and Professionalization in American Culture* (Madison: University of Wisconsin Press, 1989), 4–6.

21 Ibid., 140–60; Altenbaugh and Underwood, "The Evolution of Normal Schools," 139–44; and William S. Learned et al., "Purpose of the Normal School," in *Teacher Education in America: A Documentary History*, 184–207.

22 John Goodlad et al., "Connecting the Present to the Past," in *Places Where Teachers Are Taught*, 18–19.

23 Herbst, *And Sadly Teach*, 6–8.

24 Wayne J. Urban, *Gender, Race, and the National Education Association* (New York: Routledge and Falmer, 2000), 3–9.

25 Wayne J. Urban, *Why Teachers Organized* (Detroit: Wayne State University Press, 1982), 154–72.

26 Urban, *Gender, Race, and the NEA*, 57–74.

27 William Edward Eaton, *The American Federation of Teachers, 1916–1961: A History of the Movement* (Carbondale: Southern Illinois University, 1975), 2–17; and see George Herbert Mead, "The Educational Situation in the Chicago Public Schools [1907]," at http://www.brocku.ca/MeadProject/Mead/pubs/Mead_1907f.html (accessed on January 20, 2010).

28 Eaton, *The American Federation of Teachers, 1916–1961*, 19–29, 35.

29 Ibid., 140–55, 161–6.

30 Urban, *Gender, Race, and the NEA*, 177–9.

31 Ibid., 267–74; Jeff Archer, "NEA Board Approves AFT Partnership Pact," *Newsweek*, vol. 20, no. 23 (February 21, 2001): 3; and NEAFT Merger Caucus, at http://www.neaft.org (accessed on January 20, 2010).

32 Stuart J. Foster, *Red Alert!: Educators Confront the Red Scare in American Public Schools, 1947–1954* (New York: Peter Lang, 2000) and Fraser, *Preparing America's Teachers*, 207–13.

33 See Jonathan Kozol, *Death at an Early Age: the Destruction of the Hearts and Minds of Negro Children in the Boston Public Schools* (Boston, MA: Houghton Mifflin, 1967); Nat Hentoff, *Our Children Are Dying* (New York: Viking Press, 1966); and Colin Greer, *The Solution as Part of the Problem: Urban Education Reform in the 1960s* (New York: Harper & Row, 1973).

34 National Commission on Excellence in Education, *A Nation at Risk: The Imperative of Educational Reform, An Open Letter to the American People* (Washington, DC: The Commission [distributed by the US Government Printing Office], 1983), 5.

35 Arthur Bestor, *Educational Wastelands: The Retreat from Learning in Our Public Schools* (Urbana: University of Illinois Press, 1953); Kozol, *Death at an Early Age*; National Commission on Excellence in Education, *A Nation at Risk: The Imperative for Educational Reform*, a report to the Nation and the Secretary of Education, United States Department of Education (Washington, DC: The Commission, 1983); Chester E. Finn Jr. et al., eds, *Against Mediocrity: The Humanities in America's High Schools*, foreword by William Bennett (New York: Holmes and Meier, 1984).

36 David F. Labaree, "Educational Researchers: Living with a Lesser Form of Knowledge," in *The Life and Work of Teachers: International Perspectives in Changing Times*, Christopher Day et al., eds (London and New York: Falmer Press, 2000), 55–8.

37 The Holmes Group, *Tomorrow's Teachers: A Report of the Holmes Group* (East Lansing, MI: The Holmes Group, Inc., 1989), 4.

38 AACTE, *Governance & History: Holmes Program History.* Governance & History—American Association of Colleges for Teacher Education (AACTE) (accessed on 11/05/2024).

39 National Board for Professional Teaching Standards, *National Board Certification Overview.* NBPTS Main Site National Board Certification Overview—NBPTS Main Site (accessed on May 11, 2024).

40 Gerald Grant and Christine E. Murray, *Teaching in America: The Slow Revolution* (Cambridge, MA: Harvard University Press, 1999), 182–5.

41 Matthew A. Kraft and Melissa Arnold Lyon, The Rise and Fall of the Teaching Profession: Prestige, Interest, Preparation, and Satisfaction over the Last Half Century (EdWorkingPaper: 22–679). Retrieved from Annenberg Institute at Brown University: https://doi.org/10.26300/7b1a-vk92 (2024).

42 US Department of Education, "Raise the Bar Policy Brief," https://www.ed.gov/raisethebar/Eliminating-Educator-Shortages-through-Increasing-Educator-Diversity (accessed on November 2023).

43 Kraft and Lyon, The Rise and Fall of the Teaching Profession, 1.

44 Michelle Croft, Gretchen Guffy, and Dan Vitale, "Encouraging More High School Students to Consider Teaching," *ACT Research & Policy*, at https://www.act.org/

content/dam/act/unsecured/documents/pdfs/Encouraging-More-HS-Students-to-Consider-Teaching.pdf (June 2018).

45 Ibid., 5.

46 Phi Delta Kappan, "Teaching: Respect but Dwindling Appeal: The 50th Annual of the Public's Attitudes Toward the Public Schools," at https://kappanonline.org/wp-content/uploads/2018/08/PDK-Poll-2018.pdf (September 2018).

47 Katie Reilly, "Exactly How Teachers Came to Be So Underpaid in America," *Time*, at https://time.com/longform/teaching-in-america/ (September 13, 2018).

48 Sylvia Allegretto, "The Teacher Pay Penalty Has Hit a New High," *Economic Policy Institute*, at https://www.epi.org/publication/teacher-pay-penalty-2022/ (August 16, 2022); Madeline Will, "The Gap Between Teacher Pay and Other Professions Hits a New High. How Bad Is It?" *Education Week*, at https://www.edweek.org/teaching-learning/the-gap-between-teacher-pay-and-other-professions-hits-a-new-high-how-bad-is-it/2022/08#:~:text=Teachers%20earn%2023.5%20percent%20less%20than%20comparable%20college%20graduates (August 22, 2022).

49 Ellen Sherratt, Lisa Lachlan, and Keane Alavi, "Raising the Bar on Teacher Pay: Center on Great Teachers and Leaders at AIR & The Teacher Salary Project," *American Institutes for Research*, at https://www.air.org/sites/default/files/2023-05/Raising_the_Bar_on_Teacher_Pay.pdf (May 2023).

50 Doris Santoro, "Good Teaching in Difficult Times: Demoralization in the Pursuit of Good Work," *American Journal of Education*, vol. 118, no. 2 (November 2011): 1–23.

51 Meira Levinson, *No Citizen Left Behind* (Cambridge, MA: Harvard University Press, 2012).

52 Wayne Au, "High-Stakes Testing, Standardization, and Inequality in the United States," *Oxford Research Encyclopedia of Education* (2020).

53 Brooke B. Eisenbach, "Teacher Belief and Practice in a Scripted Curriculum," *The Clearing House: A Journal of Educational Strategies, Issues and Ideas*, vol. 85, no. 4 (2012): 153–6; Anita Ede, "Scripted Curriculum: Is It a Prescription for Success?" *Childhood Education*, vol. 83, no. 1 (Fall 2006): 29–32.

54 Julie A. Fitz and A. C. Nikolaidis, "A Democratic Critique of Scripted Curriculum," *Journal of Curriculum Studies*, vol. 52, no. 2 (2020): 195–213, 207.

55 Ede, "Scripted Curriculum: Is It a Prescription for Success?" 31–2.

56 Jodi Wood Jewell, "From Inspection, Supervision, and Observation to Value-Added Evaluation: A Brief History of U.S. Teacher Performance Evaluations," *Drake Law Review*, vol. 65, no. 2 (2017): 363–420; Cory Koedel, (2009). "An Empirical Analysis of Teacher Spillover Effects in Secondary School," *Econ. Educ. Rev.* 28 (2009): 682–92; Drew H. Gitomer and Brittany L. Marshall, "The Sizzle and Fizzle of Teacher Evaluation in the United States and the Selective Use of Research Evidence," *Frontiers in Education*, vol. 8 (2023): 1–12.

57 Gary K. Clabaugh, "Teacher Merit Pay: Is It a Good Idea?" *Educational Horizons*, vol. 88, no. 1 (Fall 2009): 16–20; Rosemary Chamberlin, Ted Wragg, Gill Haynes, and Caroline Wragg, "Performance-Related Pay and the Teaching Profession: A Review of the Literature," *Research Papers in Education*, vol. 17, no. 1 (2002): 31–49.

58 Andrew Leigh, "The Economics and Politics of Teacher Merit Pay," *CESifo Economic Studies*, vol. 59, no. 1 (March 2012): 1–33, at doi:10.1093/cesifo/ifs007; Lam D. Pham, Tuan D. Nguyen, and Matthew G. Springer, "Teacher Merit Pay: A Meta-Analysis," *American Educational Research Journal*, vol. 58, no. 3 (2020): 527–66; Mark Gius, "The Effects of Teacher Merit Pay on Academic Attainment: An Analysis Using District-Level Data," *Journal of Economics and Economic Education Research*, vol. 13, no. 3 (2012): 93–108.

59 Milbrey Wallin McLaughlin, "What Matters Most in Teachers' Workplace Context?" *Teachers' Work*, 79–103.

60 Associated Press, "Osmo Survey Shows 80% of U.S. Parents Have Newfound Respect Towards Teachers as a Result of Stay-at-Home Mandates," *AP News* (April 30, 2020), at https://apnews.com/press-release/business-wire/technology-lifestyle-palo-alto-d7d10eb8c3cb4ee1bb757abf3a2c5421 (accessed on September 17, 2024).

61 Maria Ferguson, "Washington View: Stop Blaming Teachers for School Closures," *Phi Delta Kappan*, vol. 102, no. 8 (2021): 62–3, at https://journals.sagepub.com/doi/pdf/10.1177/00317217211013942

62 Hannah Natanson, "Parental Say in Schools, Resonant in Va. Governor's Race, Bound for GOP National Playbook," *Washington Post* (November 3, 2021), at https://www.washingtonpost.com/local/education/parent-control-schools-republican-virginia/2021/11/03/313e8a68-3cc3-11ec-a493-51b0252dea0c_story.html (accessed on September 17, 2024).

63 Sarah Schwartz, "Who's Really Driving Critical Race Theory Legislation? An Investigation," *Education Week* (July 19, 2021), at https://www.edweek.org/policy-politics/whos-really-driving-critical-race-theory-legislation-an-investigation/2021/07 (accessed on September 19, 2024).

64 Ibid; Mica Pollock et al., "The Conflict Campaign: Exploring Local Experiences of the Campaign to Ban 'Critical Race Theory,'" in *Public K–12 Education in the U.S., 2020–2021* (Los Angeles, CA: UCLA's Institute for Democracy, Education, and Access, 2022).

65 CRT Forward Tracking Project, at https://crtforward.law.ucla.edu/ (accessed on September 18, 2024).

66 Sarah Schwartz, "Map: Where Critical Race Theory Is Under Attack," *Education Week* at https://www.edweek.org/policy-politics/map-where-critical-race-theory-is-under-attack/2021/06 (accessed on September 19, 2024).

67 Christopher Rufo, *X.com*. X (formerly Twitter), https://x.com/realchrisrufo/status/1371541044592996352 (March 15, 2021).

68 Pollock et al, "The Conflict Campaign."

69 https://www.edweek.org/teaching-learning/what-educators-think-about-classroom-controversy-in-charts/2024/08?utm_source=nl&utm_medium=eml&utm_campaign=tu&M=11036560&UUID=46ba8b9d18bf81f6851ba67c1e3dbacc&T=14527623

70 PDK Poll, "PDK Poll of the Public's Attitudes Toward the Public Schools," https://pdkpoll.org/2023-pdk-poll-results/ on (accessed on September 20, 2024).

71 Thea L. Racelis and Hillary E. Parkhouse, "Locating Our Role in the Struggle: Lessons from the Past and Present on Teachers' Persistence, Solidarity, and Activism for the Common Good," *Education Sciences*, vol. 14, no. 1 (2024): 11.

72 Ibid.

73 Elaine S. Povich, "Plagued by Teacher Shortages, Some States Turn to Fast-Track Credentialing," *National Conference of State Legislatures*, https://www.ncsl.org/state-legislatures-news/details/plagued-by-teacher-shortages-some-states-turn-to-fast-track-credentialing (accessed on July 26, 2023).

74 Richard M. Ingersoll, Lisa Merrill, and Henry May, "What Are the Effects of Teacher Education and Preparation on Beginning Teacher Attrition?" in *Research Report (#RR-82)* (Philadelphia: University of Pennsylvania, Consortium for Policy Research in Education, 2014).

75 Desiree Carver-Thomas, *Diversifying the Teaching Profession: How to Recruit and Retain Teachers of Color* (Palo Alto, CA: Learning Policy Institute, 2018); US Department of Education, "Brief: Eliminating Educator Shortages Through Increasing Educator Diversity and Addressing High-need Shortage Areas," https://www.ed.gov/about/ed-initiatives/raise-the-bar/raise-the-bar-policy-brief-2#_ftn10 (accessed on November 2023).

76 Connor P. Williams, "America's Missing Bilingual Teachers," *The Century Foundation*, https://tcf.org/content/commentary/americas-missing-bilingual-teachers/#:~:text=Just%2013%20percent%20of%20U.S.,21%20percent%20of%20U.S.%20children (accessed on November 16, 2023).

77 Carver-Thomas, *Diversifying the Teaching Profession*, vi–viii and 17–29.

78 Chris Geary et al., "What to Know About Education Funding in Biden's Budget," New America (March 10, 2023), at https://www.newamerica.org/insights/what-to-know-about-education-funding-in-bidens-budget/

79 National Center for Teacher Residencies (NCTR), "Annual Report 2023–2024," https://nctresidencies.org/impact-results/ on (accessed on September 24, 2024).

80 Roneeta Guha, Maria E. Hyler, and Linda Darling-Hammond, "The Power and Potential of Teacher Residencies," *Phi Delta Kappan*, vol. 98, no. 8 (May 2017): 31–7.

81 National Center for Teacher Residencies (NCTR), "Our Impact," https://nctresidencies.org/impact-results/ on (accessed on September 24, 2024).

82 Guha et al.,"The Power and Potential of Teacher Residencies," 35–7.

83 National Center for Teacher Residencies, "Annual Report 2023-2024," 5.

84 Lois Kimmel, Cheryl Krohn, Cassandra Herring, and Patricia Alvarez McHatton, "Creating Pathways into the Profession While Building Diversity with Registered Apprenticeship Programs," Branch Alliance for Educator Diversity and Center on Great Teachers and Leaders at the American Institutes for Research, https://www.educatordiversity.org/wp-content/uploads/2024/02/RTAP_Diveristy_BranchED_GTL.pdf (accessed on 2024).

85 National Center for Grow Your Own, accessed on https://ncgyo.org/ on October 2, 2024.

86 Angela Valenzuela, "Grow Your Own Educator Programs: A Review of the Literature with an Emphasis on Equity-Based Approaches. Literature Review," *Equity Assistance Center Region II, Intercultural Development Research Association* (2017); Conra D. Fist, Margarita Bianco, and Marvin Lynn, "Examining Grow Your Own Programs Across the Teacher Development Continuum: Mining Research on Teachers of Color and Nontraditional Educator Pipelines," *Journal of Teacher Education*, vol. 70, no. 1 (2019): 13–25.

87 Lee S. Shulman, "Foreword," in *Teaching as the Learning Profession: Handbook of Policy and Practice*, Linda Darling-Hammond and Gary Sykes, eds (San Francisco, CA: Jossey-Bass Publishers,1999), xiii.

88 Henry A. Giroux, *Teachers as Intellectuals: Toward a Critical Pedagogy of Learning* (New York: Bergin & Garvey, 1988), 121–8.

89 Santoro, "Good Teaching"; Welker, *The Teacher as Expert*, 129–35.

90 Roger Soder, "The Rhetoric of Teacher Professionalization," in *The Moral Dimensions of Teaching*, John I. Goodlad, Roger Soder, and Kenneth A. Sirotnik, eds (San Francisco, CA: Jossey-Bass Publishers, 1990), 35–86.

91 Ibid.

92 Gary D. Fenstermacher, "Some Moral Considerations on Teaching as a Profession," in *The Moral Dimensions of Teaching*, John I. Goodlad et al., eds (San Francisco, CA: Jossey-Bass Publishers, 1991), 136–8.

93 Paulo Freire, *Pedagogy of Freedom: Ethics, Democracy, and Civic Courage* (Lanham, MD: Rowman & Littlefield, 1998).

94 Paulo Freire, *Pedagogy of the Oppressed*, Ramos Myra Bergman, trans. (New York: Herder and Herder, 1970).

95 Aristotle, *The Politics*, Trevor J. Saunders, trans. (London: Penguin Books, 1981), 453–4.

96 Aristotle, *Ethics*, J. A. K. Thomson, trans. (London: Penguin Books, 1976), 64, 66, 69, 73–6, and 100–10.

97 Nel Noddings, *Happiness and Education* (New York: Cambridge University Press, 2003).

98 John Dewey, *Theory of the Moral Life* (reprint, New York: Holt, Rinehart and Winston, [1932] 1960), viii.

99 Ibid., ix–xii; and Kenneth A. Strike and Jonas F. Soltis, *The Ethics of Teaching*, 3rd edn, Thinking about Education Series (New York: Teachers College Press, 1998), 6.

100 Michael D. Bayles, *Professional Ethics*, 2nd edn (Belmont, CA: Wadsworth, Inc., 1989), 17–27.ff. Indebtedness in this and the following paragraphs is acknowledged to Bayles, particularly terminology related to general ethical obligations, which here are adapted to the teaching profession.

101 This idea dates back to Hippocrates, a physician in ancient Greece. See N. S. Gill, "Is 'First Do No Harm' from the Hippocratic Oath? Myth vs. Fact," at http://ancienthistory.about.com/od/greekmedicine/f/HippocraticOath.htm (accessed on January 20, 2010).

102 Bayles, *Professional Ethics*, 111–27.

103 Ibid., 136–57.

104 Ibid., 166–78.

105 National Education Association, "About NEA," at https://www.nea.org/ (accessed on October 10, 2024); and American Federation of Teachers, "About AFT," at http://www.aft.org/about/ (accessed on October 10, 2024).

106 Peter Brimelow, *The Worm in the Apple: How the Teachers Unions Are Destroying American Education* (New York: HarperCollins, 2003); G. Gregory Moo, *Power Grab: How the National Education Association Is Betraying Our Children* (Washington, DC: Regnery Publishing, 1999), xi–xii; and Myron Lieber-man, *The Teacher Unions: How the NEA and AFT Sabotage Reform and Hold Students, Parents, and Teachers, and Taxpayers Hostage to Bureaucracy* (New York: The Free Press, 1997).

107 Clifford B. Donn, Rachel E. Donn, Lloyd Goldberg, and Brenda J. Kirby, "Teacher Working Conditions With and Without Collective Bargaining," *Nevada Law Journal*, vol. 14, no. 2 (2014): 11.

108 Todd E. Vachon and Josef Ma, "Bargaining for Success: Examining the Relationship Between Teacher Unions and Student Achievement," *Sociological Forum*, vol. 30, no. 2 (June 2015): 391–414.

109 Eunice S. Han and Jeffrey Keefe, "Teachers' Unions: Engaging Teachers and Improving Student Achievement in States That Prohibit Collective Bargaining," *Educational Policy*, vol. 36, no. 2 (2022): 407–39.

2

School Governance and Control

Chapter contents

Chapter objectives

Readers should be able to:

- understand the concept of school governance and varying viewpoints on it.
- explore the history of school governance to uncover the roots of school governance today.
- analyze the current governance structure, its strengths and weaknesses.
- gain an understanding of how funding sources impact school governance.
- become attuned to contemporary reform issues and their impact on school governance.

Opening questions

1. What characteristics of school governance have changed, and what have endured? Why and how have leading economic and political theories shaped school governance?
2. What are the major factors of continuity and change in contemporary school governance?
3. How are the schools funded, and what consequences for governance flow from the existing funding system?
4. In what ways should both school governance and funding be reformed?
5. What are the pros and cons of both existing governance practices and leading reforms that impact how schools are governed?

The issue

Prior to the American Revolution, responsibility for education was considered an individual, family, or church concern, with little government involvement. The end of the eighteenth century saw rising calls for greater educational opportunity, but how to organize and finance it remained elusive. A major nineteenth-century development was the common school movement (from the late 1830s into the 1850s), which resulted in state systems of tax-supported, public elementary schools. Although these systems were created by legislation on a state-by-state basis, they were typically financed by local taxes and overseen by local **school boards** or **school committees**. After the 1870s, public high schools were added to this configuration. In the early twentieth century, critics of the organizational frameworks of school systems carried out school governance reforms modeled after corporations, which they believed would make school operations more efficient. With persistent tinkering, public school systems continue to operate within this kind of hierarchical structure.

According to David Tyack, in the twentieth century, Americans built a network of public school systems that made education available to more people of greater diversity than in any previous period, an accomplishment in which they rightly could take pride. Yet, criticism of the schools has not diminished. For example, how funds are allocated is one issue, with some critics arguing that public school systems are **bureaucratic** and limit parental choices of the schools their children may attend. As taxpayers, parents (or guardians) should have public funds made available for the schools of their choice, including private schools. Others want publicly financed school systems to remain the option of choice, but they argue for more choice within that framework. Some see publicly funded **charter schools** that operate independently of local boards and central offices as a good expansion of choice. There are also concerns about whether existing forms of governance adequately address educational needs and whether the schools use what they now receive to best effect.[1]

Criticism also emerges over what roles local, state, and federal governments should have, not only in funding but also in curriculum requirements, testing and evaluation, and other details of school operation. Critics aside, there are many who favor public, tax-supported schools, and they make strong arguments that the schools must represent all of society and expose all students to common experiences. Students need to understand local conditions and cultural communities, of course, but they also need the benefits of state and national participation and support too. Some supporters caution against too much centralized control, however. It weakens direct accountability of schools to their local communities at a time when citizens need to "own" their schools, not surrender them to distant bureaucracies. As can be seen, debate swirls around governance and control. It is a controversy prospective educators will almost certainly face as professionals.

For Further Reflection: What is a healthy balance between the power of parents and citizens versus that of educational professionals concerning school governance? What factors need to be taken into account in order to achieve such balance?

Historical background

There is difficulty in concisely describing the American system of educational governance and control, because in actuality there are fifty state systems, with each state further subdivided into numerous local systems.[2] All the state systems share much in common, but each also has its unique characteristics.

Origins of American school governance and control

Although there were educational commonalities among the British colonies in what is now the United States, there were also significant differences. The

New England colonies (Connecticut, Massachusetts, New Hampshire, and Rhode Island) shared cultural and religious assumptions that helped unify attitudes about education. The middle colonies (New York, Pennsylvania, New Jersey, Delaware, and Maryland) were more diverse. New York, for example, began as a Dutch colony, then came under British control, and attracted people from various other cultural origins, in addition to being the home of a sizable portion of Native Americans. Similarly, Pennsylvania began under the Quakers but welcomed other religious persuasions and national origins as well. Likewise, the population of Maryland was comprised of a mixture of national origins, composed of Protestants and a sizable number of Catholics. Such conditions meant diversity in educational provisions in the middle colonies. The southern colonies also contained religious and cultural variety, but most southern colonists accepted the English tradition of schooling as a duty of home and church, not government. Southern colonies also did not see the same benefits of government-provided schools because they did not need educated workers, since they used slave labor, and did not need educated consumers, since they sent raw goods elsewhere to be transformed into products for sale.[3]

Colonial Massachusetts and Virginia: A comparison

In 1647, the General Court of the Massachusetts Bay Colony passed a law attributing responsibility for education to the townships and, in turn, left each township relatively free to meet requirements as it saw fit. In Virginia, the House of Burgesses placed responsibility for education on various sources, including families, local pastors, justices of the peace, and county commissioners.[4] Although there were similarities among the colonies in following the English tradition of parish (township) and shire (county) forms of organization, differences still occurred in how schools were governed.

In Massachusetts, the local governing body for schools became the "school committee" and, depending on the township, its members were either locally elected or appointed by a township's selectmen or governing council. Some townships ignored elements of the 1647 law, particularly secondary grammar schools with a Latin and classics-based curriculum. This was partially offset by the development of township-supported English-based "writing" schools, as well as private "venture" schools that usually emphasized mathematical and technical studies (e.g., geometry, surveying, navigation, bookkeeping, foreign currency exchange rates, and languages). Despite the decline of grammar schools, Massachusetts achieved a high degree of literacy by the 1770s.[5]

In comparison, Virginia relied primarily on private initiatives, with school governance evolving along the lines of the privately endowed "free schools," the first of which was established in a 1635 bequest of 200 acres of land and the "increase and produce" of eight cows to support the education of poor white children in the Hampton area. In 1659, a heftier bequest left 500 acres, twenty hogs, twelve cows, and two bulls, as well as two enslaved people, for another free school for poor white children in the same county but in a different parish. Each school was governed by a board of trustees composed of the county commissioners and the ministers and church wardens of each respective parish. Important as these schools were, however, only a small number of children benefited while most Virginia young people received little or no education beyond what an individual family, local church, or private tutor might provide. Private venture schools also developed, but most were short lived and never extensive.[6]

Variety in school governance and control

During colonial times, no single widespread mode of governance and financial support emerged, and this probably discouraged greater uniformity in the methods of control. Thus, school governance varied from one region, locale, and school to the next. Despite the lack of uniformity, however, some aspects of school governance at the time endured. One was a growing recognition that responsibility for education rested with society as a whole, not only portions of it. A pattern was emerging of school committees and boards of trustees, which set the stage for school boards today.[7]

Suggested Activity: Discuss with other students to what extent school governance practices still vary among localities or regions today. Compare experiences and views that may differ in your group, depending on where individual members grew up.

Emergence of public school systems

In the decades following the American Revolution, the United States adopted a new constitution, extended its territory, and fought a second war with the British, but as the nineteenth century unfolded, attention was given to education.

At first, there was a mixture of sectarian schools, elite academies, private venture schools, charity schools, and municipal schools inherited from colonial times, but state systems of public schools would become dominant by midcentury.

Jeffersonian model

One of the first attempts at a statewide system of public schools was made by Thomas Jefferson in Virginia. As Jefferson envisioned it, each county would elect three aldermen who would divide their county into small geographical units (or "hundreds," Jefferson called them), each containing enough free (excluding enslaved) children to justify a school. The aldermen were also to select a site and erect a schoolhouse where the children could be taught reading, writing, and common arithmetic, with reading materials to be drawn from Greek, Roman, English, and American history. Finally, for every ten "hundreds" in a county, the aldermen were to appoint a qualified "visitor" to hire and oversee teachers and to visit each school periodically to examine students and see that the curriculum was followed.[8] Although Jefferson's plan never materialized, it provided ideas for others to consider. One can see hints of his proposal today: the aldermen are similar to local boards of education, the hundreds akin to school attendance zones, and the visitors similar to superintendents.

Public schools and local control

After experience with various private and public ventures, most Americans embraced the idea of public, tax-supported "common schools." Public common schools gained wide acceptance by the 1850s as significant instruments for producing virtuous citizens at the local level, supplementing the roles of families and churches. Perhaps these kinds of connections helped solidify public opinion that the schools should be locally controlled. As it evolved, the ideal (if not always the reality) was nonsectarian and nonpartisan local boards. Although the legal authority to establish public schools came from the state, the source of financial and moral support came from local citizens, and **local control** became the operational mode of governance.[9]

Local control was not without its problems, however. As noted by Horace Mann, as crucial as local control was, it could be deleterious if a local community was apathetic, riven by partisan divisions, or fearful of public expenditures for education. There was a need for at least some state control to invigorate local support, not replace it.[10]

Suggested Activity: Discuss the following statements: While the concept of community conjures up many positive associations such as family and friends, togetherness and support, sometimes communities can be oppressive and suspicious of differences. These two sides of local community need to be considered when deciding how best to balance localized and centralized controls over schooling.

Local school boards

Four out of five citizens lived in rural areas by 1860, but the leading developments in school governance emerged from urban areas. Between 1818 and 1853, most cities established some form of citywide school board. Large cities typically divided themselves into wards (or districts) that, in turn, provided local school governance, usually by means of an elected school committee in each ward. This body was responsible for collecting school taxes, purchasing sites, constructing and maintaining school buildings, and hiring and supervising teachers. Many cities also allowed a ward to elect a representative to serve on the central city school boards. In big cities with numerous wards, this meant large, unwieldy central school boards where political bickering and competition for city resources sometimes paralyzed effective action. In addition, some wards were dominated by corrupt political machines that used political patronage to control contracts for school supplies, the hiring of personnel, and other such functions. Reformers, dissatisfied with what they called the "inefficiencies" of ward control, successfully pushed for smaller, more powerful central city boards of education.[11] As it turned out, however, this proved to be double edged, for as ward control weakened, so also did local citizen feelings about ownership and control of the neighborhood schools.

Origins of the school superintendency

A second major development was to place administrative control in the hands of a single person, from which the modern school **superintendent** emerged. Before, local boards of education did the supervisory work, usually with one or more members doing the actual on-site visits and other supervisory duties. As the population increased and school-age children became more numerous, supervision consumed more time than most board members (usually unpaid for their services) were willing to provide, and so the idea of a paid, full-time school supervisor or superintendent became an attractive alternative for most boards.

It was in 1837 that the first superintendents were hired, in Buffalo, New York, and Louisville, Kentucky. In the 1840s, St. Louis, Missouri, appointed a superintendent, followed in due course by Boston, Chicago, Cleveland, Detroit, New York City, and San Francisco. By the 1880s, Pittsburgh, Philadelphia, and Los Angeles also joined the trend. At first, the job was ill-defined: Buffalo desired someone to gather reliable information about the schools for board deliberations, Baltimore wanted someone to provide oversight of textbook adoptions, while San Francisco sought someone to take charge of renting and provisioning adequate schoolhouses. Other places needed a full-time board secretary. By 1900, the title of superintendent (or some other approximation, such as director or secretary of the board) was common. As the job evolved, it took several forms: In some locales, boards directly hired superintendents as employees; in others, superintendents were elected officials. Regardless of title or method of appointment, the idea of having a full-time person responsible for general administrative duties of public school systems gained popularity.[12]

Urbanization, industrialization, and school reform

The *Gilded Age* is a term coined by Mark Twain in an 1873 book about the rampant materialism and corruption in the years following the Civil War.[13] It has since been used to designate the period from roughly 1865 to 1900, when American society experienced rapid urban and industrial development that brought far-reaching changes to institutions and social life.

Population growth and urbanization

One important change was massive population growth, which made it difficult for existing institutions to meet increased demands. Population in the United States almost doubled in the thirty years from 1870 to 1900 (see Table 2.1). Some of this increase was due to higher fertility rates, but a significant part was from immigration. Although a portion of the population growth stretched to the rural frontiers, most centered on the urban areas, which attracted both foreign and domestic newcomers. The number of foreign immigrants greatly changed the United States, and its ethnic variety has become an oft-told part of the American story. Less well known was the migration of native-born farm workers and marginal farmers from the rural areas into the cities, particularly during periods of agricultural recession or depression. Both foreign-born immigrants and native-born migrants were lured to the cities by the promise of better jobs and greater economic opportunity. As the cities experienced this growth, however, there were shortages as existing institutions struggled to meet the new demands. In addition, the newcomers—many of whom came from rural backgrounds—often faced difficulties adjusting to city life as they confronted unfamiliar customs and lifestyles. As they poured into the cities, they also faced insufficient numbers of schools to meet their needs because educational institutions and their governance structures were unable to respond effectively.

Table 2.1 United States Population, 1870–1900

Year	Total population	Numerical increase	Percent increase
1870	38,558,371	N/A	N/A
1880	50,189,209	11,630,838	30.2%
1890	62,979,766	12,790,557	25.5%
1900	76,212,168	13,232,402	21%

Note: Adapted from US Census Bureau, "Decennial Census Population and Housing Counts" (1990), at http://www.census.gov/population/censusdata/table-2.pdf (accessed on March 20, 2009). https://www.census.gov/programs-surveys/decennial-census/decade.1880.html#list-tab-693908974 (accessed on March 1, 2025)

Figure 2.1 Orchard Street, Manhattan, sometime between 1865 and 1899.

Compulsory attendance

In a time of subsistence wages for the working class and extreme wealth for a small group of industrialists and investors, many working-class families needed income from all family members, including their children. Some reformers saw this as child exploitation, and they pushed compulsory attendance laws as a way to get children in schools and out of factories and sweatshops. However, due to a combination of factors, including rapid changes and ineffective political leadership, many hard-pressed city school systems were unable to accommodate all eligible children. Though well-intentioned, compulsory attendance laws sometimes exacerbated the hardships of working-class families. Not only did poor families need the extra income children earned, but poor children themselves often resisted attending because they found schools unpleasant places biased against poor and immigrant children.[14]

Compulsory attendance was also complicated by legal variations from state to state. Some states required as much as full nine-month term, some required no more than 16 weeks, while others had no attendance laws at all. Legal age of compulsory attendance also varied, from 7 to 16 in Wyoming but only 10 to 14 in Utah. Few states provided any serious enforcement, and many laws included exemptions ranging from travel distance, poverty, and lack of clothing (commonly recognized exemptions) to such vague ones as "inability to send" and "urgent reasons."[15]

In addition, many cities proved so unable (or unwilling) to provide adequate financial support that schools were forced to operate on double sessions each day and on shortened annual terms just to keep expenditures in line with funding. While the boom-and-bust economic fluctuations of that era made financial planning difficult for schools, many Gilded Age school "reforms" were little more than cutbacks driven by political resistance to school taxes. Simply put, inadequate financial resources meant the lack of facilities, materials, and professional personnel sufficient to accommodate all eligible children.[16]

For Further Reflection: Look at compulsory school attendance from an ethical perspective; human beings are forced to do something (go to school) regardless of their wishes. How can such laws be ethically justified given the infringement on the liberties of individuals? Does society have an obligation to educate children whether they want it or not? Does the social group have ethical responsibilities for its individual members?

For Further Reflection: Although the phenomena described here date back more than a century, some of the problems sound quite familiar today. Is history repeating itself? Do certain things never change, or do we simply fail to solve problems? How else can apparent similarities between the early twentieth century and the twenty-first century in regard to the problems of education be explained?

Progressive education reform

At the close of the nineteenth century, progressivism became the name for a series of reforms that affected many areas of American life. The progressive movement was not anchored in a single philosophy, and progressive education was only one part of the larger movement.[17] For purposes of illustration, two broad philosophical views on school governance are examined: the **pedagogical progressives** and the **administrative progressives.**[18]

Pedagogical progressives

One of the hallmarks of pedagogical progressivism was "child-centered" education, and it helped make progressive education a household term at the time. Child-centered education had its roots in European educational thought, particularly that of Jean-Jacques Rousseau and his followers Johann Pestalozzi and Friedrich Froebel.

Rousseau rejected the old theological doctrine of original sin, that the child was corrupted by Adam and Eve's behavior in the Garden of Eden. On the contrary, Rousseau maintained that the child was innately good in the original natural state and was only corrupted by the artifices of society, such as an overly bookish, abstract, and unnatural education; therefore, the child's education should occur in natural settings away from society. Of course, Rousseau did not reject all civilization, but he insisted on education where the child is free to explore and learn from their experiences, with adult intervention limited to such things as safety, well-being, and educational guidance as needed. Implements of civilization, such as books, should be introduced only when the child is able developmentally to benefit.[19] This may seem highly impractical, but what attracted educational thinkers to Rousseau was his insight into the need to fit education to the child's natural growth stages, learning from experiences, and higher levels of intellectual education as development allows.

Pestalozzi put Rousseau's ideas into practice with child activities, observations, and manipulations of instructional objects at the schools he ran. He encouraged child-initiated activities but also teacher-designed activities that respected the child's natural development. A properly educated child's potential would develop naturally, just as a sprouting seed unfolds its full potential as a mature plant. To aid the child's development, their natural senses should be stimulated through observations and hands-on activities that gradually move from concrete experience to abstract, reflective thought. Pestalozzi emphasized that kindness rather than harshness must be the rule. From such ideas, Friedrich Froebel developed the idea of the kindergarten, a "garden" for children replete with carefully structured activities and instructional objects in a nurturing environment. Froebel believed that a child is in harmony with God's natural order, and he stressed the need for play and learning activities to stimulate the physical and intellectual growth of the child.[20]

These theories were among the educational outlooks of American pedagogical progressives, or what some proponents called the "new education." Among the contributors were educator Francis W. Parker and psychologist G. Stanley Hall. As superintendent of schools in Quincy, Massachusetts, Parker stressed that, rather than primary reliance on textbooks, students should also use supplementary materials such as newspapers, magazines, and teacher-devised materials; rather than memorizing scientific laws and principles, they should be taken on field trips for direct observations and specimen collection; and rather than rote learning of such things as multiplication tables, they should learn inductive problem-solving with objects and examples. The Quincy System, as it was called, emphasized learning through observation, description, and understanding before moving students into more abstract approaches. G. Stanley Hall did pioneering work in child development that had a major impact on progressive education. Although influenced by predecessors, Hall's psychological research convinced him that the content of the curriculum should be determined by the developmental needs of the child. As Hall viewed it, education was too school centered, with the child forced to adapt to school demands; instead, school should be adapted to the child's needs. Hall's use of empirical research gave him an aura of scientific legitimacy, and his child-centered views appealed to the pedagogical progressives.[21]

Perhaps the person most often identified with pedagogical progressivism, however, is **John Dewey**, who believed that philosophers should help people break from outmoded ways of thinking in order to solve major problems they actually faced. While Dewey valued child-centeredness, he took a broadened approach that included the social as well as the individual needs of the children, who become educated through their experiences of both the natural and the social world. The urban, corporate, industrial society of Dewey's day contained the elements for increased communication and interaction, but it was also too ruthless, competitive, and inhumane. Changes were needed so that schools could operate as protective environments where the capacities of children could be developed. To accomplish this, schools must be environments where, instead of imposing traditional rote instruction and harsh discipline, pupils can learn, shape, and test ideas in humane environments that foster the development of reflective personal and social judgment.[22]

Dewey's philosophy was complex and his writings not always easily understood, but he also had followers who sometimes took his ideas in directions he never intended. For example, some disciples understood Dewey's criticism of traditional education to mean that knowledge acquisition was unimportant. Some took his stress on the social to mean children should mainly be taught social roles and relationships. A closer reading, however, shows Dewey's firm insistence that education should help the young understand the world and the changes it undergoes by such things as scientific and technological development, industrialization, and urbanization. He placed particular focus on the social nature of education because he saw it as an important pathway to build a more democratic society with humane social conditions. New approaches to organizing and teaching the curriculum were needed, and they should begin with children's ordinary shared experiences. As their intellectual skills and social understandings grow, they should increasingly become immersed in the cumulative knowledge of the human race and in using it to better understand the larger society and its problems. Dewey thought that the true value of administration, curriculum, and instruction resided in operating schools as learning communities animated by a democratic social spirit and shared learning experiences.[23]

In many respects, the First World War was a watershed for progressivism. After several decades of reform, topped off by a war that was supposed to "make the world safe for democracy," many Americans were weary of reformist slogans, and a new generation was ascending that was attuned to jazz music, get-rich-quick schemes, Prohibition and bootleggers, and other markers of the Roaring Twenties, all of which took people's attention away from educational reform.

Pedagogical progressivism did not disappear, but in the struggle to control the governance and direction of American schools, pedagogical progressivism lost out to administrative progressivism.[24] In other words, pedagogical progressivism helped shape how we continue to think and talk about curriculum and instruction, but administrative progressivism shaped how we actually govern and control the schools.

Yet there have been revivals of progressivism, such as the open education movement of the late 1960s and early 1970s, which focused on the active engagement of children in the learning process. The movement faltered in the mid-1970s, however, as economic stagnation and the war in Vietnam drew public attention away from children's education. By the 1980s, the country was in a conservative, "back to basics" swing, with high-stakes testing and accountability becoming reform bywords. Still, pedagogical progressivism's legacy continues in such emphases as active student learning, small group projects, and cross-disciplinary studies.[25]

Administrative progressives

Many administrative progressives found child-centered education lacking when it came to learning the prescribed curriculum. They also found the views on democracy—such as Dewey's—too impractical for what they believed the "real" world required. They saw themselves as individuals of action akin to the corporate captains of industry who supposedly saw the world as it truly was. They formed what Raymond Callahan termed the "cult of efficiency."[26]

The administrative progressives were concerned about the problems facing large urban school systems, but where pedagogical progressives looked to democratic expansion for remedies, administrative progressives sought answers in what they believed were the most successful institutions of their time, the industrial corporations. Like Dewey, they worried that the country's rapidly growing urban population was swamping existing institutions, but they thought local neighborhood control was both corrupt and inefficient, and it should be replaced by centralized expert management. They believed their approach was progressive because, guided by their scientific and technological expertise, it would lead to efficiently managed school systems.

The administrative progressives were attracted to philosophical realism, a view that ultimate reality is external to human consciousness and independent of internal human needs and desires. A branch of philosophical realism is scientific realism (sometimes called positivism), which holds that the material world is the only objective reality, it can be measured and quantified, and rigorous scientific investigation uncovers the operating principles of that reality. Moreover, human well-being depends on understanding those operating principles and bringing human behavior into conformity with them.[27]

Figure 2.2 Winchell School 3rd grade class, 1926.

Although most administrative progressives were not philosophers, they reflected some of the main currents of philosophical realism during their time. In addition, the administrative and management theories from which they borrowed or which they created also reflected important elements of realist thinking.

> **For Further Reflection:** Do you still perceive a tension between pedagogical and administrative progressivism in schools today?

Scientific, technological, and industrial developments

Most administrative progressives believed that the truly successful changes in modern society appeared to be based on scientific "laws." The thinking went something like this: Since the corporation was the most successful institution of the day, and since it used scientific management and technology to operate in predictable and efficient ways, then the corporate form of organization must reflect the correct way to operate all kinds of institutions, even schools.

Likewise, since "survival of the fittest" seemed to be a "law of nature" (as backed by some scientific claims of the times), then it must also be a law of human nature as well (see Chapter 3 for more on the idea of "survival of the fittest"). These kinds of assumptions led some to conclude that, if science measured natural conditions and reduced them to their true descriptions and classifications, then properly trained educational experts should be able to measure (test) and classify (group) pupils from their "lower" to their "higher" forms, and schools would then operate predictably and educate efficiently at the lowest possible cost.[28]

Efficiency movement

One development in American business that gained the attention of many administrative progressives, and one with mixed blessings, was "scientific management," or simply "Taylorism" after its prime spokesman, industrial engineer Frederick W. Taylor. Scientific management involved time-motion studies of how workers performed their jobs, along with detailed recommendations on how they might become more productive in less time and with less wasted motion. Indeed, scientific management helped make American industries among the most productive in the world, and its success attracted followers, including many administrative progressives who hoped it might bring similar gains to school systems.

> **For Further Reflection:** To what extent can today's testing and accountability movement be traced back to the social efficiency movement just described? To put it differently, what are the parallels between the two movements and eras?

Corporate model of school governance and control

Armed with a strong belief in the power of their ideas and assuming that scientific management and the corporate model would help them better organize schools and instruct pupils, administrative progressives set out to discover the "one best system" for urban schools and to implement it everywhere.[29]

However, the mixed-blessing by-products were centralized authority, hierarchical divisions, organizational stratification, and increased specialization among administrators and support staff. In 1920, for example, there was one supervisor for every thirty-five teachers; by 1930, it had increased to one for every twenty-two teachers; by 1974, it was one for every sixteen teachers; and by 1985, it was one for every eleven teachers.[30]

The drive toward the "one best system" of schools was characterized by an **ideological orientation**—a set of beliefs about social institutions, human behavior, and knowledge. "One best" advocates believed that, with the right kinds of knowledge about organizational structures and human psychological and social conditioning, they could solve troubling educational problems by making schools more efficient.

School systems came to look like corporations: a small board of directors at the top (the school board), a chief executive officer (the superintendent), professional managers (various levels of administrators), experts (specialists and supervisors), and assembly line workers (classroom teachers). The new structures brought changes many teachers welcomed, including specialized courses, subject-area departments, and classes organized by age and grade levels, but gradually new stresses emerged as bureaucratic controls eroded teacher autonomy and professional judgment in classrooms. Teacher objections to the contrary, by the 1950s, the organizational revolution was fairly complete: Centralized, bureaucratic, and corporation-mimicking organizational patterns became deeply rooted in every major school system in the United States.[31]

For Further Reflection: Does the corporate model actually work efficiently and effectively for schools, or are there distinct differences between schools, on the one hand, and businesses and industries, on the other hand, that make such comparisons between the two problematic? In other words, is educating children and youth the same as making automobiles, or are the two operations distinctly different?

School board change

As originally intended, school committees or boards of education were to provide representative public control over schools at the local level. Despite the dedicated public service demonstrated by most boards, some systems experienced corruption and political favoritism, which helped fuel reformist fires. Consider, for example, the situations in San Francisco and Philadelphia.

At one point, the San Francisco school board hired and fired teachers as much for political connections as professional competence. Also, teachers were hired on annual contracts only, and every year the board divided the hiring task equally among its twelve members. Those wishing to be re-employed had to take an annual examination with questions so arbitrary that the board could pass or fail applicants at will.

Arbitrary control was also present in Philadelphia, divided into forty-two wards, each with its own school committee. Ward bosses often intervened in such matters as hiring or firing and who got lucrative school contracts (for school repairs, heating, and supplies, for example). Such conditions hastened calls for civil service reform, merit-based hiring, elimination of graft and corruption, and rational management by qualified professionals. The goal was laudable: incorruptible, orderly, and efficient school systems.[32]

One outcome was the reduction of ward control in favor of centralized city school boards. The idea caught on that central school boards, composed of only 7–15 citizens chosen at large rather than by ward, would be as efficient as reformers believed corporate boards to be. As early as 1872, San Francisco and Chicago abolished ward representation and reduced the size of their central school boards. Boston reduced its level of ward representation in 1875, and Detroit followed in 1881 (only to restore it in 1889). By the early twentieth century, most major cities had either modified or abolished ward representation, and small central school boards with elite memberships, whether elected or appointed, became the chief educational policy-making bodies in most American cities.[33]

This was a pattern that would, with periodic tinkering, remain intact into the twenty-first century. A major problem, however, was that elite centralized school boards meant elite viewpoints (and biases) in the making of educational policies and directions.

The changing superintendency

The superintendent's job became more complex, involving not only the business end of school operations but also oversight of instruction, curriculum development, and personnel. Reformers successfully argued that superintendents should be in charge of all school operations, and in large school systems, assistant superintendents and other assorted administrative support staff were added. With the growth of large administrative bureaucracies, school superintendents truly became chief executive officers (CEOs), as bureaucratic in some respects as corporations.

Trained in the universities and armed with "scientific" psychology and testing technology, the new breed of school superintendents organized urban school systems into corporate-style bureaucracies with educational production separated into three lines: elementary schools, junior high schools, and high schools. Curriculum and instruction at the secondary levels were organized like assembly lines, with curriculum divided into discrete subjects taught by teachers specialized in those areas, with bells ringing to signal class changes and students marching from one specialized teacher and classroom to another. Quality control was managed by grouping students according to age and tested abilities and with curriculum specifically designed (or "differentiated") so that each ability level received the kind of academic or vocational preparation deemed appropriate. Such developments, with structural tinkering and terminological changes over succeeding decades, set the standards by which most school systems continue to operate today. Improvements were made, but reformers failed to recognize that centralized school boards and powerful superintendents meant neighborhood control and citizen identity with the schools would wither.[34]

Suggested Activity: Discuss with others: Well-intended structural changes often produce results neither planned nor desired. Brainstorm examples related to education, historical and contemporary, that illustrate this phenomenon, and discuss whether or not things could have been done differently.

Teachers and school reform

There is a need to recognize that teachers—not administrators, supervisors, specialists, boards, scholars, reformers, or critics—are the ones who deliver instruction. This is not meant to imply that the other groups fail in providing important services, but since instruction is the central function of schools, then teachers ought to be recognized as the significant professionals in the schooling process. Powerful representatives of the elite and centralized bureaucracies continue to control American public schools in ways that leave teachers out of the loop. Until better engagement of teachers occurs, instructional reforms orchestrated by elites in government, corporations, academia, and superintendents' offices will probably continue top-down. If the historical record is any indication, it promises little more than "tinkering toward Utopia," an approach that "has rarely worked well."[35]

Financial control of education

In many ways, the most powerful aspect of control is school finance. As can be seen in Table 2.2, the bulk of school finance continues to come from the state and local levels, with the federal government being the third. It is said that "the person who pays the piper calls the tune," so it would appear that the state and local levels exert the most control over schools. The way federal control is exercised over education, however cannot be so neatly drawn, because its influence over policy is far heftier than its percentage of financial contribution would suggest. In early twentieth-century reforms, educational governance was devised for boards and superintendents that served to shield them from interference by mayors and city councils. Similar shields existed for state superintendents and state boards as well. Most local boards were elected rather than appointed, and so were some superintendents. Election by voters entailed loyalty to constituents, and it provided a degree of independence from higher authorities. Prior to the 1950s, most state and federal authorities were content to allow localities to exert the lion's share of control over curriculum, personnel, and finances.

Table 2.2 Percentage of Revenues Provided to Elementary and Secondary Schools by Government Level in Selected Academic Years in the United States

School year	Federal %	State %	Local %
1919–20	0.3	16.5	83
1929–30	0.4	16.9	82.7
1939–40	1.8	30.3	68
1949–50	2.9	39.8	57.3
1959–60	4.4	39.1	56.5
1969–70	8.0	39.9	52.1
1979–80	9.8	46.8	42.4
1989–90	6.1	47.1	46.6
2000–01	7.3	49.7	43.0
2010–11	12.5	43.1	44.3
2020–21	11	46	44

Sources: Adapted from National Center for Educational Statistics, "Table 172: Revenues for Public Elementary and Secondary Schools, by Source of Funds: Selected Years, 1919–20 to 2006–2007," *Digest of Educational Statistics, 2009*, at http://nces.ed.gov/programs/digest/d09/tables/dt09_172.asp (accessed on January 1, 2010); National Center for Education Statistics, "Public School Revenue Sources." *Condition of Education*. US Department of Education, Institute of Education Sciences. https://nces.ed.gov/programs/coe/indicator/cma/public-school-revenue (accessed on January 29, 2025); National Center for Education Statistics. (2024). Public School Revenue Sources. *Condition of Education*. US Department of Education, Institute of Education Sciences. Retrieved [date], from https://nces.ed.gov/programs/coe/indicator/cma. (accessed on January 29, 2025)

In the second half of the twentieth century, however, governors found good schools to be a major lure to bring businesses and jobs to their states, and achieving a competitive edge helped push states toward more control of schools. During the Cold War, federal leaders faced increased international scrutiny when, for example, the United States was compared unfavorably to the Soviet Union over racially segregated schools. Later, as global economic competition threatened American power, negative international comparisons of American educational achievement with those of competitor nations stimulated even greater federal control of education. Thus, state and national controls over the schools increased in the latter half of the twentieth century.[36]

There was an important shift in financial control from localities to state and federal levels, with a growing gap occurring between those who made school policy and those held accountable for results. Between the early 1980s and the early twenty-first century, governors and state legislators imposed statewide reforms to raise student achievement and require high-stakes testing. In addition, several US presidents since the 1980s—Ronald Reagan, George H. W. Bush, William J. Clinton, George W. Bush, and Barack H. Obama—all pushed national education reforms and policies. When such state and federal demands lack adequate funding, however, critics hurl the charge of "unfunded mandates." Schools, teachers, and even students get blamed if they do not meet the demands, but the evidence is thin that governors, state legislatures, presidents, or congresses ever accept blame when school performance does not improve under policies they imposed.[37]

Local control

Although local control has popular appeal, from a legal standpoint the constitutional power to establish public schools is a state responsibility. Historically, most governance and control were delegated to localities, and so it was well into the twentieth century.

The growth of state control over education was never a straight line of progression but more of a perpetual balancing act between state and local authority.[38] From colonial times through the first decades of the twentieth century, localities maintained dominant control but with a slow drain of power toward the state level by the middle decades of the twentieth century. During the 1930s, local control was particularly eroded when Depression-wracked localities had to appeal to state governments for financial aid. Financial outlays are highly significant ways and means of governance. As seen in Table 2.2, during the

1929–30 school year (the beginning of the Great Depression), local financial outlays were a whopping 82.7 percent, with state outlays only 16.9 percent, but by the 1939–40 school year (as the Great Depression was coming to an end), local outlays had shrunk to 68 percent, while state outlays almost doubled to 30.3 percent. By 1949–50, state outlays increased to 39.8 percent, where they more or less hovered until the 1979–80 school year, when for the first time state financial outlays (46.8 percent) actually exceeded those of the localities (42.4 percent). In the 1980s, the local share increased slightly as federal contributions decreased, but by the 2000–1 school year, the state clearly had the lion's share at 49.7 percent. Since 2000, federal funding initially increased but decreased slightly between 2010 and 2020, while state funding initially decreased and then increased slightly between 2010 and 2020, and local funding remained relatively stable.

State control

The idea of ultimate state responsibility for public education has long been recognized by the courts. In the landmark decision of *Brown v. Board of Education, Topeka* (1954), for example, the US Supreme Court held that a state may delegate responsibility for public schools to its local governments, but it cannot abrogate its ultimate responsibility for those schools and, therefore, a state must ensure that its laws and policies are consistent with the requirements of the Constitution.[39] The force of court decisions along such lines has contributed to an increase in state control of public education.

However, this is not as clear-cut as it seems. Two notable decisions on financial resources for schools, one by a state supreme court (*Serrano v. Priest* [1971]) and the other by the US Supreme Court (*San Antonio Independent School District v. Rodriguez* [1973]) help illustrate the point. The Serrano case, brought before the California State Supreme Court in 1971, concerned that state's heavy reliance on local property taxes to finance education and how this method of financing created educational inequalities between wealthy and poor school districts. Although the case would reassert itself in the California courts several times over the years, *Serrano v. Priest* helped focus nationwide attention on state responsibility for equitable public education provisions at the local level.[40]

The issues were similar in *Rodriguez*, a case originating in Texas, particularly the inequities from relying on local property taxes, except *Rodriguez* was appealed to the US Supreme Court, which held that, while education is one of the most important services provided by a state, it is not a federal right guaranteed by the

Constitution. The court concluded that issues of taxation for public education are reserved to state legislatures, in effect upholding state responsibility for public education.[41]

Both of these cases reinforce the view that public education is squarely the responsibility of states; however, criticisms continue. For example, there is the argument that state responsibility under the Tenth Amendment is no match for the spending power of the US Congress. Over time, the federal government has slowly increased expenditures for schools, and Congress has come to exert growing influence over education through the **power of the purse**, even moving toward a national curriculum and a national testing program. Viewed in this light, the tradition of strong local and state control is facing increasing pressure.[42]

Perhaps there has been a loss of confidence in local control by both the state and federal levels of policy making. Near the end of the twentieth century, driven by fears of global competition and domestic economic decline, many states instituted massive statewide testing programs to make local educational authorities and teachers accountable for the educational achievement of their students. At its onset, this movement was spurred by critics charging that the schools were failing to meet the challenges of global market competition. There was also an intense economic rivalry among the states for businesses and jobs, and strong accountability and testing programs were seen as indicators of good schools. Pressures to lower local property taxes and the clamor over standards and accountability only encouraged more centralization, an enhancement of state and federal control, and a diminution of local control.[43]

For those who fear federal control, however, it should be kept in mind that as late as the academic year 2020–1, the federal government contributed only 11 percent of the nation's public school funding, while state governments contributed, on average, 46 percent, and local governments put up 44 percent (see Table 2.2). The lion's share (90 percent) was still provided by localities and states.

Federal control

Although the federal government has no specific constitutional authority for schools, it has long been involved. Although never as substantial as local or state involvement (see Table 2.2), federal involvement came about primarily in initiating or providing crucial support for educational activities that state and local governments could not or would not undertake.

In its earliest educational forays following the American Revolution, the federal government was debt ridden and short of cash. It did, however, have federal land, although much of it had been taken from indigenous peoples. While still operating under the Articles of Confederation, Congress passed the Ordinance of 1785, concerning the Northwest Territory between the Ohio River and the Great Lakes, to wit: "There shall be reserved the lot No. 16, of every township, for the maintenance of public schools, within the said township."[44] In 1862, Congress passed the Morrill Act to dispense land in the Louisiana Purchase by apportioning large swaths to each individual state to sell, using the proceeds for "the endowment, support, and maintenance of at least one college." The colleges, now referred to as land-grant colleges, were to provide instruction in "agriculture and the mechanic arts" (not excluding other "scientific or classical subjects") and to promote "the liberal and practical education of the industrial classes."[45] Through the late eighteenth and into the nineteenth centuries, most federal support for education came through federal lands. While these actions were also intended to bring lands into economic production, and relieve population pressures east of the Mississippi River, educational objectives were clearly important.

Federal funds for education were extended by the Smith-Hughes Act of 1917, which helped (and pushed) states to provide high school vocational and technical education "in agriculture and the trades and industries" and which also included funds for "the preparation of teachers of vocational subjects" at the higher education level.[46] Most federal education legislation coming after 1917 continued to provide financial aid, one of the more significant being the G.I. Bill (officially the Serviceman's Readjustment Act of 1944), which provided financial support for the Second World War veterans to attend postsecondary educational institutions.[47]

More federal financial aid came after the Second World War in legislation such as the National Defense Education Act of 1958 (NDEA), which supported math, science, and foreign language instruction and was to some extent an outgrowth of the Cold War "space race" with the Soviet Union. Another major expansion occurred with the Elementary and Secondary Education Act of 1965 (ESEA), which was a significant part of President Lyndon Johnson's Great Society program and what he called the War on Poverty. A decade later came the Education for All Handicapped Children Act of 1975 (later revised and renamed the Individuals with Disabilities Act [IDEA] in 1990), which expanded federal aid to include equal educational opportunities for persons with disabilities. All these acts expanded federal involvement, and they also increased federal controls.

Cross-reference: For more on Johnson's Great Society and War on Poverty, see Chapter 3. For more on the Individuals with Disabilities Act (IDEA), see Chapter 7.

Since there is no explicit education power laid out in the Constitution, federal aid must be channeled through other powers, such as national defense (the National Defense Education Act of 1958), general welfare (the Elementary and Secondary Education Act of 1965), and equal protection of the laws (the Individuals with Disabilities Education Act of 1990).[48] Federal funds must be allocated according to the Constitution and as specified by congressional legislation; consequently, most federal funding for education is through **categorical grants**, or federal funding of education for narrowly defined purposes and programs, rather than **general grants** (as provided by state and local governments).

In sum, general financial support for education continues to rest with local and state governments, but pressures for greater federal aid have grown. In the 1980s, there was an effort to relax restrictions on federal funding with block grants, or grants that allow more state and local discretion to spend federal funds. Although **block grants** did not loosen restrictions as much as supporters hoped, they were extended by the **No Child Left Behind (NCLB)** Act of 2002 under President George W. Bush.[49] In 2009, President Barack Obama made it clear that strong federal involvement in education would continue during his administration.

Matters became complicated during the administration of President Donald Trump. Within the first month of the second administration, for example, the government discontinued hundreds of millions of dollars in federal investments in education and pledged to shut down the US Department of Education. Although closing the department would require an act of Congress, the presidential administration can significantly reduce its activities.

Contemporary conditions

Schools are institutions controlled at several levels in both direct and indirect ways, but the most direct form of control comes at the local level. The primary policy-making local body is the school board, which provides general oversight of policies, operations, and professional personnel (superintendents, other administrators and support personnel, and classroom teachers) to deliver day-to-day operations and instruction. However, local school systems must not only carry out local board policies and directives but also state and federal laws and regulations as well. State governance is more indirect than local, but local schools are dependent on the state because it is the significant source of policy, legislation, and funding. In comparison, the federal government has been a secondary player, but its influence over educational policies and practices often exceeds the financial support it actually provides.

Local school systems

While schools differ by state and locality, they share much in common in regard to organizational and physical structures, as well as curriculum and instruction. For example, local school systems are organized hierarchically, with the school board setting policy at the top and the superintendent serving as the chief administrative (or executive) officer. Authority and power flow downward to central office staff and outward to building principals and then to teachers. In physical structure, schools are typically constructed with individual classrooms along hallways in a configuration that has been likened to an "egg crate" or "motel-like" design, a feature that has utility but may hamper communication among teachers and serve as a physical barrier to innovative instructional practices. In addition to classrooms, there is usually a central office and an auditorium, cafeteria, gymnasium, and perhaps spaces designed specifically for music, theater, art, shop, and other activities. In other words, the typical school is arranged by the functions and activities that take place.[50]

> **Suggested Activity:** Consider the high school you attended and describe the physical layout. Compare notes with other students and discuss your findings.

The "motel-like" structure of many school buildings facilitates what has been described as the "autonomy of the closed door."[51] In other words, teachers may have limited control over the curriculum and other factors impacting their professional lives, but when classroom doors are closed, they are able to determine much of what goes on within.

School districts

While states set the general parameters for school operations, significant control is still exercised at the local level. **Local school districts** (sometimes *school divisions* or similar terms) vary by size, number of schools served, and function. In addition, there is variation in terminology: As used here, a school district is a local school system with a board, superintendent, administrative support staff, and classroom teachers in a network of elementary, middle, and high schools (see Figure 2.3).

Of course, large school systems are more complex and subdivided than smaller ones. Denver public schools, for example, are part of a single system divided into five director districts. An immense and subdivided school system like Los Angeles might also be called a unified school district. New York City, the country's largest school system, is subdivided into ten regions that are further subdivided into school districts.[52]

Among the variety of school districts, student enrollments range from a few hundred students in the smaller districts that may serve only a handful of schools to thousands of students in the larger ones serving hundreds of schools. For example, New York City has almost 1,600 schools currently serving over 900,000 students in grades kindergarten through 12; on the other hand, Winooski, Vermont, encompasses approximately 1 square mile of territory served by three schools serving just 803 students.[53]

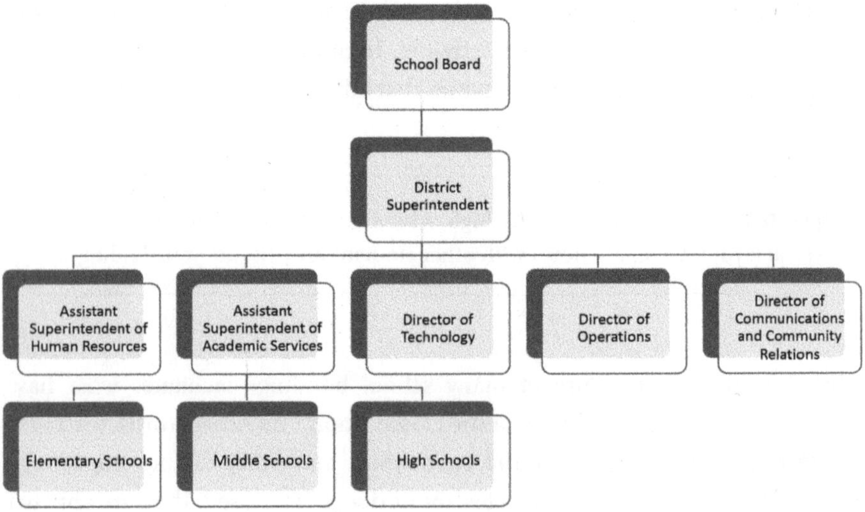

Figure 2.3 Sample organizational chart of a school district.

The organizational structure of local school districts varies according to such things as state requirements and local needs and conditions. Generally, local school districts mirror state law requirements; states usually define in general terms how their local school systems must be structured, how school board members must be selected, and what their general roles and responsibilities must be.

School boards

The majority of **local school boards** are elected by local citizens, although in some instances boards may be appointed by local judges, mayors, city councils, or county commissioners or supervisors. Elected or appointed, however, school board members are supposed to be public servants representing the people, rather than a narrowly defined constituency. Sometimes professional educators may serve on boards, but they generally cannot serve on boards that employ them because of conflict of interest laws. The idea is that education should serve the public interest, and public school systems should be governed by citizens, not professional employees. Professionals certainly exercise influence through their services and advice, but according to democratic theory, citizens are the ultimate source of legal authority, not educational professionals.[54]

The roles and responsibilities of local school boards may vary by state, but usually boards operate at the level of policy rather than hands-on daily operations. Although local board controls diminished as state and federal control grew over the years, boards still exercise significant influence. In many respects, democratically elected school boards provide a "nursery" for self-government, allowing citizens an opportunity for direct involvement in public policy making that impacts their lives in the close personal terms of children, families, and homes. School board meetings are always open to the public, except when addressing such legally protected areas as confidential personnel matters. Local school boards must be conducted in accordance with applicable local, state, and federal statutes. According to the **National School Boards Association (NSBA)**, some of the key responsibilities of local school boards include:

- Employing the superintendent
- Developing and adopting policies, curriculum, and the budget
- Overseeing facilities issues
- Adopting collective bargaining agreements.[55]

Suggested Activity: Attend a school board meeting, take notes of any discussions related to governance, and discuss your observations and reflections in class.

Superintendents

Traditionally, some of the earliest **local superintendents** were elected by voters, but in most states today they are directly hired by school boards; consequently, superintendents and local school boards typically share similar educational philosophies, and superintendents tend to be concerned with maintaining the support of their board. Superintendents serve as chief executive officers of local school districts, and their primary responsibility is to keep the schools working smoothly and lawfully. They also provide professional advice and data to their boards to help them shape policies, plan budgets, and articulate educational goals. Superintendents serve at the pleasure of the board, and they should be cognizant of community constituencies and interest groups, understanding that they will often face forceful special interests that try to influence curriculum, policies, personnel, and operations. Not surprisingly, the turnover rate for local superintendents tends to be high, particularly in large school districts.[56]

Principals

At the school level, the principal must see that the policies of the board and the administrative directives of the superintendent are carried out and then report back on the effects and ongoing needs. In another sense, however, the term *principal* means "first" teacher (or sometimes "head" teacher), that is, one who serves as the **instructional leader** who also has duties as the **school administrator**. Principals are instructional leaders who must encourage professional growth, commitment to goals, and innovative teaching and curriculum practices; they are school administrators who must manage professional staff, students, programs, community relationships, and the general operation of the school. Principals report directly to the local superintendent or a designated assistant superintendent. Depending on the number of faculty, students, and the needs of a school, principals may be supported by assistant principals and other support staff.[57]

For Further Reflection: What do you see as the pros and cons of school principals holding both the role of instructional leader and the role of school administrator at the same time? Do you think it would be better to have instructional coaching and guidance provided by a different person than the school administrator?

Teachers

Schools are often organized by departments at the secondary school level and grade levels at the elementary level—often called **professional learning communities**. High school departments are typically organized around subjects or disciplines. Department chairs or team leaders are generally full-time teachers who facilitate team efforts and communications to and from the principal's office.

Teachers comprise the largest group of professionals in any school, yet they may work independently of one another in their individual classrooms. Individualization of work affords teachers a certain degree of autonomy, but this can foster professional isolation if it restricts cooperative interaction with professional colleagues.[58] Interactive collaboration and professional autonomy are not mutually exclusive. Professional autonomy does not mean all-powerful teachers in isolated classrooms; instead, it means competent teachers using their best professional judgment in conducting professional duties and activities in line with the lawful directives of employers and administrative supervisors. At the same time, the work of teachers may well be enhanced by exchange and collaboration with their colleagues.

Cross-Reference: see Chapter 1: The Teaching Profession for a discussion of professional organizations and unions. pp. 1—60.

For Further Discussion: Think about the potential ethical dilemmas resulting from the tension between professional autonomy and democratic control over education. How much input should laypersons have when it comes to educational decision-making? How would you, as a teacher, feel if your opinion ran counter to the opinion of the local school board, which does not consist of educational professionals but of local citizens? How would you feel as a parent?

Special interest groups

Every community has **special interests**, and they emerge from parents, local communities, and/or the larger society. Special interest individuals and groups exert pressures on schools by pleading various causes and ideologies. They lobby legislatures, school boards, councils, and individuals; and they speak out at public meetings, circulate petitions, organize media campaigns, and work behind the scenes to further their agendas.

The existence of special interest groups can be a sign of a healthy democracy in action where various elements of the community play vital roles in educational decision-making, but some special interests can become obstructive or even destructive of the public interest, particularly when they dominate public dialogue to the detriment of vital but less vociferous views. When this occurs, there is a need for both patience and a concerted effort to ensure public participation under the rules of fair play.

> **Suggested Activity**: Research a special interest group that has recently attempted to exert influence over public schools. What interests were they trying to advance, and what were their strategies for doing so?

Parents and caregivers

Parents and other caregivers might be involved in schools in many ways, but it is particularly important for them to ensure that their children have a caring and supportive home environment that encourages learning and that fulfills such specific practical needs as getting the children ready and prepared for school each day. Caregivers also attend parent-teacher conferences and work supportively with teachers to ensure their children's success. Other forms of parental participation can include volunteer activities, such as chaperoning field trips or helping with special classroom or school events. Caregivers often organize fundraisers, support sports teams and other extracurricular activities, and work in parent-teacher organizations such as the school's Parent-Teacher Association (PTA).

There has been an increased awareness of the ways in which parental involvement has been narrowly defined and based on white middle-class norms. Thus, recent studies have expanded popular conceptions of what "counts" as engagement or involvement. For example, several studies have pointed to the ways in which Black parents of children in under-resourced schools have engaged primarily through advocacy for equity-oriented reforms. Other studies have illuminated how Latinx families organized and built coalitions with Latinx activists in order to promote dignity and justice in schools.[59]

It must be recognized that caregivers, not just professionals, have rights and duties. After all, the schools actually belong to citizens and taxpayers, including caregivers, and they, too, have ethical obligations and feelings of responsibility for their children that must not be undervalued by professionals. Studies have repeatedly demonstrated significant correlations of parental participation with the academic success of their children.[60]

For Further Reflection: How would you define the most productive form of parental involvement in schools that is not only in the best interest of children but also respects teacher professionalism as well as parental rights?

For Further Reflection: To what extent should parents be advocates for their children? Should they influence school governance and shape educational policy?

State governance of schools

As noted, states have the implied power to establish public schools under the Tenth Amendment of the US Constitution. "Implied" means the power is not explicitly stated; in fact, the Constitution does not contain the word *education*. The Tenth Amendment simply states that "the powers not delegated to the United States by the Constitution, nor prohibited by it to the States, are reserved to the States respectively, or to the People."

At the present time, the most significant source of governance and control over education remains at the state level. State legislatures are by far the most influential because they control a large portion of school funding. Governors also play significant roles through executive powers and personal powers of persuasion that can stir public opinion to action. State governance is also exercised through a **state board of education**, a **state superintendent**, and a **state department of education**, which provide central state-level oversight and regulatory roles concerning state laws, policies, regulations, and general operations. State government decides crucial aspects of funding, curriculum requirements, student promotion and graduation requirements, and teacher licensing. Over the past few decades, state power has expanded in these areas, and state funds and sanctions have become increasingly tied to high-stakes testing results.

> **Suggested Activity**: Research your own state department of education. Based on a review of their website, what are some of their current priorities?

Federal control of schools

Although federal government participation is limited, it does have power and influence through Congressional funding. Four important ways are:

- Categorical aid—funding that supports specific programs, such as compensatory education, bilingual education, special needs education, and vocational-technical education.
- Power of the purse—technically, all federal funds to education are "purse" related, but here the expression reflects funding to uphold constitutional powers and the laws of Congress, such as the Fourteenth Amendment's "equal protection of the laws" and congressional statutes supporting equal educational opportunity.
- Education research—funding of research on federally endorsed educational projects, the collection and dispersal of national education statistics and other general information useful to citizens, educators, and all levels of government.
- Moral suasion—developing a national vision for education by example through leadership, programs and policies, national discussion and debate, lawmaking, and the collection and dispersal of information.[61]

No Child Left Behind

Until after the Second World War, education was rarely, if ever, a national political issue, but beginning in the 1950s, education gained increasing national importance, even becoming the source of major initiatives in presidential administrations. One of the most ambitious presidential initiatives was President Lyndon Johnson's Great Society, of which the 1965 Elementary and Secondary Education Act (ESEA) was a part. There have been a number of other federal education reform efforts, an example being President George W. Bush's **No Child Left Behind (NCLB)**, a revision of ESEA, signed into law on January 8, 2002. It contained four key elements:

- Stronger accountability—schools are accountable for monitoring and ensuring that all students become academically proficient, both as a whole group and within specified subgroups. States and school districts must release public information annually about school progress, and under-performing schools must take corrective actions (such as tutoring and after-school and summer programs).
- Increased flexibility for school districts—in exchange for stronger accountability, states and school districts must have more freedom to shift and combine funds to serve different purposes (such as hiring, salaries, and professional development).
- Scientifically supported educational methods—rigorous research should determine the effectiveness of programs and practices (such as teaching skills in preschool and elementary reading instruction), and federal funds will be targeted at successful ones.
- School choice—families should be able to choose a different school or free tutoring if their child attends a school deemed unsafe or in need of improvement. The law encourages charter schools and supports selected services in private schools as well as **homeschooling**.[62]

Every Student Succeeds Act

After NCLB, the next reauthorization of ESEA—called the **Every Student Succeeds Act (ESSA)**—was signed into law by President Barack Obama on December 10, 2015. ESSA attempted to address the federal financing issue by moving accountability from the federal government to the states. Under ESSA, each state has to develop and submit an accountability plan to the US Education Department. These plans have to include long-term and short-term goals addressing graduation rates, English-language proficiency, and proficiency on tests as well as gaps in these areas. ESSA still requires states to test students in reading and math in grades 3 through 8 and once in high school, and it requires states to intervene in the lowest performing schools. ESSA also removed the requirement for states to include student test scores in their teacher evaluation systems.[63]

Unintended consequences of federal accountability measures

The emphasis by the federal government on standards, accountability, and testing has certainly affected public education. Some observers see federal accountability measures as welcome reform, but others are skeptical or even opposed, and some have changed their minds over time. Diane Ravitch, for instance, who was initially instrumental in paving the way for NCLB, later viewed the legislation's narrow focus on testing as undermining what public education really needs: a focus on the aims of education and a strong curriculum. Other critics argue that NCLB and ESSA fail to address social and emotional risk factors that prevent student success in school. Some maintain that the statistical procedures used to measure student proficiency are flawed. Still others complain that the system of local-state-federal control is too complex for top-down management, and high-stakes testing is problematic because there is little agreement on the best way to measure school performance.

A great deal of criticism is directed at high-stakes testing itself: It does not effectively measure what students actually learn; it skews instruction toward teaching to the test, which distracts teachers from helping students pursue knowledge of interest; and there is a "saw-tooth-effect" of testing in which performance improves over time because both teachers and students become "test smart," rather than students actually learning and retaining knowledge. Finally, critics point out that the punitive provisions in NCLB and ESSA encourage states to lower standards so enough students pass to keep federal funds flowing.[64]

One troublesome problem is that accountability measured by test scores may be particularly detrimental to low-income students of color because such students are not underprivileged by their own doings but by the history of racialization and capitalism in the United States. Instead of reducing inequities, the accountability movement exacerbates them with its sorting and ranking, which determine how federal funding rewards and penalties are doled out to the schools. In its accountability measures, NCLB and ESSA seem to assume that low academic achievement results from personal irresponsibility and that poverty results from the poor choices of individual children rather than pre-existing economic inequities.[65]

In other words, while students from marginalized communities might eventually shape their own destinies, as children they have no choice about their socioeconomic conditions, which impact their test performance differently than those students whose luck of birth environment makes school achievement more likely. In sum, the accountability movement encourages moral and academic judgments about students and their teachers and schools but not about children's socioeconomic conditions and the adult world of power that created them.[66]

> **For Further Reflection:** What do you think is the best way for schools to be held accountable for student learning?

Federal financing

Legal challenges have been launched against the way American schools are financed, although their full impact remains to be seen. Since the late 1980s, following a pattern set by the Serrano case in 1971, but also reflecting the more recent accountability movement, state supreme courts in Kentucky, New Hampshire, Tennessee, Arkansas, Ohio, and New Jersey have ruled that their respective state constitutions require each state to provide resources necessary to meet state-mandated standards. In other words, if a state is going to require higher standards, and if it expects schools to actually achieve them, then it must provide the requisite financial resources. However, if it is difficult for a state to determine what it will cost to meet its own standards, it is even more difficult for the federal government, because it must adapt its requirements to each state's unique educational system and each state's unique accountability standards, and this makes it challenging to determine a fair mode of dispensing federal funds.[67]

This points to a major school governance dilemma: How do localities, states, and the federal government sort through all the pressures from politically hot education issues and the economic realities faced in funding and governing education?

Debate over school governance reform

Public school governance has been criticized for years from a variety of vantage points, and numerous reforms have been suggested. Some proposals advocate a simplified reform that leaves some traditional structure while increasing local community and even individual school control over curriculum and teaching. Others call for a more radical restructuring that seems to leave few vestiges of traditional modes of governance.

For example, there are critics who argue that public schools are top-down, hierarchical systems that overload teachers with supervisors and negate teacher professionalism, but the primary reason this approach continues is "the trap of favored ways of thinking." The greatest concentration of bureaucratic decision-making power has occurred at the state level, when what is needed is more control over curriculum and instruction at the local level. The role of school principals must be redefined as facilitators of teaching, and teachers must be more fully engaged in decisions not only on curriculum and instruction but also on administrative acts impacting their professional duties. If teachers had more control, they could break out of their current isolation and work in teams to meet unique needs at each individual school. Old ways of scheduling class periods and organizing by age-grade levels should be scrapped in favor of organizing around student needs and progress. Parents should be more involved in governance, with individual schools deciding how to define this involvement.[68]

Other critics, however, propose not simply restructuring but complete reshaping. For example, it has been observed that existing school systems are not, and never were intended to be, very efficacious. In the early 1900s, they were designed based upon an assembly line approach to socialize large numbers of immigrant children to the urban industrial environment, without much regard for productive learning. What is needed now is a new school governance system designed for productive learning, with teachers and parents exercising far more authority over local schools than currently. More research and evaluation should be conducted to better understand how teachers and students interact and how productive learning occurs. Schools should be open to public scrutiny and be accountable to the communities they serve. School principals might become superfluous, because faculty would be directly involved in running schools and could assume administrative responsibilities.[69]

> **Suggested Activity**: Divide into two groups and debate the two perspectives described in the above section.

Other critics idealize the past, seeking to recover lost traditions and better times. Advocates of school vouchers and stringent accountability standards, for example, appear to believe that education was once wide open to private choice, and academic standards were once very high. As the historical record shows, however, before there were any public school systems, school choice was mostly dependent on the ability to pay at a time when few could afford it. No serious effort was made to educate everyone, and there were never enough private schools to accommodate the demand if all parents had tried to enroll their children. Criticism of schools for lack of academic achievement has a long history, and would-be reformers who seek to return to a golden age of academic achievement actually look for a past that never existed.[70]

Although criticism has a valuable role to play, it sometimes seems the critics know everything about public school improvement but very little about financing it. For example, in the 1980s, critics proclaimed that global economic competitors were surpassing the United States and pointed their fingers at the schools. About a decade later, however, the National Assessment of Educational Progress (NAEP) reported that reading and math scores were at a thirty-year high, and by 2000, the dropout rate neared an all-time low. Critics then complained about the "merely average" performance of American students on international tests of reading, math, and science achievement. These same critics seemed strangely silent when an international comparison showed the United States rated only average in the percentage of gross domestic product invested in elementary education, and well into the bottom half in secondary education.[71]

Some assumptions of reformers

Sometimes it helps to examine reform vocabulary and rhetoric. It has been observed that the current school accountability movement is based less on **accountability to the public** (which ordinary citizens might expect the term to mean), and more on **technical-managerial accountability** in which auditable accounts are reviewed by state or federal authorities instead of parents or community. It is a market-style view of accountability that defines schools as producers of commodities and students and parents as consumers; hence, educational quality is associated with accounting processes and procedures rather than academic substance. Parents are made to feel that they should be preoccupied with whether their children are prepared for the needs of competitive economic interests rather than their children's own educational growth and development or the larger common good.[72]

Defining school accountability in terms of market theory reflects what has been called the **consumerization of citizenship**. It is based on promotional, top-down communication, with service delivery geared at maximizing customer preferences based on market competition.[73]

Charter schools, voucher plans, and school choice

The impact of market ideology on the public possibly helps explain such developments as **school choice**, **voucher plans,** and charter schools, which are all consumer-driven views of education.[74]

School choice refers to programs that allow families to use public money to choose education beyond their locally districted public school, including private schools. More than 25 percent of K12 students attend a school other than their local assigned school.[75] This number does not include the many children whose families have moved into or out of a particular neighborhood primarily because of the quality of the schools there, though one could argue this is another form of "school choice."

Some public school choice options include magnet schools, open enrollment, and charter schools. **Magnet schools** typically specialize in a particular area of study, such as STEM or the arts, and were originally designed to integrate schools through drawing in families from higher-income neighborhoods to schools established in lower-income neighborhoods. **Open enrollment** is a system that allows families to choose public schools outside of their assigned school.

Beginning in the 1990s, states made it easier for parents to homeschool their children. Homeschooling rates doubled during the COVID-19 pandemic, and many families never went back to their public schools. Many other families switched their children from public to private schools during the pandemic.[76]

The 1990s also saw the emergence of charter schools. Charter schools are publicly funded in the same way as district schools; however, they operate with more flexibility and independence than district schools. In exchange for this flexibility, charter schools are expected to be more accountable to parents and their authorizers. Proponents argue that this flexibility, paired with the competition they face from other schools, spurs innovative approaches. Critics argue that the independence of charter schools has led to financial mismanagement, that charters educate fewer students with disabilities and English language learning needs, that they rely on more punitive disciplinary practices, and that they increase racial segregation. About 7 percent of all public school students were enrolled in charter schools in the 2021–2 school year.[77]

The laws regulating charter schools vary from state to state. For example, in some states like Virginia, the local district has to approve the creation of new charter schools in their area; however, in other states charter schools are authorized by a state education agency, independent chartering board, or other authorizer. Some states allow for-profit companies to run charter schools, which leads to confusion over the profit status of charters. Although the schools themselves are not-for-profit, the companies running the schools can earn profits from services such as creating curricula and providing school facilities.[78]

School voucher plans are perhaps the most controversial type of school choice. These allow parents to use government monies, called vouchers, for private school tuition or other education costs such as tutoring or materials for homeschooling. Since private schools are legally permitted to discriminate on the basis of religion, LGBTQI+, English proficiency, disability, and other factors, critics argue that publicly funded vouchers should not support them. Because private schools can select their students, the director of Public Funds Public Schools has argued that "so-called school choice is really the schools' choice."[79]

Rural communities tend especially to oppose these plans, since families in sparsely populated areas often have no other choice than the local public school. Although vouchers were historically intended for lower-income families, more recent voucher plans allow public monies to flow to parents already sending their children to private schools. Some have called this a reverse Robin Hood scheme in that it takes money from already systematically underfunded schools and gives it to families who least need it.[80]

For Further Reflection: What are your thoughts about school choice? What types of choices, if any, did your caregivers have with regard to the school you attended? For example, did they move to a neighborhood for its schools? Did they opt not to send you to the local school? Did other caregivers have the same choices? What do you see as the advantages and disadvantages of school choice plans?

Taken together, this movement toward greater school choice, charter schools, and voucher plans (which are accompanied by a weakening of teachers' unions) has been called school **privatization.** Proponents of privatization argue that the government is less efficient than the private sector and that parents, as consumers, should be able to select the school their child attends. Critics, on the other hand, point out that these efforts are being bankrolled by companies standing to make a profit and that privatization allows the erosion of civil rights protections for students.[81]

Suggested Activity: Conduct some research into school choice plans, either in your local state/area, or other parts of the country. What are the arguments for and against these plans?

Market logic applied to school governance

Applications of market theories to school governance assume that public schools exist fundamentally to serve economic ends. What gets lost is public education's vital importance in preparing future citizens of a democratic society. Schools never had and do not now have the singular, eternal purpose of serving economic interests, despite what is loudly proclaimed. The historical record shows no such singular purpose. What it actually reveals is multiple purposes in which economic benefit was only one (and very often *not* the most important one). In the end, the fact remains that values are not biologically transmitted; they must be passed from one generation to the next through some means of education. Education to develop competent and knowledgeable citizens may be the *most* important goal of education in any society that aspires to be democratic.[82]

Rather than mere submission to the drumbeat of market ideologues, greater emphasis is needed on education for a deliberative democracy. Perhaps the greatest need is the education of future citizens who take citizenship responsibilities as seriously as private rights and privileges.[83]

> **For Further Reflection:** The above section describes two purposes of schools being the preparation of democratic citizens and support for individual and national economic security. What other purposes do schools serve? How can these multiple purposes be balanced?

Value of criticism

While school critics might need criticism themselves, and while they might seem to ignore too easily the accomplishments of schools and their governing agencies, it still remains that the schools face daunting problems that need serious attention. In the final analysis, American education is neither as hopeless as detractors proclaim nor as flawless as admirers pronounce. Both the public and professional educators alike need to understand that valuable service is provided by critics when their efforts become stimuli for creative thought and action about the aims of education and better ways to accomplish them.

Summary and conclusions

Understanding school governance and control is central to comprehending the ways schools work today. Prior to the emergence of public school systems, there was considerable variety in how American schools were governed. For the most part, education was seen as the responsibility of individuals, families, or religions, not governments. The nineteenth-century idea of universal, tax-supported public schools, available to virtually all children, became accepted and widely implemented. Among the driving forces were industrialization, urbanization, and the immigration of diverse peoples. As the population became more heterogeneous, it soon became obvious that some common experiences were needed to reduce social divisions and provide a stronger sense of the common good. Public common schools were considered a central part of such reform efforts, with most of the financial support and governance provided by localities and with oversight by local boards of education or school committees. The idea of public, tax-supported education eventually spread to secondary and higher education as well.

High fertility rates and increasing immigration caused rapid population growth in the late nineteenth and early twentieth centuries, and public schools had to expand accordingly. Seeking to manage this population impact on schools, progressive reformers opted for the corporate model of governance, which resulted in bureaucratized school systems governed by small elite boards and operated by trained professionals, a development that shaped the kinds of school governance existing today.

An important aspect of school control is finance, and while the proportions provided by the local, state, and federal levels have changed over time, the lion's share of funding continues to come from the local and state levels. Traditionally, the power to establish public schools was a state responsibility, with actual control delegated to the local levels. At one time, localities were the major source of funding, but by the late twentieth century, state funding exceeded that of local funding. Federal funding has always been less than that contributed on the local and state levels, and it usually provides only categorical rather than general funding. In earlier times, the federal government gave land to encourage educational development, but in the twentieth century, it started contributing funds for certain specific programs. Today, the federal government is involved in significant ways, with such programs as the Individuals with Disabilities Act (IDEA; see Chapter 7) and Every Student Succeeds Act (ESSA).

Individual schools are administered by principals and assistant principals who function as instructional leaders, supervise teachers, deal with student discipline, manage school budgets, maintain community relations, and more. Department chairs and team leaders facilitate coordination and communication among teachers and administrators, while support staff help ensure smooth operation. At the local level, school boards make budgets, purchase school sites, decide curriculum questions, among many other duties. The boards hire local superintendents who serve as chief administrators of the schools. Interest groups also shape school governance through such activities as lobbying and raising public attention. Accreditation agencies exert control through monitoring activities at the local, state, regional, and national levels.

At the state level, governance is performed through legislatures, governors, courts, state superintendents, state boards of education, and state departments of education. Crucial decisions are made involving such issues as state financial support for schools, content of the curriculum, teacher licensure, and student promotion and graduation criteria. Finally, the federal level shapes education through promoting a national perspective for schools across the country, gathering educational data, providing categorical aid, and funding education research, among other things.

Throughout history, school governance has been modified, overhauled, and reformed. Reform proposals during recent years encompass ideas ranging from centralization to decentralization, from increasing the scope of public options to privatization and school choice, and from strengthening the status quo to completely rebuilding it. Despite all the criticism, debate, and reforms over the years, schools and school governance seem to be fairly resistant to radical change. Perhaps some fundamental change will come, but time will tell what changes take root and what conditions remain the same.

Vocabulary

accountability to the public
accreditation agencies
administrative progressives
block grants
categorical grants
charter schools
consumerization of citizenship
Every Student Succeeds Act (ESSA)
general grants
ideological orientation
instructional leader
John Dewey
local control

local superintendents
local school boards
local school districts
magnet schools
National School Boards Association (NSBA)
No Child Left Behind (NCLB)
open enrollment
pedagogical progressives
power of the purse
privatization
professional learning communities
school administrator
school choice
school committee
special interests
state board of education
state department of education
state superintendent
superintendent
technical-managerial accountability
voucher plans

Notes

1 David Tyack, *Seeking Common Ground: Public Schools in a Diverse Society* (Cambridge, MA: Harvard University Press, 2003).

2 US Department of Education (USDOE), "About Us," at http://doe.k12.hi.us/about/index.htm (accessed on February 1, 2010).

3 Glenn Weaver, "Benjamin Franklin and the Pennsylvania Germans," *The William and Mary Quarterly*, 3rd ser., vol. 14, no. 4 (October, 1957): 536–59; and Patricia U. Bonomi, "The Middle Colonies as the Birthplace of American Religious Pluralism," at http://nationalhumanitiescenter.org/tserve/eighteen/ekeyinfo/midcol.htm (accessed on February 2, 2010); Heather McGhee, *The Sum of Us: What Racism Costs Everyone and How We Can Prosper Together* (New York: One World, 2022).

4 S. Alexander Rippa, ed., "The Massachusetts School Law of 1647," in *Educational Ideas in America: A Documentary History* (New York: David McKay, 1969), 162; Daniel Calhoun, ed., "Enforcement of Pious Teaching [Laws of Virginia, March 1645–6]," in *The Educating of Americans: A Documentary History* (Boston, MA:

Houghton Mifflin, 1969), 18; and "Labor for Poor Children [Laws of Virginia, October 1646]," in Calhoun, 18.

5 Jon Teaford, "The Transformation of Massachusetts Education, 1670–1780," in *The Social History of American Education*, B. Edward McClellan and William J. Reese, eds (Chicago: University of Illinois Press, 1988), 31–5; and William J. Gilmore, *Elementary Literacy on the Eve of the Industrial Revolution: Trends in Rural New England* (Worchester, MA: American Antiquarian Society, 1982), 87–178.

6 Lawrence Cremin, *American Education: The Colonial Experience, 1607–1783* (New York: Harper Torchbooks, Harper and Row, 1970), 177–8, 530–1; and J. L. Blair Buck, *The Development of Public Schools in Virginia, 1607–1952* (Richmond: Commonwealth of Virginia State Board of Education, 1952), 14–18. In 1805, the Syms and Eaton schools combined to form Hampton Academy, which in 1852 became a part of the public school system of the city of Hampton, Virginia.

7 Cremin, *American Education: The Colonial Experience, 1607–1783,* 517–43 and 544–63; R. Freeman Butts and Lawrence A. Cremin, *A History of Education in American Culture* (New York: Holt, Rinehart and Winston, 1953), 97–115.

8 Thomas Jefferson, *Crusade Against Ignorance: Thomas Jefferson on Education*, Gordon C. Lee, ed, Classics in Education, No. 6 (New York: Teachers College Press, 1961), 84–6.

9 Thomas Timar and David Tyack, *The Invisible Hand of Ideology: Perspectives from the History of School Governance* (Denver: Education Commission of the States, 1999), 11.

10 Lawrence Cremin, "Horace Mann's Legacy," in Horace Mann, *The Republic and the School Horace Mann on the Education of Free Men*, Lawrence Cremin, ed., Classics in Education, No. 1 (New York: Teachers College Press, 1957), 20; Horace Mann, "First Annual Report (1837)," in ibid., 29–30.

11 Joseph M. Cronin, *The Control of Urban Schools: Perspectives on the Power of Educational Reformers* (New York: The Free Press, 1973), 39–52.

12 Ibid., 52–7; and Joseph M. Cronin and Michael D. Usdan, "Rethinking the Urban School Superintendency: Non-Traditional Leaders and New Models of Leadership," in *American Educational Governance on Trial: Change and Challenges*, William Lowe Boyd and Debra Miretsky, eds (Chicago, IL: National Society for the Study of Education, 2003), 177–8.

13 Mark Twain (Samuel Clemens) and Charles Dudley White, *The Gilded Age: A Tale of To-Day* (Hartford, CT: American Publishing, 1873).

14 David Tyack, *The One Best System of Education: A History of American Urban Education* (Cambridge, MA: Harvard University Press, 1974), 177–81.

15 William A. Bullough, *Cities and Schools in the Gilded Age: The Evolution of an Urban Institution* (Port Washington, NY: Kennikat Press, 1974), 15–18.

16 Ibid., 22–6.

17 Lawrence Cremin, *The Transformation of the School: Progressivism in American Education, 1876–1957* (New York: Vintage Books, 1961), vii–x.
18 Tyack, *One Best System*, 126–32ff. The terms "pedagogical progressives" and "administrative progressives" are borrowed from this source.
19 Jean-Jacques Rousseau, *The Émile of Jean Jacques Rousseau: Selections*, William Boyd, trans. and ed. (New York: Teachers College Press, [1956] 1976); and Howard Ozmon and Samuel M. Craver, *Philosophical Foundations of Education*, 7th edn (Columbus, OH: Merrill Prentice Hall, 2003), 131–2.
20 Johann Heinrich Pestalozzi, *The Education of Man: Aphorisms* (New York: Greenwood Press, [1951] 1969); and Friedrich Froebel, *The Education of Man* (Clifton, NJ: A. M. Kelley, 1974).
21 Cremin, *The Transformation of the School*, 101–3 and 128–35.
22 John Dewey, *Democracy and Education: An Introduction to the Philosophy of Education* (New York: Macmillan, 1916), 100–2, and 130–45; John Dewey, *Experience and Education*. Kappa Delta Pi Lecture Series (New York: Collier Books, [1938] 1963), 43–4; and Dewey, *Moral Principles in Education*. With a New Preface by Sidney Hook (Carbondale: Southern Illinois University Press, 1975), 2, 11–13.
23 Ibid., 414–18; and Ibid., 78–84.
24 David F. Labaree, "Progressivism, Schools and Schools of Education: An American Romance," *Pedagogica Historica*, vol. 41, nos. 1 and 2 (February 2005): 275–88. See also Labaree, *The Trouble with Ed Schools* (New Haven, CT: Yale University Press, 2004).
25 Larry Cuban, "The Open Classroom," *Education Next*, vol. 4, no. 2 (Spring 2004): 68–72, at http://educationnext.org/theopenclassroom/ (accessed on February 24, 2009).
26 Raymond E. Callahan, *Education and the Cult of Efficiency: A Study of the Social Forces That Have Shaped the Administration of the Public Schools* (Chicago, IL: University of Chicago Press, 1962).
27 John T. Wahlquist, *The Philosophy of American Education* (New York: The Ronald Press, 1942), 56–70; and John Wild, "Education and Human Society: A Realistic View," in *Modern Philosophies and Education: The Fifty-Fourth yearbook of the National Society for the Study of Education, Part I*, Nelson B. Henry, ed. (Chicago, IL: University of Chicago Press, 1955), 17–56.
28 See Leonard Ayres, *Laggards in Our Schools: A Study of Retardation and Elimination in City Schools Systems* (New York: Russell Sage Foundation, Charities Publication Committee, 1909).
29 Ibid., 28–9, 39–40.
30 Welker, *The Teacher as Expert*, 7.
31 Tyack, *One Best System*, 142–7.
32 Ibid., 97–104.
33 Cronin, *The Control of Urban Schools*, 44–52.

34 David Tyack and Larry Cuban, *Tinkering Toward Utopia: A Century of Public School Reform* (Cambridge, MA: Harvard University Press, 1995); and Michael Engel, *The Struggle for Control of Public Education: Market Ideology and Democratic Values* (Philadelphia, PA: Temple University Press, 2000).

35 Tyack and Cuban, *Tinkering Toward Utopia*, 15–22, 44–7, 54–9, 134–40.

36 Michael Kirst, "A History of School Governance," in *Who's in Charge Here? The Tangled Web of School Governance and Policy*, Noel Epstein, ed. (Denver: Education Commission of the States, 2004), 20–4, 28–32, 36–7.

37 Noel Epstein, "Introduction: Who Should Be in Charge of Our Schools?" in *Who's in Charge Here?*, 2–3.

38 Nancy Beadie, "The Limits of Standardization and the Importance of Constituencies: Historical Tensions in the Relationship Between State Authority and Local Control," in *Balancing Local Control and State Responsibility for K-12 Education. 2000 Yearbook of the American Education Finance Association*, Neil Theobald and Betty Malen, eds (Larchmont, NY: Eye on Education, 2000), 47–120.

39 Although the Court's *Brown* decision rested on the "equal protection" clause of the Fourteenth Amendment, and not on the Tenth Amendment, the idea of state responsibility was clearly a part of the Court's thinking. In reference to the right to "the opportunity of an education," the Court held, "Such an opportunity, where the state has undertaken to provide it, is a right which must be made available to all on equal terms" (p. 493). See *Brown v. Board of Education Topeka* (1954), 347 US 483, also at http://supct.law.cornell.edu/supct/search/display.html?terms=brown&url=/supct/html/historics/USSC_CR_0347_0483_ZO.html (accessed on February 2, 2010).

40 *Serrano v. Priest* (1971) 5 C3d 584, and at http://online.ceb.com/CalCases/C3/5C3d584.htm (accessed on February 2, 2010). See also *Serrano II* (1976) 18 Cal. 3d 728, for a later ruling.

41 *San Antonio Independent School District v. Rodriguez* (1973) 411 US 1, at http://supct.law.cornell.edu/supct/html/historics/USSC_CR_0411_0001_ZO.html (accessed on February 2, 2010).

42 James E. Ryan, "The Tenth Amendment and Other Paper Tigers: The Legal Boundaries of Education Governance," in *Who's in Charge Here*, 42–74.

43 Michael Kirst, "Turning Points: A History of American School Governance," in *Who's in Charge Here?*, 14–5.

44 "Land Ordinance of 1785," at http://west.stanford.edu/cgi-bin/pager.php?id=49 (accessed on February 2, 2010).

45 "Transcript of the Morrill Act of 1862," at http://ourdocuments.gov/doc.php?flash=true&doc=33& page=transcript (accessed on February 2, 2010); and Scott Key, "Economics or Education: The Establishment of American Land-Grant

Universities," *Journal of Higher Education*, vol. 67, no. 2 (March–April 1996): 196(25).

46 "The National Vocational Education (Smith-Hughes) Act," at http://www.cals.ncsu.edu/agexed/sae/smithugh.html (accessed on February 2, 2010).

47 Serviceman's Readjustment Act ("G. I. Bill") of 1944, *United States Statutes at Large* 58 Stat. L. 284; Michael J. Bennett, *When Dreams Came True: The GI Bill and the Making of Modern America* (Washington, DC: Brassey's, 1996); and Reginald Wilson, "The G.I. Bill and the Transformation of America," *National Forum*, vol. 75, no. 4 (Fall 1995): 20(3).

48 For a general overview of federal government powers, see the Constitution's Preamble: "to form a more perfect Union, establish Justice, insure domestic Tranquility, provide for the common defense, promote the general Welfare, and secure the Blessings of Liberty." Other, more specific powers that have been applied to education are granted in the body of the document and in its amendments (such as the "equal protection of the laws" clause of Amendment XIV).

49 See, for example, Kenneth Finegold, Laura Wherry, and Stephanie Schardin, "Block Grants: Historical Overview and Lessons Learned," Urban Institute, No. A-63 in Series, "New Federalism: Issues and Options for States" (April 21, 2004), at http://www.urban.org/url.cfm?ID=310991 (accessed on February 2, 2010).

50 James A. Johnson et al., *An Introduction to the Foundations of American Education*, 12th edn (Boston, MA: Allyn and Bacon, 2002), 176. The "egg crate" characterization probably dates back to John Philbrick's creation of a specially designed, age-graded school in Boston, Massachusetts, in 1848. See Tyack, *One Best* System, 44–5.

51 Kathleen Bennett deMarrais and Margaret D. LeCompte, *The Way Schools Work: A Sociological Analysis of Education* (White Plains, NY: Longman Publishers, 1995), 48–9.

52 "Denver Public Schools Director Districts," at http://planning.dpsk12.org/DistrictMaps/Director-Districts.pdf (accessed on January 28, 2010); Los Angeles Unified School District, at http://notebook.lausd.net/portal/page?_pageid=33,47493&_dad=ptl&_schema=PTL_EP (accessed on January 28, 2010); The Legal Aid Society, "Questions About the NYC School Structure," http://www.legal-aid.org/selfhelp/education/structure/structure_ny_schools.html (accessed on January 28, 2010).

53 NYC Department of Education, "About Us" at https://www.schools.nyc.gov/about-us (accessed on February 7, 2025) and "Winooski School District," https://www.wsdvt.org (accessed on February 7, 2025).

54 For ethical tensions between "professionals" and "the public," see Kenneth Strike and Jonas F. Soltis, *The Ethics of Teaching*, 4th edn (New York: Teachers College, 2004), 94–11.

55 Education Commission of the States, *Effective School Governance: A Look at Today's Practice and Tomorrow's Promise*, at http://www.ecs.org/clearinghouse/13/20/1320.htm (accessed on January 28, 2010).

56 J. H. Snider, "The Superintendent as Scapegoat," *Education Week*, vol. 25, no. 18 (January 11, 2006): 31, 40.

57 Ibid., 177.

58 Ibid., 178.

59 Lori Delale-O'Connor et al., "Racialized Compensatory Cultivation: Centering Race in Parental Educational Engagement and Enrichment," *American Educational Research Journal*, vol. 57, no. 5 (October 2020): 1912–53; Samantha M. Paredes Scribner and Erica Fernández, "Organizational Politics of Parental Engagement: The Intersections of School Reform, Anti-Immigration Policies, and Latinx Parent Organizing," *Educational Policy*, vol. 31, no. 6 (July 2017): 895–920.

60 Maike Philipsen, ed., *Parental Involvement in the Schools: Ideas That Work*. Hot Topics Series (Bloomington, IN: Phi Delta Kappa, 1997), 3.

61 US Department of Education, "No Child Left Behind Act of 2001," at http://www.ed.gov./nclb/overview/intro/execsumm.doc (accessed on January 28, 2010); and "Four Pillars of NCLB," at http://www.ed.gov/print/nclb/overview/intro/4pillars.html (accessed on January 28, 2010).

62 William J. Mathis, "No Child Left Behind: Costs and Benefits," *Phi Delta Kappan*, vol. 84, no. 9 (May 2003): 679–86, 680–2, 684–6.

63 Alyson Klein, "The Every Student Succeeds Act: An ESSA Overview," *Education Week* (March 31, 2016).

64 Jane Hannaway, "Accountability, Assessment, and Performance Issues: We've Come A Long Way … or Have We?" in *American Educational Governance on Trial: Change and Challenges*, 25; and deMarrais and LeCompte, *The Way Schools Work*, 25–34, 49.

65 Diane Ravitch, *The Death and Life of the Great American School System: How Testing and Choice Are Undermining Education* (New York: Basic Books, 2010).

66 Ibid.

67 Ibid. Christine Lagana-Riordan and Jemel P. Aguilar, "What's Missing from No Child Left Behind? A Policy Analysis from a Social Work Perspective," *Children & Schools*, vol. 31, no. 3 (July 2009): 135–44; and Andrew Dean Ho, "The Problem with 'Proficiency': Limitations of Statistics and Policy Under No Child Left Behind," *Educational Researcher*, vol. 37, no. 6 (August/September 2008): 351–60.

68 Seymour B. Sarason, *How Schools Might Be Governed and Why* (New York: Teachers College Press, 1997), 35–94.

69 William J. Bailey, *Organizing* Schools (Lancaster, PA: Technomic Publishing, 1997), 22, 49–108.

70 Robert Nelson Reddick, "History, Myth, and the Politics of Educational Reform," *Educational Theory*, vol. 54, no. 1 (February 2004): 73–87.

71 Mathis, "No Child Left Behind: Costs and Benefits," 679–80. See also the National Center for Education Statistics (NCES), "National Assessment of Educational Progress (NAEP) Overview," at http://nces.ed.gov/nationsreportcard/about/#overview (accessed October 31, 2010).

72 Gert J. J. Biesta, "Education, Accountability, and the Ethical Demand: Can the Democratic Potential of Accountability Be Regained?" *Educational Theory*, vol. 54, no. 3 (August 2004): 233–50.

73 Michael A. Peters, "The New Prudentialism in Education: Actuarial Rationality and the Entrepreneurial Self," *Educational Theory*, vol. 55, no. 2 (May 2005): 135–6; and Catherine Needham, "Citizen-Consumers: New Labour's Marketplace Democracy," working paper, *Catalyst* (April 2003), at http://editiondesign.com/catalyst/pubs/pub10a.html (accessed on October 24, 2010).

74 Michael Barzelay, *The New Public Management: Improving Research and Policy Dialogue* (Berkeley: University of California Press, 2001), xi–xii, 2–3, 9; Laurence E. Jr. Lynn, *Public Management: Old and New* (New York: Taylor and Routledge, 2006), 107, 143–4.

75 Douglas N. Harris, "How Free Market Logic Fails in Schooling—And What It Means for the Role of Government," *Educational Researcher*, vol. 53, no. 2 (March 2024): 111–22.

76 Laura Newmberry, "The Pandemic Pushed More Families to Home School. Many Are Sticking with It," *Education Week*, https://www.edweek.org/policy-politics/the-pandemic-pushed-more-families-to-home-school-many-are-sticking-with-it/2022/01 (accessed on January 28, 2022).

77 Arianna Prothero, "What Are Charter Schools?" *Education Week* (August 9, 2018); Jacob Fischler and Cole Claybourn, "Understanding Charter Schools vs. Public Schools," *US News & World Report*, https://www.usnews.com/education/k12/articles/understanding-charter-schools-vs-public-schools (accessed on November 14, 2023); Adrienne D. Dixson, Camika Royal, and Kevin Lawrence Henry Jr., "School Reform and School Choice," in *Handbook of Urban Education*, H. Richard Milner IV and Kofi Lomotey, eds (New York: Routledge, 2013), 512–41.

78 Prothero, "What Are Charter Schools?"

79 Anayat Durrani, "What School Choice Is and How It Works," *US News & World Report*, https://www.usnews.com/education/k12/articles/what-school-choice-is-and-how-it-works (accessed on April 14, 2023); Harris, "How Free Market Logic Fails in Schooling," 112–14.

80 Jack Schneider and Jennifer C. Berkshire, "Robbing from the Poor to Educate the Rich," *The Nation*, https://www.thenation.com/article/society/vouchers-attack-public-education/ (accessed on February 13, 2023).

81 Tim Walker, "Fewer and Fewer States Escaping School Privatization's Reach," *NEAToday*, https://www.nea.org/nea-today/all-news-articles/fewer-and-fewer-states-escaping-school-privatizations-reach (accessed on August 17, 2018).

82 Michael Mintrom, "Educational Governance and Democratic Practice," *Educational Policy*, vol. 15, no. 5 (November 2001): 616–17, 639–40. See also Amy Gutmann, *Democratic Education* (Princeton, NJ: Princeton University Press, 1987).

83 Abe Feuerstein, "Elections, Voting, and Democracy in Local Schools District Governance," *Educational Policy*, vol. 16, no. 1 (January and March 2002): 29–35.

3

Social Class and Education

Chapter contents

Chapter objectives

Readers should be able to:

- understand the concept of social class and varying viewpoints on it.
- appreciate the historical influence of social class on educational policy.
- analyze social class and its impact on educational opportunity and attainment.
- explore leading research studies on how social class shapes the realities of schooling.
- gain an understanding of major contemporary controversies over social class and education such as school funding and access.
- explore ethical and philosophical ramifications of social class in education.

Opening questions

1. What is social class and its importance in education, past and present?
2. How has social class affected access to and the quality of education over time?
3. How have views on social class shaped educational policy?
4. What is the relationship between educational attainment and social mobility?
5. How do people's attitudes about social class affect their views on education?

The issue

Providing a simple definition of *social class* is difficult because it consists of many attributes. Class membership may be defined by income and financial assets, such as inherited wealth, property, and investments (or the lack thereof); it may also be defined by educational attainment and professional or occupational status. Class may be characterized by attributes difficult to measure, such as power, prestige, and tastes in style and language. People speak of "middle-class values" or "working-class neighborhoods," indicating that those who belong to a particular social class share not only material but also cultural characteristics. To identify solely with one particular social class could prove difficult because any given individual might belong to several categories at once. Raised in a middle-class family, for example, a person may achieve a high educational status, such as a PhD in English, yet not be able to find full-time employment. Teaching as an adjunct college professor, they might make little more than minimum wage and actually earn less than many entry-level workers, their low earnings forcing them into a poor standard of living. Another person may grow up in poverty and barely succeed in graduating from high school, but she may develop interests and skills in a growing economic field where she earns a good salary and enjoys a lifestyle that places her in the middle class.

These examples illustrate not only the complexity of social class but also the point that educational expansion per se does not guarantee economic success and increased social mobility.[1] In addition, class membership can change over the life span as people experience significant changes in income, earn degrees, obtain (or lose) jobs, experience the economic consequences of marriage and divorce, and generally feel the effects of changes as broad as the global economy and as personal as aging or illness.

Historically as well as presently, social class both reflects and causes significant differences among individuals, regarding income, wealth, status, education, and lifestyle, influencing how they are perceived and treated by others. Similar to racism and sexism, this treatment may manifest in both personal discrimination, like stereotyping, and structural discrimination embedded, for example, in schooling or employment. Regarding education specifically, social class also shapes such aspects as educational attainment, teaching methods, and both the formal and hidden curricula.[2]

Due to the legacy of slavery and the various forms of discrimination that followed it (e.g., Black Codes during Reconstruction, Jim Crow laws of the twentieth century), social class is tied to race in the United States. After the Civil Rights legislation of the 1960s, new barriers to social mobility replaced the explicitly racial barriers of the past. These included measures such as cuts to social safety net spending and the so-called War on Crime which led to the mass incarceration of Black Americans.[3] Chapter 4 of this book will further explore the impacts of racial inequality on education. However, we note here that class and racial hierarchies are best understood together when considering the context of the United States.

For Further Reflection: In your own experience, has social class affected your educational opportunities and if so, how and why? Consider the even broader question of how social class might impact your future.

Historical background

Early colonial period

The Virginia colonists followed the English tradition that education was a responsibility of home and church, not government. When the Virginia House of Burgesses dealt with the plight of destitute children in the 1631–2 session, they chose religious instruction. In the 1642–3 session, legislation was enacted for the education of orphaned children in "the rudiments of learning," and in 1646 this was revised to include preparing destitute children "in honest and profitable trades and manufactures." A major intent was "to avoid sloth and idleness" by employing the children in the "public flax houses" to learn cloth making. Despite such legislative efforts, there is scant evidence that the laws had any great salutary effect on the children.[4]

> **Suggested Activity:** Does our society continue to see schooling as a means to prevent "sloth and idleness" or, as more contemporary language would put it, "keep kids off the streets"? Should schools be used for that purpose? Do you think schools are effective in that regard?

To an inquiry in 1671, Virginia governor Sir William Berkeley replied that there were "no free schools nor printing" in Virginia, for learning brought "disobedience, heresy, and sects into the world" while printing "divulged them, and libels against the best government. God keep us from both!"[5] The attitude of Virginia's aristocratic leaders, at least as reflected by Governor Berkeley, was to do as little as possible.

Of all the measures to promote education in the early colonial period, none had the sweep of those in the Massachusetts Bay Colony. The first college founded in the English-speaking colonies was Harvard College in 1636. A large donation of money and books was made by John Harvard, while others contributed lesser amounts "and the publique hand of the State added the rest." Still, despite the "publique hand," social class strongly influenced who gained access to Harvard College for generations to come.[6]

Perhaps the most inclusive educational action taken by Massachusetts was the Old Deluder Act of 1647, which required townships of more than "50 householders" to appoint a reading and writing teacher whose wages were to be paid "either by the parents and masters of such children, or by the inhabitants in general." Although the means of financing were vague and there was lax compliance with the law, the act helped establish a pattern across New England, such that by the late eighteenth and early nineteenth centuries that region had a higher literacy rate than either the middle or the southern colonies.[7]

Cross-reference: See Chapter 4, Race, Ethnicity and Education, for an extended discussion of Native Americans and their views on education, pp. 180–2.

Late colonial period

Some observers date the beginnings of free public schools from the Old Deluder Act of 1647, but in fact it did not establish either free or universal public schools. The primary financial obligation still remained with parents, although it became common practice for some towns to give limited public support to their schools to lower tuition costs, and a few localities allowed very poor children to attend tuition-free. In these communities, at least some schooling was available to all classes, but whether a family was able to take advantage of it depended on that family's circumstances. Despite shortcomings, a network of schools developed in New England that ranged from elementary petty schools, to secondary grammar schools, to Harvard College.

In the southern colonies, legislation for education was intended to help poor people and orphaned children become employable adults, but lawmakers were mostly silent on the education of other classes. A notable exception was the founding of the College of William and Mary in Virginia in 1693, primarily intended to prepare candidates for the ministry. Generally, the southern assumption was that education should be provided by private means. A similar pattern was found in the middle colonies, which relied mainly on voluntary efforts, religious charity, and traditional forms of schooling. If New England took the lead in public support for schools, and if the middle and southern colonies relied on charitable and private approaches, it was still the case that in each region the schools served the requirements of a hierarchically divided society.[8]

Class and colonial education

The offspring of the gentry and the upper middle class, particularly the sons, were usually educated in classical (Greek and Latin) literature and languages, with some attention to mathematics, rudimentary science, and a few other general subjects. Lower-middle-class youth of European descent, again mostly young men, were likely to get a basic education and then be apprenticed in skilled trades or businesses. Lower-class children of European descent received some religious instruction, and a few might receive some rudimentary reading instruction.

African Americans had little access to education in the North or South. Most Southern states outlawed the education of enslaved people and in some cases free Black people as well. Slave owners feared that literacy would expose enslaved people to ideas of freedom and lead to uprisings. Nevertheless, some enslaved people did secretly teach themselves and each other to read and write, despite the grave risks of doing so.[9]

During colonial times, many youth did not attend school: instruction might be provided in the home if a parent had both the knowledge and the time to do it, while wealthy families often had private tutors for their children. In the churches, most pastors provided religious education, and a few might include helping the children learn to read and perhaps even to write. In other words, many colonists were illiterate, some possessed a moderate degree of literacy, and a few were well educated.

Suggested Activity: Interview a teacher or school counselor. Do they see a correlation between parents' social class and that of their children? To what extent, in other words, does social class continue to influence the type and quality of education a student receives?

Where schools were available, the most common were the so-called petty schools for young children that taught the rudiments of reading, writing, and arithmetic, usually with a strong religious emphasis. Typically, petty schools were located in substantial villages or towns and provided instruction in English. Most depended on tuition payments, but some received public funding as well. There were a few "free" schools for the very poor, institutions that relied on bequeaths, endowments, and other charitable contributions for support.

At the secondary level were the grammar schools, which taught Latin and Greek languages and literature along with other academic subjects. Coming late in the colonial period were the academies, secondary schools that offered a college-preparatory curriculum and a more practical curriculum as well. At the higher education level were the colleges, of which nine had been established by the time of the American Revolution, that offered studies leading to the bachelor of arts degree. In addition, there was a variety of private, entrepreneurial forms of instruction, or private venture schools. For example, skilled tradespersons, ministers, physicians, lawyers, or others might give instruction in the evenings for a fee, teaching general subjects or their particular knowledge and skills to interested learners. With few exceptions in colonial times, educational opportunity was most available to those who could pay for it.[10]

Class and education from the early republic to the Civil War

As the new American republic sought to gain its footing, the classical tradition of education remained strong, but there was also a growing desire for education more attuned to contemporary interests, as signified by Benjamin Franklin (1706–90) who was one of those Americans whose hopes for the future were emboldened by Enlightenment ideas of progress. While he lived most of his life during the colonial period, his views help illustrate some of the influences that impacted education in the early United States.

Franklin only received one year of formal schooling but he eventually made a name for himself as a master printer and a widely read author, acquiring both wealth and international fame as a statesman and scientist. Yet he always viewed himself as a "leather apron" man, a tradesman, and a printer. He strongly identified with "the middling sorts" of people who sought to build up the community with useful knowledge, a class-based point of view that helps explain his educational ideas.[11]

A critic of traditional education, Franklin once observed of Harvard College that, with all its classical languages and religious emphases, it produced graduates who could neither "dig for a living nor live by their wits," and who finished "as great Blockheads as ever, only more proud and self-conceited." Despite the popular image of Franklin as thoroughly utilitarian, however, broad social responsibility was at the top of his educational objectives. "*True merit*," he believed, consisted of "an *Inclination* join'd with an *Ability* to serve Mankind, one's Country, Friends, and Family," an ability "greatly increased by *true Learning*" and one that should be "the great *Aim* and *End* of all Learning."[12]

In 1749, Franklin advocated a new kind of secondary education designed to serve the interests of the rising American middle class, and from his efforts and those of his associates, the Philadelphia Academy emerged in 1751. Franklin maintained that the academy should help students enter "the several Professions for which they are intended." Others associated with the founding retained the classical curriculum at the academy, but Franklin's "practical studies" became an option, including such subjects as arithmetic, accounting, geometry, astronomy, logic, ethics, English, modern foreign languages, writing, speaking, history, gardening, and "mechanics" or practical physics.[13]

Shortly before the colonies declared independence from Britain, the school changed its name to the College of Philadelphia, and after the revolution it became the University of Pennsylvania. Still, the idea of secondary schools with practical as well as classical studies appealed to the "middling" parts of society, and academies became the standard for American secondary schools until displaced by public high schools in the late nineteenth century.

For Further Reflection: What is the relationship between classical and practical studies today? Is the college-preparatory curriculum the modern equivalent of the traditional classical curriculum, and are current vocational/technical studies equivalent to what Franklin meant by "practical studies"? What does the American public expect its high school and college graduates to be able to do? To what extent are they class based, and do they "promote the well-being of society"?

In the nineteenth century, the United States transformed from an agrarian into an industrialized nation, and the need for a more inclusive system of education that served students from all levels of society became a rallying cry for reformers. Various alternatives were put forward to educate more people: charity schools, free schools, subscription schools, Sunday schools, and Lancastrian schools (in which more advanced students would teach those less advanced). But each had serious drawbacks, and none seemed to meet the goal of universal education.[14]

Public common schools

Although Massachusetts had a strong record in education from early colonial days, by the 1820s its schools had deteriorated. As industrialization spread, cities and towns around Massachusetts attracted both poor people from rural areas and immigrants from Europe looking for work in the new factories. Among the results were poor living conditions, unemployment, low wages, and increased crime and violence. People feared social disintegration, and a number of reformers rose up who embraced the idea of public, tax-supported common schools (as they were then called) for all children as the way to alleviate social conditions. These schools were intended to be socially inclusive and to widely distribute literacy, social unity, and sturdy "republican" values. From Massachusetts and surrounding states, the common school idea spread.

The most representative spokesman for common schools was **Horace Mann** of Massachusetts, who addressed existing socioeconomic divisions. He noted that in European tradition, "men are divided into classes—some to toil and earn, others to seize and enjoy," but in a free republic all are supposed "to have an equal chance for earning, and equal security in the enjoyment of what they earn." A new kind of feudalism lay in American industrialism's "vast and overshadowing private fortunes," one potentially "more oppressive and unrelenting than that of the Middle Ages." Massachusetts was "exposed, far beyond any other state in the Union, to the fatal extremes of overgrown wealth and desperate poverty," Mann argued, and he proclaimed that "nothing but Universal Education can counterwork this tendency to the domination of capital and the servility of labor." Indeed, it "would do more than all things else to obliterate factitious [class] distinctions in society."[15]

For Further Reflection: What are examples where education has, indeed, alleviated social and economic tensions? To what extent can education solve social problems? Does education truly provide each rising generation with "a brighter and more plentiful future"?

For Further Reflection: Research current rates of wealth inequality in the United States and the degree to which it affects class distinctions in current society and within schools.

An indication of how the education/social-class relationship actually played out, however, may be seen in the example of St. Louis, Missouri. Between 1840 and 1880, St. Louis public schools grew from a few struggling common schools to a diversified school system of kindergartens, elementary schools, evening schools, high schools, and normal (or teacher-preparation) schools. The student body swelled from a mere 266 students in 1840 to 55,870 by 1880. For all this growth, however, many parents still allowed their children to drop out after only a few years of elementary school, despite the fact that free public education in St. Louis was available up through high school. Why? A major variable in how long students attended school was the occupations of their fathers. The majority of students attending the district elementary schools had fathers in skilled and unskilled occupations, but the majority of students continuing to high school and normal school had fathers in white collar, business, managerial, or professional occupations. This was prior to the establishment of child labor laws; consequently, after age 13, the dropout rate dramatically increased until, after age 16, only about 15 percent of all eligible children remained in school. The lower a child's socioeconomic class, the greater the possibility of dropping out and entering the workforce, usually in unskilled or semiskilled jobs. Children of professionals were far more likely to complete high school.[16]

Thus, almost a half century after Mann called public education the "**great equalizer**," cases such as St. Louis questioned this notion. Nevertheless, through the efforts of educational reformers and people's growing recognition that changing conditions called for better educational opportunities, the belief that education and social conditions were causally linked became an enduring part of the American outlook.

Such belief has been subject to criticism, however. For one thing, it seems doubtful that schools by themselves are capable of solving deep-seated socioeconomic conditions, and there is a danger in viewing the schools as a cure-all. Obviously, schools do not and cannot exercise full control over society, because many influences help shape the directions a society takes. In their zeal, the common school reformers overemphasized the ability of education to ameliorate socioeconomic inequities.[17]

Be that as it may, the use of education to increase people's knowledge and to help them pursue desirable personal and social goals seems preferable to either doing nothing or resorting to authoritarian force to bring about social change. Experience seems to show, moreover, that schooling usually has a positive impact on people's futures, and it usually results in individual and social good. Finally, many if not most Americans continue to believe that having good schools is one of the ways for their children to have brighter futures.

Class and education in the late nineteenth and early twentieth centuries

The influence of socioeconomic class on economic, social, and political power increased during the period of growing wealth inequality that began in the 1880s. This began to change after the end of the Second World War in 1945, as available jobs, higher take-home pay, affordable consumer goods, and increased educational opportunity all helped make more Americans consider themselves part of the middle class. However, social class continued to shape American social life as one of many forms of inequality.[18] These changes were accompanied by various developments reflected in the schools.

Education and social Darwinism

Social Darwinism is a term usually applied to the belief that, similar to Darwin's account of the evolution of biological species through natural selection over eons of time, human society itself is shaped by a no less intense struggle, one that British philosopher Herbert Spencer called the **survival of the fittest**. In other words, in the competition among people in the movement up and down the social strata, those who "survive" best, who enjoy wealth, power, and prestige, are deemed the "fittest." Thus, the term *social Darwinism* (although Darwin himself never made such a generalized application of his theory). Spencer also saw no need for state intervention to help the poor through public housing or public education, because he believed it disrupted the "natural" evolutionary process of social survival. According to the theory, the poor who were seen as "unfit" should be allowed to die out in the evolutionary process, making way for only the fit members of society to survive, reproduce, and evolve. Spencer's writings attracted an American following, possibly because his ideas seemed to describe the desperate nature of Gilded Age competition. Such "robber baron" industrialists as Andrew Carnegie and John D. Rockefeller were attracted to his ideas, possibly because he helped them justify their own ruthless economic acquisitions. Spencer's ideas also seemed to appeal to those who feared social, political, and economic reform.[19]

Social Darwinism bolstered the so-called **heredity thesis**, which claimed scientific backing for its view that heredity was the single most important factor determining human intelligence. The heredity thesis emerged at a time when science was rapidly gaining prestige, and by wrapping themselves in the cloak of "objective science," heredity advocates exerted an important influence over social and educational policies. However, as noted by critics at the time, there was no reason to believe that the lower economic classes were genetically weaker than the upper classes, mainly because environmental factors, not genes, made the difference.

Increasingly, many scholars found social Darwinism to be unsatisfactory, and the weight of opinion came down on the view that, while various individual physical and mental characteristics might be biologically inherited, social characteristics were not.[20]

Nevertheless, some scholars were fascinated with the heredity thesis, including researchers in the field of intelligence testing, such as psychologists Lewis Terman, Robert Yerkes, Henry Goddard, Carl Brigham, and Madison Grant. Some adherents raised alarms about what they believed was a decline in American intelligence due to the influx of what they called "inferior," lower-class immigrants, and supported the use of intelligence tests for purposes of social control. Once again, criticism swelled in the scholarly community, and prominent thinkers disavowed the Spencerian version of heredity, which they believed was based on emotional appeals to class, race, and ethnic prejudice, not scientific inquiry. Unfortunately, many laws and policies had by then been put in place that fostered various classifications, groupings, and selection processes in schools and other institutions, including laws enacted in twenty-seven states that allowed authorities to sterilize people who had been diagnosed with intellectual disabilities. Moreover, such laws remained in effect in some states until the 1970s.[21]

From rags to riches: The role of success literature

In the boom-and-bust upheavals of the late nineteenth century, a new form of **success literature** emerged that appealed to those experiencing economic instability and social change. The genre grew to include such widely popular developments as the Horatio Alger stories, "rags to riches" novels for adolescents. Success manuals for adults also sold well in what appeared to be an insatiable market between 1870 and 1910.[22]

Some of the authors were influenced by the view of social life as a competitive struggle for survival, but most of them rejected social Darwinist determinism; instead, they promoted such things as hard work, frugality, dependability, and character as proper pathways to success. They shunned social revolution and advocated traditional values as the best way for people to fit themselves into the corporate industrial order and to make it work, at least in some small way, to their advantage.

Many authors of success literature upheld basic education but were wary of higher education because a "self-made" person was expected to learn the ropes by hard work and struggle, not academic study. Besides, at a time when even a high school education was a luxury for most people, few of the readers of success literature could afford college. Indeed, the projected goal of most success literature was not great wealth but middle-class respectability; it was a middle-class ideology of "self-made" individuals and middle-class status achieved by decent, law-abiding Americans who believed in progress and the new industrial order behind it. If economic struggle was a reality, so also was the fluid nature of the American class system, which encouraged aspirations to higher status.[23]

> **For Further Reflection:** In what ways are the ideas reflected in success literature of the nineteenth century still present today?

Changes in work and the rise of vocational education

Prior to the 1880s, schools were seldom viewed as institutions directly involved in job preparation, although most people recognized the economic benefits of education. Still, many people doubted the value of education beyond the elementary grades, because by 1890 only 3.5 percent of 17-year-olds graduated from high schools. As the twentieth century dawned, reformers charged that traditional schools were irrelevant to the new economic realities, because they failed to teach skills necessary for occupational advancement and they ignored the needs of industrial society. From business, labor, agriculture, and education came reformers demanding that schools must de-emphasize traditional academic subjects and become vocationally oriented. They advanced the view that the main job of schools was to train the young for the world of work, and they achieved a great deal of success in their efforts.

> **For Further Reflection:** On the one hand, vocational education is seen as an opportunity to make school more relevant; on the other hand, it is criticized as mere training rather than true education. What are your thoughts?

As the new type of education reformers insisted, the central role of the schools now became one of integrating youth into the hierarchical occupational structures of corporate industrial society, and one of the major ways to accomplish this was through what was called vocational education.

Where once it was the salvation of souls, then the making of useful citizens, or even the promotion of equal opportunity, the central goal of schools increasingly seemed to be preparing youth for the new corporate economy. To accomplish this, the schools were also expected to integrate immigrants into the workforce, reduce worker alienation, lessen the possibility of labor conflict, and increase job capabilities for working-class youth and youth living in poverty. But if vocational education proponents saw their solution as scrapping an outmoded academic curriculum and replacing it with practical understandings and skills demanded by the corporate industrial order, the history of those reforms reveals that vocational education solved few problems. Poverty, unemployment, and inequality remained, mainly because their roots were in the larger social, political, and economic system, not in the educational system.[24]

As industrialization, urbanization, and population increased, traditional small businesses gave way to giant corporations and big business trusts. With all these changes there came a slackening in the traditional belief that individuals could get by solely through their own efforts. Growing numbers of Americans found themselves living in urban environments where opportunities were limited.

Social class divisions were a central part of the problem. For example, a study of city school boards in the 1920s found them dominated by the wealthier classes, with 76 percent of all members coming from the proprietorial (31 percent), professional (31 percent), and managerial (14 percent) occupations, while only 22 percent came from commercial (6 percent), clerical (6 percent), manual labor (8 percent), and agricultural service (2 percent) occupations (the remaining 2 percent were unknown). Overall, whether city, county, or state school boards, the dominant classes of society were in control. The formulation of school policies by an unrepresentative portion of society was problematic. A leading counter-proposal was a system of control in which schools were not the subservient tools of powerful community interests,[25] but during the 1920s, when risky speculation and careless financial investment were rampant, it was a proposal that largely went ignored.

Suggested Activity: Research the social class composition of school board members in your school district; compare and analyze the meaning of your findings with others.

Depression, war, and the rise of the middle class

There were signs of economic distress during the 1920s, but dire trouble became obvious after the stock market crashed on Black Tuesday, October 29, 1929. Americans had experienced economic depressions before but never on the scale of the **Great Depression** that lasted from 1929 to 1940. From 1929 to 1934, the gross national product went from $85.9 billion to $47 billion, and the official unemployment figure (no one knew the actual number) increased from 3.2 percent to 24.9 percent of the civilian workforce.[26]

The economic meltdown affected not only corporations, banks, and small businesses but also people's incomes and retirement savings, all of which threatened basic necessities for countless families. The depressed economy depressed tax revenues, which forced state and local governments to cut services and payrolls. Thus, school budgets suffered extreme cuts all across the nation, such that during the winter of the 1932–3 school year, for example, Chicago was unable to pay its teachers.[27] As the deprivations of the Depression increased, disaffection mounted. Some observers looked for solutions in the corporate business world of **capitalism** so popular in the 1920s, and some looked to remedies in **socialism**.[28]

A heightened sense of **class consciousness**, meaning an awareness of one's socioeconomic standing in society, emerged from the Depression years. However, it did not generate sustained assaults on existing institutions; instead, people demanded reforms that allowed them to exercise greater participation in institutions. A 1939 poll showed that workers understood their own practical economic circumstances, with more than half placing themselves in the lower income levels. When it came to social class identity, however, the overwhelming majority claimed they were middle class. In short, workers could accurately appraise their own economic circumstances, but many held on to the American view of upward **social mobility** and the American Dream.[29]

The Depression and the schools

From 1930 to 1940, a declining birth rate meant fewer students enrolling in elementary schools. Yet high school enrollment increased as students in the school pipeline came of age, and the number of students graduating annually nearly doubled. Due to the circumstances, one might expect students to avoid schooling and seek jobs to help their struggling families, but jobs were difficult to find, and schools offered attractive benefits.

Some enticements came from New Deal programs under the administration of President Franklin Roosevelt. For example, the National Youth Administration (NYA) provided funds to schools for work-study opportunities for students in need, 95 percent of whom came from families who received public financial assistance. The amount was small (on average only about $5.41 per ten-hour work week) in school-related jobs such as cafeteria and laboratory assistants, clerical aides to teachers, and school grounds landscaping, but it helped keep many high school students and some college students in school. Another program was the Works Progress Administration (WPA), a mostly adult-related

Figure 3.1 Unemployed men queued outside a depression soup kitchen opened in Chicago by Al Capone, 1931.

program to provide work to unemployed professional and technical people who would serve the public good as, for example, teachers, nurses, librarians, and artists. Its most direct contributions to public schools were its provisions for school health services, supplementary teachers, and surplus food programs that provided hot lunches to school children in need.[30]

Despite New Deal programs and other efforts to restore economic health, social class divisions continued. A study conducted in a mid-Western town in the late 1930s provides insight on how social class impacted the lives of students at a local high school. The study found that the social behavior of students was closely related to the class position of their families in the community. Socioeconomic status conditioned what curriculum students pursued (college prep, general, or vocational) and how students were steered toward a curriculum. Class also impacted how grades were assigned, with higher grades more often assigned to upper-class students and failing grades to lower-class students. A similar pattern was found in disciplinary practices, with detention and expulsion most often meted out to students with lower-class backgrounds. Overall, the study noted, "The class system is far more vital as a social force in our society than the American creed."[31]

> **For Further Reflection:** To what degree might these findings still hold true if the study were repeated today?

As the Great Depression lingered, critics emerged who charged that educators and educational policy makers had become bogged down in inexcusable inaction. Sometimes called **reconstructionists**, these critics maintained that educators occupied strategic positions to help society break free from the Depression by teaching the young to question the status quo and preparing them to change society as adults. Traditionalists replied that educators and schools were ill equipped to ease the Depression, much less remake society. Reconstructionists countered that, while education was only a formative step, it was crucial: schools might not change society immediately, but they could and should help the young learn the knowledge and critical-thinking skills needed to rationally scrutinize society, develop visions of future possibilities, and work to change society for the better. Educators should serve as examples by providing community leadership, demanding reforms and better public policies, or even pursuing important public offices to achieve the goals of change. Indeed, educators should work for a radical reconstruction of the larger society, and it should be widespread and thorough.[32] These and other calls for change were made, but they did not achieve sufficient public support to effect major policy changes.

> **For Further Reflection:** In your opinion, can schools truly rebuild the social order? Compare your ideas with those of your peers.

Rise of the middle class

The Second World War helped end the Depression by stimulating American economic capacities with wartime production, and it refocused attention away from economic worries to the global tragedies of a world at war. In 1944, in anticipation of the war's end, Congress passed the Servicemen's Readjustment Act of 1944, or what came to be popularly called the **GI Bill of Rights**. This legislation provided unprecedented levels of funding for millions of war veterans to pursue further education upon their return. Although the language of the legislation was race-neutral, in practice many Black veterans were unable to take advantage of the GI Bill due to discrimination and segregation in higher education institutions. As a result, the GI bill exacerbated disparities in education and wealth between white and Black men in the South.[33]

Overall, the GI Bill expended approximately $14.5 billion on the education of veterans before it ended. It also stimulated an educational boom, with almost 500,000 university degrees awarded in the 1949–50 academic year alone (as compared to only 216,500 in 1939–40). Many veterans who took advantage of the GI Bill were the first in their families to pursue higher education. Many also expected their children to gain even more, which helped boost the large increase in college attendance in the second half of the twentieth century. From a financial standpoint, the money was well spent, because what most veterans received under the GI Bill was far exceeded by the taxes they paid back into the federal treasury from their increased earnings over succeeding years.[34]

Despite such successes in the postwar years, however, the problem of class-related inequality in educational opportunity persisted. A leading study in the early 1960s examined the relationship between the educational success of students and the socioeconomic status of their families. Among the findings were the following: teacher-student ratios were higher in low-income neighborhoods than in other neighborhoods. In low-income high schools, the reading scores of tenth graders averaged at least 2.6 grade levels below the norm. For every scholarship awarded to lower-income students, ten were awarded to higher-income students, with low-income students who most needed financial help getting it the least. In regard to virtually all the significant factors, higher-income students consistently seemed to be in better positions.[35]

In the 1960s, equal educational opportunity became a major policy quest. Presidents John F. Kennedy and Lyndon B. Johnson each sought to remedy existing inequalities through federal initiatives. The Johnson administration significantly increased federal aid to schools in poverty-impacted areas with the **Elementary and Secondary Education Act (ESEA)** of 1965, which was an important part of Johnson's **War on Poverty**. A former schoolteacher, Johnson believed a comprehensive effort was needed to use education to overcome poverty, and his administration launched such programs as Adult Basic Education (ABE) for adults learning literacy skills, Head Start programs for preschool children living in poverty, and financial aid for students living in poverty and seeking to go to college.[36]

Figure 3.2 President Johnson's poverty tour in 1964. Note: President Lyndon B. Johnson shakes the hand of one of the residents of Appalachia as Agent Rufus Youngblood (far left) looks on.

The intent was to break the cycle of poverty by educating people living in poverty to move out of it. Financial assistance was given to school districts and non-school programs (such as Head Start and ABE) that served poverty impacted areas. It was assumed that strong correlations existed between poverty and educational underachievement. The legislation was characterized by both flexibility and accountability: flexibility for states, school districts, and educational programs to use the funds but with more accountability for educational results. This "flexibility and accountability" theme came to characterize subsequent federal education initiatives as well, including the programs of Presidents George H.W. Bush, Bill Clinton, George W. Bush, and Barack Obama.[37]

Social class in the late twentieth and early twenty-first centuries

Two theories of class have played significant roles in education scholarship—those of **Karl Marx**, who viewed the history of industrial capitalism as leading to increased exploitation of the working class, and of **Max Weber**, who saw class as one of the ways people relate to one another socially.

Marx was the more controversial, a revolutionary whose theory of historical materialism held that one must first understand the "material forces of production" (such as agriculture, industries, and trades) before one can understand the "superstructure" of society (such as institutions, political authority, and the class system). Since scientific, technological, and industrial innovations emerge from the material forces, the superstructure must accommodate them in order for social life to flourish; however, those who benefit from the existing superstructure usually try to thwart change, which results in people getting caught in conditions beyond their control. For example, the Industrial Revolution produced unprecedented levels of new wealth that could have helped create a better life for all, but powerful interests in the superstructure refused to relinquish their privileges. Instead, they used capitalist traditions of private property and monopolistic practices to control society while they also gathered the bulk of the new wealth to themselves.[38]

Where Marx was a revolutionary who saw the fundamental conflict of capitalist industrial society occurring between the haves (capitalistic owners, or the bourgeoisie), and the have-nots (industrial workers, or the proletariat), Weber was an academic sociologist who recognized class conflict but also investigated education and its relationship to industrial society. He believed that industrialism and its organizational structures had produced a bureaucratized "rational" society. A main function of schools had become one of teaching particular "status cultures" to "insiders," whose status was reinforced, and "outsiders," whose status was restricted.[39]

Education and training had become identified with a system of special examinations to assess the training of experts to serve emerging bureaucracies. This system supposedly allowed individuals a chance to move up rather than remain in a particular class, but it also produced a privileged class whose degrees, certificates, and diplomas enabled them to monopolize society's advantageous positions. Weber understood that prestige based on education was nothing new, but where the educational ideal of traditional society was to produce "cultured" people, the educational ideal of industrial society was to produce bureaucratic "specialists."[40]

Among the important features of Weber's ideas was his insight into how mass schooling was being used to sort and select students for bureaucratized corporate society, bestowing social mobility on some while denying it to others. More recent sociological theory takes a diversified approach, seeking to explain how individual experience is shaped—but not completely determined—by larger social and cultural conditions. For example, French sociologist **Pierre Bourdieu** maintains that individual lives are akin to roles played in various social and cultural "fields," and an individual may be involved in several fields at once. For instance, a schoolteacher might not only be a school employee but also a church member, a Little League coach, and a volunteer firefighter. Each of these "fields" has its own implicit and explicit rules and expectations, and together they form dynamic domains where individual participants are not entirely free agents but are at least partially defined by the expectations and roles inherent in each organization.[41]

Many thinkers view social class as not nearly so dependent on economic conflict between **haves and have-nots**, as Marx assumed, or on specialist roles in bureaucratic structures, as Weber would have it. Rather, as Bourdieu saw it, a person's status or class in various social and cultural fields is dependent on a combination of factors. They include material possessions and "things" as well as untouchable features such as social prestige and authority (which Bourdieu called **symbolic capital**), and education, command of language, and "taste" in artistic and cultural matters (which Bourdieu called **cultural capital**). Thus, many criteria impact a person's status in a society, because it is influenced by a complex network of relations between individual agency and various social, economic, and political factors.[42] What educators need to understand is what roles education and schooling play in this process.

Of course, people have behaved along class lines throughout history, and while Marx may have been correct that capitalism created a greater sense of class consciousness, it seems clear that capitalism itself did not create social classes. Class consciousness historically arose from people's everyday experiences of subordination and exploitation long before industrial capitalism appeared on the scene. Thus, subordination and exploitation can be found throughout history, not only in economic relations but in many other kinds as well, including kinship, gender, politics, and religion.[43]

Nevertheless, economic factors are significant in any consideration of social class. Marxism viewed class as capitalist owners and proletarian workers, largely ignoring other classes or strata of society. Capitalism viewed classes along occupational lines (as managers, supervisors, skilled workers, and unskilled workers), but this ignored the fact that any occupational group could itself be stratified. Where owners once stood out as powerful individuals who both owned the means of production and exercised direct control over it, during the second half of the twentieth century, ownership was significantly institutionalized by such things as mutual funds, insurance funds, and retirement systems, with ownership becoming dispersed and largely hidden from public notice. Actual control over production processes impacting class consciousness was now wielded not by conspicuous owners themselves but by hired managers and specialists who worked on behalf of owners and/or stockholders. Of course, the major beneficiaries of such conditions were very wealthy individuals or institutions, and so the issue of inequalities of income and wealth continued into the twenty-first century.[44]

By the end of the twentieth century, some observers saw new forms of social stratification developing. For example, as class-based social hierarchies supposedly weakened, people's political behavior seemed less defined by occupational identities. As economic affluence increased after the Second World War, people appeared to assume that their basic needs would be met by the corporate welfare state, and many shifted their political attention away from economic issues to "lifestyle" issues. This new individualism reflected beliefs that social class no longer counted; now it was all about ability and education. As class structures became more complex and as class relations underwent significant changes, society seemed to be entering a new stage of historical development where much higher levels of education and work autonomy were needed.[45]

However, other observers called attention to the growing downward mobility of the American middle class, as witnessed by trends beginning in the 1970s and accelerating in the 1980s, 1990s, and 2000s. This period was characterized by **neoliberal economic policies** such as deregulation of businesses and reduction of publicly funded economic and social support services.[46] While the middle-class share of wealth increased from 1950 to 1970, by the 1990s it was decidedly shrunken. Several reasons were proffered for this, including higher costs of living, corporate downsizing, exportation of industrial jobs to low-wage foreign countries, and the erosion of people's retirement savings by corporate greed and dishonest financial practices.[47]

As American society entered the twenty-first century, it confronted an era as filled with inequalities and exaggerated lifestyles as during the Gilded Age. Few Americans seemed aware of it, even though most of them experienced only modest income increases after 1970. Average annual salaries went from approximately $32,522 in 1970 to only $35,864 in 1998, a mere 10 percent increase (adjusted for inflation). During that same time, the average annual income of leading corporate executives moved from $1.3 million (or about 39 times the average income of American workers in 1970) to $37.5 million (or 1,000 times the average income of workers in 1998). This was far different from the income direction between 1945 and 1970, when the middle class grew and income gaps actually narrowed between ordinary Americans and the very rich. After 1970, however, the big winners were the very rich who experienced a massive transfer of wealth to themselves.[48] By 2023, the top 10 percent of households by wealth in the United States held 69 percent of total household wealth while the bottom 50 percent held only 2.4 percent of total household wealth.[49]

Contemporary conditions

When asked about their social class background, most Americans proclaim to be middle class despite significant income disparities and the ongoing existence of poverty. For example, at the 90th percentile, 10 percent of households in 2022 had incomes exceeding $216,000 while at the 10th percentile, 10 percent of households had incomes at or below $17,100.[50]

The general and childhood poverty rates in the United States are some of the highest among industrialized nations. The official poverty rate in 2022 was 11.5 percent, and 37.9 million people lived in poverty, according to US Census Bureau statistics.[51] The poverty rate for children under the age of 18 was 16.3 percent in 2022.[52] The United States has the third highest childhood poverty rate of the thirty-four OECD (Organization for Economic Co-operation and Development) nations.[53] Childhood poverty more than doubled from 2021–2 due to the expiration of COVID-19 programs, such as a child tax credit, which had dropped the poverty rate to a historic low of 5.2 percent in 2021.[54] In other words, the high poverty rates are not a result of lack of knowledge or tools to address them, but rather lack of political will to fund social safety net programs.

At the same time, education maintains a persistent connection with social class in several ways. One that is often measured and discussed is the economic relationship between education and income. As indicated in Table 3.1, statistical data strongly suggest that the more educational attainment, the higher one's earnings. However, interpreting the education-earnings relationship is complex because there are usually multiple factors involved in a person's socioeconomic status.

While statistics clearly depict existing class divisions, Americans tend to avoid thinking of themselves along class lines, and class consciousness is relatively low. Feudalistic Europe may be seen as the epitome of class stratification, while the American Dream idea of **meritocracy** has long held that social class should not be the determining factor in an individual's pursuit of success. Therefore, actual **class differences** are seldom challenged and, if addressed at all, are usually

Table 3.1 Median Annual Earnings of Full-Time, Year-Round Workers Ages 25–34, by Educational Attainment: 2021

Educational attainment	Dollars
All educational attainment levels	$54,210
Less than high school completion	$35,470
High school completion	$41,790
Some college, no degree	$45, 230
Associate's degree	$49, 470
Bachelor's or higher degree	$71,060
Bachelor's degree	$66, 610
Master's or higher degree	$80,180

Source: Adapted from National Center for Education Statistics. *Digest of Education Statistics*, table 502.30. Median annual earnings of full-time year-round workers 25–34 years old and full-time year-round workers as a percentage of the labor force, by sex, race/ethnicity, and educational attainment: Selected years, 2005 through 2022 (accessed on May 28, 2025).

explained as natural occurrences in a society that assumes the capable tend to rise to the top.

Individuals in the United States may not be legally prevented from rising through society's ranks, but some have greater opportunities than others, and class plays an important role. The circumstances of a child's birth, whether born into poverty or comfortable economic conditions, or born to parents with or without educational credentials, have important ramifications for a child's life chances. There is considerable research affirming that parental social class contributes to a child's educational attainment that, in turn, contributes to the child's future attainments. Social class also impacts access to health care, child care, and numerous other services that affect the quality of life. Privilege tends to breed more privilege, which greatly improves opportunities and assistance should a privileged person encounter obstacles in life. Contrarily, poverty and material deprivation usually have a negative impact on people, limiting their access to adequate care, goods, services, and education.[55]

A recent illustration of class privilege can be found in the relative advantage middle-class parents had over parents in working-class occupations during the COVID-19 pandemic. Based upon their economic, social, and cultural capital, they were better able to respond to challenges experienced by students and parents generally, such as a lack of structure, a lack of communication with the school, and student isolation. They had more resources and flexibility to deal with the problems, thereby further exacerbating the inequalities based on social class.[56]

Out-of-school factors (OSFs) are often directly related to school success, and class is indicative of many of those OSFs (for example, low birth weight, inadequate medical care, food insecurity, environmental pollutants, family stress, and neighborhood characteristics), any and all of which can significantly affect the learning opportunities of children. Indeed, poverty exacts a strong toll on communities, neighborhoods, families, and, therefore, schools and children.[57] In short, socioeconomic conditions shape life chances, a factual condition that has received inadequate attention in many leading school reform movements in the closing decades of the twentieth century and the beginning of the twenty-first century, a time characterized by policy shifts from concerns about equality of educational opportunity to concerns about school achievement as measured by test scores.

For Further Reflection: Think about your own life and the people you know. How clear-cut are definitions of class? To what extent do people identify with a class? Based on your observations and understandings, why do they exhibit a class identity? Have any crossed class lines or changed their class identities?

It has been argued that the traditional classification of middle class or lower class no longer adequately describes the job structure in the United States. Rather, the emerging class structure consists of a permanent inner ring of skilled workers and an outer ring of semi-skilled part-time workers without such benefits as health insurance, retirement funds, vacations, or sick leave. The two-tiered job structure is not confined to any one sector of the economy. In academia, for instance, tenured faculty constitute an inner core while those in the outer core of temporary and poorly paid adjunct professors are hired by the course, moving from one job to the next. The "new economy" is said to demand a more flexible workforce willing to work long hours and perform at a high level of productivity. This is supposed to make the economy more productive, but job security and fringe benefits have suffered greatly, with employees always subject to being laid off. One might think about the role of the schools and wonder whether or not schools should be expected to produce the "human bricks with which the global economy is being built."[58]

In general, American society is neither quite as open nor as socially mobile as the traditional American Dream would suggest. While social class is not all-important, it can exert lasting effects on educational opportunities and other aspects of life. Social class often strongly influences school funding, educational resources, quality of teachers, extracurricular options, postsecondary opportunities, and more. Ever since the rise of the public school in the nineteenth century, there have been claims it could serve as the "great equalizer." In 1848, Horace Mann stated his belief that public education would do " … better than to disarm the poor of their hostility toward the rich: it prevents being poor."[59] The common schools, as they were then called, were intended to counteract the influence social class had in shaping individual lives. They were seen as essential instruments in providing a common set of experiences to help knit a diverse society together and provide better opportunities for everyone regardless of class background.

However, schools themselves continue to be marred by deep inequities, far from able to provide all students equitably with needed resources.[60] The following sections will analyze key aspects of these realities.

For Further Reflection: What types of economic reforms would it take to reduce the effects of class divisions and alleviate the most detrimental effects of poverty and economic deprivation?

School funding

K-12 schools are funded through a mix of federal, state, and local monies; and while the exact percentages vary from year to year, the lion's share has consistently been derived from state funds and local tax revenue. In 2022, for example, the federal government contributed only 7.5 percent to total K-12 spending; the rest was based on state and local funding.[61]

How much each state is supported by the federal government also varies, and so does per-pupil spending. As for the latter, in fiscal year 2021, New York, for example, spent $28,571 per pupil, while Idaho spent $9,053.[62] Vast differences that existed prior to the Civil War between free and slave states in investments in public services, such as schools and libraries, have had lasting impacts to this day. In her book, *The Sum of Us: What Racism Costs Everyone and How We Can Prosper Together*, Heather McGee draws from research showing how investing in public services in free states was in the financial interest of the wealthy: they relied on these to attract and retain workers and customers for their businesses. However, the wealthy slave-owners of the South needed neither workers nor customers—they exploited unpaid labor and exported their raw goods to the north and around the world. In fact, an educated populace was against their financial interest. In the 1850s, while New Hampshire had 2,381 public schools, Mississippi had only 782. After slavery was abolished, the deficit in public infrastructure proved difficult to overcome. Today, not only are nine out of ten of the poorest states in the South, but even within states, the counties that relied more on slave labor in 1860 had lower per capita incomes in 2000.[63]

School funding has long been fraught with systemic characteristics leading to inequalities. For one, since local funding remains a significant source in the funding formula, and it depends heavily on property taxes for revenues, community wealth disparities directly affect the schools. Affluent communities are able to generate far more funds for their schools than low-income communities, a phenomenon that neither state nor federal funds effectively equalize.

A seminal piece of work showing how inequities in school funding affect public schools is Jonathan Kozol's *Savage Inequalities*, an indictment of public education's funding structure circa 1991. While written more than three decades ago, Kozol's observations unfortunately remain largely valid today. Among the school systems he studied was East St. Louis, Illinois, whose public schools were in disrepair and lacked essential resources, reflecting the grim poverty of the larger community. One school was evacuated because of sewage flooding, while another's sports facilities lacked "almost everything," including goalposts on the football field. East St. Louis High School's science labs were thirty to fifty years outdated, the heating system did not work correctly, supplies and texts were scarce, and teachers often had to pay for materials out of their own pockets. Overall, Kozol captured the deteriorating conditions of poor schools across the country and compared them with schools in wealthier communities. Wealthy communities had large numbers of class offerings, enjoyed sophisticated facilities such as greenhouses and swimming pools, and made use of services to perfect students' music and athletic skills. Legal challenges to the funding inequities remained largely ineffective in altering systems marred by "savage inequalities." A central conclusion was that many inequalities are built into school systems by their dependence on property taxes as their main source of local funding.[64]

For Further Reflection: To what degree do you think the phrase "savage inequalities" accurately captures the conditions of today's public schools in the United States?

As mentioned above, Kozol's work remains relevant today although it has also been critiqued for ignoring the majority of schools that represent the middle, being neither poorly funded nor wealthy. Not seeing the extreme conditions at either end of the spectrum in their own schools may be one of the reasons why many parents are "lulled into inaction" when it comes to addressing unequal school funding.[65]

Despite attempts over time to support students from low-income families, school finance policy choices at all levels—federal, state, and district—tend to systematically disadvantage the most vulnerable students. At the federal level, for example, the Elementary and Secondary Education Act (ESEA), signed into law in 1965 and re-authorized many times since, was intended to address disparities among high-poverty and low-poverty schools. In order to improve educational equity, funding for school districts serving low-income students continues to be authorized under Title I of the Act. However, these goals remain unrealized today for various reasons.[66] One reason is insufficient funding. In addition, Congress continues to struggle with meeting the original intent of Title I, which is to support schools and school districts with high concentrations of poverty. The counter-pull for Congress is political in nature: the goal to secure widespread public support through spreading federal funding more broadly.[67]

Various recommendations to remedy the funding gap include: increasing federal funding and providing equitable educational opportunities to all students; monitoring and evaluating how well federal spending enhances student achievement and closes the opportunity gap; and updating and revising the formulas according to which Title I funds are being distributed.[68]

At the state level, reforms have been implemented in response to funding inequity lawsuits, and yet stark funding inequities continue to exist. One reason is that the majority of states do not provide more funding to high-poverty school districts, with several states even allocating more funding to affluent districts than districts serving low-income students (a system called "regressive funding").[69]

Considering race in addition to social class, the data show that school districts serving large populations of low-income students and students of color tend to receive far less funding than those serving white students and students from more affluent families. Overall, school districts serving the largest populations of students of color receive 13 percent less per student in state and local funding than those serving the fewest students of color.[70]

Desegregation efforts have attempted to remedy these inequalities through measures such as opening up the boundaries between urban and suburban schools to address resource inequalities between the two. However, beginning in the 1970s, a series of Supreme Court decisions protected the physical separation of the property-rich suburban districts. To reach this conclusion in cases such as *San Antonio v. Rodriguez* (1973), the Court essentially had to reject the proposition that education is a fundamental right.[71]

In terms of wealth disparities, the difference is smaller, with the United States spending approximately 7 percent less per student in the nation's highest poverty districts compared to those educated in the wealthiest districts. This gap is nevertheless significant as it results in funding disparities of about $1000 per child. Some states have begun to address these funding inequities: the state of Utah, for instance, ensures that districts with the highest poverty levels receive approximately 21 percent more state and local dollars than school districts with the lowest levels of poverty. However, when engaging in the debate about school funding one also needs to take into account that there are added costs for students growing up in low-income households, such as high-quality early learning opportunities, **wraparound services** (various supports for students, including those that are academic, behavioral, or social), and other selected student supports. A prominent recommendation to close the funding gap is for states to reduce their reliance on local property taxes, assume more state responsibility for education funding, and target more funds specifically for the education of low-income students.[72]

At the district level, the trend continues, and it matters greatly because almost half of public school funding is drawn from local government revenue, highly correlated with local property values. As mentioned above, wealth disparities among school districts have led to significant inequities in school funding between high and low-poverty districts. What this means is that high-poverty districts are less able to afford hiring and retaining high-quality teachers and high-quality instruction, among other important factors related to schooling.

In order to address the problem, states and districts can equalize funding based upon formulas that provide additional funds to districts with lower property values. In addition, they can pursue other strategies such as investing in educator skill development and early childhood programs.[73]

For Further Reflection: Some people say, "Throwing money at the public schools is not going to improve their quality." Others counter, "We have never tried it. So, how do we know?" What do you think? How central is adequate financial support to address shortcomings in public education?

Social class and school choice

School choice is the idea that students should be able to select their school rather than have a neighborhood school assigned to them. The person often credited with originally proposing the idea of school choice, specifically **vouchers**, was economist Milton Friedman. Guided by free market principles, he argued that families should receive school vouchers which would enable them to choose their children's schools rather than being assigned to public schools based upon residence. The way choice supporters view it, this form of school choice permits public funds to follow the students to schools or services that best fit their needs, whether these are public, private, homeschooling, or any other learning environment.[74]

Proponents argue that school choice revives antiquated, bureaucratic public school systems through healthy competition and thus greater efficiency. It enhances power at the most local level because parents and students are able to make school choices. Advocates also contend that choice has the potential to equalize education by providing new alternatives to low-income families who, without school choice programs, are the ones most relegated to low-quality public schools, unable to afford what wealthier families take for granted: the opportunity to choose a high-quality private school education for their children.

Those who oppose school choice argue that many forms of school choice actually exacerbate rather than address inequities. To truly increase fairness and efficiency, as proponents argue school choice would do, students would need to be able to choose any school within a reasonable distance, whether public or private. In reality, school choice plans are usually within single—typically urban—districts and allow schools to only accept students when space is available. This means students in districts with few successful schools have little real choice. In addition, few plans require schools to inform parents of their options and few states provide transportation across district lines, effectively limiting choice to those parents who can transport their children to a non-neighborhood school.[75]

Other concerns arise about the idea that principles of market competition should be applied to a public service such as education. Do parents have access to enough information to make informed decisions, or are choices based on less than credible sources? Countering the pro school choice argument that competition will force underperforming schools to be closed, opponents warn that school closures are different from business closures: states are unable to simply rely on outside organizations or the market alone to educate students in case an underperforming school is closed. In addition, not only do families choose schools, but schools may also choose students through such things as targeted advertising or strategic placement of campuses. Consequently, the highest performing schools may not accept or even push out students who are low-performing or require relatively many resources, such as students with disabilities and multilingual learners. Also, inequitable markets will lead to lower-quality schooling options in low-income neighborhoods when compared to high-income ones.[76]

Many variations of school choice exist. They include inter- and intra-district public school choice, charter schools, magnet schools, homeschooling, hybrid homeschooling, online learning, microschooling, town tuitioning, as well as personalized learning and learning pods. To support primarily private schooling, programs include school vouchers, education savings accounts, tax credit education savings accounts, tax-credit scholarships, and individual tax credits and deductions.[77]

One important form of school choice that is often omitted from these discussions is the choice that parents make when purchasing a home in order to be in a particular school zone or district. Conservative estimates place the rate of this type of informal school choice around 25 percent—higher than any other form of choice.[78] Some have argued that this reality undermines the "publicness" of public schools because schools in more affluent areas exclude those who cannot afford to live there. Below we discuss in more detail two types of formal school choice: vouchers and charter schools.

School choice and vouchers

Some choice advocates embrace the idea of vouchers, that is, parents or guardians being able to use public funds allocated for their children's education to choose private schools, including religious schools.

School vouchers were initially offered only in a limited number of states and provided to specific groups of students only. In Arkansas, for example, private school vouchers are offered to students in foster care, students with disabilities and children of active-duty or reserve members of the military. In Maine, a town tuitioning program allows students to attend a public school in another town, or a private school, if their own town does not have a public school. Another example is Ohio, where an income-based scholarship program allows certain income-qualified students to receive vouchers that enable them to attend private schools.[79]

Recent voucher legislation in states like Arizona, Iowa, and New Hampshire, however, reimburses families who are already sending their children to private schools, effectively transferring millions of dollars annually from state funds into the hands of families who could already afford private school tuition.[80] These bills were made possible by the 2020 Supreme Court Decision, *Espinoza v. Montana Department of Revenue,* which held that states must allow private religious schools to participate in any voucher programs despite the "no-aid" clause of the state constitution which barred state funding of religious institutions.[81] As an example of this ruling and the subsequent legislation it enabled, small private schools (many of which are religious), across New Hampshire, received 63.4 percent of the grants in the first year.[82] In other words, the tax dollars funding the program were largely diverted to private institutions.

Central arguments for vouchers are that this system bestows all parents with a degree of freedom traditionally only enjoyed by families with the means to pay for private schooling. They also argue that vouchers have the potential to improve students' academic performance, promote both more racial and socioeconomic integration, and improve students' civic values.[83]

In contrast, opponents warn that school choice exercised through vouchers is, in the final analysis, little more than tax-paid supplements for wealthier patrons. Only the wealthier families are able to supplement their vouchers to exercise genuine choice among a variety of schools, including those that charge considerably more than a voucher alone would pay. Under such conditions, the gap between the wealthy and low-income families might actually increase, and rather than equalizing educational opportunity, school choice could lead to further stratification and inequality along racial and socioeconomic lines.

An important argument against school vouchers is also steeped in the notion that schools are qualitatively different from businesses.[84] A central problem with vouchers is that they supposedly rely on market forces, but it seems that market forces seldom if ever work in favor of those living in poverty. In a market economy, people buy what they can afford, not what they might truly want or choose. Simply put, to use the word *choice* to describe such conditions seems misleading.[85]

Along the same lines, while the purposes of consumer products tend to be rather clear, the purpose of education is not. Parents, for example, may differ as to whether schools are mainly supposed to impart basic academic skills, prepare students to function in society, or instill values, including religious beliefs. Historically, elected school boards discussed the purposes of education and translated them into school policies, but school choice programs shift the locus of control to the parents. They can now select schools based upon their own personal definition of educational purpose, but much information is needed to not only clearly articulate educational purpose, but also judge whether schools are meeting them. Parents may not have sufficient access to this kind of information or may choose to rely on individual preferences to guide their decision-making instead.[86]

Thus far, studies of the impacts of voucher programs on student achievement have not produced the results proponents predicted they would. Two decades of research on the impacts of voucher programs have found that test scores of students using vouchers differ very little from their non-voucher peers.[87] Most studies that have reported positive effects of voucher programs were funded by private foundations advocating school choice.[88]

Charter schools

Another option frequently advanced as a way to provide school choice is public **charter schools**. Those are publicly funded and run by a group or organization under a legislative contract (or charter) with the state, district, or other entity. The school enjoys a relatively large degree of freedom since it is granted exemption from certain state or local regulations, but it must meet accountability standards as specified by its charter. In 2021, all but seven states had public charter schools. There were about 7800 charter schools in the 2021–2 school year in the United States, and between 2010 and 2021, public charter school enrollment more than doubled (from 1.8 to 3.7 million students) while students attending traditional public schools decreased by 4 percent, or 2 million students during that time.[89] Although the total share of public students who attend charter schools is only 6 percent, within nineteen cities the rate is above 30 percent.[90]

Advocates of charter schools view them as providing families with the opportunity to find schools that best fit the needs of their children, within a school culture supportive of the surrounding community. Teachers have opportunities to provide innovative, high-quality instruction while school leaders are able to pursue new ideas. Supporters claim that charter school students outperform their peers in other types of public schools.[91]

Critics argue that charter schools are, in many respects, as unsatisfactory as vouchers because they take tax money away from regular public schools that so desperately need it. Some states allow for-profit companies to run charter schools.[92] Charter schools are often exempt from the same teacher licensure requirements as regular public schools and in unionized states can hire teachers outside the union.[93] In addition, where charter schools are targeted for a specific group, they tend to operate in an exclusive manner. Advocates reply that charter schools are still *public* schools and are not exempt from public control in the way private schools are. Rather than being exclusive, many charter schools attempt to target the special needs of particular groups, but outside the centralized bureaucratic control of public school systems. However, in some states charter schools are not required to provide transportation, limiting accessibility to only those families who can drop off and pick up their children each day.[94]

While the independence of charter schools can be an asset, some charter schools have engaged in financial or academic mismanagement and ultimately had to be shuttered.[95] Billionaire philanthropy has been a major source of charter school funding, especially for urban charter school networks such as Uncommon Schools, KIPP, and Achievement First. These networks have been dubbed "no excuses" charters due to their philosophy that longer school days and strict disciplinary practices will benefit low-income students of color. This approach has been criticized as racist, and in response some charter leaders have shifted these practices.[96]

The research on the impacts of charter schools on student achievement has been mixed and difficult to carry out due to the variation among school models and challenges in comparing district to charter school students.[97]

School choice programs in operation

Programs involving school choice have been implemented in most states, although not all of them support private school choice. California, for example, provides charter and magnet schools, as well as homeschooling and limited public school choice via open enrollment, but it does not have any private school choice programs. Wisconsin, on the other hand, provides several types of school choice programs, including five private school choice programs, charter and magnet schools, homeschooling, and both inter- and intra-district public school choice.[98]

An in-depth look at school choice in New York City reveals the sometimes surprising complexities potentially inherent in school choice programs. Looking at elementary schools in particular, a recent report found that the number of kindergartners attending their zoned public schools is shrinking. Rapidly growing school choice programs have led to an increasing number of children leaving their zoned schools every day to attend charter schools, gifted programs, dual language programs, and traditional public schools outside of their school zones. Many attend schools close to home but many also migrate, usually toward higher-income neighborhoods. Race, ethnicity, and social class makeup of the neighborhood influence who opts out and who stays in their zoned school: in New York City, the school choice rate is significantly higher for Black children than white, Asian, or Hispanic, and it is much higher for free-lunch eligible students than higher-income and English-proficient students. Students who leave their zoned schools typically start attending schools with fewer students from low-income families. Students who stay, however, tend to be left behind in schools with higher concentrations of poverty with declining enrollment and, because funding is based upon enrollment, with dwindling resources. In addition, school choice in New York City appears to lead to increased racial segregation. The report concludes that school choice may have led to a paradoxical situation: thousands of students are able to enjoy better educational opportunities because they can leave low-performing schools, but those who are left behind may face increased challenges.[99]

A central question remains whether it is possible within school choice systems to send every child to a high-quality school of choice without leaving anybody behind. Critics of school choice argue that rather than dismantling public school systems through draining resources, the nation's energies and resources would be better spent on strengthening them.

Tracking and ability grouping

Social class not only influences funding and overall school quality but also many within-school experiences students have. Two curriculum approaches that involve social class are **tracking** and **ability grouping**. Tracking is a traditional practice in secondary education of assessing students and separating them into particular curriculum programs such as general, vocational-technical, and college preparatory. Placement decisions usually involved grades, test scores, teacher recommendations, and school counseling among other factors, but it has become clear that one of the most prominent factors was the social class, race, gender, ethnic origin, disability, as well as ESOL (English as a second language) status of students. After legal restrictions were placed on tracking, the practice fell out of favor, but vestiges of it are retained in the practice of ability grouping. Sometimes the terms are used interchangeably.

A leading factor that changed curriculum tracking in the United States was the district court decision in *Hobson v. Hansen* (1967), which ordered the Washington, DC, public school system to abolish its tracking system. The court held that the tracking system and its use of intelligence quotient (IQ) test scores as a primary basis for placements were racially and socioeconomically biased against students in violation of the equal protection of the laws, a decision that discouraged traditional tracking programs nationwide.[100]

However, *Hobson* did not end tracking altogether, with ability grouping soon replacing it, although the latter was applied mostly to specific courses rather than curriculum programs. The end result was still a differentiated curriculum within academic courses (for example, basic math, general math, advanced math, and honors math courses), but one more implicit than the previous tracking system, one that continues to have profound effects on students today.

Ability grouping, i.e., grouping students based upon academic achievement, has the purpose of providing appropriate instruction for individual students, although critics question whether the practice achieves this purpose. Many different varieties exist, including multi-level ability grouping, cross-grade grouping, school-wide cluster grouping, and within-class grouping. The main distinction is between-class grouping which separates students into different classrooms on the one hand, and within-class grouping which divides students within a classroom on the other.[101]

During the 2017–18 school year, roughly one-third of public schools reported assigning students based on their ability. Numbers vary by school level: nearly half of all middle schools assign students based upon perceived ability, 40 percent of high schools, 32 percent of combined schools, and 24 percent of elementary schools.[102]

Children sometimes experience ability grouping as early as pre-school and kindergarten levels. In the early elementary grades, students are typically grouped by ability for reading and math instruction, but as they proceed up the grade levels, they are increasingly placed in courses associated with such labels as advanced, general, or remedial.

Suggested Activity: Think about your personal experiences with tracking or ability grouping. How prevalent were these practices in the schools you attended? What effect may they have had on you? Compare your experiences with those of your peers and/or those of members of older generations, for example, your parents or grandparents. What do these intergenerational comparisons suggest about how schools have changed and how much has stayed the same?

Research on ability grouping at the elementary school level indicates that some teachers employ this approach seeking to meet individual students' needs, improve student learning, and increase test scores. Other educators believe it negatively affects student achievement and self-concept. They prefer whole-group instruction over ability grouping. Ability grouping may in some instances be academically and psychologically beneficial, but it can also be harmful, depending upon students' background and levels.[103]

Critics of ability grouping have long pointed out that this kind of sorting is nothing more than tracking by another name, and may be deeply flawed. Some have even described it as "the new IQism," because it reflects similarities with the pseudoscientific claims of social Darwinism and certain aspects of the testing movement of the late nineteenth and early twentieth centuries.[104] One effect of this form of tracking is that students in higher-level courses tend to be taught with pedagogically superior methods and materials; they develop more positive attitudes toward themselves and toward school, and they are more likely to be positively received by the wider society. Social class continues to play a role in this kind of tracking because students from advantaged family backgrounds almost always receive the best placements, and their parents are most likely to intervene on behalf of their children to influence decisions about their children's placement in advanced courses. These parents also tend to have considerable educational experience themselves, and they know how to navigate school systems and obtain information about courses beneficial for their children's future, a form of status and influence that lower-income parents may lack. In other words, social class has an educational impact that advantages some people and disadvantages others.[105]

Opponents of ability grouping and tracking argue that even if educational policy makers are well intentioned and assume that ability grouping is beneficial for students, the practice is nothing more than an unquestioned habit, a tradition with harmful consequences. Contrary to the assumption that it helps students learn better in homogeneous groups, opponents bring evidence that most advanced students are not held back by mixed classrooms, and slower learners actually learn better in mixed classrooms. There are research findings indicating that tracking deflates the self-esteem of lower-track students while inflating it in the upper tracks. The behavior of lower-track students tends to be influenced by their placement: they participate less in extracurricular activities, drop out in higher numbers, and experience more alienation from school than their upper-track peers.

A seminal study of twenty-five schools found that upper-track students were exposed to a higher quality of knowledge (they read works of literature while lower-track students worked with reading kits); their teachers spent more time on instruction in the classroom (instead of discipline or social activities); they perceived their teachers to be more concerned about them (and less punitive than teachers in lower-track classes); and they reported more positive peer relationships than did lower-track students. Tracking results in stigmatizing labels such as slow, basic, remedial, or fast, bright, and honors. Labeling often leads to self-fulfilling prophecies with students placed in lower tracks tending to find it difficult to free themselves from the label and escape the track. Tracking also tends to separate students along socioeconomic lines as well as racial and ethnic lines. In sum, low-income and minority students are over-represented in the lower tracks and underrepresented in the higher tracks, low-income students seem to be negatively affected by tracking, and tracking seriously interferes with achieving equality of educational opportunity.[106]

These critiques have stood the test of time. A more recent examination of the literature on ability grouping in the Western world generally indicates that dividing learners into academic groups contributes to broadening socioeconomic divisions.[107]

In addition, international research studies have shown mixed results concerning ability grouping and academic achievement, with benefits typically being seen mostly for students in so-called gifted-and-talented programs rather than students placed in mid- or low-ability groups.[108]

Specific to the United States, recent research suggests similarly that ability grouping may exacerbate inequalities while alternatives potentially improve learning for all students. Concerning the former, it has been shown, for example, that ability grouping in the early grades leads to educational paths that grow further apart over time with multiple years of grouping. Educational inequalities, in other words, are reproduced over time.[109]

As far as alternatives to ability-grouping are concerned, the literature documents various efforts. One case study focused on elementary mathematics instruction, for example, shows how teachers use alternate grouping practices such as forming collaborative learning groups with students grouped by mixed ability levels, or random grouping of students; partnering students across abilities rather than grouping them by ability; and inviting students to share problem solving strategies with the whole class. Positive effects, particularly for historically marginalized students, include increased confidence and perseverance because mixed-ability groups may be experienced as safe spaces to ask questions and experiment with new problem-solving strategies. There is improved positivity toward the subject, and more inclusive participation. Students may benefit from mixed-ability grouping that allows teachers to see not just the cognitive development of their students, but also their social and identity development, acknowledging academic as well as interpersonal strengths and life experiences.

Challenges remain, however, such as school policies in favor of ability grouping. Since ability grouping tends to disadvantage mostly low-income students and students of color, challenging this practice also means challenging teachers, who continue to be predominantly white and of middle-class background, and who work in systems of education that have mostly benefited them.[110]

In addition, supporters of tracking and ability grouping argue that de-tracking (or differentiation) does not work. It is a losing proposition; unrealistic and impossible to implement because teachers are unable to effectively teach in classes that comprise diverse groups of learners, including so-called gifted and average students, alongside multilingual learners.[111]

Some researchers argue that resistance to de-tracking is one way in which upper- and middle-class parents help create educational advantages for their children. One seminal study of ten socioeconomically mixed schools undergoing de-tracking reforms concluded that "elite" parents tended to oppose de-tracking for fear that it could undermine their children's relative advantages. They based their resistance on labels, on the "symbolic mixing of high deserving and low deserving" students, rather than on information about the results in de-tracked classrooms. They were convinced that their children's placements in advanced programs were a result of merit or the children's academic achievement, not their privileged social-class status or the fact that the placements were often a result of parental pressure and influence. Because of the resources (including tax monies) that elite parents brought to the system, they seemed to take for granted that their children were entitled to better educational opportunities than others. In addition, they used several strategies to undermine de-tracking efforts, including: threatening to pull their children out of public schools should educators alter the existing talented and gifted programs, co-opting educational administrators, and receiving special privileges in return for allowing small degrees of de-tracking to take place in the schools.[112]

The issue of tracking and ability grouping is far from resolved. It goes to the heart of discussions about how deeply embedded class-based practices persist in the schools, what roles people play in such processes, and how some educational practices continue to exist because they serve certain interests. At the same time, change is initiated and sustained only through people's actions. How to better understand this interplay of people's actions and school programs and practices, and how to make it work for good education, ought to be continuing quests for educators.

Summary and conclusions

As difficult as it may be to define the concept of social class, both historical and contemporary analyses show that social class significantly impacts educational policy and practice. It complicates education in many ways, from equal access and attainment all the way to individual success and failure in the educational process.

During American colonial times, access to education among the European colonists was usually connected to one's class status; that is, it was primarily the wealthier classes that received any extensive **formal education**. Nevertheless, there were trends and developments that encouraged a broadening of educational opportunity, including the education of so-called common people. One such example was the religious notion that the salvation of the soul was to a significant degree dependent on one's ability to read the Scriptures, which helped spur the founding of schools in the early colonial period. A more secular influence was the fact that the vast majority of colonists were common people who came to the United States in hopes of improving the circumstances of their lives, and education was seen as one way of helping achieve this. Finally, a growing sense of distinctly American identity and self-reliance contributed even further to the notion that education ought to be more widely available and not be restricted to only the elite.

In the nineteenth century, these ideas were further developed, and many people came to see public schools as the "great equalizer." There was a sizable expansion of schools to more and more people, though schools remained segregated with those serving white students receiving most funding.

By the late nineteenth and early twentieth centuries, reformers pushed education as a servant of industrial expansion, and they built large urban educational systems modeled along the lines of the modern corporation. Some policy makers, perhaps influenced by claims that existing social inequities resulted from natural competition and the survival of the fittest, saw no need to expand education or expend many resources on those from low socioeconomic classes. Others, enamored with a testing movement that promised to "scientifically" sort and track students into the vocational and academic curriculum programs they were most suited for, saw such differentiation as a more "efficient" way to run schools; however, the end results usually reflected the social-class conditions of students more than their actual abilities or goals. Repelled by the excesses of urban industrial society, still other reformers called for using education to democratize industrial society and to make it more humane and livable.

Economic setbacks such as the Great Depression aggravated class differences, but it also renewed calls for education as a means of social betterment. The expansion of educational opportunity in higher education following the Second World War helped further democratize access to a greater extent than ever before, at least for white veterans. It could be argued that, despite some detours and setbacks, the twentieth century witnessed the expansion of educational opportunity from the elementary to the secondary and higher-education levels, which all contributed significantly to the growth of the American middle class.

By the beginning of the twenty-first century, however, it appeared that the middle class was losing ground, and critics feared that American society was becoming characterized once more by a growing gap between the rich and the poor. The gap can be seen in unequal funding and in practices such as tracking and ability grouping, and school "choice" schemes such as vouchers promise to widen it further.

Many contemporary policies and practices seem to be undermining past educational advances achieved through arduous efforts over the years. For example, the current system of local school funding is marred by inequities, one reason being that it depends on taxes on local wealth and property, which determines how much funding can be generated. Efforts have been made to equalize funding among localities by injecting more state and federal monies into poor districts. The War on Poverty during the 1960s increased federal monies to poverty-impacted areas in an attempt to reduce socioeconomic inequities. Despite such efforts, the results have been mixed, one reason being poorly enforced programs over the long term. Perhaps reform of educational institutions alone is not enough to change socioeconomic conditions without some fundamental changes also being made in other, more powerful social, economic, and political institutions.

Recent educational reforms include the controversial school choice movement. Proponents argue that choice, particularly when exercised with school vouchers, will help bridge the gap between the wealthy and the poor. Critics argue that vouchers will not enable poor families to send their children to good private schools because, in fact, the actual voucher plans put into operation could not pay the costs of existing public schools, much less high-quality private schools. In short, the question of how school choice programs in operation thus far can possibly ameliorate class-based differences in educational opportunity remains unanswered.

Controversy also swirls around the issues of tracking and ability grouping. While most research on the issue indicates that tracking and ability grouping do not benefit the majority of students, these practices nevertheless continue in many school systems. Efforts to de-track the schools are typically met with resistance by the parents of students in the higher tracks, who appear to be the ones most benefiting from tracking. Social-class lines also become pronounced because middle- and upper-class students are disproportionately represented in the higher tracks.

In conclusion, social class continues to impact provisions for education in the United States, although many reforms and expansions of schooling opportunities over the years have been instituted. The long-term American hope that education might alleviate if not overcome the effects of social class has not been without some success, but the struggle is far from over. Social class continues to impact the life chances of Americans, including their educational chances.

Vocabulary

ability grouping
capitalism
charter schools
class consciousness
class differences
cultural capital
Elementary and Secondary Education Act (ESEA)
formal education

great equalizer
Great Depression
haves and have-nots
heredity thesis
Horace Mann
Karl Marx
Max Weber
meritocracy
neoliberal economic policies
Out-of-school factors (OSFs)
Pierre Bourdieu
reconstructionists
school choice
Servicemen's Readjustment Act of 1944 (known as GI Bill of Rights)
social Darwinism
socialism
social mobility
success literature
survival of the fittest
symbolic capital
tracking
vouchers
War on Poverty
wraparound services

Notes

1 Ron Thompson, *Education, Inequality and Social Class: Expansion and Stratification* (New York: Routledge, 2019), 12.

2 Dave Hill, "Social Class and Education," in *Considering Class*, Deirdre O'Neill and Mike Wayne, eds (Boston, MA: BRILL, 2017), 31–50

3 Elizabeth Hinton, *From the War on Poverty to the War on Crime: The Making of Mass Incarceration in America* (Cambridge, MA: Harvard University Press, 2016).

4 "Piety for Virginia Households [Laws of Virginia, Feb. 1631–2]," in Calhoun, 17; "Protection for Public Wards [Laws of Virginia, March 1642–43]," in *Educational Ideas in America: A Documentary History*, S. Alexander Rippa, ed. (New York: David McKay Co., Inc., 1969), 17, hereafter referred to as "Rippa;"

"Enforcement of Pious Teaching [*Laws of Virginia*, March 1645–6]" and "Labor for Poor Children [*Laws of Virginia*, October 1646]," in Calhoun, 18.

5 Sir William Berkeley, "A Governor of Virginia Takes Pleasure in Colonial Backwardness [from 'Answers to Inquiries from the Lords Commissioner of Foreign Plantations (1671)],'" in Calhoun, 76.

6 "New England's First Fruits [1643]," in *American Higher Education: A Documentary History*, vol. 1, Richard Hofstadter and Wilson Smith, eds (Chicago, IL: University of Chicago Press, 1961), 5–6.

7 "The Massachusetts School Law of 1647," in Rippa, 162; and William J. Gilmore, *Elementary Literacy on the Eve of the Industrial Revolution: Trends in Rural New England* (Worchester, MA: American Antiquarian Society, 1982), 87–178.

8 Rush Welter, *Popular Education and Democratic Thought in America* (New York: Columbia University Press, 1962), 12, 18–21.

9 https://encyclopediavirginia.org/entries/slave-literacy-and-education-in-virginia/#:~:text=A%20small%20number%20of%20enslaved,often%20tied%20to%20religious%20teaching

10 Lawrence Cremin, *American Education: The Colonial Experience, 1607–1783* (New York: Harper Torchbooks, 1970), 167–224, 400–7, and 499–506; Merle Curti, *The Social Ideas of American Educators, With a New Chapter on the Last Twenty-Five Years* (Totowa, NJ: Littlefield, Adams, 1968), 3–10; and Bernard Bailyn, *Education in the Forming of American Society: Needs and Opportunities for Study* (Chapel Hill: University of North Carolina Press, 1960), 20–1, 41–4.

11 Walter Isaacson, *Benjamin Franklin: An American Life* (New York: Simon and Schuster, 2003).

12 Benjamin Franklin, "Silence Dogood, No. 4 on the Higher Learning," in *Benjamin Franklin on Education*, John Hardin Best, ed. Classics in Education, No. 14 (New York: Teachers College Press, 1962), 38; and Benjamin Franklin, "Proposals Relating to the Education of Youth in Pensilvania [1749]," in Rippa, 108.

13 Franklin, "Proposals Relating to the Education of Youth in Pensilvania [1749]," in Rippa, 105, 106, 108; and "The Idea of the English School, Sketch'd out for the Consideration of the Trustees of the Philadelphia Academy [1751]," in *Benjamin Franklin on Education*, 150. See also Benjamin Franklin, *Educational Views of Benjamin Franklin*, Thomas Woody, ed. (New York: McGraw-Hill, 1931). See also Cremin, *American Education: The Colonial Experience, 1607–1783*, 376–8.

14 See, for example, Stanley William Rothstein, *Schooling the Poor: A Social Inquiry into the American Educational Experience* (Westport, CT: Bergin and Garvey, 1994), 1–9.

15 Horace Mann, "Twelfth Annual Report [1848]," in *The Republic and the School: Horace Mann on the Education of Free Men*, Lawrence A. Cremin, ed. Classics in Education, No. 1 (New York: Teachers College Press, 1957), 84–7. For biographies

of Mann, see Jonathan Messerli, *Horace Mann: A Biography* (New York: Alfred A. Knopf, 1972); and Robert B. Downs, *Horace Mann: Champion of Public Schools* (New York: Twayne Publishers, 1974).

16 Selwyn K. Troen, "Popular Education in Nineteenth-Century St. Louis," in *The Social History of American Education*, B. Edward McClellan and William J. Reese, eds (Urbana: University of Illinois Press, 1988), 119–36.

17 Henry J. Perkinson, *The Imperfect Panacea: American Faith in Education*, 4th edn (Boston, MA: McGraw- Hill, 1995). See also Michael B. Katz, *Class, Bureaucracy, and Schools* (New York: Praeger Publishers, 1971). For a critical treatment of early twentieth century reforms, see Clarence J. Karier, Paul C. Violas, and Joel Spring, *Roots of Crisis: American Education in the Twentieth Century* (Chicago, IL: Rand McNally, 1973).

18 Ronald Schultz, "A Class Society? The Nature of Inequality in Early America," in *Inequality in Early America*, Carla Gardena Patina and Sharon V. Slinger, eds (Hanover, NH: University Press of New England, 1999), 216.

19 Richard Hofstadter, *Social Darwinism in American Thought*, revd edn (Boston, MA: Beacon Press, 1955), 35–50.

20 Carl N. Degler, *Search of Human Nature: The Decline and Revival of Darwinism in American Social Thought* (New York: Oxford University Press, 1991), 79, 128–9, 145–8.

21 Ibid., 50–1, 150–1; and Peter Quinn, "Race Cleansing in America," *American Heritage*, vol. 54, no. 1 (February/March 2003): 34–43.

22 Judy Hilkey, *Character Is Capital: Success Manuals and Manhood in Gilded Age America* (Chapel Hill: University of North Carolina Press, 1997), 2–7.

23 Ibid., 25–7, 90, 107, and 137–8.

24 Harvey Kantor and David Tyack, "Introduction: Historical Perspectives on Vocationalism in American Education," in *Work, Youth, and Schooling: Historical Perspectives on Vocationalism in American Education*, Harvey Kantor and David Tyack, eds (Stanford, CA: Stanford University Press, 1982), 1–3.

25 George Sylvester Counts, *The Social Composition of Boards of Education.* American Education: Its Men, Ideas, and Institutions, Lawrence Cremin, ed. (reprint, New York: Arno Press, [1927] 1969), 66ff, 78–80, 83–5, 90–1.

26 David Tyack, Robert Lowe, and Elisabeth Hansot, *Public Schools in Hard Times: The Great Depression and Recent Years* (Cambridge, MA: Harvard University Press, 1984), 3–7, 10–14.

27 David M. Kennedy, *Freedom from Fear: The American People in Depression and War, 1929–1945*. The Oxford History of the United States, vol. 9, C. Vann Woodward, gen. ed. (New York: Oxford University Press, 1999), 163.

28 Tyack, Lowe, and Hansot, *Public Schools in Hard Times*, 6–17.

29 Kennedy, *Freedom from Fear*, 322.

30 Tyack, Hansot, and Lowe, *Public Schools in Hard Times*, 122–32.

31 August B. Hollingshead, *Elmtown's Youth: The Impact of Social Classes on Adolescents* (New York: John Wiley and Sons, Inc., Science Editions, 1961), 452.

32 George Sylvester Counts, *Dare the Schools Build a New Social Order?* (New York: Arno Press, 1969). See also Tyack, Lowe, and Hansot, *Public Schools in Hard Times,* 18–27.

33 https://www.nber.org/digest/dec02/gi-bill-world-war-ii-and-education-black-americans

34 James T. Patterson, *Grand Expectations: The United States, 1945–1974*, vol. 10, The Oxford History of the United States, C. Vann Woodward, gen. ed. (New York: Oxford University Press, Inc., 1996), 68–9.

35 Patricia Cayo Sexton, *Education and Income: Inequalities of Opportunity in Our Public Schools* (New York: Viking Press, 1964), 114, 120, 124, 157, and 159.

36 John F. Jennings, "Title I: Its Legislative History and Its Promise," in *Title I: Compensatory Education at the Crossroads*, Geoffrey D. Borman et al., eds (Mahwah, NJ: Lawrence Erlbaum Associates, 2001), 2–5.

37 Ibid., 6–21.

38 For a synopsis of Marxism and education, see Howard A. Ozmon and Samuel M. Craver, *Philosophical Foundations of Education*, 7th edn (Upper Saddle River, NJ: Pearson Education, 2003), 307–12, 317–18, and 320–3.

39 Jeanne H. Ballantine, *The Sociology of Education: A Systematic Analysis*, 4th edn (Upper Saddle River, NJ: Prentice Hall, 1997), 9.

40 Max Weber, "The 'Rationalization' of Education and Training," in *The Structure of Schooling: Readings in the Sociology of Education*, Richard Arum and Irenee R. Beattie, eds (Mountain View, CA: Mayfield Publishing, 2000), 16–19.

41 Chelen Mahar, Richard Harker, and Chris Wilkes, *An Introduction to the Work of Pierre Bourdieu: The Practice of Theory* (New York: St. Martin's Press, 1990), 6–11.

42 Ibid., 7, 13, 14.

43 Schultz, "A Class Society? The Nature of Inequality in Early America," 203–8.

44 Richard Scase, *Class. Concepts in Social Thought* (Minneapolis: University of Minnesota Press, 1992), 2–3, 33–4, and 41.

45 Terry Nichols Clark and Seymour Martin Lipset, "Are Social Classes Dying?" in *The Breakdown of Class Politics: A Debate on Post Industrial Stratification*, Terry Nichols Clark and Seymour Martin Lipset, eds (Washington, DC: Woodrow Wilson Center Press, 2001), 39–54; and Erik Olin Wright, *Class Counts: Comparative Studies in Class Analysis* (New York: Cambridge University Press, 1997), 18–19, 73, 101, 110–11.

46 Vicente Navarro, "Neoliberalism as a Class Ideology; or, the Political Causes of the Growth of Inequalities," *International Journal of Health Services*, vol. 37, no. 1 (2007): 47–62.

47 Frederick R. Strobel, *Upward Dreams, Downward Mobility: The Economic Decline of the American Middle Class* (Lanham, MD: Rowman and Littlefield, 1993).

48 Paul Krugman, "For Richer: How the Permissive Capitalism of the Boom Destroyed American Equality," *New York Times Magazine* (October 20, 2002), 62(10).

49 Ana Hernández Kent and Lowell R. Ricketts, "The State of U.S. Wealth Inequality," *Federal Reserve Back of St. Louis* (July 31, 2023), https://www.stlouisfed.org/institute-for-economic-equity/the-state-of-us-wealth-inequality (accessed on February 10, 2023).

50 US Census Bureau, "Income Inequality Down Due to Drops in Real Incomes at the Middle and Top, but Post-tax Income Estimates Tell a Different Story," https://www.census.gov/library/stories/2023/09/income-inequality.html#:~:text=The%20ratio%20of%20the%2090th,a%206.7%25%20decrease%20from%202021 (accessed on March 10, 2023).

51 United States Census Bureau, "Poverty in the United States: 2022," at https://www.census.gov/library/publications/2023/demo/p.60-280.html (accessed on February 10, 2023).

52 United States Census Bureau, https://www.census.gov/search-results.html?q=children+living+in+poverty&page=1&stateGeo=none&searchtype=web&cssp=SERP&_charset_=UTF-8 (accessed on March 10, 2023).

53 Collyer, Sophie, Megan Curran, Irwin Garfinkel, David Harris, Dominic Richardson, and Christopher Wimer. A step in the right direction: The expanded Child Tax Credit would move the United States' high child poverty rate closer to peer nations. Poverty and Social Policy Report, vol. 6, no 7. New York: Columbia University, Center on Poverty and Social Policy and UNICEF Innocenti, Global Office of Research and Foresight. 2022.

54 https://www.nytimes.com/2023/09/12/business/economy/income-poverty-health-insurance.html (accessed on March 12, 2023).

55 See, for example, Wendy Johnson, Caroline E. Brett, and Ian J. Deary, "The Pivotal Role of Education in the Association Between Ability and Social Class Attainment: A Look Across Three Generations," *Intelligence*, vol. 38, no. 1 (January–February, 2010): 55–65; and Maike Ingrid Philipsen, "The Problem of Poverty: Shifting the Attention to the Non-Poor," in *Late to Class: Social Class and Schooling in the New Economy*, Jane A. Van Galen and George W. Noblit, eds (Albany: State University of New York Press, 2007), 269.

56 Max Antony-Newman, S. Niyozov, and K. Pashchenko, "Middle-Class Parental Engagement in Pandemic Times: Developing Strategies and Mobilizing Capitals," *British Journal of Sociology of Education*, vol. 45, no. 2 (2023): 193–209, https://doi.org/10.1080/01425692.2023.2294687

57 David C. Berliner, *Poverty and Potential: Out-of-School Factors and School Success* (Boulder, CO: Education and the Public Interest Center & Education Policy Research Unit), http://epicpolicy.org/publication/ poverty-and-potential (accessed on March 16, 2010); and Sue Books, *Poverty and Schooling in the*

U.S.: Contexts and Consequences (Mahwah, NJ: Lawrence Erlbaum Associates, 2004), 134.

58 Martin Packer, *Changing Classes: School Reform and the New Economy* (Cambridge: Cambridge University Press, 2001), 278–9.

59 Mann, "Twelfth Annual Report [1848]," 84–7.

60 Christina Samuels, "Data Reveal Deep Inequities in School," *Education Week* (March 3, 2020), https://www.edweek.org/leadership/data-reveal-deep-inequities-in-schools/2020/03 (accessed on October 26, 2023).

61 Education Week, "How Much Money Do Public Schools Get? The Latest Numbers," (June 2009, 2023), https://www.edweek.org/leadership/how-much-money-do-public-schools-get-the-latest-numbers/2023/06 (accessed on October 14, 2023).

62 United States Census Bureau, "Public School Spending Per Pupil Experiences Largest Year-to-Year Increase in More than a Decade," (May 18, 2023), https://www.census.gov/newsroom/press-releases/2023/public-school-spending.html (accessed on October 14, 2023).

63 Heather McGee, *The Sum of Us: What Racism Costs Everyone and How We Can Prosper Together* (New York: One World, 2021).

64 Jonathan Kozol, *Savage Inequalities: Children in America's Schools* (New York: Crown Publishers, 1991).

65 Harman Singh, "Savage Inequalities: Children in America's Schools," Review in NACADA (National Academic Advising Association) (June 1, 2020), https://nacada.ksu.edu/Resources/Book-Reviews/Current-Past-Book-Reviews/Savage-inequalities-children-in-Americas-schools.aspx#:~:text=Kozol%20takes%20a%20qualitative%2C%20ethnographic,American%20school%20system%20faces%20today (accessed on October 14, 2023).

66 US Commission on Civil Rights: Public Education Funding Inequity: In an Era of Increasing Concentration of Poverty and Resegregation. Washington, DC: January 2018, https://www.usccr.gov/files/pubs/2018/2018-01-10-Education-Inequity.pdf (accessed on October 23, 2023).

67 ALL4Ed. Understanding and Improving Title I of ESEA. Rebecca Shackleford and Anne Hyslop. January 23, 2023, https://all4ed.org/publication/improvetitlei/ (accessed on October 26, 2023).

68 US Commission on Civil Rights (accessed on October 27, 2023).

69 US Commission on Civil Rights (accessed on October 30, 2023).

70 The Education Trust. Funding Gaps 2018, https://edtrust.org/rti/funding-gaps-2018/?utm_source=chatgpt.com.

71 James Ryan, *Five Miles Away: A World Apart* (New York: Oxford University Press, 2010).

72 Ivy Morgan and Ari Amerikaner, "An Analysis of School Funding Equity Across the U.S. and Within Each State," *Funding Gaps 2018*, at https://edtrust.org/resource/funding-gaps-2018 (accessed on October 20, 2023).

73 American University, School of Education. Inequality in Public School Funding: Key I issues & Solutions for Closing the Gap. September 10, 2020, https://soeonline.american.edu/blog/inequality-in-public-school-funding/ (accessed on March 7, 2025).

74 edCHOICE School Choice FAQ's- https://www.edchoice.org/school-choice/faqs/ (accessed on November 3, 2023).

75 Ryan, *Five Miles Away*.

76 David Garcia, *School Choice* (MIT Press, 2018), 72–4.

77 *ed*CHOICE Types of School Choice, https://www.edchoice.org/school-choice/types-of-school-choice/ (accessed on October 31, 2023).

78 Ryan, *Five Miles Away*.

79 EdCHOICE What Are School Vouchers? https://www.edchoice.org/school-choice/types-of-school-choice/what-are-school-vouchers-2/ (accessed on November 11, 2023).

80 https://www.thenation.com/article/society/vouchers-attack-public-education/ (accessed on December 6, 2023).

81 National Coalition for Public Education, https://static1.squarespace.com/static/582f7c15f7e0ab3a3c7fb141/t/6018701f8a33bc20f2e229c9/1612214310823/NCPE+Espinoza+and+Vouchers+Toolkit+.pdf.

82 Dewitt, 2022, https://newhampshirebulletin.com/2022/04/05/private-christian-academies-see-boost-from-education-freedom-account-funds/ (accessed on December 6, 2023).

83 edCHOICE, "What Are School Vouchers?" https://www.edchoice.org/school-choice/types-of-school-choice/what-are-school-vouchers-2 (accessed on November 10, 2023).

84 Maike Philipsen and George Noblit, "Tricky Business: Corporate Conceptions of Educational Reform," *The High School Journal*, Vol. 76, no. 4(1993): 260–72.

85 Interview of Amy Wilkins, "School Colors: The Racial Politics of Public Education," *The Nation* (June 5, 2000), 14.

86 David Garcia, *School Choice* (Cambridge, MA: MIT Press, 2088), 24–7.

87 https://hechingerreport.org/opinion-after-two-decades-of-studying-voucher-programs-im-now-firmly-opposed-to-them/ (accessed on December 6, 2023).

88 Ibid.

89 National Center for Education Statistics, Fast Facts: Charter Schools, https://nces.ed.gov/fastfacts/display.asp?id=30#:~:text=Between%20school%20years%202010%E2%80%9311,decreased%20from%2093%2C500%20to%2091%2C400 (accessed on November 3, 2023).

90 https://www.edweek.org/policy-politics/what-are-charter-schools/2018/08 (accessed on December 7, 2023).

91 National Alliance for Public Charter Schools, About Charter Schools, https://publiccharters.org/about-charter-schools (accessed on November 6, 2023).

92 https://www.edweek.org/policy-politics/what-are-charter-schools/2018/08 (accessed on December 7, 2023).

93 https://www.edweek.org/policy-politics/why-and-where-charter-school-teachers-unionize/2019/03 (accessed on December 7, 2023).

94 https://www.readingrockets.org/topics/learning-disabilities/articles/facts-charter-schools-and-students-disabilities (accessed on December 7, 2023).

95 https://www.edweek.org/policy-politics/what-are-charter-schools/2018/08 (accessed on December 7, 2023).

96 https://www.washingtonpost.com/education/2019/08/29/some-no-excuses-charter-schools-say-they-are-changing-are-they-can-they/ (accessed on December 8, 2023).

97 https://www.edweek.org/policy-politics/what-are-charter-schools/2018/08 (accessed on December 8, 2023).

98 edCHOICE, School Choice in America. How to use our Dashboard, https://www.edchoice.org/school-choice-in-america-dashboard-scia/ (accessed on November 3, 2023).

99 The New School, Center for New York City Affairs. The Paradox of School Choice: How School Choice Divides New York City Elementary Schools, https://static1.squarespace.com/static/53ee4f0be4b015b9c3690d84/t/5aecb1c3352f537d3541623b/1525461450469/The+Paradox+of+Choice.pdf (accessed on November 11, 2023).

100 *Hobson v Hansen*, 269 F. Supp. 401 (D.D.C. 1967); and Beatrice A. Moulton, "Hobson v. Hansen: The De Facto Limits on Judicial Power," *Stanford Law Review*, vol. 20, no. 6 (June 1968): 1249, 1256–8, 1262, and 1266.

101 Kristina N. Bolick and Beth A. Rogowsky, "Ability Grouping Is on the Rise, but Should It Be?" *Journal of Education and Human Development*, vol. 5, no. 2 (June 2016): 40–51, http://jehdnet.com/journals/jehd/Vol_5_No_2_June_2016/6.pdf. (accessed on November 14, 2023).

102 Institute of Education Sciences, Pre-Covid Ability Groupings in U.S. Public School Classrooms, https://permanent.fdlp.gov/gpo155450/2021139.pdf (accessed on November 13, 2023).

103 Bolick and Rogowsky, "Ability Grouping Is on the Rise, but Should It Be?" 40–51.

104 Jeannie Oakes, *Keeping Track: How Schools Structure Inequality* (New Haven, CT: Yale University Press, 1985); Kathleen Bennett deMarrais and Margaret D. LeCompte, *The Ways Schools Work: A Sociological Analysis*, 2nd edn (White Plains, NY: Longman, 1995); and David Gillborn and Deborah Youdell, "The

New IQism: Intelligence, 'Ability' and the Rationing of Education," in *Sociology of Education Today*, Jack Demaine, ed. (New York: Palgrave, 2001), 65–99.

105 Samuel Roundfield Lucas, *Tracking Inequality: Stratification and Mobility in American High Schools* (New York: Teachers College Press, 1999); and Ellen Brantlinger, *Dividing Classes* (New York: Routledge, 2003).

106 Oakes, *Keeping Track*.

107 Muhammad Zubair, Ambreen Alam, and Samir Dukmak. "Harvesting the Crops of Ability Grouping Practice in Schools from the Field of Literature," *Cogent Education*, vol. 10, no. 1 (2023), doi: 10.1080/2331186X.2023.2198478 https://www.tandfonline.com/doi/full/10.1080/2331186X.2023.2198478, (accessed on November 16, 2023).

108 Jodie Hunter, Roberta Hunter, and Glenda Anthony, "Shifting Towards Equity: Challenging Teacher Views About Student Capability in Mathematics," *Mathematics Education Research Journal*, vol. 32 (2020): 37–55, https://doi.org/10.1007/s13394-019-00293-y

109 Anthony Buttaro, Jr. and Sophia Catsambis, "Ability Grouping in the Early Grades: Long-Term Consequences for Educational Equity in the United States," *Teachers College*, vol. 121, no. 2 (2019): 1–50, https://doi.org/10.1177/016146811912100204

110 Corey Webel, Jennifer Woldruff, Katherine Daugherty, Brendan Dames, Leah Lindaman, and Jennifer Brown, "Field-Based Perspectives on Enacting Alternatives to Ability Grouping in Elementary Mathematics Education," *Mathematics Teacher Education and Development*, vol. 23, no. 3 (2021): 111–31, https://files.eric.ed.gov/fulltext/EJ1321121.pdf (accessed on November 19, 2023).

111 James R. Delisle, "Differentiation Doesn't Work. Commentary," *Education Week* (January 6, 2015), https://www.giftedguru.com/wp-content/uploads/2018/03/Differentiation-Doesnt-Work-Education-Week.pdf (accessed on November 26, 2023).

112 Amy Stuart Wells and Irena Serna, "The Politics of Culture: Understanding Local Political Resistance in Racially Mixed Schools," *Harvard Educational Review*, Vol. 66, no. 1 (Spring 1996): 93–118.

4

Race, Ethnicity, and Education

Chapter contents

Chapter objectives

- To better understand the origins of the terms *race* and *ethnicity* and how their meanings have changed over time.
- To explore the impact of race and ethnicity on educational institutions, laws, policies, and practices, both historically and at present.
- To analyze major historical eras related to race and education.
- To describe the educational experiences of various ethnic-racial groups.
- To explore significant philosophical views on the educational implications of race and ethnicity.
- To better understand how leading problems in education are related to social constructs of race.
- To analyze contemporary reform movements addressing race and educational opportunity.

Opening questions

1. Why is it important to understand race, ethnicity, and racism in discussions of contemporary education?
2. How and why has the meaning of the term *race* changed over time?
3. What were some of the major historical developments associated with race, ethnicity, and education?
4. What court cases and policy developments most influenced how race and ethnicity shaped America's schools over time?
5. What are some leading reform efforts addressing inequalities related to race and ethnicity?

The issue

The definition of race is complex and has evolved greatly over time. The American Psychological Association (APA) defines **race** as

> the social construction and categorization of people based on perceived shared physical traits that result in the maintenance of a sociopolitical hierarchy. The term is also loosely applied to geographic, cultural, religious or national groups. The significance often accorded to racial categories might suggest that such groups are objectively defined and homogeneous; however, there is much heterogeneity within categories, and the categories themselves differ across groups and cultures. Moreover, self-reported race frequently varies owing to changing social contexts and an individual's possible identification with more than one race.[1]

The definition's complexity illustrates the difficulty of knowing whether people are using the concept in the same way in discussions of race and racism. Some cling to an idea that race refers to inherited traits, while others wish to dispense of the concept entirely now that geneticists have found there is no biological basis for the racial categories we assign to people.[2] There is a growing body of genetic evidence indicating that all modern human chromosomes contain genetic markers originating in eastern Africa with a female about 150,000 years ago and a male about 59,000 years ago. The descendants of each gradually migrated around the globe to produce the wide variety of peoples we see today. In light of this evidence, the concept of race as discrete human groups originating independently of each other simply makes no sense.[3] Historians have traced the origins of the concept of race to the creation by Europeans of categories used to subjugate African, Native American, Asian, and other people.[4]

Education scholars tend to operate from the belief that, while race and racial categories are social constructions (i.e., created by people, and not objective or inherent), we nevertheless cannot dispense with them, as long as racial inequities need to be redressed. In other words, "race matters," as Cornel West so pointedly put it.[5] For generations after slavery was officially abolished, white Americans maintained white supremacy through Black codes, Jim Crow laws, voting restrictions, intimidation, vigilante public lynchings, segregation, redlining, and other means. As a result, American society to this day is characterized by a racial hierarchy so entrenched that it has been compared to the caste system in India.[6] **Racism** can be defined as a system of advantage based on race or the belief that race is a primary determinant of basic human characteristics and capabilities and that one or more races have inherent superiorities over other races. When the term is being used to describe a *system* of advantage, that system is characterized by unequal access to better schools, housing, jobs, health care, financial security, and social status. People who enjoy advantages may fervently defend them, even when they themselves do not personally affirm racist beliefs or openly exhibit racist attitudes.

Within the United States, white Americans are advantaged on virtually every social indicator, from access to high-quality schools and higher education to health outcomes and life expectancy.[7] This is often referred to as **white privilege**, meaning that whites benefit from this system even when they may personally oppose racism and be disadvantaged along other lines such as class, gender, or disability. Acknowledging this can be painful for many white people, in part due to what psychologists call "belief in a just world"—or the understandable desire to believe we deserve the good things in our lives and that others deserve what they get as well.[8]

The term **ethnicity** is sometimes used interchangeably or in conjunction with race. The APA defines ethnicity as "a characterization of people based on having a shared culture (e.g., language, food, music, dress, values, and beliefs) related to common ancestry and shared history."[9] Because race is also associated with ancestry, ethnicity, and race are intertwined, though they refer to distinct concepts. African Americans (specifically those with multigenerational ancestry in the United States) have been described both as a racial group and an ethnic group, while Hispanic is defined within the US Census as an ethnic group that includes multiple racial groups such as Afro-Latinos and white Hispanics. However, the ambiguous boundaries between the two concepts can be seen in the many terms that conjoin the two, such as "racial/ethnic category," commonly used in health research.[10] Psychologists use the term "ethnic-racial socialization" rather than choose between "ethnic socialization" or "racial socialization," arguing that the latter two terms overlap and are "too broad and nonspecific to be conceptually or empirically useful."[11] Thus, in this book, we also use phrases like "ethnic-racial" to denote individuals' affiliations with ancestral groups.

Ethnic-racial socialization refers to processes through which individuals learn about their ethnic and racial identities, as well as the values, norms, behaviors, and attitudes associated with their ethnic and racial groups. It encompasses the transmission of cultural knowledge, heritage, and experiences from one generation to the next within a particular ethnic or racial community. Racial attitudes and beliefs filter through to students, sometimes from school programs and long-held educational beliefs and traditions but also from sources outside the schools, such as the entertainment industry, other mass media, and even family and community environments. Such influences inevitably affect how students think and act. Consider, for example, how sources in the larger society transmit notions about Black and white communication styles, musical preferences, clothing, and peer associations, and consider also how these are internalized by students and enforced by their peers.

Racial and ethnic inequalities in education are central to understanding schooling in the United States. Although both race and ethnicity intersect significantly with other social identities, such as gender, class, and ability/disability, in this chapter we focus on the roles race and ethnicity specifically have played in the history of education in the United States and contemporary conditions.

> **For Further Reflection:** How do racial identities affect you and your friends and acquaintances? How do racial identities get shaped, and what causal factors in the larger society influence such developments? To what extent are those identities socially based, and to what extent are they matters of individual choice? What impact, if any, has this had on your education?

Historical background

It was not until the European expansion into the Western Hemisphere that a concept of race was developed to differentiate between slave owners and enslaved people. Prior to this, differentiation between groups usually occurred along such lines as religion, ethnicity, geography, and tribal or national identities. If the term *race* was used at all, it was usually in a nationalistic sense, such as "the Spanish race" or "the French race." Beginning with colonial expansion, Europeans' belief in the inherent superiority of people of European descent ("white" people) over all others was used to provide a rationalization for the enslavement of Africans and forced removal of American Indians from their land.

Although slavery was abolished in 1865 and equal protection under the law was guaranteed three years later when the Fourteenth Amendment was ratified, challenges to achieving full equal protection for people of color in the United States persist. Since the beginning of public education in the United States, access and quality have been unequally distributed among white Americans, Black Americans, American Indians, and Hispanic Americans, as well as immigrants, which will be discussed in Chapter 5. Collective struggles for more equal education and opportunities have come from all of these groups and others. The next section will describe inequalities and fights for better education, first among the Black American community, followed by American Indian, Latine American, and Asian American communities.

Education and African Americans

Education during slavery

The system of chattel slavery that would impact American life throughout history and into the present is often traced to the year 1619. This was the year the first recorded enslaved Africans were brought to the English colonies, landing in Point Comfort, near present-day Hampton, VA. Between 1619 and 1776, slavery greatly expanded and became an integral part of the colonial economy. Colonial legislatures began institutionalizing slavery by defining enslaved individuals as property and tying slavery to African descent. Slave codes in Southern colonies severely restricted the rights of enslaved people, including the right to education and even assembly.

During the first half of the nineteenth century, two contradictory views about education existed in American society: one was that a democratic society depended upon having an educated citizenry, and the other was that the education of enslaved people posed a threat to society. At a time when free public schools were appearing in the northern United States, restrictive laws making it a crime to teach enslaved people to read and write were appearing in most of the southern states.[12]

Despite slavery's powerful grip on southern society, it exhibited some profound contradictions that are informative. Some slave owners chose to educate as many as they deemed necessary to conduct their affairs, such as in bookkeeping and other trades that required certain levels of literacy and numeracy. In addition, the children of enslavers often played school with their enslaved playmates, teaching what they were taught. However, the odds against most enslaved people acquiring any formal education were huge. The majority of enslaved people experienced lives of unremitting toil and illiteracy, but this does not mean they placed no value on education. On the contrary, most were eager to have what was denied them, for they saw education as one of the chief benchmarks of freedom and equality.[13]

A few educated Black people received recognition and acceptance during the era of slavery. One was **John Chavis**, a free man who led an extraordinary life as a soldier during the American Revolution, an ordained Presbyterian minister, and a respected teacher who taught both white and free Black students in Raleigh, North Carolina. His work was of such quality that he and his school became widely respected. Following the 1831 slave revolt led by Nat Turner (also an educated Black man), laws restricting the education of Black people were tightened across the South. However, Chavis remained an active educator until his death in 1838. During his life, Chavis taught many students, and while his impact on his Black students is unknown, among his white students were a future US senator and governors of North Carolina and New Mexico.[14]

Growth of schools for Black Southerners during Reconstruction

The Union victory over the Confederacy in 1865 ended the Civil War and toppled the "slavocracy" regimes of the southern states. In relatively quick fashion, the Constitution of the United States had three important amendments added: the Thirteenth Amendment, which abolished slavery (1865); the Fourteenth Amendment, which provided the rights of citizenship and **equal protection of the laws** to all persons born or naturalized in the United States (1868); and the Fifteenth Amendment, which declared that citizenship rights could not be denied or abridged because of race, color, or previous condition of servitude (1870). Despite the Union victory and these constitutional amendments, however, at the time most Black Americans continued to exist as a distinct underclass in which race was the distinguishing factor.

After the war, Congress enacted a series of laws called **Reconstruction**, which lasted from 1865 to 1877, when the last Union troops were withdrawn from the southern states. During Reconstruction, African Americans made significant political and educational gains, such as elective and appointive offices in government and the admission of Black children in relatively high numbers into public schools. During that time, Black people neither achieved full equality with whites nor did all white people readily accept the changes; nevertheless, some progress was made.

One important agency of change was the **Freedmen's Bureau** (officially called the Bureau of Freedmen, Refugees, and Abandoned Lands), which proved to be one of the most important educational developments during Reconstruction. The bureau was established by Congress on March 3, 1865. Originally intended to last only one year, the bureau was extended until 1870, when most of its major functions ended. Among other things, it distributed food to the formerly enslaved, regulated their labor contracts, ensured justice for them in legal matters, and encouraged the development of their churches.

Two obstacles for the Freedmen's Bureau were that it was obviously intended to be of short duration, and it had resources to get schools started, but it had no authority for their long-term operations and eventually had to turn them over to other agencies.

One of the most significant and long-lasting works of the Freedmen's Bureau was the founding and/or support of numerous schools for Black students.[15] As Reconstruction advanced, Black men gained seats in state legislatures and appointments to public boards and administrative posts, from which they were a significant force for public education. A major outcome for both Black and white people was the establishment of statewide public school systems across the South during Reconstruction.[16]

Black people were staunch supporters of the new schools, but after Reconstruction ended, Black schools faced some major hurdles. For example, the main sources of employment for most of the formerly enslaved in the rural South were the plantations and large farms, where they often worked for no pay but rather a small share of the harvest (called **sharecropping**) or the ability to live on the land, though rent was still collected (called **tenant farming).** Both systems, sometimes referred to as "slavery by another name," contributed to the perpetuation of poverty and limited economic opportunities for Black southerners. Many employers opposed education for the formerly enslaved and their children because they feared it would lead them to leave for better work. Some employers actually fired employees whose children attended school. As Southern whites regained control of state governments after Reconstruction, Black schools became grossly underfunded, enrollments fell, and Black people faced increasing restrictions on their recently gained freedoms.[17]

Education in the Jim Crow era

In the late 1880s and early 1890s, an ideology of the **New South** emerged. This was an outlook composed of northern-style industrial capitalism and social reform along with a reaffirmation of white political power. Aristocratic rural interests had dominated politics in the Old South, but now it was a growing urban middle class and emerging industrial interests that were ascendant. In the 1880s, a level of prosperity emerged that promised better funding for education. However, it was short-circuited by an economic recession and the increasingly restrictive racist politics in the 1890s that gave rise to the era of **Jim Crow**, a term used to denote the harsh laws, policies, and attitudes of a white supremacy that redefined the place of Black people in the late nineteenth and early twentieth centuries.[18]

During the Jim Crow era, racial segregation that was formerly nonexistent or simply a matter of custom now became required by law. For example, prior to 1885, no southern state legally required racially segregated railway facilities, but from 1887 to 1891, at least eight states enacted such laws. With its ruling in ***Plessy v. Ferguson* (1896)**, the US Supreme Court gave constitutional approval for state laws requiring racial segregation if the separate accommodations were equal. In effect, *Plessy* provided constitutional cover for legalized racial segregation throughout the country, having perhaps its greatest impact in those states wishing to erect **dual school systems**, one for Black students and one for white students. Although the terminology in the law was "**separate but equal**," racially segregated schools were never equal in terms of funding, resources, or public opinion.

Not all southern whites opposed the equal protection of the laws and full rights of citizenship for Black people. In an 1889 book titled *The Prosperity of the South Dependent upon the Elevation of the Negro*, a merchant named Lewis Blair from Richmond, Virginia, argued that Black equality was an economic necessity for the prosperity of all. As it turned out, Blair's words proved prophetic, but he faced such social ostracism from his peers that he recanted and embraced a more orthodox view. Advocates could also be found in other states, such as Robert Flournoy in Mississippi, but their examples were few, and the scornful intimidation they received from their own social circles helped Jim Crow tighten its grip.[19]

Debates over the aims of education for Black Americans

Once the fetters of slavery were removed, most Black Americans embraced the hope that education would be the great equalizer of society. There were disagreements, however, over what kind of education should be available and to what effect. This is illustrated in the views of **Booker T. Washington** and **W. E. B. Du Bois**, two prominent educators who struggled in difficult times to shape the condition of African Americans through education.

Booker Taliaferro Washington was born enslaved in 1856 on a farm in Franklin County, Virginia. After gaining freedom in 1865, the family moved to Malden, West Virginia, where they eked out a living in the nearby salt furnaces and coal mines.[20] Though Washington received lessons from the mine owner's wife and attended school part time, the most important educational influence on Washington was probably Samuel Chapman Armstrong, the founder of Hampton Institute in Virginia. The Institute reflected Armstrong's **paternalistic**

Figure 4.1 Monroe Elementary School, a segregated school in Topeka, Kansas, 1949.

belief that Black people needed industrial education, meaning an education in the virtues of industriousness, thrift, and self-sufficiency, as much if not more than academic and technical/industrial understanding. After attending Hampton Institute and later serving as a postgraduate student and teacher there, Washington was the head of **Tuskegee Institute** (now Tuskegee University) until his death in 1915. Washington expanded Tuskegee from a normal school specializing in teacher education to a school for agriculture, mechanics and trades, domestic science, nursing, music, and Bible training.

Washington believed that the most immediate goal for Black people should be economic self-sufficiency.[21] While most Black people expected education to help lift them out of their unrelenting poverty, Washington was convinced that hard work and economic uplift would help Black people survive in the South's social system. With his pleasing personality and tireless capacity for work, Washington assuaged white fears while building Tuskegee into arguably the most influential Black institution of the time, but his pathway was precarious. He was dedicated to the advancement of Black people, but he had to avoid antagonizing a white power structure that could close Tuskegee at any time. As Washington saw it, insistence on social and political equality only served to inflame white reaction, so Black people needed to focus first on their own economic uplift through diligent work and through educational development in such institutions as Tuskegee.[22]

For Further Reflection: Throughout much of human history, the upper portion of society received a formal academic education, while the lower classes, if they received anything more than on-the-job training, got some sort of vocational training. What was Washington's rationale for "industrial education"? Were his objectives primarily vocational, or did he have additional objectives? If politics is "the art of the possible," was Washington simply trying to get what was possible for his people under very trying political conditions, or was he being too cautious and conservative?

Some Black leaders came to view Washington's concessions to white power as a hindrance to Black advancement. The most prominent of these critics was William Edward Burghardt (W.E.B.) Du Bois. Du Bois was born on February 23, 1868, in Great Barrington, Massachusetts. His childhood playmates were mostly white, and along with them he attended the local public schools where he was a high achiever. In 1888, he graduated from Fisk University in Nashville, Tennessee, and then taught briefly in a nearby rural school where he observed the grinding poverty so many Black people endured in the rural South. That same year, he was admitted to Harvard University, where he received a BA in 1890, an MA in 1891, and a PhD in 1895. After teaching at several colleges, Du Bois became a professor at Atlanta University (now Clark Atlanta University), where his sociological studies established his reputation as a scholar and where he gained widespread recognition as a leading Black intellectual. He was one of the cofounders of the **National Association for the Advancement of Colored People (NAACP)** in 1910 and served for many years as the editor of *The Crisis*, its official publication. He moved to Ghana and became a citizen in 1963, then died shortly thereafter at age 95.[23]

Du Bois consistently argued for three democratic principles: the right to vote, civic equality, and the right to educational opportunity. He opposed Washington not for his industrial education model, but for his views on Black higher education and his failure to push the importance of equality and voting rights. Du Bois suspected that financial aid for Tuskegee from northern industrialists was proffered mainly in hopes of cultivating cheap, nonunion Black labor as a hedge against pro-union white labor in the South. Such donors did not want liberally educated Black college graduates who could raise troublesome questions about race, labor, and wages.[24]

Du Bois strongly advocated higher liberal education for the able few, the so-called **Talented Tenth**, to provide much-needed Black leaders. He believed that the Talented Tenth would then extend democracy and promote racial solidarity. Over time, however, it became clear to him that in the competitive economic climate of the time, graduates of the Black liberal arts colleges behaved little differently from their white counterparts in advancing their own self-interests. He became disillusioned with the Talented Tenth idea and, by 1938, was calling for "the perfection of the Negro elementary school" as the essential issue deserving attention. Although he never repudiated his belief in the value of liberal higher education, by the 1950s, he expressed disappointment with Black intellectuals and maintained that true leaders must come from intelligent members of the Black working class.[25]

In sum, both Washington and Du Bois were strong advocates of educational opportunity and full citizenship rights for Black people, but each came from a different perspective and with a different timetable in mind. Washington's aim was long-term, but perhaps he compromised too much with the white power structure. Du Bois wanted more immediate change, but he put his faith in developing Black intellectuals, a plan that failed to exert the socially conscious leadership he envisioned. Both men saw education as a producer of good citizens and as a social equalizer, but in the end had their hopes frustrated by the entrenched nature of racism.

> **For Further Reflection:** Compare and contrast Washington and Du Bois. Do you think either man "won" the debate, considering how things actually turned out? Justify your position with evidence and argument.

Education for Black Americans in the early twentieth century

In the early 1900s, a reform movement in the South aimed to improve public education, driven by northern industrialist-philanthropists and southern educator-reformers. This movement expanded schools for Black children, though the schools and teachers were woefully underfunded in comparison with

Figure 4.2 Law graduating class at Howard University, Washington, D.C., ca. 1900.

their white counterparts. In the early 1900s, a popular myth circulated among whites that Blacks paid so little in taxes that the costs of their schools largely fell on white taxpayers. This myth encouraged many white taxpayers to support reduced funding for Black schools. However, a study of North Carolina's school tax collections and allocations for the 1905–6 school year found that Black schools actually received less state funding than what was collected from Black taxpayers for schools.[26] Under such conditions, Black citizens had to develop private ways of financing their schools. This is what is meant by **double taxation**, for not only did Black people pay their lawful taxes, and not only were they denied their legitimate share of school funds, but they had to "tax" themselves again through their own private contributions and efforts.

These kinds of conditions continued until the mid-century. Per pupil expenditures in the South in 1945 were twice as high for white children as for Black children, and four times as much was invested for the construction and upkeep of white schools as for Black schools. Salaries for white teachers were 30 percent higher than for Black teachers, and only a fraction of the transportation cost spent on white children was spent on Black children.[27]

School desegregation

With the passage of time, it became clear to many observers that the "separate but equal" doctrine established in *Plessy v. Ferguson* only produced unequal schools. The NAACP began an all-out effort to end segregation, and they chose to challenge the constitutionality of racially segregated public schools. Prior lawsuits had slowly chipped away at *Plessy*, with lower-court rulings that pushed states to provide more equitable facilities for Black and white alike. None of those rulings were definitive, but their constitutional implications helped NAACP lawyers build a better legal foundation for **desegregation** leading up to the landmark US Supreme Court case ***Brown v. Board of Education*** **(1954)**.

Linda Brown, the lead plaintiff in the case, sued for access to a nearby white school rather than having to cross railroad tracks and walk to a distant Black school. Her case was consolidated with three similar cases from other states, all involving Black children who, because of their race, were denied admission to their nearest local public school. The argument was that segregated schooling was not and could not be equal, and it denied students the equal protection of the laws as guaranteed by the Constitution's Fourteenth Amendment. In a unanimous (9-0) decision, the Supreme Court concluded that, "in the field of public education the doctrine of 'separate but equal' has no place. Therefore, we hold that the plaintiffs ... are ... deprived of the equal protection of the laws guaranteed by the Fourteenth Amendment."[28]

Brown failed to state how soon desegregation should begin, and it provided no guidance on legally acceptable desegregation measures. Thus, on May 31, 1955, the Court reconvened to consider implementation measures (sometimes called ***Brown II***), but it only said that school desegregation must occur with "all deliberate speed." Providing no deadlines or guidance for state and local school authorities, the court simply made federal district courts responsible for implementation.[29]

One result was that some school districts desegregated soon afterward, while others delayed as long as possible. Ten years after the *Brown* decision, just 2 percent of Black students in the South attended majority-white schools.[30] Political leaders in Virginia launched a campaign of **massive resistance** to circumvent *Brown* with state legislation to close any public schools that desegregated. The most extreme example of resistance was in Prince Edward County, Virginia, which closed its entire county public school system for five years to avoid desegregation. Ultimately, Virginia's own Supreme Court of Appeals declared the legislation in violation of the Virginia Constitution, which required the state to provide free public schools.[31]

In *Swann v. Charlotte-Mecklenburg Board of Education* (1972), the Supreme Court ruled that constructing new schools in more strategic locations, rearranging attendance zones, and using transportation capacities such as busing could be effective tools of desegregation.[32] Busing helped desegregate schools in many communities, but the efficacy of cross-district busing came under increasing scrutiny. In part, this was due to the reemergence of political conservatism at the national level in the 1980s, with school desegregation not among the priorities. It was also due to changing demographics, with racial minorities becoming concentrated in urban areas as the white middle class relocated to suburbia. By the end of the 1980s, court-ordered busing was being abandoned by federal district courts, sometimes by the same judges who ordered it in the early 1970s.[33]

Suggested Activity: Research the racial demographics of at least five schools in your state. If possible, include schools in urban, suburban, and rural communities. To what degree would you say racial segregation is still an issue in these schools? If applicable, research the degree to which policy makers in your area have attempted to desegregate schools and the impacts of these attempts on school demographics.

Figure 4.3 Deputy US Marshals escort Ruby Bridges to and from school in 1960, while segregationist protests continued.

Education and American Indians

The education of American Indians, following the arrival of Christopher Columbus in 1492, has been described as:

> a battle for the hearts and minds of Indigenous nations; (2) a colonial call for assimilation; and (3) a responsibility of the federal government arising from a series of agreements between Indian nations and the United States meant to open up land bases to a burgeoning immigrant population. In short, the education of Indigenous peoples is intricately intertwined with the legal/political relationship between Indigenous peoples and the U.S. government, as well as myriad racist policies and practices that have devastated Indian children and communities.[34]

American Indians represent more than 560 federally recognized tribes, and members of these tribes are citizens of both the United States and their specific tribe. Historically, Indigenous people in the United States have not sought inclusion in the same ways as other marginalized groups but rather asserted their right to maintain their tribal sovereignty.[35] No one knows exactly how many Indigenous people were present in 1492, but their population clearly shrank to a historic low in the 1890s, from which many feared they could not recover. A century later, however, the 1990 census reported approximately 1,937,000 American Indians in at least 556 recognized tribal entities, with names that reach across time: Apache, Cherokee, Cheyenne, Choctaw, Iroquois, Navaho, Seminole, Sioux, and Shoshone, to name a few. In 2000, the Census Bureau combined the population count of both the American Indian and Alaska Native (AIAN) into one population category (AIAN), which then stood at approximately 2.66 million persons. By 2022, the AIAN population estimate was approximately 4.3 million.[36]

American Indian education before 1492

Prior to the arrival of Europeans, American Indian youth learned their tribe's way of life from their elders, from tribal lore and legends, and from observation and participation in daily life. A glimpse into this process may be seen in the oral traditions of the Catawbas, a small tribe in the Catawba River valley along the border of the Carolinas. The Catawbas believed that stories developed children's minds and showed them how to live. Oral traditions were passed down through generations, with stories about tribal adventures, trials, and triumphs, and with children taken to old town sites, battlefields, and other locales to drive home the lessons. There were also stories about nature and the spirit world: how the chipmunk got its stripes and the robin its red breast, what caused storms or cured disease, or what pleased or displeased the spirit world.[37]

Education after 1492: Cherokee education as an example

The Cherokees were a large, powerful tribe in the Appalachian highlands stretching from Georgia to Kentucky. Around 1820, a Cherokee named **Sequoyah** encountered printed English books and became convinced that a writing system was possible for the Cherokee language as well. He developed a system of eighty-six abstract symbols representing the syllable sounds of the Cherokee language (called a syllabet). In 1821, the Cherokee Council (the Cherokee governing body) officially adopted the writing system Sequoyah provided, and its use can be seen in the Cherokee translation of the Bible in 1825, a Cherokee constitution in 1827, and the newspaper *Cherokee Phoenix*, which began publication in 1828. Today, the Cherokee people hold Sequoyah in high regard, and his syllabary occupies an honored position in Cherokee cultural and educational traditions. Furthermore, his statue in the US Capitol and the giant redwood tree named after him (the sequoia) serve to commemorate his work.[38]

Christian missionaries attempted to assimilate Cherokees and other American Indian tribes into European religion and culture. Cherokee society became divided between those who accepted Christianity and schooling (about 25 percent of the population) and those who remained committed to traditional tribal ways (about 75 percent of the population). Among the missionaries sent to the Cherokee homeland was the father-son team of Evan and John B. Jones, who sympathized with the traditionalists and went with the tribe to Oklahoma in 1838. When the Cherokee Council established a public school system in 1841, the Joneses championed bilingual education, but it was not until 1866 that the younger Jones was authorized to write bilingual textbooks; thus, the Cherokees developed the first bilingual and bicultural school system in the United States. By the end of the nineteenth century, most Cherokees were better educated than many white Oklahoma neighbors. The Cherokee school system remained in operation until tribal control dissolved with the creation of the state of Oklahoma in 1907, at which time Cherokee children began attending that new state's public schools.[39]

National policy and American Indian education

Where education was a part of national policy concerning American Indians, it was viewed as a way to **acculturate** them to Euro-American ways. In 1879,

Figure 4.4 Group of Omaha boys in cadet uniforms, Carlisle Indian School, Pennsylvania, 1880.

Richard Henry Pratt established the first Bureau of Indian Affairs (BIA) off-reservation boarding school, the most infamous of which was the **Carlisle Indian School** in Pennsylvania. The purpose of these schools was to isolate students from tribal influences and "to educate the Indian out of them." Children were forcibly removed from their families and communities, leading to the loss of cultural identity and intergenerational trauma. Once a child entered the school, Americanization started with baths, haircuts, uniforms, military discipline, English names, and English-only language enforcement. Rigid rules, strict discipline, and homesick students produced runaways and anguished parents. Children were often physically, emotionally, and sexually abused, with many dying as a result.[40]

In the 1930s, reforms by both the Hoover and Roosevelt administrations brought changes, such as reservation community schools, cross-cultural education in both tribal and outside cultures, Indian art and culture in the schools, and better Indian access to and federal funding for public schools that accepted Indian students. Unfortunately, the economic realities of the Great Depression hampered those reforms, and the Second World War brought them to a standstill.[41]

During the war, American Indians provided valuable military service to the country, and some policy makers wanted to give them greater independence as American citizens. Afterward, however, the onset of the Cold War drew public focus onto international affairs, and the BIA fell back on the Americanization track, with vocational education and job-training programs to move people off reservations into urban job markets. That policy weakened the previous reforms, and movement off the reservations threatened tribal cultures and properties. In the 1960s, a new generation of activist leaders arose, aided by such organizations as the National Congress of American Indians (NCAI) and the American Indian Movement (AIM), and they helped redirect Indian education through the remainder of the twentieth century.[42] Congress passed the Indian Education Act of 1972 with funds stipulated for community-based schools and bilingual and culturally relevant curriculum materials, and the **Indian Self-Determination and Education Assistance Act of 1975** allowed the BIA to make contracts with tribal governments to run their own schools, giving them greater control over curriculum, instruction, and school management. Federal government presence continues through the BIA and its Bureau of Indian Education (BIE).

Federal government presence continues through the BIA and its BIE. The BIE funds 183 elementary and secondary schools located on 64 reservations in 23 states. The BIE also provides support for tribal colleges and universities and directly operates two of them, the Haskell Indian Nations University in Lawrence, Kansas, and the Southwest Indian Polytechnic Institute in Albuquerque, New Mexico.[43] Despite these positive developments, issues such as inadequate funding, low graduation rates, and limited access to quality education resources continue to affect Indigenous communities.[44]

Education and Latine Americans

The largest ethnic-racial minority group in the United States is the Hispanic group at $6.2 million, or 18.9 percent of the population, according to 2020 Census data.[45] However, the label Hispanic has shifted in definition over time, and many prefer the category of Latino/a/e over Hispanic—though the two terms are not fully interchangeable. Note also that the Census asks about race separately from this question, considering Hispanic to be an ethnic origin, not a racial category. Much debate surrounds this delineation, however.[46]

The Census Bureau defines Hispanic as "a person of Cuban, Mexican, Puerto Rican, South or Central American, or other Spanish culture or origin regardless of race." It is important to note that not all people from these countries necessarily trace their origins to Spanish culture. Individuals with Indigenous roots, for example, might instead identify as Latine (also sometimes Latinx), which is a gender-inclusive variation of Latino/Latina and generally includes any person of Latin American descent. This would include, for instance, Brazilians—who typically speak Portuguese rather than Spanish. Alternatively, someone from Spain would be defined by the Census as Hispanic but not Latine because they have Spanish—but not Latin American—origins.

However, how people choose to identify themselves can differ from the boxes the Census offers as choices. A Pew Research survey found that about half of those who identify as Hispanic most often prefer to describe themselves by their country of heritage, using terms such as "Mexican," "Cuban," or "Salvadoran" rather than "Hispanic" or "Latino." Another 23 percent prefer to describe themselves as American, and the remaining 23 percent use the label of Hispanic or Latino. However, these numbers vary across groups. First-generation immigrant Latinos most often use their country of origin, whereas the proportion using "American" to describe themselves rises in the second and third generations. Moreover, some Americans with Hispanic ancestry do not identify as Hispanic for various reasons, such as viewing their Hispanic ancestry as too distant or having no link to Hispanic relatives or culture.[47]

Further complicating matters, separating race and ethnicity is not always simple or desirable. For example, 2 percent of adults in the United States identify as Afro-Latino, and not all of these also identify as Hispanic or Latino. Fifteen times as many enslaved people from Africa were taken to Spanish and Portuguese colonies than to the United States; about a quarter of the population of Latin America is of African descent.[48] In short, ethnic and racial demographics in the United States are much more complex than they may appear in government or research reports, in part because of potential contradictions between how people choose to identify and how others identify them (i.e., their subscribed vs. ascribed ethnic-racial group).

As a whole, students of Hispanic or Latin American descent tend to graduate at lower rates (83 percent) than their white and Asian American counterparts (90 and 93 percent, respectively),[49] and this disparity is generally attributed to inequitable school funding and opportunities afforded to this group. The following section will use the case of Mexican Americans to illustrate the history of discrimination, segregation, and other inequities that are necessary to understand current educational injustices for this group. Although this history is unique to Mexican Americans, the discrimination and **deficit ideologies** they faced—and continue to face—are unfortunately common experiences among members of other Latine subgroups as well.

For Further Reflection: It is potentially misleading to make generalizations involving large numbers of people; however, academic disciplines such as sociology and anthropology are dependent on research-based generalizations intended to capture significant group characteristics. Without such generalizations, the social sciences could not exist, and many social phenomena might be perceived as coincidental and go unexamined. Think about this dilemma. How can one make sense of society without generalizations? How does one avoid the trap of inappropriate generalizations?

Education and Mexican Americans as an example

Whereas the current societal status of African Americans is rooted in slavery and the status of American Indians is rooted in conquest, the status of Mexican Americans (also sometimes referred to as Chicanos) is rooted in conquest and colonization. Spain's conquest of present-day Mexico began in the 1500s and later expanded into present-day Texas, New Mexico, Arizona, and California. Mexico gained independence from Spain in 1821, but expansionism in the newly formed United States quickly led to the loss of much of its territory. The Mexican-American War (1846–8) resulted in the signing of the Treaty of Guadalupe Hidalgo in 1848, which ceded a significant portion of Mexican territory, including California, Texas, Arizona, New Mexico, Nevada, Utah, and parts of Colorado, Wyoming, Kansas, and Oklahoma, to the United States. Mexicans who remained in the newly acquired territory had to decide whether to maintain their Mexican citizenship or become American citizens. Most chose the latter, thus becoming the first Mexican Americans. The treaty also obligated the United States to protect its new citizens' rights, such as ensuring the retention of their language, religion, customs, and property claims; however, many of them saw their status reduced rather than enhanced.[50]

The descendants of these first Mexican Americans would eventually be joined by many others in search of jobs and economic improvement during the early twentieth century. Most were unskilled laborers, but some were members of the middle class fleeing the Mexican Revolution of 1910. Generally, stereotyping and prejudice made it difficult for Mexican Americans to move up socially and economically. Mexican immigrants were exploited as cheap labor in the factories and fields, but during the Great Depression of the 1930s, they were often viewed as unfair competition to native-born American laborers. The federal government deported Mexican workers in the 1930s to free up jobs for unemployed American workers, but when production increased during the Second World War, the government once again recruited Mexican agricultural workers as short-term emergency labor. This "bracero program" actually continued until 1964 and involved a sizable labor pool, but American growers controlled workers' wages and prevented them from organizing to improve working conditions. When the bracero program ended, however, the migration of Mexican job seekers did not. Some of them resided in Mexico and daily commuted to work in the United States on work permits called green cards. Others were migrant farmworkers who legally entered the United States on short-term work permits during harvest seasons.

Suggested Activity: Many countries recruit foreign workers in times of labor shortages but tend to expose them to much discrimination. Read about so-called guest workers in Germany, for example. Consider how such foreign labor policies come about and what implications those policies might have for the workers' families, in particular their children.

In many respects, the history of Mexican American schooling during the first half of the twentieth century was one of segregation. Most Mexican American children were placed in segregated classrooms or schools, similar to what African American children experienced, but the segregation Mexican Americans faced was more often based on language and cultural differences than physical attributes. One consequence of segregated and unequal schools was an extraordinarily high dropout rate. For example, during the 1930s, there were few Mexican American students attending California high schools, and those who did were often tracked into vocational education programs, boys for manual labor and girls for domestic work. **Culturally biased testing** bolstered the tracking system, with test scores used to justify placement decisions. A disproportionate number of Mexican American students were thus separated from their non-Mexican peers and denied equal access to academic programs, particularly the children of migrant farmworkers who, following the cycle of harvests, could not remain in a given school very long. They had to attend schools operating on shortened days and terms, or they were simply denied access on the claim that their frequent moves created problems for the schools. Sometimes, school boards collaborated with local agricultural and business interests to ensure the availability of sufficient hands during harvests. Mexican migrant workers were easily exploited as cheap labor, and, if considered at all, the children's education was a secondary concern.[51]

For Mexican Americans who were a permanent part of the American population, policy makers embraced an Americanization approach. In the southwestern United States, the Americanization of Mexican Americans was particularly emphasized because of their significant numbers and because policy makers assumed that their cultural backgrounds were inferior and in need of "cultural illumination." As the Los Angeles superintendent of schools put it in 1923, "if we Americanize them, we can live with them." Such views reflected a common sentiment of the time that "the American way" was the only right way. Colleges and universities instituted courses to prepare teachers to deal with the special problems that children of Mexican origin were thought to have. Teachers were to encourage the children to substitute "desirable" traits for "undesirable" ones, such as the use of English, not Spanish, in school. In effect, the policy was to replace Mexican culture with the norms and values of Anglo-American society.[52]

Organizations such as the League of United Latin American Citizens (LULAC) and the American GI Forum (AGIF) helped combat the rising discrimination against Mexican Americans. In education, lawsuits were brought not only against segregated schools but also against tracking and ability grouping practices that denied equal educational opportunity. Many participants hoped that the 1946 court decision in *Mendez v. Westminster School District* (1946) would end legal school segregation for Mexican American students in California, but the court decision was circumvented by local school districts that used such evasive practices as school choice plans and the classification of students by ability.[53]

The situation was aggravated by some of the arguments advanced by LULAC and AGIF that Mexican Americans were, if not "Caucasian," then at least "other white." Local school districts used the other white argument to "desegregate" the schools simply by mixing African American and Mexican American students, claiming they had desegregated the schools while they also still maintained exclusive schools in white neighborhoods. In the 1960s and 1970s, however, the Mexican American "other white" argument changed to the "equal protection of the laws" strategy so successfully used by African Americans in their desegregation cases. Thus, in *Cisneros v. Corpus Christi Independent School District* (1972), the California court ruled that Mexican Americans were an identifiable ethnic minority group. The 1954 *Brown* decision, with its legal obligation to desegregate African American students, was now applied to

Mexican Americans as well. In ***Keyes v. School District No. 1, Denver, Colorado* (1973)**, the US Supreme Court held that Hispanic students in Denver experienced difficulties similar to African American students because both faced educational inequalities when compared to the majority of white students. Moreover, since Denver school authorities historically manipulated policies and rules in order to have racially and ethnically segregated schools, the entire school district must be desegregated.

Despite these important legal successes, however, desegregation proceeded slowly for Mexican Americans, with de facto segregation actually increasing in some locales between the 1960s and 1980s. Moreover, schools serving largely Mexican American students tended to be overcrowded, dilapidated, and staffed by underqualified teachers. This was the case in the schools of East Los Angeles, California, which was 75 percent Latine, where a student walkout protested these conditions. **Sal Castro**, a Mexican American social studies teacher in the district, organized students in requesting better conditions from school administrators. When their requests went unanswered, the students organized a walkout that ultimately led to between 15,000 and 20,000 students across multiple schools leaving class in protest. Parents and community members attended in support as well.[54] Overall, educational justice efforts made by Mexican Americans and others helped change old patterns of educational discrimination, but equal educational opportunity for Mexican American students still remained elusive.[55]

Suggested Activity: View and discuss the HBO feature film *Walkout,* which profiles the 1968 walkouts, also referred to as the East L.A. Blowouts.

For Further Reflection: What similarities and differences do you notice between the struggle for educational justice for African Americans and for Mexican Americans throughout US history? How might these two struggles have influenced one another?

Education and Asian Americans

Asian Americans have a long history in the United States, with some Chinese and Filipino individuals arriving as early as the 1500s, and Asian Americans as a whole constituting a significant portion of the population since the mid-nineteenth century.[56] Today, the proportion of the population that identifies as Asian American is growing significantly, having nearly doubled between 2000 and 2019. This population is very diverse, tracing roots to over two dozen countries and including new immigrants as well as many with long-standing and deep histories in the country.[57] Beginning in the mid-nineteenth century, when young men from Southern China were recruited as contract laborers, Asian Americans have played a crucial role in the development of the United States through farming, mining, and railroad and factory work.[58]

The Asian American and Pacific Islander (AAPI) group includes, among others, the following American ethnic groups: Asian Indian, Burmese, Chinese, Filipino, Indonesian, Japanese, Korean, Lao, Malaysian, Maldivian, Native Hawaiian, Nepalese, Okinawan, Pakistani, Singaporean, Samoan, Taiwanese, Thai, and Vietnamese. In spite of significant differences in languages, nationalities, and cultures, Asian American groups have often been lumped together and faced similar challenges related to discrimination and inequitable schooling.[59] The next section describes the history of education for Chinese and Japanese Americans to illustrate some of these issues.

Education of Chinese and Japanese Americans as examples

Today, Chinese Americans are the largest Asian origin group in the United States, making up about 24 percent of the Asian American population, with Indian Americans and Filipinos representing the second and third largest (21 percent and 19 percent, respectively). Japanese Americans make up 7 percent of the Asian American population, with Vietnamese and Korean communities being slightly higher at 10 and 9 percent, respectively.

Anti-Asian discrimination has led to Chinese and Japanese children being barred from schools at various points throughout US history. For example, in the 1880s, Chinese students were refused admission to the San Francisco public schools, and the parents of Mamie Tape took the issue to court in ***Tape v. Hurley* (1885)**. The California State Supreme Court ruled that Chinese children could not be excluded from public schools, but the San Francisco school board evaded the court's decision by establishing the segregated Oriental Public School. The school grew in enrollment but employed few Chinese or bilingual teachers. Although the school proved ineffective in teaching English, students were forbidden to speak their native language in the school or on the playground.[60] Nevertheless, this case helped pave the way for future challenges and serves as an illustration of the ways in which Asian Americans fought for educational justice as early as the nineteenth century.

Amid the anti-Japanese fear and suspicion of the Second World War, President Roosevelt forced virtually all of the 120,000 Japanese Americans living in the United States into internment camps. About two-thirds were citizens born in the United States. A 23-year-old Japanese American citizen named **Fred Korematsu** challenged the constitutionality of Roosevelt's order. However, the Supreme Court ruled in *Korematsu v. United States* (1944) that the detention was a "military necessity" and not based on race. Although a US District Court judge overturned the decision in 1983, the Supreme Court ruling still stands as precedent.[61] Korematsu went on to lobby for reparations, ultimately leading the US government, in 1988, to compensate $20,000 to each surviving Japanese American who was incarcerated. President Bill Clinton awarded Korematsu the Presidential Medal of Freedom in 1998. This medal is the nation's highest civilian honor.[62] Through struggles for equality and civil rights such as these, Asian Americans have expanded democracy in the United States and recognition that American identities extend beyond white and Black.[63] Education scholars have advocated for greater inclusion of this history in school curriculum to increase awareness of the contributions Asian Americans have made to the United States.[64]

One of the other aims of scholars over the last several decades has been to dispel the **model minority myth.** This is the commonly held stereotype that Asian Americans are smarter, more polite, or otherwise more capable students than those from other ethnic or racial backgrounds. Though this may seem to be a positive assumption, like all stereotypes, it can be harmful in many ways. It ignores the individuality of Asian Americans and diversity within the group, obscures the history of discrimination they have endured, and reinforces other harmful stereotypes, such as Asian Americans as perpetual foreigners.[65]

Historical efforts to address racial and ethnic inequities in education

As long as there have been racial and ethnic inequities in education in the United States, there have been individuals and groups, some famous and many not, who have struggled for educational justice. Booker T. Washington, W.E.B. DuBois, Sal Castro, and the families behind the court cases described in the prior sections all contributed to a gradual expansion of education to more Americans. Important figures in this movement include Carter G. Woodson, James Banks, Geneva Gay, Sonia Nieto, Gloria Ladson-Billings, and others—each of whom increased public awareness of the unequal opportunities afforded to students from ethno-racially minoritized groups and offered concrete ideas to equalize education in the United States.

Ethnic studies, Afrocentric and multicultural education

Ethnic studies refers to the interdisciplinary study of the experiences and contributions of people of color, with emphasis on social movements and historical struggles, US colonialism, the construction of race and racism, and critical examinations of knowledge and power.[66] Its roots can be traced back to such works as Charles C. Wesley's (1922) *The Negro in Our History* and **Carter G. Woodson's** (1933) *The Mis-Education of the Negro*, which were among the first texts to call for greater inclusion of Black history in school curriculum. These scholars argued that the inclusion only of European history caused emotional and psychological distress for Black children and robbed them of knowledge of their own people.[67] Woodson also started Negro History Week, which would later evolve into African American History Month.

During the postwar economic boom of the 1940s and 1950s, many Black and Mexican Americans moved to northern and western cities for newly created jobs. This resulted in racial tensions that prompted the intergroup or **intercultural education movement**. As part of this movement, leading social scientists of the day developed theories about the types of instruction that could promote interracial harmony and cooperation and a shared, common culture. For example, Allport's 1954 study, *The Nature of Prejudice*, posited that harmony required interracial contact characterized by four conditions: (a) equal status, (b) common goals, (c) intergroup cooperation, and (d) the support of authorities. The intercultural education movement differed from the early ethnic studies movement of Carter G. Woodson and others in that only the latter attended to issues of power and structural inequality and aimed for ethnic empowerment.[68] In addition, most of the leaders of the intercultural education movement were white, while most of the leaders of the early ethnic studies movement were people of color.

By the 1960s, many African Americans were becoming impatient with the limited progress of desegregation and began advocating instead for separatism, Black power, and Black studies in colleges and schools. Parallel goals began to emerge among Puerto Ricans, Mexican Americans, American Indians, and Asian Americans. Books examining institutionalized discrimination against specific groups were published and widely read, such as *The Story of the Chinese in America* by Betty Lee Sung (1967), *Custer Died for Your Sins: An Indian*

Manifesto by Vine Deloria, Jr. (1969), and *Occupied America: The Chicano's Struggle toward Liberation* by Rudy Acuña (1972). Women's rights and LGBTQ+ groups joined the efforts to diversify the curriculum and educational leadership. Colleges and universities began offering ethnic studies courses and programs.[69]

In the 1970s, a number of scholars and organizations began questioning the Eurocentric curriculum in schools and teacher education. This marked the beginning of the **multicultural education movement**. Leaders of the movement tended to be scholars working in ethnic studies programs as well as teacher education. These scholars began challenging long-held dominant curricular narratives, such as the idea that the American West was empty land to which European settlers brought civilization and that enslaved people were contented and well cared for. Professional organizations for teachers began publishing curricular guidelines for teaching ethnic studies and multiethnic education. Textbook publishers also began to address omissions and stereotypes.[70]

Many attempts to diversify the curriculum were superficial, for instance, sprinkling into lessons a few token heroes of a particular group rather than questioning dominant perspectives on history. Leaders of multicultural education, such as James Banks, Carl Grant, Christine Sleeter, Geneva Gay, and Sonia Nieto, pushed for deeper, more comprehensive reforms to the entire institution of schooling, including tracking, testing, school funding formulas, discriminatory discipline practices, hiring, and others.

Still others, beginning in the 1960s, argued for **Afrocentric education**. Afrocentric education involves an African-centered pedagogy that recognizes the place of Indigenous languages and fosters individual ties and services to family, community, nation, race, and world. A major goal of Afrocentric education was to infuse the African legacy into social and political change. It was concerned with Africans and people of African origins speaking for themselves rather than having their experiences analyzed only from a Western or Eurocentric view. It emphasized "other ways of knowing" than just the accepted concepts of Western thought; instead, Afrocentric thinkers linked knowledge with cosmology, society, religion, medicine, and tradition to arrive at "intellectual wholeness." An Afrocentric view of literature and orature (oral traditions and stories) differs from the Western view because the Afrocentric writer or speaker seeks peace, balance, and harmony among disparate views. As advocates saw it, African Americans need to be understood in terms of African history, and Africans must be posited as subjects rather than objects of human history. In order to do this, Western cultural and scientific paradigms need to be questioned as the only true or valid approaches to any kind of study.[71]

Afrocentricity as a pedagogical approach fostered both cultural continuity and critical consciousness, a major goal of which is to help Black American students overcome the "double consciousness" described by W.E.B. Du Bois, that is, Black people having to view themselves as individuals and as stereotyped images projected by others. The pedagogy focused on African American cultural conventions, speech patterns, storytelling schemas, and traditions of play in order to teach literacy, numeracy, and other subjects more effectively. Children's ways of thinking and knowing were used as cognitive scaffolding to provide a structural basis for teaching.[72]

The Afrocentric idea was met with criticism. Opponents such as African scholar Kwame Anthony Appiah argued that Afrocentricity makes the same error that Eurocentricity did in viewing all cultures outside of itself as inferior and that it ignores that all human understandings of the world are limited in some ways.[73] Conservative white critics challenged Afrocentricity on the grounds that it distorted history and fragmented and divided the nation. Proponents countered that the goal was actually "to unite the country based on mutual respect for the cultural agency of all its peoples."[74]

Critical race theory and applications to education

Many approaches to improving racial equity in schools, including ethnic studies and multicultural education, have been influenced by **critical race theory (CRT)**. CRT has its origins in critical legal studies. Legal scholars in the 1970s and 1980s observed that the new legislation of the civil rights movement had not achieved its intended effects of eradicating racism from policies and institutions. It became clear that something else was going on that could not be solved through legislation and litigation alone, and the existing social theories were inadequate to explain it. Social theories being used at the time, for example, Marxism and post-Marxism, failed to adequately explain the persistence and ubiquitousness of racism as an oppressive force that cannot be explained by, much less reduced to, class oppression (see Chapter 3 for a description of Marxism and its analysis of social class).[75]

CRT scholars have both theorized race and provided tools that can be used to understand how racism continues to operate in society as well as in particular social institutions, such as schools, despite the legal gains achieved during the civil rights movement. Their work builds on the intellectual contributions of W.E.B. DuBois and Carter G. Woodson described earlier in this chapter. One tenet of CRT is that racism is institutionalized (rather than merely a characteristic within individuals) and endemic in American life, upheld by cultural, legal, and psychological forces. A second tenet is that US society is not truly based on human rights but actually property rights. CRT challenges dominant ideologies perpetuated in schools, such as objectivity, meritocracy, race neutrality, and equal opportunity, which mask the ways in which racism protects the power and interest of the dominant group (which in the United States is whites). In other words, school practices such as disciplinary procedures and tracking are widely believed to be race-neutral because there is no conscious attempt to sort students by race. However, studies have shown that these practices can nevertheless have racially disproportionate effects on students because of the entrenched and often invisible ways that racism operates in US society. As a result, CRT also advocates for broadening social science research beyond quantitative methods and incorporating opportunities for people to name their own reality through methods such as storytelling, counternarratives, *testimonios*, family histories, poetry, and others.[76] These methods reflect CRT's challenge to Eurocentric epistemologies, or systems of knowing. In these ways, CRT has provided valuable tools for both researchers and education practitioners, such as teachers and school leaders, to better understand and challenge racism.

After Gloria Ladson-Billings and William Tate wrote a seminal article applying CRT to education in 1995, the theory became widely used within educational scholarship to answer questions such as how—forty years after the *Brown v. Board* ruling—schools were more segregated than prior to the ruling. Paralleling critical legal scholars' observations of the failure of incremental civil rights law to transform society, Ladson-Billings and Tate argued that multicultural education was too moderate and incremental to equalize educational opportunities for students of color. A more radical approach, such as CRT, was needed in their view.[77] In response, multicultural education theorists have asserted that their field's conceptual moorings were indeed in the critical analysis of power relations, despite the apparent neglect of this in many places where multicultural education is purportedly practiced. Some began using the term **critical multicultural education** to emphasize that multicultural education must actively challenge racial oppression, not merely celebrate difference and reduce prejudice.[78]

Many scholars have applied CRT to analyze educational issues, and some have developed and used complementary theories for specific groups or fields of study, such as Latina/o critical race theory (LatCrit), critical race feminism (FemCrit), Tribal Crit, AsianCrit, and QuantCrit—which is an attempt to rethink the quantitative research paradigm with a more critical analysis of power and claims to objectivity.[79] Critical Whiteness Studies also emerged as a means of interrogating the ways whiteness is assumed to be normative or neutral and the inherent privileges and power dynamics associated with being white. Later in this chapter is a discussion of the backlash to the use of CRT in education.

Contemporary conditions

A misconception that the United States had finally achieved a post-racial society took hold after the 2008 election of Barack Obama as the president of the United States. Obama's mother was white, and his father was Kenyan, making him the first person of color to be elected to the nation's highest office. Many Americans wanted to believe that, if a person of color could be elected president, then the country must have successfully overcome the racism of its past.

Unfortunately, racial inequality persists in wealth, education, housing, employment, health, and many other realms of life. In 2019, the poverty rate for non-Hispanic white Americans was 7.3, while the rate for Hispanic Americans was 15.7 and for Black Americans, 18.8. The wealth gap is even more stark, with Hispanic and Black households possessing only 15–20 percent of the net wealth of white households. The unemployment rate for Black Americans is double the rate of white Americans. Racial inequality is also evident in health outcomes. Black and Hispanic Americans have significantly higher rates of infant mortality, pregnancy-related death, childhood lead exposure, and chronic illness in adulthood than white Americans.[80] These inequalities don't just affect racial and ethnic minorities—they actually inhibit the growth of the US economy as a whole and thus the lives of every American.

Current segregation and its educational consequences

Despite the legal victory over state-imposed segregation in *Brown v. Board of Education*, full-scale desegregation has yet to be achieved, particularly in large urban centers where almost no white children are found in many public schools. Racial segregation continues to impact American education, but too few Americans seem concerned about its effects or seek new policies to address its institutional roots. It appears that many Americans think of racial segregation as part of a distant past, with lingering pockets of segregation due to insufficient time for civil rights laws to take full effect. Such outlooks stand in sharp contrast to the serious consequences of segregation, which include concentrations of poverty, barriers to social mobility, and educational failure.[81]

Race not only affects economic opportunity but educational opportunity as well. African Americans have used public schools to their advantage, and their educational attainment rates have improved since the 1954 *Brown* decision; however, dropout rates remain significantly higher for Black students than for white students. In the 2019–20 school year, the on-time graduation rate for white students was 90 percent, Asian/Pacific Islander 93 percent, Hispanic 83 percent, Black 81 percent, and American Indian/Alaska Native 75 percent. These percentages are national figures, and one must understand that dropout rates vary from one locality to another and tend to be low in wealthy school districts and high in poor districts. For example, the on-time graduation rate for Black students ranges from 66 percent in Wyoming to 88 percent in Alabama.[82]

Although there has been improvement over time, racial discrepancies in educational achievement continue to occur. The percentage of white students scoring at or above proficient on fourth-grade reading on the 2022 National Assessment of Educational Progress (NAEP) was fifty-two, while the percentage of Black students scoring at or above proficient was eighteen and Hispanic students twenty-four.[83] One major explanation for racial disparities in educational achievement is socioeconomic disparities between white, Black, and Hispanic families. However, even in states where these socioeconomic disparities are near zero (typically in states with small Black and Hispanic populations), achievement disparities remain.[84]

Some education scholars have argued that the focus on the so-called achievement gap hinders our ability to understand persistent inequalities in schools and points us toward short-term solutions that have thus far been ineffective in ameliorating these inequalities (e.g., high-stakes testing, scripted curriculum, and takeovers or closures of schools). Gloria Ladson-Billings proposed that we, instead, focus on the **education debt** that has accumulated over time and is owed to Black and Latine students. Such a shift in focus would allow us to understand how intergenerational effects of separate and unequal schooling have compounded to produce the educational outcome disparities we see today.[85]

For Further Reflection: Discuss the argument that the phrase "achievement gap" should be replaced by the term "education debt." How do the two terms frame the problem differently and point to contrasting solutions for the problem?

Unintended consequences of Brown

While *Brown* provided important legal precedents to overcome educational inequalities based on race, the decision was implemented in ways that exacted a high price for any gains accruing to the Black community. Prior to desegregation, most Black educators usually had access to all teaching and administrative opportunities in the schools of their own communities, but desegregation curtailed careers for many Black educators. For example, African Americans lost 31,000 teaching jobs when their schools were closed or consolidated with white schools. Black teachers also faced nonrenewal of contracts more often than white teachers. If they did not lose their jobs, Black educators were frequently reassigned to other functions not of their choosing, as when principals of former all-Black schools were reassigned as assistants to white principals. Such developments restricted many Black educators from cultivating academic achievement among Black students as they once had.[86]

While community members were keenly aware of the second-rate facilities and resources of Black schools in the segregated South, they trusted their teachers as professionals who cared about the children, imparted values shared by the community, and kept in close contact with parents about student progress. The teachers made regular home visits and encouraged parents to reinforce the norms taught at school, while schools were perceived as havens where students were prepared to live as best as they could in a segregated society. This trust was lost as schools were closed and students were bused out to other schools to meet desegregation requirements. Students then had teachers who often lacked the traditional personal and social missions involved in "uplifting the race."[87]

One study of school desegregation in Richmond, Virginia, describes how citywide busing after *Brown* failed. Whites not only protested forced busing, but most of them transferred their children from public to private schools or moved from the city to adjacent and predominantly white counties for their children to attend public schools. Soon, busing in Richmond did little more than transport Black children from their neighborhood schools across town to another school with predominantly Black students. Cross-town busing was finally abandoned in 1986, ironically by the same federal district judge who first ordered it back in 1970.[88]

A leading purpose of *Brown* was to ensure that children would no longer be required by law to attend racially segregated schools. A second purpose, to extend the equal protection of the laws, proved more difficult to fulfill. After all the struggle to desegregate the schools, in many locales a new type of dual education system developed that consisted of private schools for predominantly white affluent citizens and public schools for predominantly poor Black and white children.[89] One might argue that a division of public and private schools existed ever since public schools appeared, but the older pattern was based primarily on socioeconomic class lines. Certainly, the new type of division included class lines, but race was now central because **white flight** from desegregation was a leading stimulus behind it.

Resegregation

What happened in Richmond reflected similar developments in most urban school systems around the country. This was **resegregation**, the process of formerly desegregated schools undergoing demographic changes in student bodies that resulted in a predominance of racial and ethnic minorities. The resegregation of schools noticeably increased during the 1980s and 1990s as a series of court and legislative decisions weakened prior desegregation efforts. As the example of Richmond shows, the South became relatively desegregated as a result of court orders, federal legislation, and their implementation, but its urban school systems resegregated due to white flight and other forms of affluent resistance. A consequence is that children living in urban areas at present are often more segregated in racially unequal schools than they were in the 1970s. Furthermore, at the federal level, no major national desegregation policies have been implemented since the 1980s.[90]

As a consequence of this inaction, the 1990s saw an increase in racial and socioeconomic isolation across schools. A 2023 US Department of Education report stated that the majority of Black and Latino students attend schools in which 75 percent or more of the population are students of color. These schools tend to receive less funding due to the history of using local property taxes to fund schools in the United States. Studies have found that districts with the highest percentage of Black, Latino, or Native American students receive $1,800 less per pupil than do districts with fewer students of color.[91]

One result of this increase in racial and socioeconomic isolation has been an increase in racial disparities in achievement.[92] Schools receiving less funding have less access to extracurricular and academic opportunities and fewer high-quality, experienced teachers. When school desegregation efforts were most successful in the 1980s, the achievement gap for Black 13-year-old students, for example, decreased by more than half in reading and almost half in math. However, as resegregation has increased, so too have racial disparities in graduation rates and achievement in math, science, and language arts.[93]

A relatively recent phenomenon contributing to resegregation is known as **school district secession.** This refers to the political process in which new, small school districts are carved out of existing districts in order to serve higher rates of affluent and white residents than the existing district. This not only increases school segregation but residential segregation as well. School district secession is most common in the southern states, though it occurs throughout the country.[94]

> **Suggested Activity:** Read up on the Civil Rights Project, which began at Harvard University in 1996 as a multidisciplinary research and policy think tank and as a clearinghouse for intellectual resources for academics, policy makers, civil rights advocates, and journalists, among others. Education reform and related efforts are central to its mission. In 2007, it was moved to the University of California at Los Angeles and renamed as the Civil Rights Project/Proyecto Derechos Civiles. Its website is https://www.civilrightsproject.ucla.edu/ (accessed on September 18, 2024).

One approach that has shown success in desegregating schools is the creation of magnet schools.[95] The US Department of Education defines a **magnet school** as a public school "that offers a special curriculum capable of attracting substantial numbers of students of different racial backgrounds" in order "to desegregate racially isolated schools or to reduce racial isolation in a district or consortia of districts." Approximately one in fifteen public school students attends a magnet school. Following legal challenges to race-based school assignments, magnet schools have become less supported, contributing to resegregation.[96]

The benefits of integrated schools for children of all ethnic and racial backgrounds are well established in the research literature. These benefits include:

- prejudice reduction
- higher achievement in math, science, language, and reading
- increased likelihood of graduating from both high school and college
- higher income
- more advanced critical, social, and historical thinking and civic engagement
- increased civic engagement and better learning outcomes in general.

These do not result simply from the presence of racial diversity but also from the increased resources that accompany schools with higher shares of white students. Even when schools in high-poverty neighborhoods are provided more funding, this has proved insufficient to overcome long-standing resource inequities. Thus, the goal of desegregation is not just to change the racial composition of schools but also to increase access to high-quality resources.[97]

> **For Further Reflection**: Reflect on your own school experience, past and present. Were (or are) students segregated by racial background? If so, why might this be the case, and what could be done about it?

Ongoing racial inequities within schools

In addition to the negative effects of segregation on the educational outcomes of children of color, racial biases and the cultural mismatch between schools and homes can further disadvantage students of color. Although the majority of school-aged children in the United States are now children of color, the vast majority of the teaching force remains white. Despite the fact that teacher preparation programs and many school districts have emphasized culturally sensitive teaching approaches, school curriculum and norms remain highly influenced by white, middle-class cultural norms and values. History textbooks, children's literature, and other curricular materials continue to underrepresent the histories and perspectives of Black, Indigenous, Latine, and Asian Americans. Some of the white cultural norms that are assumed to be "neutral" or "normal" within schools include communication styles and emphasis on individual achievement and autonomy, as opposed to the more collectivist values of many Black, Indigenous, Latine, and Asian cultures.[98]

Variance from dominant norms is often interpreted not just as cultural difference, but as deficiency or even disobedience. For example, in some East Asian cultures, it is considered disrespectful for a young person to look an elder in the eyes while the elder is speaking to them. However, in dominant white American culture, this can be interpreted as avoiding eye contact and not fully listening.[99] When the culture of the school staff differs from that of the students, intercultural misunderstandings such as this can occur. In addition, educators of the dominant culture often fail to understand the education debt discussed earlier, instead placing the blame for low educational achievement on students or their cultures, rather than on the history of inequitable schooling.

Family engagement and cultural disconnects

Research on school reform has found that schools improve academic outcomes when they foster trusting and collaborative relationships with families and the community. However, such trusting relationships are often absent in schools serving predominantly students of color. Studies have shown that African American parents face greater obstacles to parent involvement than white parents. White school staff may differ from caregivers of color in their beliefs about what family engagement looks like. White conceptions are often limited to participation in parent-teacher conferences and supporting children with their homework.[100] However, families from other cultural backgrounds may defer to school professionals for academic instruction and view the family's role as providing guidance in realms like character, morality, and spirituality. For example, in Mexican homes, family needs may be valued over individual needs, and parents may be reluctant to divert attention from family events to a child's school project.[101]

Racial biases and deficit-based assumptions about the degree to which caregivers of color care about their children's education also play a role. While educators may assume parents who do not attend parent-teacher conferences are not invested in their children's learning, the reality may be that their work schedules or childcare needs prohibit them from attending or that they have not been made to feel welcome in the school environment. Several studies have shown the positive effects when schools build culturally responsive family partnerships through recognizing and valuing caregivers' funds of knowledge and expertise in their own children's learning.[102]

For Further Reflection: What are your personal experiences with family engagement in schools, either from a student's or parent's/caregiver's perspective? Reflect on and compare your own experiences with those of your peers in class.

Effects of high-stakes testing on students of color

One of the major aims of the No Child Left Behind (NCLB) legislation of 2002 was to close the so-called achievement gaps among students. NCLB was grounded in the principles of accountability, transparency, and choice, and the primary accountability mechanism was high-stakes, standardized tests.

Through requiring schools to report test scores for students as a whole, as well as subgroups of students, NCLB was supposed to catalyze change and raise student achievement nationwide. Yet even NCLB proponents report that the achievement gap between white and Black students (as measured by NAEP scores) actually increased after the introduction of NCLB accountability measures. Many have argued that NCLB made impossible-to-achieve demands on the nation's schools that serve minoritized and low-income students.

The legislation that replaced NCLB during the Obama administration, called the Every Student Succeeds Act (ESSA), allowed states greater flexibility in determining the academic achievement of their students, as states would submit ESSA plans describing their strategies for supporting achievement and equity. However, ESSA still relied heavily on standardized test scores as the primary measure of achievement, and a review of ESSA plans found that many states ignored requirements for interventions supportive of equity. The US Department of Education, led at that time by Secretary of Education Betsy DeVos, approved those plans anyway.[103]

Ample research has demonstrated the undesirable consequences of high-stakes testing on students of color and low-income students. The high-stakes testing movement has increased apathy and dropout rates and led to narrower curricula and harsher discipline policies, especially for students of color.[104] The emphasis on test preparation squelches critical thinking, and the use of punitive accountability measures for teachers serves to drive creative teachers away from the schools that most need them.

Cross-reference: For a more detailed discussion of NCLB and ESSA, see Chapter 2, School Governance and Control, pp. 84–97

Quality and diversity of the teacher workforce

A National Academy of Sciences report from 2019 suggested several indicators that could be used to monitor progress toward educational equity in the United States, several of which related to teacher quality and diversity. In terms of teacher quality, the authors found that Latine students are twice as likely and Black students are four times as likely as their white peers to attend schools where at least 20 percent of their teachers have not met state licensing requirements. Black and Latine students were also more likely to attend schools with higher proportions of teachers in their first year of teaching. The report recommended monitoring teacher diversity to address equity. Although white students now make up less than half of the national student population, only 20 percent of teachers are not white, and an estimated 40 percent of schools had no nonwhite teachers in 2011.[105] Research has demonstrated sizable positive effects of teacher-student racial match for students of color. These include short-term impacts, such as test scores, and long-term impacts, such as completing high school.[106] Thus, many states, districts, and universities are implementing measures to diversify the teacher workforce, such as improving working conditions for teachers of color, redesigning teacher education programs, and removing licensure exams as a barrier to entry.[107]

Cross-reference: For further discussion of current efforts to diversify the teacher workforce, see Chapter 1, Teaching as a Profession, pp. 35–6

Racial disproportionality in exclusionary discipline practices

Despite decades of documented disproportionality in the rates at which Black students are suspended and expelled from schools, and efforts to address this problem, disparities remain. The 2013–14 report from Civil Rights Data Collection reported that Black students made up 40 percent of suspensions, though they account for only 16 percent of school enrollment nationally. Numerous studies have revealed links between such practices and contact with the criminal justice system, funneling far more students of color than white students on what has been called "the school-to-prison pipeline."[108]

A 2014 letter jointly issued by the US Department of Education and Department of Justice explained that differences in behaviors do not explain the gap in exclusionary discipline practices and cited their investigations into civil rights violations that have revealed discrimination in the use of these practices. Studies have also found that these gaps are higher when looking specifically at Black students who come from high-poverty backgrounds and that the differences exist within, not just across, schools. In other words, the gaps are not caused by Black and white students attending schools with different discipline practices. Further supporting the claim that the gap is at least in part due to discrimination, one study found that Black students were less likely to be suspended or expelled when they had Black teachers rather than white teachers. The study authors recommended changes to disciplinary practices, including limiting the use of suspension to only those behaviors threatening school safety, and replacing exclusionary practices with positive behavioral supports and **restorative justice** practices.[109] Restorative justice is grounded in the belief that punitive approaches do little to repair the harm that occurred or the relationships among those involved. Restorative practices often begin with conversation circles of all those involved in an incident sharing what happened from their perspective and expressing their understanding of the others' perspectives.

To date, few of these measures have shown large-scale reductions in racial disparities in discipline, though some can lead to an overall reduction in disciplinary incidents and suspensions. One challenge to effectiveness may be that these approaches are often implemented *alongside* rather than *as a replacement for* existing disciplinary practices. Staff are often able to select from traditional and more restorative responses, and the subjectivity involved can then increase racial disproportionality in exclusionary discipline. Without transformative organizational change, the impact of these approaches may be limited. However, in those cases where these approaches were paired with cultural and racial consciousness training, they have been able to reduce racial disparities.[110]

> **For Further Reflection:** What were your experiences with discipline in your elementary and secondary schools? Were discipline practices more punitive or more restorative? Did you notice any differences in how discipline practices affected various groups of students?

Addressing racial justice in education

Community schools

One promising initiative for addressing racial inequalities in education is the community schools movement. Community schools are public schools that tailor their services and support to meet the specific needs of their school or neighborhood, fostering collaboration among educators, local community members, families, and students to improve conditions for learning and healthy development. This concept originates in John Dewey's vision of schools as "social centers," capable of addressing students' needs comprehensively. Recent research has demonstrated that community schools not only enhance student outcomes but also promote educational equity.

Various models of community schools exist, all acknowledging schools' central role in community infrastructure and the importance of access to a range of community and social supports, particularly in areas affected by historical and ongoing social and economic disparities. The COVID-19 pandemic underscored the significance of the bond between schools and communities, particularly in addressing education equity gaps. Models such as Communities in Schools and the Whole School, Whole Community, Whole Child Model have shown improvements in various measures, from attendance rates to academic achievement. In 2023, the Biden administration provided $63 million in grants for forty-two Full-Service Community Schools.[111]

Culturally relevant and antiracist pedagogy

Other approaches to addressing racial inequities in education focus on teachers' mindsets and practices. In the 1990s, two major concepts that gained traction in teacher education were *culturally relevant pedagogy* (developed by Gloria Ladson-Billings) and *culturally responsive teaching* (developed by Geneva Gay). **Culturally relevant pedagogy** draws from critical pedagogy and CRT and served initially as a framework for education with African American students intended to enhance their sociopolitical consciousness while also promoting academic achievement and cultural competence. Ladson-Billings emphasized that culturally relevant pedagogy is not a set of practices or a teaching methodology but rather a theoretical approach—a way of thinking rather than a prescription for doing.[112]

Overlapping in some ways is *culturally responsive teaching*. Geneva Gay defined it as "using the cultural characteristics, experiences, and perspectives of ethnically diverse students as conduits for teaching them more effectively."[113] Thus, Gay's framework speaks more directly to teaching methods and competencies, whereas Ladson-Billings' framework applies more to teachers' dispositions. More recently, Django Paris and Samuel Alim put forward a framework called *culturally sustaining pedagogy* to address two shortcomings of earlier models. First, according to Paris and Alim, the terms "responsive" and "relevant" do not go far enough; they argue that nondominant cultures should be actively maintained, not just tolerated and accepted. Second, these earlier frameworks often rested on static and abstract notions of culture.[114]

Although there are important distinctions among these three approaches, all fundamentally aim to refocus attention on educational equity, appreciate the under-recognized assets of culturally diverse students, and foster the critical citizenship skills necessary for addressing social issues. Studies have generally found that these approaches benefit students of all backgrounds and students from racially minoritized backgrounds in particular.[115]

Whereas culturally relevant education focuses broadly on affirming students' knowledge and cultural assets and developing their cultural competence and academic skills, **antiracist pedagogy** focuses more specifically on engaging students in critical dialogue about racism and white supremacy and becoming activists against racism in schools and beyond. Some research suggests that the latter term can reduce color-evasive practices and increase possibilities for transforming the status quo. When educators in one study used the term "antiracism," they were more likely to grapple with racism, oppression, and whiteness rather than trying to avoid these topics.[116]

However, teacher confidence and skill in the use of culturally relevant and antiracist pedagogies in PK-12 school approaches are generally low, and these approaches are not widespread in schools.[117] Professional development for teachers and other school-based practitioners is a key lever for supporting schools as they promote culturally relevant and antiracist pedagogies. This is especially true when considering the growing cultural mismatch between a diversifying student population and a teaching force that remains predominantly white and female.

Another barrier to culturally relevant and antiracist pedagogies is the prescriptive curricula many teachers are expected to use. The amount of autonomy teachers have over what they can teach varies greatly by state and district. In those communities where teachers can select their materials, free antiracist lesson plans and activities are available from organizations such as Learning for Justice, Facing History and Ourselves, and Rethinking Schools. The Pulitzer Prize-winning *New York Times* publication *The 1619 Project* has also evolved into a curriculum for teaching a more comprehensive and accurate history of the legacy of slavery and contributions of Black Americans.

Suggested Activity: Locate the websites of the curricular organizations listed above and explore the various resources they offer. Consider ways you might be able to use some of these resources in the future.

However, the growth of antiracist teaching efforts has spurred a backlash that has attempted to restrict these efforts. Between January 2021 and June 2023, measures restricting discussions on racism and sexism were introduced in forty-four states, with eighteen states enacting such measures. Even states without explicit prohibitions have seen a chilling effect—numerous districts and schools have scaled back their efforts to address racism, and teachers are more hesitant to talk about race or diversity-related subjects. Research suggests that approximately 35 percent of K-12 students nationwide have been affected by local initiatives linked to these restrictions, with students in rapidly changing districts being three times as likely to be impacted. Furthermore, book bans were enforced in twenty-one states and sixty-six school districts during the first half of the 2022–3 academic year alone. On average, around 100 books were removed from student access monthly during this period, predominantly focusing on LGBTQ+ individuals and people of color. This period has been labeled the "ed scare" by PEN America due to the vague language in these policies causing educators to avoid potentially contentious content and instructional practices.[118]

Nine days after his second inauguration, President Donald Trump issued an executive order entitled "Ending Radical Indoctrination in K-12 Schooling," which threatened to withhold funding from any K-12 school that teaches "radical anti-American ideologies" or "discriminatory equity ideology" and legal action against any school that acknowledges the existence of more than two genders. The executive order defines "discriminatory equity ideology" as "ideology that treats individuals as members of preferred or disfavored groups, rather than as individuals, and minimizes agency, merit, and capability in favor of immoral generalization."[119] While public schools have historically been arenas for ideological clashes, this nationwide policy effort has been uniquely restrictive.

For Further Reflection: How do the tensions between efforts to implement culturally relevant and antiracist teaching approaches and the recent legislative restrictions impact students' ability to learn a comprehensive and nuanced understanding of history and social issues? Consider the potential long-term educational and social consequences of limiting discussions about race, diversity, and historical experiences.

Summary and conclusions

Americans today are perhaps the most divided they have been in a half-century on how to address the problem of race in school and society. Some advocate addressing it head-on, with programs and policies directed at equalizing educational conditions across groups. Others argue that these programs and policies are discriminatory and make some people feel uncomfortable because they involve explicit discussions of past and present mistreatment by white people.

Part of the problem faced by American society is that racial categorizations and racialization are rooted in the nation's unique history of slavery, particularly the way racism developed as a supporting ideology for it. Race was an important condition for a nation built on the myth of white superiority and Black inferiority, and one of its long-term legacies was racial segregation.

African Americans made some important advances after the Civil War, particularly in public education during Reconstruction, aided by the Freedmen's Bureau and northern missionary societies. A major factor was the desire of the freed people to educate themselves and their children for a new life of freedom. As the New South recovered from the war and became more industrialized and urbanized, new possibilities seemed ascendant, but the era of Jim Crow segregation brought white supremacy laws, Black suppression, and segregated public institutions, conditions that endured for decades to come.

Booker T. Washington attempted to make industrial education the model of choice for the education of African Americans and their children, emphasizing the values of industriousness, hard work, and economic goals over the acquisition of knowledge or social and political power. Washington made Tuskegee Institute the center for his policies, but his efforts to advance the cause of Black people were severely hampered by Jim Crowism, and his attempts to appease the power structure, his Atlanta Compromise, came to haunt his efforts. W.E.B. Du Bois struggled with Washington over the direction education should take, particularly in the value of liberal higher education and the development of Black intellectual leaders who would push for voting rights, civic equality, and educational opportunity for all.

In 1896, Jim Crow was bolstered by the Supreme Court's "separate but equal" doctrine in *Plessy v. Ferguson*. Segregated (but never equal) schools became legal and social fixtures until *Brown v. Board of Education* in 1954. This case, spearheaded by the NAACP, struck down state laws requiring racially segregated schools, while segregation caused by housing patterns and other socioeconomic conditions remained. Some education reformers then advocated programs (such as multicultural education and Afrocentric education) to better integrate Black people and culture into the American mainstream. However, rapid change seemed elusive, and conditions continued to exist that stymied social and cultural integration.

One difficulty in addressing contemporary challenges arising from race is that the magnitude of the problem often seems insurmountable. However, improvements have been made over time, more often than not in small incremental steps rather than dramatic leaps. The problem of race was centuries in the making, and it is unlikely to be solved in short order. Education alone cannot solve the remaining problems of race, but it can help if the lines of free inquiry and public debate are kept open. In other words, educational efforts to address lingering racial issues are not hopeless, but they will take commitment, patience, and broad societal support.

Vocabulary

acculturate
Afrocentric Education
antiracist pedagogy
Brown v. Board of Education (1954)
Brown II
Carlisle Indian School
Castro, Sal
Chavis, John
critical multicultural education
critical race theory (CRT)
culturally biased testing
culturally relevant pedagogy
deficit ideology
desegregation
double taxation
Du Bois, W. E. B.
education debt
equal protection of the law
ethnic-racial socialization
ethnic studies
ethnicity
dual school systems
Freedmen's Bureau
Indian Self-Determination and Education Assistance Act of 1975
intercultural education movement
Jim Crow
John Chavis
Keyes v. School District No. 1, Denver, Colorado (1973)
Korematsu, Fred

magnet school
massive resistance
model minority myth
multicultural education
National Association for the Advancement of Colored People (NAACP)
New South
paternalistic
Plessy v. Ferguson (1896)
race
racialization
racism
Reconstruction
resegregation
restorative justice
segregation
separate but equal
Sequoyah
school district secession
sharecropping
social construct
Talented Tenth
Tape v. Hurley (1885)
tenant farming
Tuskegee Institute
Washington, Booker T.
white flight
white privilege
Woodson, Carter G.

Notes

1 APA Dictionary of Psychology, at https://dictionary.apa.org/race?_gl=1*td5ufo*_ga*ODAwMjU0NzY3LjE3MDI1NjQzMDQ.*_ga_SZXLGDJGNB*MTcwMjU2NDMxMi4xLjAuMTcwMjU2NDMxMi4wLjAuMA (accessed on December 14, 2023).

2 Alan H. Goodman, "Why Genes Don't Count (for Racial Differences in Health)," *Health Psychology*, vol. 90, no. 11 (November 2000): 161–6.

3 Frederick Douglass, "The Color Line," 567, Electronic Text Center, University of Virginia Library, at http://etext.virginia.edu/toc/modeng/public/DouColo.html (accessed on April 12, 2010); Dante Puzzo, "Racism and the Western Traditions," *Journal of the History of Western Ideas*, vol. 15, no. 4 (October–December 1964): 579; Audrey Smedley, *Race in North America* (Boulder, CO: Wesview Press, 1999), 17, 39; and Spencer Wells, *The Journey of Man: A Genetic Odyssey* (New York: Random House, 2002), 30–3, 53–5.

4 Laura C. Chávez-Moreno, "Toward a Relational Racialization Lens in Education: Addressing Critiques of CRT's Race Theory," *International Journal of Qualitative Studies in Education*, at https://doi.org/10.1080/09518398.2024.2365196 (published online July 1, 2024).

5 Cornel West, *Race Matters* (Boston, MA: Beacon Press, 2017).

6 Isabel Wilkerson, *Caste: The Origins of Our Discontents* (New York: Random House, 2020).

7 Beverly Tatum, *Why Are All the Black Kids Sitting Together in the Cafeteria?* (New York: Basic Books, 1997/2017), 88.

8 Ibid.

9 APA Dictionary of Psychology, at https://dictionary.apa.org/ethnicity (accessed on December 14, 2023).

10 Linda M. Hunt and Mary S. Megyesi, "The Ambiguous Meanings of the Racial/Ethnic Categories Routinely Used in Human Genetics Research," *Social Science & Medicine*, vol. 66, no. 2 (2008): 349–61.

11 Diane Hughes et al., "Parents' Ethnic–Racial Socialization Practices: A Review of Research and Directions for Future Study," *Developmental Psychology*, vol. 42, no. 5 (2006): 749.

12 James D. Anderson, *The Education of Blacks in the South, 1860–1935* (Chapel Hill: The University of North Carolina Press, 1988), 1–2.

13 Carter G. Woodson, *The Education of the Negro Prior to 1861* (Washington, DC: Associated Publishers, 1919). See particularly Chapter 4 (70–92) and Chapter IX (205–228); and Anderson, *The Education of Blacks in the South, 1860–1935,* 4–7.

14 Woodson, *The Education of the Negro Prior to 1861*, 115–117; Woodson, *The Negro in Our History*, 5th edn (Washington, DC: Associated Publishers, 1928), 159–60; Theodore Carter Delaney, Jr., "Founder's Day Lecture," Washington and Lee University (January 19, 2001), at http://home.wlu. edu/~delaneyt/Chavis.htm (accessed on April 13, 2010); "Rev. John Chavis, 1762/1763–1838" Presbyterian Heritage Center, at http://www.phcmontreat.org/chavis.html (accessed on December 19, 2023).

15 "About the Bureau," The Valley of the Shadow, at http://valley.lib.virginia.edu/VoS/fbureau/aboutbureau.html (accessed on April 23, 2010).

16 Anderson, *The Education of Blacks in the South, 1860–1935,* 5–7.

17 Ibid., 23, 285.

18 The origin of the term *Jim Crow* is obscure, but it may have originated with a stereotyped image arising from minstrels in which white actors in "black face" depicted a ragged comic figure who danced with a hopping step called the Jim Crow. See C. Vann Woodward, *The Strange Career of Jim Crow*, 3rd edn (New York: Oxford University Press, 1974); Ronald L. F. Davis, "Creating Jim Crow: In-Depth Essay," at http://www.jimcrowhistory.org/history/creating2.htm (accessed on April 13, 2010) and Susan Falck, "Jim Crow Legislation Overview," at http://www.jimcrowhistory.org/resources/lessonplans/hs_es_jim_crow_laws.htm (accessed on April 12, 2010).

19 Lewis Harvie Blair, *The Prosperity of the South Dependent Upon the Elevation of the Negro* (1889), C. Vann Woodward, ed. (Boston, MA: Little, Brown, 1964), 122–51; Charles C. Bolton, *The Hardest Deal of All: The Battle for School Integration in Mississippi, 1870–1980* (Jackson: University Press of Mississippi, 2005), 5–6; and Robert W. Flournoy to Thaddeus Stevens (November 20, 1865), at http://www.sewanee.edu/faculty/Willis/Civil_War/documents/FlournoySte vens.html (accessed on April 7, 2011).

20 Considerable reliance was made on two sources of biographical material on Booker T. Washington: Washington's autobiography, *Up from Slavery* (New York: Penguin Books, 1986), and the two-volume biography by Louis R. Harlan, *Booker T. Washington: The Making of a Black Leader, 1856–1901* (New York: Oxford University Press, 1972) and *Booker T. Washington: The Wizard of Tuskegee, 1901–1915* (New York: Oxford University Press, 1983).

21 Booker T. Washington and W. E. B. Du Bois, *The Negro in the South: His Economic Progress in Relation to His Moral and Religious Development* (New York: The Citadel Press, 1970), 46–9, hereafter cited as *The Negro in the South.*

22 Anderson, *The Education of Blacks in the South, 1860–1935,* 5–6, 71–5, and 101–7.

23 Manning Marable, *W. E. B. Du Bois: Black Radical Democrat* (Boston, MA: Twayne Publishers, 1986). See also Du Bois, *The Autobiography of W. E. B. Du Bois: A Soliloquy on Viewing My Life from the Last Decade of Its First Century*, Herbert Aptheker, ed. (New York: International Publishers, 1968).

24 Du Bois, *The Autobiography*, 223.

25 Du Bois, "The Revelation of Saint Orgne [1938]," in *W. E. B. Du Bois: Writings*, 1052–1053; and Marable, *W. E. B. Du Bois: Black Radical Democrat,* 195–6.

26 Anderson, *The Education of Blacks in the South, 1860–1935*, 154–6.

27 Richard Kluger, *Simple Justice: The History of Brown v. Board of Education and Black America's Struggle for Equality* (New York: Vintage Books, 1977), 256–7.

28 *Brown v. Board of Education of Topeka, Kansas*, 347 U.S. 483, 98 L. Ed. 873, 74 S. Ct. 686 (1954), at http://supreme.justia.com/us/347/483/case.html (accessed on April 14, 2010).

29 *Brown v. Board of Education of Topeka*, 349 U.S. 294 (1955), at http://supreme.justia.com/us/349/294/ case.html (accessed on April 14, 2010). In particular, see pp. 300, 301.

30 Kendra Taylor, Erica Frankenberg, and Genevieve Siegel-Hawley, "Racial Segregation in the Southern Schools, School Districts, and Counties Where Districts Have Seceded," *AERA Open*, vol. 5, no. 3 (2019): 1–16.

31 Robert Pratt, *The Color of Their Skin: Education and Race in Richmond, Virginia 1954–1989* (Charlottesville: University Press of Virginia, 1992), 11.

32 *Swann v. Charlotte-Mecklenburg Board of Education* (1971), 402 U.S. 1, at http://supct.law.cornell.edu/supct/html/historics/USSC_CR_0402_0001_ZO.html (accessed on April 14, 2010).

33 Pratt, *The Color of Their Skin: Education and Race in Richmond, Virginia 1954–1989*, 108–9.

34 Bryan McKinley Jones Brayboy, Susan C. Faircloth, Tiffany S. Lee, Margaret J. Maaka, and Troy A. Richardson, "Sovereignty and Education: An Overview of the Unique Nature of Indigenous Education," *Journal of American Indian Education*, vol. 54, no. 1 (Spring 2015): 1.

35 Ibid., 2.

36 US Census Bureau, "Table 1. Top 25 American Indian Tribes for the United States: 1990 and 1980," at http://www.census.gov/population/socdemo/race/indian/ailang1.txt (accessed on May 25, 2010); and "Intergovernmental Affairs: Tribal Affairs—American Indian and Alaska Native (AIAN)," at https://www.census.gov/about/cong-gov-affairs/intergovernmental-affairs/tribal-aian.html#:~:text=The%20estimated%20American%20Indian%20and,M%20on%20July%201%2C%202022 (accessed on December 26, 2023).

37 James H. Merrell, *The Indians' New World: Catawbas and Their Neighbors from European Contact through the Era of Removal* (Chapel Hill: University of North Carolina Press, 1989), viii–x; E. Fred Sanders and Thomas J. Blumer, "The Catawba Nation Under Siege: A Troubled History of Tribal Sovereignty," in *Foundations of First People's Sovereignty: History, Education and Culture*, Ulrike Wiethaus, ed. (Washington, DC: Peter Lang, 2008), 97–122.

38 Margaret Bender, *Signs of Cherokee Culture: Sequoyah's Syllabary in Eastern Cherokee Life* (Chapel Hill: The University of North Carolina Press, 2002), 25–36; Grant Foreman, *Sequoyah* (Norman: University of Oklahoma Press, 1938). See also "Sequoyah (ca. 1770–ca. 1840)," The New Georgia Encyclopedia, at http://www.georgiaencyclopedia.org/nge/Article.jsp?id=h-618 (accessed on October 13, 2010).

39 William G. McLoughlin, "An Alternative Missionary Style: Evan Jones and John B. Jones Among the Cherokees," in *Between Indian and White Worlds: The Cultural Brokers*, Margaret Connell Szasz, ed. (Norman: University of Oklahoma Press, 1994), 99–102, 104–9, 113, 116, 118–20 and Delores J. Huff, *To Live Heroically: Institutional Racism and American Indian Education* (Albany: State University of New York, 1997), 2–4.

40 David Thomas, *Skull Wars: Kennewick Man, Archaeology, and the Battle for Native American Identity* (New York: Basic Books, 2000), 49–50, 53–63, and 101–12; Richard Henry Pratt, "The Advantages of Mingling Indians and Whites," in *Americanizing the American Indians: Writings by the "Friends of the Indian" 1880–1900*, Francis Paul Prucha, ed. (Lincoln: University of Nebraska Press, 1973), 261, 266.

41 Lewis Meriam et al., *The Problem of Indian Administration* (Baltimore, MD: Johns Hopkins University Press, 1928); Margaret Connell Szasz, *Education and the American Indian: The Road to Self Determination since 1928*, 3rd edn (Albuquerque: University of New Mexico Press, 1999), 3, 18–29, 60, 89, 91, 97, 101–105, and 189; and Vine Deloria, Jr. and Clifford M. Lytle, *American Indians and American Justice* (Austin: University of Texas Press, 1983), 92–102.

42 Guy B. Senese, *Self-Determination and the Social Education of Native Americans* (New York: Praeger, 1991), 3–7, 11, 16, 19–21, and 37 and Szasz, *Education and the American Indian*, 113–14.

43 See "Bureau of Indian Education," Bureau of Indian Affairs, US Department of the Interior, at https://www.bia.gov/bie (accessed on May 27, 2025).

44 Senese, *Self-Determination and the Social Education of Native Americans,* xi–xii, 183; and David Wilkins, "Indigenous Self-Determination: A Global Perspective," in *Foundations of First People's Sovereignty: History, Education and Culture*, Ulrike Wiethaus, ed. (New York: Peter Lang, 2008), 11–20.

45 Hispanic/Latino Health. US Department of Health and Human Services Office of Minority Health, at https://minorityhealth.hhs.gov/hispaniclatino-health#:~:text=Overview%20(Demographics)&text=According%20to%20 2020%20Census%20data,group%20after%20non%2DHispanic%20whites. (accessed on December 28, 2023).

46 2015 National Survey of Latinos. Pew Research Center, at https://www.pewresearch.org/hispanic/dataset/2015-national-survey-of-latinos/ (accessed on December 28, 2023).

47 Hispanic Identity Fades across Generations as Immigrant Connections Fall Away. Pew Research Center, at https://www.pewresearch.org/hispanic/2017/12/20/hispanic-identity-fades-across-generations-as-immigrant-connections-fall-away/ (accessed on December 28, 2023).

48 Ana Gonzalez-Barrera, "About 6 Million U.S. Adults Identify as Afro-Latino," Pew Research Center, at https://www.pewresearch.org/short-reads/2022/05/02/about-6-million-u-s-adults-identify-as-afro-latino/ (accessed on December 28, 2023).

49 Fast Facts: Hispanic Heritage Month. National Center for Educational Statistics (NCES), https://nces.ed.gov/fastfacts/display.asp?id=1142 (accessed on December 28, 2023).

50 Julian Samora and Patricia Vandel-Simon, *A History of the Mexican-American People* (Notre Dame, IN: University of Notre Dame Press, 1977), 6, 99–100.

51 Ibid; Ruben Donato, *The Other Struggle for Equal Schools: Mexican Americans During the Civil Rights Era* (Albany: State University of New York Press, 1997), 29–40.

52 Gilbert G. Gonzalez, “Culture, Language, and the Americanization of Mexican Children,” in *Latinos and Education: A Critical Reader*, Antonia Darder, Rodolfo D. Torres, and Henry Gutíerrez, eds (New York: Routledge, 1997), 162–73.

53 Guadalupe Salinas, “Mexican-Americans and the Desegregation of Schools in the Southwest,” in *Latino Language and Education: Communication and the Dream Deferred*, Antoinette Sedillo López, ed., vol. 5 (New York and London: Garland Publishing, Inc., 1995), 157; Guadalupe San Miguel, Jr., “Mexican American Organizations and the Changing Politics of School Desegregation in Texas, 1944 to 1980,” in *Latino Language and Education*, 180–6.

54 East L. A. Walkouts. Britannica, https://www.britannica.com/event/East-L-A-walkouts#ref1295643 (accessed on January 24, 2024).

55 *Cisneros v. Corpus Christi Independent School District*, 467 F.2d 142 (CA5 1972); and *Keyes v. School District No. 1, Denver, Colorado*, 413 US 189 (1973), at http://supct.law.cornell.edu/supct/html/ historics/USSC_CR_0413_0189_ZO1.html (accessed on May 15, 2010); Richard R. Valencia, “The Plight of Chicano Students: An Overview of Schooling Conditions and Outcomes,” in *Chicano School Failure and Success: Research and Policy Agendas for the 1990s*, Richard R. Valencia, ed. (London: The Falmer Press, 1991), 7; and San Miguel, “Mexican American Organizations and the Changing Politics of School Desegregation in Texas, 1944 to 1980,” 186–92.

56 Eilieen H. Tamura, “Introduction: Asian Americans and Educational History,” *History of Education Quarterly*, vol. 43, no. 1 (Spring 2003): 1–9; Roland Sintos Coloma, “Disorienting Race and Education: Changing Paradigms on the Schooling of Asian Americans and Pacific Islanders,” *Race Ethnicity and Education*, vol. 9, no. 1 (2006): 1–15, t$, doi: 10.1080/13613320500490606

57 Abby Budiman and Neil Ruiz, “Key Facts About Asian Americans, a Diverse and Growing Population,” *Pew Research Center*, https://www.pewresearch.org/short-reads/2021/04/29/key-facts-about-asian-americans/ (accessed on December 28, 2023).

58 “Asian Americans Then and Now: Linking Past to Present,” Asia Society, https://asiasociety.org/education/asian-americans-then-and-now (accessed on December 28, 2023).

59 Valeria Ooka Pang, Peggy P. Han, and Jennifer M. Pang, “Asian American and Pacific Islander Students: Equity and the Achievement Gap,” *Educational Researcher*, vol. 40, no. 8 (2011): 378–89.

60 Meyer Weinberg, *Asian-American Education: Historical Background and Current Realities* (Mahwah, NJ: Lawrence Erlbaum Associates, 1997), 17–20.

61 Facts and Case Summary—Korematsu v. US, https://www.uscourts.gov/educational-resources/educational-activities/facts-and-case-summary-korematsu-v-us (accessed on January 12, 2024).

62 Fred Korematsu's Story, https://korematsuinstitute.org/freds-story/ (accessed on January 12, 2024).

63 Tamura, "Introduction: Asian Americans and Educational History," 9.

64 Coloma, "Disorienting Race."

65 Sarah-Soonling Blackburn, "What Is the Model Minority Myth?" *Learning for Justice* (March 21, 2019), https://www.learningforjustice.org/magazine/what-is-the-model-minority-myth

66 Thomas S. Dee and Emily K. Penner, "The Causal Effects of Cultural Relevance: Evidence from an Ethnic Studies Curriculum," *American Educational Research Journal*, vol. 54, no. 1 (February 2017): 127–66; Nolan L. Cabrera, Elisa L. Meza, and Cintli Rodriguez, "Missing the (Student Achievement) Forest for All the (Political) Trees: Empiricism and the Mexican American Studies Controversy in Tucson," *American Educational Research Journal*, vol. 51, no. 6 (December 2014): 1084–118.

67 James A. Banks, "Multicultural Education: Historical Development, Dimensions, and Practice," in *Handbook of Research on Multicultural Education*, J. A. Banks and C. A. McGee Banks, eds, 2nd edn (San Francisco, CA: John Wiley & Sons, 2004).

68 Ibid., 10–11.

69 Ibid., 12–13; Paul Gorski, Hamline University and Ed Change, "A Brief History of Multicultural Education" *Critical Multicultural Pavilion Research Room* (November 1999), http://www.edchange.org/multicultural/papers/edchange_history.html

70 Banks, "Multicultural Education: Historical Development, Dimensions, and Practice," 13; Gorski, "A Brief History of Multicultural Education"; Christine Sleeter, "The Academic and Social Value of Ethnic Studies: A Research Review," National Education Association (2011), https://vtechworks.lib.vt.edu/server/api/core/bitstreams/aa6716dd-b7a4-404f-8e62-a92e343d013f/content

71 Molefi Kete Asante, *The Afrocentric Idea* (Philadelphia, PA: Temple University Press, 1998).

72 Haki Madhubuti and Safisha Madhubuti, *African-Centered Education: Its Value, Importance, and Necessity in the Development of Black Children* (Chicago, IL: Third World Press, 1994), 21–3.

73 Tytianna Nikia Maria Ringstaff, "Afrocentric Education for Liberation in the Classroom: It Takes a Village to Raise a Child," *MDPI*, vol. 13, no. 6 (2023): 532.

74 Asante, *The Afrocentric Idea*, xi.

75 Gloria Ladson-Billings and William F. Tate, "Toward a Critical Race Theory of Education," *Teachers College Record*, vol. 97, no. 1 (1995): 47–68.

76 Daniel G. Solorzano and Tara J. Yosso, "Critical Race and LatCrit Theory and Method: Counterstorytelling," *International Journal of Qualitative Studies in Education*, vol. 13, no. 4 (2001): 472–3.

77 Ladson-Billings and Tate, "Toward a Critical Race Theory of Education," 62.

78 Christine E. Sleeter and Dolores Delgado-Bernal, "Critical Pedagogy, Critical Race Theory, and Antiracist Education: Implications for Multicultural Education," in *Handbook of Research on Multicultural Education*, James A. Banks and Cherry A. McGee Banks, eds, 2nd edn (San Francisco, CA: John Wiley & Sons, 2004), 240–1.

79 Nichole Garcia, Nancy López, and Verónica N. Vélez, "QuantCrit: Rectifying Quantitative Methods Through Critical Race Theory," *Race Ethnicity and Education*, vol. 21, no. 2 (2018): 149–57.

80 Aditya Aladangady and Akila Forde, "Wealth Inequality and the Racial Wealth Gap," Board of Governors of the Federal Reserve System (October 22, 2021), https://www.federalreserve.gov/econres/notes/feds-notes/wealth-inequality-and-the-racial-wealth-gap-20211022.html; Samantha Artiga, "Health Disparities Are a Symptom of Broader Social and Economic Inequities," KFF (June 1, 2020), https://www.kff.org/policy-watch/health-disparities-symptom-broader-social-economic-inequities/

81 Jonathan Kozol, *The Shame of the Nation: The Restoration of Apartheid Schooling in America* (New York: Crown Publishers, 2005), 10; and Douglas S. Massey and Nancy A. Denton, *American Apartheid: Segregation and the Making of the Underclass* (Cambridge, MA: Harvard University Press, 1993), 1–2.

82 National Center for Education Statistics, "Public High School Graduation Rates," *Condition of Education*. US Department of Education, Institute of Education Sciences, at https://nces.ed.gov/programs/coe/indicator/coi (accessed on February 6, 2024).

83 US Department of Education, Institute of Education Sciences, National Center for Education Statistics, National Assessment of Educational Progress (NAEP), 1998–2022 Reading Assessments, at https://nces.ed.gov/nationsreportcard/subject/publications/stt2022/pdf/2023010NP4.pdf (accessed on February 6, 2024).

84 Racial and Ethnic Achievement Gaps. The Educational Opportunity Monitoring Project. Stanford Center for Education Policy Analysis, at https://cepa.stanford.edu/educational-opportunity-monitoring-project/achievement-gaps/race/ (accessed on February 6, 2024).

85 Gloria Ladson-Billings, "From the Achievement Gap to the Education Debt: Understanding Achievement in U.S. Schools," *Educational Researcher*, vol. 35, no. 7 (2006): 3–12.

86 Nancy Levi Arnez, "Desegregation of Public Schools: A Discriminatory Process," *Journal of Afro-American Issues*, vol. 4, no. 2 (Spring 1976): 274–82 and Michele

Foster, "The Politics of Race: Through the Eyes of African-American Teachers," *Journal of Education*, vol. 172, no. 3 (1990): 123–41.

87 Vanessa Siddle Walker, *Their Highest Potential—An African American School Community in the Segregated South* (Chapel Hill: The University of North Carolina Press, 1996); Maike Philipsen, *Race and the Cultural Consequences of a School Closing* (Cresskill, NJ: Hampton Press, 1999).

88 Pratt, *The Color of Their Skin: Education and Race in Richmond, Virginia 1954–1989*, 108–9.

89 See, for example, what happened in Richmond, Virginia, in Pratt, *The Color of Their Skin: Education and Race in Richmond, Virginia 1954–1989*, 108–9.

90 Gary Orfield and Chungmei Lee, *Historic Reversals, Accelerating Resegregation, and the Need for New Integration Strategies*, A Report of the Civil Rights Project, UCLA, August 2007, 5–8, at http:// www.civilrightsproject.ucla.edu/research/deseg/reversals_reseg_need.pdf (accessed on April 20, 2010). See also Gary Orfield and Chungmei Lee, "Segregation 50 Years After Brown: A Metropolitan Change," in *Beyond Silenced Voices: Class, Race, and Gender in United States Schools*, Lois Weis and Michelle Fine, eds, rev. edn (Albany: State University of New York Press, 2005), 17–20.

91 Miguel A. Cardona and Roberto J. Rodriguez, "The State of School Diversity in the United States," Report of the US Department of Education and the Office of Planning Evaluation and Policy Development, at https://www.ed.gov/sites/ed/files/rschstat/eval/resources/diversity.pdf (May 2023).

92 Erica Frankenberg, Genevieve Siegel-Hawley, and Jia Wang, *Choice Without Equity: Charter School Segregation and the Need for Civil Rights Standards*, A Report of The Civil Rights Project/Proyecto Derechos Civiles at UCLA (2010), www.civilrightsproject.ucla.edu.

93 Cardona and Rodriguez, "The State of School Diversity in the United States," 4–7.

94 Taylor, Frankenberg, and Siegel-Hawley, "Beth Ford, Jennifer Lapointe, and Nancy Balow Racial Segregation in the Southern Schools, School Districts, and Counties Where Districts Have Seceded."

95 Frankenberg et al., *Choice Without Equity: Charter School Segregation and the Need for Civil Rights Standards.*

96 Manya Walton, Beth Ford, Jennifer Lapointe, and Nancy Balow, "Magnet School Development Framework," Magnet Schools Assistance Program Technical Assistance Center. US Department of Education Office Innovation and Improvement Parental Options and Improvement (2018), 4; Barbara DeLollis, "What Is a Magnet School?" *U.S. News and World Report* (November 16, 2021), https://www.usnews.com/education/k12/articles/what-is-a-magnet-school

97 Janel George and Linda Darling-Hammond, "Advancing Integration and Equity Through Magnet Schools," *Learning Policy Institute* (2021), 4; Frankenberg et al., *Choice Without Equity: Charter School Segregation and the Need for Civil Rights Standards.*

98 Banks, "Multicultural Education: Historical Development, Dimensions, and Practice," 20–22.

99 Shota Uono and Jari K. Hietanen, "Eye Contact Perception in the West and East: A Cross-Cultural Study," *PLoS One*, vol. 10, no. 2 (2015): e0118094.

100 Amy L. Cook, Alveena Shah, Lauren Brodsky, and Laura J. Morizio, "Strengthening School-Family-Community Engagement Through Community Dialogues," *Journal for Social Action in Counseling & Psychology*, vol. 9, no. 1 (2017): 9–37; Abigail Kayser, Brian Kayser, Lars Holmstrom, and Barbara Leilani Brazil Keys, "We Appreciate What You Are Doing, but You Are Doing It Wrong": Two Schools Address School-Family Tensions Through Culturally Responsive Family Partnerships," *Taboo: The Journal of Culture and Education*, vol. 20, no. 2 (2021): 9–27.

101 Gualdalupe Valdés, *Con Respecto: Bridging the Distances Between Culturally Diverse Families and Schools, An Ethnographic Portrait* (New York: Teachers College Press, 1996), 29, 160–205.

102 Cook et al., "Strengthening"; Kayser et al., "We Appreciate What You Are Doing, but You Are Doing It Wrong," 9-11.

103 Denise Forte, "Under ESSA, Achieving Equity in Education Is Still Challenging," The Century Foundation (July 23, 2018), https://tcf.org/content/commentary/essa-achieving-equity-education-still-challenging/

104 George F. Madaus and Marguerite Clarke, "The Adverse Impact of High Stakes Testing on Minority Students: Evidence from 100 Years of Test Data," Report for Institute of Education Sciences (2001), https://eric.ed.gov/?id=ED450183; Gail L. Thompson and Tawannah G. Allen, "Four Effects of the High-Stakes Testing Movement on African American K-12 Students," *Journal of Negro Education*, vol. 81 no. 3 (2012): 218–27.

105 National Academies of Sciences, Engineering, and Medicine, *Monitoring Educational Equity* (2019), accessed at https://doi.org/10.17226/25389

106 National Academies of Sciences, Engineering, and Medicine, "Federal Policy to Advance Racial, Ethnic, and Tribal Health Equity" (July 27, 2023), accessed at https://www.ncbi.nlm.nih.gov/books/NBK596406/#

107 Christine E. Sleeter and H. Richard Milner IV, "Chapter 3: Researching Successful Efforts in Teacher Education to Diversify Teachers," in *Studying Diversity in Teacher Education*, Ametha F. Ball and Cynthia Tyson, eds (Lanham, MD: Rowman and Littlefield, 2011), 81–103.

108 Miles Davison, Andrew Penner, and Emily K. Penner, "Restorative for All? Racial Disproportionality and School Discipline Under Restorative Justice," *American Educational Research Journal*, vol. 59, no. 4 (2022): 687–718.

109 Nora Gordon, "Disproportionality in Student Discipline: Connecting Policy to Research," *Brookings* (January 18, 2018), https://www.brookings.edu/articles/disproportionality-in-student-discipline-connecting-policy-to-research/

110 Davison et al., "Restorative for All?"; Gordon, "Disproportionality in Student Discipline: Connecting Policy to Research."

111 National Academies of Sciences, Engineering, and Medicine, "Federal Policy to Advance Racial, Ethnic, and Tribal Health Equity."

112 Gloria Ladson-Billings, "Toward a Theory of Culturally Relevant Pedagogy," *American Education Research Journal*, vol. 35, no. 3 (1995): 465–91.

113 Geneva Gay, "Preparing for Culturally Responsive Teaching," *Journal of Teacher Education*, vol. 53, no. 2 (2002): 106.

114 Django Paris and Samuel H. Alim, eds, *Culturally Sustaining Pedagogies: Teaching and Learning for Justice in a Changing World* (New York: Teachers College Press, 2017).

115 Dee and Penner, "The Causal Effects"; Cabrera et al., "Missing"; Brittany Aronson and Judson Laughter, "The Theory and Practice of Culturally Relevant Education: A Synthesis of Research Across Content Areas," *Review of Educational Research*, vol. 86, no. 1 (2016): 163–206.

116 Mollie K. Galloway, Petra Callin, Shay James, Harriette Vimegnon, and Lisa McCall, "Culturally Responsive, Antiracist, or Anti-oppressive? How Language Matters for School Change Efforts," *Equity & Excellence in Education*, vol. 52, no. 4 (2019): 485–501.

117 Enid Lee, Deborah Menkart, and Margo Okazawa-Rey, *Beyond Heroes and Holidays: A Practical Guide to K-12 Anti-Racist, Multicultural Education and Staff Development* (Washington, DC: Network of Educators on the Americas, 1997); Huanshu Yuan, "Preparing Teachers for Diversity: A Literature Review and Implications from Community-Based Teacher Education," *Higher Education Studies*, vol. 8, no. 1 (2018): 9–17.

118 Sarah Schwartz, "Map: Where Critical Race Theory Is Under Attack," *Education Week* (June 11, 2021 | Updated: March 21, 2025), at https://www.edweek.org/policy-politics/map-where-critical-race-theory-is-under-attack/2021/06 (accessed on March 24, 2025); Mica Pollock et al., *The Conflict Campaign: Exploring Local Experiences of the Campaign to Ban "Critical Race Theory" in Public K–12 Education in the U.S., 2020–2021*, A Report of UCLA's Institute for Democracy, Education, and Access (2022); PEN America, "Banned in the USA: State Laws Supercharge Book Suppression in Schools," (April 20, 2023), https://pen.org/report/banned-in-the-usa-state-laws-supercharge-book-suppression-in-schools/

119 The White House, "Ending Radical Indoctrination in K-12 Schooling" (January 29, 2025), https://www.whitehouse.gov/presidential-actions/2025/01/ending-radical-indoctrination-in-k-12-schooling/

5

Immigration, Language, and Education

Chapter contents

Chapter objectives

- To explore the meaning and usage of such terms as *pluralism, acculturation*, and *assimilation.*
- To clarify the significance of immigration in shaping educational institutions, laws, policies, and practices.
- To analyze the historical and political contexts of bilingual education in the United States, including pertinent federal and state legislation, significant court cases related to bilingual education, and ideological conflict related to bilingual education.
- To contextualize bilingual education within broader historical and contemporary struggles for educational reform.
- To analyze the policies, political contexts, and discourses affecting immigrant students in today's schools, and how these vary by state.
- To demonstrate understanding of equity issues in multilingual education in the United States, and how to be an effective advocate for multilingual learners and immigrant students.

Opening questions

1. What roles have assimilation and Americanization played in US education, past and present?
2. What effect does immigration have on schooling and education?
3. Why is bilingual education controversial, and how does the controversy relate to differing understandings of the good society?
4. What conditions contribute to inequitable education for immigrant children in the United States, historically and today?
5. What conditions contribute to inequitable education for English learners in the United States, historically and today?
6. How do state-level contexts impact the education of immigrants and English learners?
7. What reforms and promising practices have been attempted to improve the educational experience of immigrant youth and English learners?

The issue

Closely related to the discussions in Chapter 4 of race, ethnicity, and educational equity in a diverse society is the issue of immigration. In 2022, approximately 27 percent of the US population were immigrants or the children of immigrants. The United States has more international migrants than the next four countries combined (Germany, Saudi Arabia, the UK, and France).[1] Although many countries have had high rates of immigration at various points in history, no other country has had as high a rate for as prolonged a period as the United States. Except for American Indians and those forcibly brought to the United States through enslavement or annexation, everyone in the United States is either an immigrant or descendant of immigrants.[2] As a result, the United States is often called a "nation of immigrants" in both a past and present sense.

Although immigration is one of the most polarizing topics in current political debates, the United States has long been thought of as a "melting pot of nations." Exactly when this metaphor originated is uncertain, but a popular play titled *The Melting Pot*, written by Israel Zangwill in 1908, certainly helped spread it. One of the characters describes America as "God's crucible," a "great Melting-pot" where immigrants from around the world are melted down and recast. They come from various national origins, languages, and histories: "But you won't be long like that, brothers, for these are the fires of God you've come to," a seething pot that mingles "East and West, and North and South, the palm and the pine, the pole and the equator, the crescent and the cross," a place where people from "all races and nations" may have hope in the future.[3]

The melting pot metaphor stuck in the popular imagination, but it proves less accurate than might first be assumed. Immigration is surrounded by contentiousness today, and so it was in Zangwill's day. For illustration, the issue may be divided into two broad perspectives. On the one hand were those who valued cultural unity. They believed that immigrants from northern and western Europe would better fit American society and that access should be limited to people from those regions. On the other hand were those who valued cultural diversity and pluralism. They believed immigrants added valuable economic and cultural perspectives and should be allowed to contribute to the development of American society. The balance between these two views has fluctuated over time, with times of war and immigration surges tipping the balance away from pluralism.

Today, similar tensions are present, found not only in political wrangling about immigration and border security but also in arguments over the most appropriate ways to educate the newcomers. Such tensions are difficult to ease, but it is helpful to remember that they have surfaced in one way or another with each new wave of immigrants. What both the unity and the diversity sides seem to forget is that society is always changed by what each immigrant group adds.[4]

Schools reflect the society that creates and supports them; hence, the unity-diversity tension is found in schools, too. The tension is evident in such current issues as whether the languages immigrant children bring with them should be recognized in school programs or whether the children should be immersed in English-only instruction.

Since the beginning of public school systems in the nineteenth century, one of their assumed obligations was **assimilation**, or fitting immigrant children as quickly as possible into American lifestyles and common values. By the early twentieth century, this process came to be called **Americanization**, or educating immigrant children to shed their parents' cultures and embrace American ways. There are those who continue to believe a top priority of the schools should be the rapid assimilation of newcomers to protect national unity from perceived internal and external threats. There are also those who champion more deliberative educational approaches that respect differences and allow cultural diversity.

In raw numbers, the United States is now undergoing the greatest immigrant wave in its history, and ethnic diversity is not only a demographic fact but also a heated political issue. Such conditions directly impact the schools, and educators need to be as knowledgeable as possible about them.

Historical background

Immigrant waves to the United States

The history of immigration to the United States may be divided into four phases, or waves. The first wave, in the late seventeenth and early eighteenth centuries, included mainly English speakers from the British Isles. In the first half of the nineteenth century, a second wave was mainly composed of Irish and German immigrants. Following the Civil War, a third wave of immigrants (lasting roughly from the 1870s to the 1920s) came from southern and eastern Europe, most of whom settled in the cities. The First World War interrupted the flow, but in the mid-1920s Congress imposed country-by-country quotas on immigration, which slowed it to a trickle. In the 1960s, however, reforms eliminated the quotas and helped set the stage for the fourth wave of immigration, which is—numerically speaking—the largest yet and which is still occurring, mostly from countries in Latin America and Asia.

The phenomenon of these "rolling waves" of newcomers has been called "the greatest migration in history." Social institutions, particularly the schools, attempted to make a united people out of many diverse peoples—or what is meant by the motto *e pluribus unum* (out of many, one). In being transplanted from their homelands to the United States, many immigrants encountered for the first time a sense of their own distinctiveness (as Irish or Italians, for example) in a new land where the cultural assumptions of their homelands were not self-evident.[5]

Immigration policies

For a century after the United States was founded, there were virtually no restrictions on immigration into the country, though *citizenship* was limited to white Europeans. It was not until the late nineteenth century that several laws were passed restricting immigration specifically from Asian countries (as described below). The Immigration Act of 1924 established quotas that favored western and northern Europeans, but the Immigration Act of 1965 abolished those discriminatory quotas, opening up large-scale immigration from Latin America and Asia. This pivotal law gave priority to individuals with family members already residing in the United States and those possessing what were deemed to be desirable skills.

Immigrant students in US schools have remained largely invisible, as neither state nor federal education agencies recognize them as a distinct group. Most policies have narrowly focused on English language acquisition, even though a significant portion—26 percent in the 2020–1 school year—of recently arrived immigrant students were already proficient in English. This singular emphasis on language overlooks the socioemotional needs of immigrant youth and fails to address potential gaps in their formal education backgrounds.[6] As described in a section below, the policy debates have largely surrounded what the aims of bilingual education should be—whether to maintain home languages, or replace them with English.

Progressive reform and education

In the late nineteenth and early twentieth centuries, many progressive education reformers saw public schools as instruments to bring about important social changes. Among the beliefs many progressives held was that education helped produce equality and that all children should be schooled to become productive citizens. In facing the problem of massive immigration, however, progressive educational reformers were split between **pluralists** and **nativists**.

The pluralists valued ethnic differences, and most wanted to avoid "denationalizing" immigrant children too quickly or in any total sense. They preferred an education that respected **cultural pluralism** while also preparing every child to become a functioning member of society. The problem with pluralist reformers, some critics charge, is that they failed to deal constructively with cultural differences and, instead, put their faith in economic remedies, the workings of the "melting pot," and slogans about the merits of cultural pluralism.[7]

On the contrary, nativists insisted on rapid Americanization or even the outright exclusion of immigrants labeled by some as "undesirable." For example, Elwood Cubberley, a professor of education at Stanford University in the early 1900s, saw the newcomers as "a very different type." Rather than the familiar immigrants from northern and western Europe, they were now from southern and eastern Europe and the Middle East (Italian, Pole, Bohemian, Slovak, Austrian, Bulgarian, Bosnian, Russian Jew, Syrian, Turk, and Armenian), peoples who Cubberley considered "largely illiterate, docile, [and] lacking in initiative," with almost no "Anglo-Saxon conception of righteousness, liberty, law, order, public decency, and government."[8] At that time, many Americans were only a generation or two away from being immigrants themselves, but the sheer numbers and diverse origins of the newcomers, combined with determined and highly vocal critics, all produced fuel for fear and prejudice.

Generally speaking, most reformers wanted education to provide cultural harmony, social mobility, and economic utility to deal with the massive industrialization, urbanization, and immigration from the late nineteenth through the mid-twentieth centuries. Both native-born and newcomer alike faced major stresses, including an increased need for greater literacy and knowledge. Hard pressed by massive economic change and population growth, most reformers did not fully comprehend either the forces of change or the plight of the immigrants. The remedies they put in place helped establish patterns of response that persist to the present time.

Examples of immigrant groups' access to education

The following sections examine the educational opportunities and access of four specific groups: Chinese, Polish, Italian, and Central American immigrants. This selection provides a glimpse of the divergent experiences of different groups based on their national origins, languages, and the time period during which they immigrated. The final group examined—undocumented immigrants—cuts across national origins and ethnicities. Many educators are likely to teach undocumented students or students with undocumented family members; therefore, it is important to understand the challenges experienced by students with this status.

Chinese immigrants

The mid-nineteenth century marked the beginning of large-scale immigration from China. Many of the first Chinese immigrants to the United States came primarily from Canton Province in China, which at the time was experiencing drought and civil war. Since then, others have not only come from mainland China but also from Hong Kong, Taiwan, the Philippines, and other countries to which Chinese people migrated historically.[9] Thus, people considered Chinese Americans may actually differ in significant ways, not only in terms of social class or educational background but national origin as well.

Despite Chinese traditions dating back to Confucius (551–479 B.C.E.) that placed a high value on education and learning, their education was impeded by xenophobia and prohibitions on their ability to become naturalized citizens or own land. The protection of white political and economic interests by the Jim Crow laws of the South was mirrored in exclusionary immigration laws against Asians. Congress passed the Chinese Exclusion Act in 1882, the only US law to restrict immigration on the basis of race. Japanese immigrants then began filling jobs on the West Coast formerly occupied by Chinese immigrants, such as fishing, farming, and building railroads. However, they too were soon met with discrimination and immigration restrictions. In 1907, the United States and Japan signed a "Gentleman's Agreement" that restricted immigration from Japan. Shortly after, in 1924, Congress passed the Oriental Exclusion Act which denied citizenship and naturalization to all Asians, as well as prevented them from marrying whites or owning land.[10]

The **Immigration Act of 1965** abolished the national-origin quota system, although immigrants with skills deemed desirable, or with relatives who were permanent residents or US citizens, continued to receive favorable treatment.

Figure 5.1 Miss April Lou, teacher at PS 1, Manhattan, with six Chinese children, recent arrivals from Hong Kong and Formosa, who are holding up placards giving his or her Chinese name (both in ideographs and in transliteration) and the name to be entered upon the official school records.

Stemming in large part from the US involvement in the Vietnam War, the Indochinese Refugee Resettlement Act of 1975 and the Refugee Act of 1980 further liberalized immigration laws, permitting the entry of close to one million additional Southeast Asian refugees.[11]

One problem for Chinese immigrant students was the lack of attention to their language needs in schools. In ***Lau v. Nichols*** **(1974)**, however, the US Supreme Court ruled that the failure of San Francisco schools to provide English-language instruction to Chinese American students denied them a meaningful education and violated the Civil Rights Act of 1964. The court did not impose a remedy, but it recognized that teaching the students English as a second language was one option and teaching them in Chinese was another. Whatever the remedy chosen, the court ruled, it was the board of education's responsibility to "apply its expertise" and "rectify the situation." The *Lau* decision also encouraged the passage of the **Equal Educational Opportunity Act of 1974**, which supported bilingual education programs in public schools.[12]

Polish immigrants

By far, the bulk of Polish immigration to the United States came between the 1880s and 1920s, with the newly arrived settling mostly in the urban areas of the Northeast. During the nineteenth century, Poland was occupied by three different powers—Germany, Russia, and Austria. In the German-occupied sector, children had access to better schools than in the other two sectors; however, after German chancellor Otto von Bismarck imposed state control over the Roman Catholic Church of Poland in 1871, the schools began reflecting anti-Catholic and anti-Polish views, which helped push the initial wave of Polish immigrants to the United States, followed by subsequent waves from the other two sectors. The fact that American public schools were free appealed to Polish immigrants, most of whom were poor. Most of them were also devout Roman Catholics; therefore, existing Catholic **parochial schools** previously established by Irish and German immigrants also proved a popular choice. Of course, not all Polish immigrants were of a single mind about either education or religion. Some Poles were secularists, some were Jews, but most were Catholics. After Catholic leaders encouraged Polish immigrants to attend existing parochial schools and to start building their own as well, most of them chose the parochial school option.[13]

> **For Further Reflection:** Should tax monies be used to support parochial schools?

Almost all Polish immigrants maintained strong affinities for Polish traditions, but this did not keep them from eventually developing loyalty to the United States. As their schools developed, they reflected an almost exclusive emphasis on the Polish language and culture, even to the point of reprinting old textbooks from Poland. With the passage of time, however, curriculum materials were developed specifically for Polish American schools, and American values came to be emphasized, even when students continued to be taught in Polish. When societal pressures emerged for the Poles to become more Americanized, such as government concerns about Polish immigrant loyalty to the Allied cause during the First World War, the Polish nationalism expressed in their curriculum materials was toned down. By the 1930s, English usage increased in both verbal instruction and printed materials, although Polish continued to be used for religious instruction. By the 1940s, English was becoming the standard language in Polish schools and communities, but a strong sense of ethnicity still flourished.[14]

Eventually, the strong Polish identity declined, and the pressures came not only from the outside. The Catholic Church served a variety of immigrant groups, and church leaders decided they had to build an American rather than an Irish, Italian, or Polish American Catholic Church. In 1916, there were more than 1200 Catholic "national" parishes in the United States, with some using a particular immigrant group's native language exclusively or else using English only occasionally. In 1918, however, the papacy stopped the creation of new national parishes, except in special cases. In addition, the maintenance of a strong Polish identity suffered because the Polish American community never founded its own higher education institutions, as the Irish did with Notre Dame University or the Jews with Brandeis University. Thus, with fewer institutional structures to cultivate Polish identity, it receded over time.[15]

Italian immigrants

The great influx of Italian immigrants occurred from the 1880s to the 1920s, when more than 4.5 million people came to the United States. Most came from southern Italy, from the regions of Abruzzi, Calabria, Campania, and the island of Sicily. They were overwhelmingly of rural origin and had a long history of poverty and exploitation. Many Italian immigrants intended to return home after "making it" in the United States, and several hundred thousand actually returned to their native land in the early 1900s. This fed negative attitudes about "ungrateful" Italian immigrants, but most Italian immigrants came to stay.[16]

In their new homeland, Italian immigrants faced an industrial society that was unfamiliar to them, a formerly rural people now living in urban areas and working in mechanized industries. Often exploited by their own *padrones* (labor bosses) and confronted with a strange and hostile social environment, many held tightly to the old ways by keeping to their families in close-knit ethnic neighborhoods where they found support and could protect their children from unwanted assimilation. For such reasons, an Italian enclave (or Little Italy, as it was often called) sprang up in many American cities.[17]

For Further Reflection: How important is family to educational success? What are some of the various ways that family impacted the educational attainment of immigrant children?

However, where Polish immigrants clung to their Catholic parish schools, the Italians did not because most of the parents preferred public schools. Since the majority of Italian immigrants were from the rural peasantry who identified with their local villages, they had little or no identity with the central church hierarchy in Rome, perhaps because it was run by the upper class that had long oppressed them. They might respect distant church leaders, but they identified church and religion with their local priest, who was usually one of them. Therefore, in the United States, the pleas of the church hierarchy for Italian parish schools yielded far less response than among Polish immigrants.[18]

American tradition holds that free public schools enabled most immigrant children to enter adult society, with at least some achieving wealth and success. Numerous immigrants left testimonials to the availability of free public education and how the American faith in education brought hope and meaning to the immigrant world of privation and want. However, this tradition has been questioned. Revisionist critics maintain that public schools were instruments designed to control immigrants, not free them. Rather than being avenues to equality and upward mobility, the schools were compulsory, bureaucratic, class-biased, and racist.[19]

Figure 5.2 An Italian home near Hull House, 1910.

The Italian immigrant experience provides a good source of material to test such views. There is evidence that the schools probably did control more than liberate, but while assimilation was slow, it was also relentless and came from a number of influences in addition to schools. Many second- and third-generation Italians eventually moved out of the old neighborhoods and into the larger society as bankers, merchants, manufacturers, builders, and members of other professions, all of which was aided by formal education. Italian immigrants did not exhibit the nationalistic identity with their origins as the Poles did, but they nevertheless took great pride in Italian culture, particularly its art and music, and they maintained close affinity with those sources of pride.[20] Today, ethnic Italian identity is still present, but most descendants of Italian immigrants perceive themselves as part and parcel of mainstream American society.

For Further Reflection: In your opinion, are schools more prone to control immigrant students today or to serve as empowering forces? Justify your position.

Central American immigrants

Since 1990, Latin America has been the top origin region for immigrants to the United States. In the 2010s and 2020s, a growing share came from the Northern Triangle countries of Guatemala, El Salvador, and Honduras, driven by a complex mix of factors. Civil wars in the 1980s, fueled in part by Cold War-era US intervention and funding of counterrevolutionary groups, precipitated initial waves of migration as violence destabilized the region. In Guatemala, for example, the 36-year war from 1960 to 1996 resulted in an estimated 200,000 deaths. The instability in these countries became fertile ground for drug trafficking and violent transnational gang activity.

As a result of drug-related gang violence, extreme poverty, climate-change related drought, and food insecurity, many Central American migrants continue to seek refuge in the United States. In the first decades of the twenty-first century, homicide rates in these countries were among the highest in the world, and femicide rates (murders of women and girls) in El Salvador and Honduras were among the highest in Latin America.[21] Many migrants have come from Mayan backgrounds and speak Spanish as a second language. While the Immigration Act of 1990 established **Temporary Protected Status (TPS)** to provide relief for those fleeing disasters or armed conflict, the complex realities driving modern

Central American migration make qualifying for asylum difficult.[22] Among those fleeing are thousands of unaccompanied children. In 2018, more than 38,000 unaccompanied minors from the Northern Triangle were apprehended at the border. Some of these children come involuntarily as labor or sex trafficking victims.[23]

In the late 2010s, the US government attempted to curb immigration from the Northern Triangle, first by partnering with Northern Triangle governments on counternarcotics and anti-smuggling initiatives and then by withholding aid to those countries. In 2018, the Trump administration issued a "zero tolerance" policy, which controversially led to the detainment of asylum seekers and the separation of children from their parents. Although most were later reunited with their parents, it is estimated that between 5,300 and 5,500 children were forced to spend some period of time separated from their parents in a new and unfamiliar country.[24]

Undocumented immigrants

Some immigrants in the United States do not have official legal status like Temporary Protected Status, a green card for permanent residency, citizenship, or other authorization to live in the country. These immigrants are considered "**undocumented immigrants**." Another term sometimes used is "illegal," though this word is dehumanizing and misleading, since residing in the country without papers is a civil violation, not a criminal one.

A major debate has been whether undocumented immigrant children should be allowed to enroll in public schools. In 1975, Texas passed a law letting school districts deny these students enrollment. Four families sued with help from the Mexican American Legal Defense and Education Fund. The case went to the Supreme Court, which ruled 5-4 in ***Plyler v. Doe* (1982)** that blocking undocumented children from public education violates the Fourteenth Amendment's Equal Protection Clause. The Court wrote that denying these children public education "imposes a lifetime hardship on a discrete class of children not accountable for their disabling status .... By denying these children a basic education, we deny them the ability to live within the structure of our civic institutions, and foreclose any realistic possibility that they will contribute in even the smallest way to the progress of our Nation."[25]

Since then, the US Department of Education has given guidance to school districts to ensure their enrollment procedures comply with federal civil rights laws. When schools seek proof of residency within their attendance zone in order to evaluate eligibility for enrollment, they are not to ask for proof of citizenship.

Instead, they can ask for lease agreements, utility bills, or other documentation that the family's address falls within the school's attendance zone. Asking for proof of citizenship, rather than just proof of address, could discourage families from enrolling and therefore have a discriminatory effect. If districts ask for social security numbers, they are required to "inform the individual that the disclosure is voluntary, provide the statutory or other basis upon which it is seeking the number, and explain what uses will be made of it."[26]

The *Plyler* decision has not prevented states and localities from attempting to exclude undocumented immigrants from schools and other public services. For example, California adopted Proposition 187, based on a popular referendum in 1994, that attempted to deny schooling and medical care to undocumented immigrants. Although the policy was deemed unconstitutional, it has served as a sample referendum other states and governments have since used in their own attempts to limit access to schools.[27] Beyond just enrolling undocumented students, schools face broader questions of true inclusion and equity for this population. This issue will resurface in the Contemporary Conditions section.

History and politics of bilingual education

Although it may surprise many to learn this, bilingual schools abounded in the first centuries after European colonization of what is now the United States. There is a widespread assumption that immigrants of prior centuries gave up their home languages upon moving to the United States in a rapid attempt to Americanize. In fact, wherever non-English speaking immigrant groups settled in the seventeenth through nineteenth centuries, home language instruction was common. For example, Spanish instruction was prevalent throughout the Southwest in the nineteenth century, and German instruction was common throughout the United States until the start of the First World War. Various communities across the United States offered programs in Cherokee, Chinese, Polish, Italian, Danish, Japanese, Czech, and other languages.

US history has seen the public attitude pendulum swing from tolerance or promotion of multilingual education to **linguistic restrictionism** and back, often dependent upon global events or rates of immigration at a given time. For instance, during the Second World War, Japanese-language schools in Hawaii and California were closed. These policies are generally focused more on social control than helping students who speak languages other than English. Enslaved Africans were not allowed to use their home languages or acquire

English literacy, and American Indians were forced into English-only boarding schools,[28] as described in Chapter 4.

The civil rights movement of the 1950s and 1960s saw increasing demands for linguistic tolerance and bilingual education. Prior to this time, students learning English as a new language were not guaranteed any instruction in the acquisition of English. They were often placed in "sink or swim" situations in which no specific instruction or materials were provided to help them develop English language proficiency. Concerned by the low graduation rates of Mexican American students in particular, communities and educators began advocating for equitable education for Spanish-speaking children. This ultimately led to the first federal legislation pertaining to bilingual education.

The **Bilingual Education Act (BEA)**, (also known as Title VII of the Elementary and Secondary Education Act, or ESEA) was signed by President Lyndon B. Johnson in 1968. Though the idea of bilingual education would later become controversial, at the time of the legislation's passage, there was bipartisan support and relatively little opposition. One contributing factor may have been that the law did not require schools to deliver instruction in languages other than English but rather funded instructional materials, teacher training, and educational programs. Another may be that the policy left unclear whether its intended goal was bilingualism or only acquisition of English. Following enactment of the law, many states began authorizing instruction in languages other than English, and in some cases, requiring such instruction when the number of students learning English passed a certain threshold.[29]

In 1970, the federal **Office of Civil Rights (OCR)** gave school districts specific guidance on how the BEA should be implemented. This guidance stated that schools should offer special language instruction for children acquiring English and to communicate with parents in a language they could understand. However, it was not until the federal courts stepped in that school districts began complying with this requirement. The most significant of these cases was Lau v. Nichols (1974). The case began as a class-action lawsuit on behalf of Chinese-background students in San Francisco who argued they were being denied equal education because of their limited English skills. The Supreme Court ruled, "There is no equality of treatment merely by providing students with the same facilities, textbooks, teachers, and curriculum, for students who do not understand English are effectively foreclosed from any meaningful education." The ruling effectively outlawed sink-or-swim approaches and led to what were called the **Lau Remedies.** These were guidelines for districts on how to identify children with limited English skills and on the instructional approaches that would meet federal standards for equal treatment. The Remedies ordered districts to provide bilingual instruction, not just **English as a Second Language (ESL)** programming, to elementary-aged children in order to attend to their affective and cognitive development, as well as linguistic and academic development. This was not required for secondary students.[30]

An ongoing debate throughout these decades was whether bilingual education should prioritize transitioning students to English or promoting bilingualism and biliteracy. The Ethnic Heritage Act of 1972 provided federal aid for curriculum materials and research centers that supported the maintenance of heritage languages and cultures, but the policy was quickly met with a backlash. Critics argued that heritage language maintenance conflicted with acquisition of English and assimilation into the mainstream. Others expressed concerns that bilingual tracks might exacerbate de facto segregation. In its amendments to the Bilingual Education Act in 1978, Congress clarified that federal funds were only to be used for transition to English, not maintenance of home languages.[31]

A 1981 court decision, ***Castañeda v. Pickard***, outlined three criteria schools must meet to be considered upholding the civil rights of language-minority children:

1. Programs serving children learning English must be based on "sound educational theory."
2. Programs must be "implemented effectively," which includes sufficient personnel and resources.
3. Programs must be evaluated for effectiveness after a trial period.

This three-prong test, as it would be called, led states to develop their own standards for compliance. However, the first prong proved too easily met, as almost any program could find some literature or scholar to support its particular approach. The second prong could also be met easily if a program required few resources, and the third allowed a number of years to pass before a program was evaluated, resulting in multiple cohorts of students experiencing ineffective models.

The public attitude pendulum swung back toward nativism in the 1980s and 1990s. Though the Cold War was over and the economy booming, economic well-being for many in the middle class was no longer as secure as it once had been, as companies merged, outsourced work, and expanded the pay gap between executives and workers. This period saw court rulings that were less sympathetic to claims of civil rights and public opposition to bilingual education, both transitional and maintenance. OCR enforcement of the Lau Remedies dramatically declined in the 1980s and 1990s as well.[32]

Language restrictionism reached a peak in the late 1990s and early 2000s when California, Arizona, and Massachusetts passed ballot measures that forbid the use of home languages for instructional purposes. Called "English-only" laws, these affected 40 percent of **English learners (ELs)**. Researchers would later find that these laws negatively impacted graduation rates and reading and math achievement for ELs.[33]

> **Suggested Activity:** To what extent have language education policies in the United States reflected best practices as identified in research versus political sentiments of the time? Do you think this balance (or imbalance) holds true for other education policies in addition to language education? Conduct research to identify other examples. Discuss what may account for this tension.

Contemporary conditions

Immigration today is different in many ways from the immigration of prior centuries. Advances in communication and transportation technologies allow immigrants to maintain more transnational identities, as many move back and forth and regularly communicate with friends and family from back home. Transnationalism and globalization affect the ways in which immigrants build new lives in the countries where they settle.

Another major shift has been the political climate surrounding immigration in the United States. Although anti-immigrant sentiment existed prior to the September 11 terrorist attacks, that moment marked a turning point. In response to the attacks, the US government eliminated the Immigration and Naturalization Service (INS) and replaced it with three new agencies under the newly formed Department of Homeland Security: US Citizenship and Immigration Services (USCIS), Immigration and Customs Enforcement (ICE), and Customs and Border Protection (CBP). CBP enforces border security, USCIS processes requests such as naturalization applications, and ICE enforces trade and immigration laws beyond the area immediately surrounding borders.[34]

ICE has increasingly come to the attention of school personnel as their enforcement activities can affect students. For example, ICE has been reported to have arrested teens awaiting their school bus and parents dropping their kids off at school. Critics say these enforcement activities traumatize children and deter families from enrolling their children in schools. In response, some school districts have issued resolutions stating that administrators will take measures to protect students from immigration enforcement activities during the school day.[35]

The debates over ICE are just one of many surrounding immigration in the United States. Congress has tried and failed to pass a new comprehensive immigration bill multiple times since the last one was enacted in 1986. After a 2013 bill was passed by the Senate but stalled in the House of Representatives, President Barack Obama began using executive actions as "stopgap" measures. One measure especially relevant for educators was the **Deferred Action for Childhood Arrivals,** or **DACA**, program. DACA was an attempt to accomplish part of the aims of the **DREAM Act**, or Development Relief and Education for Alien Minors. The DREAM Act would have provided a pathway to citizenship for undocumented individuals who were brought to the United States as children. Despite popular and bipartisan support, Congress failed to pass versions of the DREAM Act eleven times between 2001 and 2021. This led Obama to issue DACA, which provided a temporary relief from deportation and work permits for these young people, but not a pathway to citizenship. Obama also issued a similar plan for their parents, called Deferred Action for Parents of Americans (DAPA), but the Supreme Court overturned it in 2016.[36]

DACA has been challenged several times in court and was ruled unlawful in 2021.[37] Although a 2022 poll found that nearly 70 percent of Americans support a pathway to citizenship for undocumented immigrants already living in the United States, a majority in another poll believed illegal immigration is "a 'critical' threat to US national security."[38] These responses are emblematic of the public opinion divide regarding how to respond to immigration in the United States. There is general agreement that the immigration system is broken, but little consensus on how to fix it.

For Further Reflection: In what ways does the history of immigration shape your thinking about the immigration system today?

The 2016 campaign and subsequent election of Donald Trump as the 45th president ushered in a new era in which politicians would publicly espouse xenophobic views to gain voter support. Prior presidents and politicians had strategically masked appeals to tacit racism, with public endorsement of racism and xenophobia being considered politically costly in those times. By contrast, Trump regularly appealed to these sentiments in order to convince voters that only he could protect them from what he cast as "external threats." Throughout his first and second presidential campaigns and administrations, Trump frequently claimed that undocumented immigrants were stealing jobs and fueling violent crime in the United States, though research suggests they actually commit crimes at a lower rate than US citizens, and economists find that immigration boosts the economy and job growth.[39] Early in his second term, President Trump abolished a longstanding policy that ICE would not conduct enforcement activities in sensitive locations such as schools, hospitals, or churches. This has led some immigrant families to fear sending their children to school. In addition, the hostile political climate has increased undocumented students' stress and anxiety and led to increased bullying of this group in schools.[40]

Accompanying the polarization of the public on the issue of immigration has been a polarization in state responses. Conservative-led states (so-called *red states)* like Texas and Florida have taken on immigration enforcement themselves. Some of these states began busing asylum seekers to states controlled by Democrats (so-called *blue states)*, with the justification being that these states should have to share in the responsibility to receive these migrants. In 2022, Texas began busing tens of thousands of asylum seekers to self-declared sanctuary cities, like New York City. New York reported processing over 120,000 migrants in less than a year, putting a strain on resources such as shelters and schools. Other cities, including Chicago, Los Angeles, and Denver, have also received thousands of migrants bused from Texas.[41] This situation highlights the urgent need for federal comprehensive immigration reform legislation.

In addition, the second Trump administration has used a combination of threats, financial incentives, and examples of sending legal residents to a notorious prison in El Salvador as a means of reducing new immigration and encouraging self-deportations. Trump invoked the Alien Enemies Act (last used in the Second World War and only ever used during declared wars) as legal grounds for deporting alleged gang members to a notorious prison in El Salvador, even if the individuals were not from El Salvador and had not been convicted of gang-related crime. The Supreme Court ruled in April of 2025 that Trump could use the Alien Enemies Act to deport alleged gang members, but the immigrants must be given the opportunity to challenge the deportation in court, which had been denied to over a hundred deportees before that ruling. This is just one example of the many ways in which the second Trump administration has been

Figure 5.3 Hundreds of protesters gathered at the Federal Building in Westwood on June 23, 2018, in opposition to President Trump's immigration policy that resulted in more than 2,000 children being separated from their parents.

disregarding civil rights long protected in laws and court decisions in order to decrease immigration to the United States.[42] For educators, it is important to understand the national political contexts that affect the immigrant and refugee students in their classrooms.

Today's immigrant students

The 2014–15 school year marked the first time white students were the racial minority in US public schools, a change largely brought about by increases in Hispanic and Asian school-age children born in the United States. Whereas white students made up 63.4 percent of the school-age population in 1997, they made up just 45 percent by 2021.[43] Although these increases have been largely driven by US-born children, the nation also experienced dramatic growth in the foreign-born student population between 2011 and 2019, particularly in states across the South, and traditional destination states of Texas, Florida, California, and New York (See Table 5.1).

Table 5.1 States with the Highest Number of Recent Arrivals and Total Immigrant Children Ages 5–17, 2021

State	States with highest number of recent immigrant children arrivals (within last three years)	States with highest number of total immigrant children	Both
California			X
Florida			X
Illinois		X	
Massachusetts			X
New Jersey			X
New York			X
North Carolina	X		
Pennsylvania			X
Texas			X
Virginia			X
Washington			X

Source: Julie Sugarman. "Recent Immigrant Children: A Profile of New Arrivals to US Schools," Migration Policy Institute (October 23, 2023). https://www.migrationpolicy.org/sites/default/files/publications/mpi-recent-immigrant-children-2023_final.pd

In 2021, about half of recent immigrant students (those attending US schools for three years or less) were Hispanic. Although the largest share of Hispanic immigrant students is from Mexico, the number of immigrant children from the Central American countries of Guatemala, Honduras, and El Salvador increased dramatically between 2017 and 2021. Among the other top ten countries of birth of recent immigrant children are India, China, and the Philippines (See Table 5.2).[44]

Immigrant students have unique educational needs. Many arrive with limited or interrupted education and traumatic experiences in their home countries and/or while journeying to the United States. They are more likely than their peers to live in low-income households and with parents who have not completed high school, or with family members who are not their parents. An estimated 32 percent of recent immigrant children in 2019 were undocumented.[45] Three-quarters of recent immigrant students are designated as English learners. Nine percent of recent immigrant, high-school aged youth are not enrolled in school, compared to just three percent of their peers.[46]

While considering these statistics, it is important to keep in mind that immigrant youth are a diverse population that includes children of high-skilled workers, resettled refugees, and many other groups. In all of these cases,

Table 5.2 Top Ten Countries of Birth of Recent Immigrant Children Ages 5–17 in the United States, 2021

Country	Percent
Mexico	13%
Honduras	9%
Guatemala	8%
India	6%
El Salvador	5%
Dominican Republic	4%
Brazil	4%
Venezuela	3%
China/Hong Kong	3%
The Philippines	2%

Source: Julie Sugarman, "Recent Immigrant Children: A Profile of New Arrivals to US Schools," Migration Policy Institute (October 23, 2023). https://www.migrationpolicy.org/sites/default/files/publications/mpi-recent-immigrant-children-2023_final.pdf

immigrant youth bring valuable cognitive, linguistic, and cultural assets to the classroom that benefit their school communities. Although it is important for educators to understand the stressors faced by many immigrant youth and families, it is equally important to recognize and affirm their strengths, which can include multilingualism, intercultural competence, and global awareness.

For Further Reflection: Reflect on your schooling experiences and the many ways in which students from diverse backgrounds and countries enrich school culture.

Immigrant students' educational opportunities and achievement

As one might expect given the heterogeneity of immigrants to the United States, academic achievement varies widely across country of origin, generational status (e.g., first generation vs. second generation), race/ethnicity, and schooling conditions in the United States. Immigration to the United States leads to upward mobility for countless immigrant families, but many also experience poor-quality schools, discrimination, and other barriers to social mobility. These outcomes are related both to the resources immigrant families bring with them as well as the conditions of their reception in the United States. The **contexts of reception** can range from welcoming to hostile. Schools are one of the most important receiving institutions, considering they provide opportunities for integration into the new society, as well as socialization and social network development.[47] Sociologists developed the theory of **segmented assimilation** to describe how educational and other social contexts differentiate paths toward assimilation into a new society. Immigrants with lower educational attainment tend to assimilate into an underclass from which it is difficult to advance, while those with higher educational attainment can achieve the upward mobility immigrants hope for when moving for a better life.[48]

Research in the 1980s and 1990s found that first-generation immigrants performed better in schools than their second-generation peers, even though immigrants have higher-than-average rates of social and economic disadvantages. Compounding those economic disadvantages, immigrants from lower socioeconomic statuses tend to move to neighborhoods that are more segregated and have lower-resourced schools than average. These schools often have fewer qualified teachers, more teacher turnover, and higher student-teacher ratios than schools in more affluent neighborhoods, resulting in what some researchers have called a **double disadvantage**. Unsurprisingly, immigrants in these types of schools achieve lower academic outcomes than immigrants who move to more affluent school districts.[49] However, some research has suggested the neighborhood disadvantages affecting immigrant achievement are more associated with race/ethnicity than with national origin.[50]

Researchers are not sure why immigrants have performed better than peers of similar socioeconomic status, but they have generated several hypotheses. One possible explanation is the selectivity effect—in other words, that families who migrated may differ from their peers in ways that are associated with higher academic achievement (e.g., motivation, determination, optimism). Immigrant parents often move to the United States for educational and economic opportunities for their children. As a result, they tend to hold their children to high expectations and marshal additional resources, beyond those offered by the school, to support their achievement. Strong family connections and bilingualism are also associated with higher academic achievement.[51]

To explain the lower academic outcomes of second-generation immigrants, Angela Valenzuela posited a theory she called **subtractive schooling**, based on her ethnographic study of a mostly Mexican-American high school in Texas. This referred to the process by which cultural assets were subtracted from second-generation immigrants as the school assimilated these youth into dominant American culture. Whereas first-generation immigrants tended to have a strong sense of ethnic pride and a positive attitude toward education as a means of upward mobility, second-generation students had accumulated more experiences with prejudices and discrimination based on their Mexican heritage and Spanish language. These students then felt they had to choose between abandoning their heritage in order to assimilate into the dominant culture of the school and society, or disengage from school to preserve their positive ethnic identity and social capital.

Studies beginning in the early 2000s found a different pattern in educational achievement. According to this research, the math achievement scores were lower for first-generation immigrants than their third-generation peers. In general, researchers began to find that educational performance was more associated with race/ethnicity and socioeconomic status than generational status, suggesting the importance of contexts of reception in schools and communities. Recent research has found that immigrant students, on average, attend schools that are larger, enroll more poor students, and have lower shares of qualified math teachers than schools attended by their US-born counterparts. As a result, disparities in achievement between immigrant and US-born students appear to be largely attributable to the differences in school contexts.[52]

Many immigrant students in the United States are considered **migratory**, meaning that their caregivers move frequently for agricultural or industrial jobs. In June 2023, the US Department of Education Office for Civil Rights and the US Department of Justice Civil Rights Division issued a resource for families and schools explaining the barriers faced by migratory children, their civil rights, and whom to contact if one believes a migratory child has experienced discrimination based on national origin, immigration status, or English learner status. Some of the barriers described include schools asking students to provide Social Security numbers or birth certificates to enroll, or denying enrollment to children who move multiple times in the course of a year, or live in temporary labor housing that makes proof-of-residency requirements challenging. The guidance also reminds schools that they are required to offer language assistance services to students with limited English proficiency, including migratory children, and must provide information in a language parents and caregivers can understand.[53]

> **For Further Reflection:** Within schools, what can school leaders and teachers do to create positive contexts of reception for immigrant students? Discuss examples you have encountered or ideas you have for school policies and practices that might be beneficial for immigrant students, based on what you have learned in this chapter.

Impacts of state policy on immigrant achievement

One major contributor to the contexts of reception is state-level policy, which varies widely from state to state, from punitive to inclusive. Some states have taken it upon themselves to enforce immigration laws, for instance, through allowing police to detain individuals who do not produce proof of residence. In these contexts, immigrants tend to remain more self-contained within their communities, resulting in less seeking of medical care, less reporting of crime, and overall less integration into the larger society. Other states have created more inclusive contexts of reception. For example, some states have provided undocumented residents access to Medicaid-equivalent benefits since Medicaid and federally subsidized health insurance programs limit eligibility based on citizenship and immigration status.[54] Fewer than half the states issue driver's licenses to undocumented residents, which greatly influences the jobs people can secure and maintain and often the extracurricular activities their children can participate in.[55]

State-level education policies particularly affect immigrants' education outcomes. For instance, many states do not allow undocumented immigrants to pay in-state tuition rates at colleges and universities, even if they meet the requirements (typically living in the state for a number of years and graduating from a high school in that state). Out-of-state tuition rates are generally several times the cost of in-state rates, rendering college out of reach for many students in these states. Three states—Georgia, Alabama, and South Carolina—actually prohibit undocumented youth from enrolling in public institutions of higher education at all, though they may allow DACA recipients to enroll. Undocumented students in all states are currently ineligible for federal financial aid (at the time of writing). Youth frequently do not discover these barriers to their continued education until they are in the process of applying to college. The sudden realization that hard work in pursuit of college admission has been in vain may lead to depression and disengagement from school.[56]

As of 2024, twenty-five states and the District of Columbia had **tuition equity laws** that granted access to in-state tuition rates for undocumented students (see Table 5.3). Research has shown that states with tuition equity laws have higher graduation rates, higher rates of students enrolling in college, and higher student incomes and tax contributions.[57] This is just one example of state-level education policy that influences immigrant educational outcomes. When more welcoming contexts are created through education policy, combined with general immigration legislation, such as those affecting access to work authorization, health insurance and driver's licenses, immigrant youth perform better in school.[58] It is important for teachers and other school staff to be familiar with their state's policies so they can better understand challenges and opportunities for their students.

Suggested Activity: Research your state's policies regarding undocumented immigrants. In your state, are undocumented immigrants able to obtain driver's licenses and pay in-state tuition at public universities and colleges, for example? Discuss the extent to which you think your state's policies create positive contexts of reception for immigrants and the impacts this may have on immigrant educational achievement in your state.

Table 5.3 States with Tuition Equity for Undocumented Immigrant Students

State or State University System	Permits certain students who have attended and graduated from secondary schools in their state to pay the same tuition as their "in-state" classmates, regardless of their immigration status	Offers state financial aid to students who meet certain criteria, regardless of their immigration status	Both
Arizona	X		
California			X
Colorado			X
Connecticut			X
Florida	X		
Hawaii	X		
Illinois			X
Kansas	X		

State or State University System	Permits certain students who have attended and graduated from secondary schools in their state to pay the same tuition as their "in-state" classmates, regardless of their immigration status	Offers state financial aid to students who meet certain criteria, regardless of their immigration status	Both
Kentucky	X		
Maryland			X
Massachusetts			X
Minnesota			X
Nebraska	X		
Nevada	X		
New Jersey			X
New Mexico			X
New York			X
Oklahoma			X
Oregon			X
Rhode Island	X		
Texas			X
Utah	X		
Vermont			X
Virginia			X
Washington			X
District of Columbia		X	
University of Michigan system	X		

Source: National Immigration Law Center, "Basic Facts about In-State Tuition for Undocumented Immigrant Students" (Last updated June 3, 2024). https://www.nilc.org/wp-content/uploads/2024/06/instate-tuition-basicfacts-2024-06-1-1.pdf

English learner achievement

A portion of immigrant students are learning English as an additional language and thus are classified as English learners (ELs). Linguistics and education researchers have found that it generally takes at least seven years to acquire academic language. In the first one to three months, many students experience a "silent period," followed by several months of speaking in short phrases. It can then take three to four years to gain what linguists call "basic interpersonal communication skills" and four to six years to gain academic language proficiency.

This of course varies depending on students' readiness, motivation, abilities, and access to high-quality instruction.[59] Until students demonstrate proficiency, they are considered ELs and are entitled to English as a Second Language (ESL) services as established in the *Lau v. Nichols* (1974) ruling described earlier.

ELs made up 11 percent of the US public school population in 2021, which was more than a 10 percent increase from the decade prior. Of these, 76.4 percent reported Spanish as their home language, with Arabic being the second-most spoken language (See Table 5.4).[60] It may surprise many to learn that most ELs were born in the United States and are US citizens. Even among middle and high school-aged ELs, the majority are US-born.[61] They may still be classified as ELs because they lived in another country for part of their education or they may be what is called a **long-term English Learner.** This is a student who has been in US schools for at least six years but has not yet been redesignated as a former English learner, which could be for a number of reasons. Many understand and speak English well but struggle with academic reading and/or writing. In some cases, students did not attain literacy in their home language and thus do not have that important foundation on which to build. Some long-term ELs have moved multiple times either within the United States or back and forth from another country. Some may have learning

Table 5.4 Top Ten Home Languages of Recent Immigrant Children Ages 5–17 in the United States, 2021

Language	Percent
Spanish	48%
English	11%
Portuguese	4%
Arabic	3%
Chinese	3%
French	2%
Russian	2%
Tagalog	2%
Vietnamese	1%
Farsi/Persian	1%

Source: Julie Sugarman. "Recent Immigrant Children: A Profile of New Arrivals to US Schools," Migration Policy Institute (October 23, 2023). https://www.migrationpolicy.org/sites/default/files/publications/mpi-recent-immigrant-children-2023_final.pdf

disabilities that went undiagnosed because staff may have wrongly assumed the issue to be purely related to language acquisition.[62]

Differentiating between learning disabilities and language acquisition issues can be a challenge for school staff. ELs who are also diagnosed as having a disability are known as **dually identified students.** These students may not always receive the same access to dual language programs because they are viewed as not being able to succeed in multilingual environments, though research does not support that concern. Even more troubling, these placement decisions are sometimes made without input from families and students.[63]

Research has shown that ELs tend to be under-identified for special education in the elementary grades but over-identified in the secondary grades. This pattern may vary based on language, with one study finding that Spanish-speaking students were under-identified while Cantonese and Mandarin-speaking students were appropriately identified. However, another study found that Asian American students were over-identified because the students who did not fit the model minority stereotype were assumed to have a learning disability. Both under- and over-identification are problems. Under-identification means some students are not receiving the special education services they should be, while over-identification means some students are being inappropriately excluded from general education classrooms.

ELs are also significantly under-represented in gifted programs. Although 7.3 percent of non-ELs are enrolled in gifted programs nationally, only 3 percent of ELs are. Reasons for this could include under-identification of high ability, as well as reluctance to place ELs in these programs while they are still learning English.[64]

ELs graduate at lower rates than their peers; however, the gap varies significantly across states, suggesting that a complex combination of factors–beyond just language–accounts for the achievement disparities. For example, in Delaware, the EL graduation rate was 77 percent, compared to 87 percent of the total population in 2017, while in six states the EL graduation rate is less than *half* the total graduation rate. In Arizona, for example, the EL graduation rate was just 18 percent compared to 75.7 percent total graduation.[65]

Schools face many challenges in ensuring ELs have sufficient language support to succeed in all of their courses. Over half of all states reported a shortage of teachers trained or certified in **Teaching English to Speakers of Other Languages (TESOL)** in the 2023–4 school year.[66] Teachers of secondary content areas such as science and history may not have TESOL training or an ESL teacher in their classroom to assist their ELs with the challenging academic language required in these disciplines. Schools often lack enough bilingual staff to communicate with parents and caregivers who are not proficient in English. Although schools are required to provide information in a language families can understand, the degree of enforcement and compliance with this requirement varies across states and school districts. There are also constraints posed by curriculum and assessment requirements, as discussed in the next section.

For Further Reflection: What do you see as some of the biggest weaknesses in the US educational system's support for English learners? What do you see as some of the contributing causes to these weaknesses? What might be done to strengthen education for ELs?

Bilingual and ESL programs in schools

Given the common conception of the United States as "a nation of immigrants," one might expect widespread bilingual education programs like those of other multilingual nations such as France or Cyprus. However, while the percentage of students in each of those countries learning a foreign language is 100 and 99, respectively, the percentage of students in the United States learning a foreign language is only 20. Unlike most European countries, the United States has no national-level requirement that students learn a foreign language. Only ten states and the District of Columbia have foreign language graduation requirements. By contrast, over twenty European countries require students to study at least *two* foreign languages.[67]

However, as globalization dramatically changes the world of work and society in general, more English-speaking families want their children to learn a second language. One model of bilingual education growing in popularity allows English-speaking students learning a second language to study alongside language minorities learning English. Called **two-way bilingual immersion**, these programs typically balance classrooms with about 50 percent students learning English and 50 percent students learning a minority language–most often Spanish, French, or Mandarin. Half of the instruction is provided in English and half in the target language. These programs are considered **additive bilingual programs** because both groups of students have the opportunity to achieve high levels of fluency and literacy in both their first and second languages.

Two-way immersion programs also address a common problem in traditional ESL models, such as **push-in** and **pull-out** approaches, which is that language minority students are isolated from their peers and viewed as having a deficit that needs remediation. By contrast, in two-way immersion programs, language minority students are positioned as having the asset of fluency in the language their peers are trying to learn. English monolingual students thus view their peers as equals, rather than as "others" needing to be separated from the mainstream due to what is often perceived as a "language barrier." Another common ESL model in schools is **sheltered instruction.** Sheltered instruction classrooms are often mostly or entirely comprised of ELs, with the teacher using ESL strategies both to support content learning and English language acquisition.

For Further Reflection: Thinking back to your own schooling experiences, do you recall what types of ESL models your school had, e.g., push-in, pull-out, sheltered instruction, two-way immersion programs, or others? What is your assessment of your school's ESL model and supports for English learners?

Despite extensive research support for ESL models that maintain—rather than replace or subtract—home languages, most schools continue to have ESL programs that promote only the acquisition of English. For its part, the current federal education policy, the Every Student Succeeds Act (ESSA), does not encourage or discourage heritage language maintenance, but does specify that schools assess and report English proficiency progress for their English learners. ESSA recommends that states provide high-stakes assessments in students' home languages when they are in the early stages of learning English, but leaves this to the states to decide. Many states make no attempt to provide these assessments in a language students can understand. As a result, the test scores are of questionable value in reflecting the student's actual content knowledge, as they end up becoming more a test of language knowledge than science or history knowledge, for example.[68]

Another reason schools often deprioritize heritage language maintenance is that current accountability systems incentivize schools to prioritize rapid acquisition of English over the development of bilingualism and biliteracy. As we saw earlier with the arguments for "English-Only" instruction laws, there is a widespread misconception that bilingual instruction interferes with or slows English proficiency development. In fact, studies have shown that native language proficiency supports English language development and that bilingual instruction boosts test scores and grades. Bilingualism also allows children to maintain stronger connections to their older family members and communities in their home countries and a sense of ethnic pride and identity that can bolster resilience when encountering prejudice, racism, or xenophobia.[69]

Numerous studies have found that two-way immersion programs are the most effective model of teaching English as an additional language. Unfortunately, these are unavailable to many English learners (ELs) for several reasons. For one, they require a minimum number of students who share the target language and are interested in two-way immersion. Another is that it can be hard to find enough qualified bilingual teachers.

Suggested Activity: The multilingual learner population ranges widely across the states, from 0.8 percent in West Virginia to 20.2 percent in Texas.[70] Research the population in your state, both in terms of numbers and countries of origin. Then, locate and skim your state's ESSA plan for how it assesses and supports the ELs in your state. Discuss the extent to which the ESSA plan aligns with research on supporting ELs.

Promising approaches and models

Students speaking less common languages in particular may not have access to two-way immersion programs. In those cases, instruction can nevertheless draw on their home languages. A relatively recent pedagogical approach that supports home language use and is becoming more common across the United States is called **translanguaging.** Translanguaging is a way of viewing bilingualism—not as having two completely separate and distinct languages that a speaker toggles between—but rather as having a unified linguistic repertoire that can be drawn upon to communicate. Within classrooms, translanguaging is defined as a practice where students are encouraged to use their full linguistic repertoire to facilitate learning and communication, meaning that the mixing of languages is seen as a natural communicative practice rather than an error. In this way, translanguaging pedagogy is a culturally responsive and sustaining practice as well.[71]

Some schools also work with **community language schools**, which are often organized by parents and other individuals in the community to offer language instruction and heritage events on weekends and after school. For example, some Chinese communities offer Saturday Chinese Language Schools, and Jewish communities have Sunday Hebrew Schools. These may also serve as community centers, providing information on health and social welfare. Schools that do not have the resources to provide heritage language instruction in all of their students' languages can partner with these community language schools both for bilingualism and biliteracy development as well as family engagement and recruitment of bilingual teachers.

Another way states often encourage development of bilingualism is through offering the **Seal of Biliteracy**, which is an award given in recognition of students who have attained proficiency in two or more languages by high school graduation. The initiative began in California in 2008 as a means of replacing deficit views of Spanish-speaking students with appreciation for their accomplishments in becoming bilingual, as well as encouraging global competence for all students. As of 2020, all fifty states plus the District of Columbia had or were working towards establishing a state Seal of Biliteracy.[72]

Ensuring equitable opportunities and access for all students has been a challenge in the rollout of the Seal of Biliteracy initiative. In some cases, students must demonstrate proficiency using an assessment that requires a fee, such as an Advanced Placement (AP) or International Baccalaureate (IB) exam, and many ELs do not have access to AP and IB courses. Many states also lack assessments in less common languages, such as Hmong, Somali, Urdu, and Bengali. New York addressed this through offering a portfolio-based system for languages for which there is no recognized language assessment; however, states can have trouble finding individuals competent to score these portfolios. Another equity issue relates to different requirements for ELs versus non-ELs. In some states, ELs have to provide multiple pieces of evidence of English proficiency while non-ELs need only one. By contrast, New Jersey and New Mexico require only that students meet the English language arts (ELA) graduation requirements or pass their state's English language proficiency exam.[73]

One final promising model is the Internationals Network, which is a school development organization dedicated to addressing the needs of recently arrived immigrants and refugees. Since starting in New York in 2004, Internationals Network has partnered with school districts and community organizations across the country to open new schools as well as provide professional development and other types of school support related to multilingual learners' academic achievement, sense of belonging, and sense of community. The organization provides a model for how entire schools can be designed to meet unique needs and promote high academic achievement for immigrant and refugee students.[74]

Suggested Activity: Research the programs and organizations in your local community that support immigrant students and/or families in some way, either within or beyond schools. What types of resources are available? What role, if any, do you think schools should play in helping immigrant families learn about local resources and programs?

Summary and conclusions

The United States has undergone several significant demographic shifts over time, caused in part by changing immigration patterns. Prior to the late twentieth century, most immigrants came from Europe, but today it is Latin America and Asia that provide the majority of immigrants. The history of immigration has been marked by tension between assimilation and pluralism, unity and diversity. A continuing challenge is how best to integrate or ameliorate these contesting forces.

Each wave of immigrants encountered a unique set of challenges after they arrived. For example, the Poles struggled with poverty and low educational attainment, and while they sought to maintain their ethnic identity through parochial schools reflecting Polish traditions, their children's education was compromised by pressing economic needs. Italian immigrants from mostly rural backgrounds had to make some harsh adjustments as they entered American urban industrial society. More recently, Central American immigrants have fled violence in countries destabilized in part by Cold War-era US interventions.

The history of sentiments about immigration has fluctuated between openness and xenophobia, and at the time of writing we are experiencing an intensely xenophobic period. Deportations have been prioritized over respect for civil rights such as the right to due process, and many are now choosing to remain in dangerous situations in their home countries rather than risk the peril of migrating to the United States.

Teachers, counselors, school leaders, and all staff in today's schools need to understand issues surrounding the education of immigrants and language minority students as these represent significant proportions of the student body that are likely to continue growing. Immigration is a heated political topic not only in the United States, but increasingly in other Western countries, and thus educators should be aware of how media coverage and anti-immigrant attitudes may be affecting their students. Xenophobic, nativist, and racist discourses—which circulate not only outside schools but often inside them as well—can affect youth's identity development and academic and socioemotional outcomes. Compounding these effects are the social and educational policies that reduce immigrant and English learners' access to opportunities such as higher education, gifted programs, and advanced coursework.

However, schools can be sites of advocacy and sanctuary. For instance, some school districts have issued resolutions reassuring families that they will protect their children from immigration enforcement activities at school, and teachers have organized UndocuAlly trainings to learn more about how they can support their undocumented students. By understanding the histories and contemporary conditions of immigrant and language minority students, educators can critically reflect on their instruction and beliefs, develop affirming relationships and effective practices, and advocate for more socially just school policies.

Clear and accurate explanations of problems and their causes are hard to come by, but they are necessary for successful reform efforts. For example, advocates of bilingual and multicultural education see their programs as ways to promote both majority and minority cultures in education in ways that help bridge social and cultural divisions, while critics see such education approaches as threats to social unity and as devices that encourage ethnic tensions and erect new forms of internal dissension. At present, there seems to be little common ground between the contending sides, but American society has confronted such divisions before, and the hope is that it will successfully do so again.

Vocabulary

acculturate
Americanization
additive bilingual programs
assimilation
Bilingual Education Act
Castañeda v. Pickard (1981)
community language schools
contexts of reception
cultural pluralism
Deferred Action for Childhood Arrivals (DACA)
double disadvantage
DREAM Act

dually identified students
English as a Second Language (ESL)
English learner (EL)
Equal Educational Opportunity Act of 1974
Immigration Act of 1965
linguistic restrictionism
Lau v. Nichols (1970)
Lau Remedies
long-term English learner
nativists
Office of Civil Rights (OCR)
parochial schools
pluralists
Plyler v. Doe (1982)
push-in and pull-out ESL programs
Seal of Biliteracy
segmented assimilation
sheltered instruction
subtractive schooling
Teaching English to Speakers of Other Languages (TESOL)
Temporary Protected Status (TPS)
translanguaging
tuition equity laws
two-way bilingual immersion
undocumented immigrants

Notes

1 Jeanne Batalova, Frequently Requested Statistics on Immigrant and Immigration in the United States, Migration Policy Institute, at https://www.migrationpolicy.org/article/frequently-requested-statistics-immigrants-and-immigration-united-states#:~:text=This%20Spotlight%20offers%20information%20about,are%20in%20the%20country%20legally (accessed on March 28, 2025).

2 Xue L. Rong and Judith Preissle, *Educating Immigrant Students in the 21st Century: What Educators Need to Know*, 2nd edn (Thousand Oaks, CA: Corwin Press, 2009), 1–2.

3 Israel Zangwill, *The Melting Pot* (New York: Macmillan, 1923).

4 Peter D. Salins, "Assimilation, American Style," *Reason Magazine*, vol. 28, no. 9 (February 1, 1997): 20–7, at http://www.reason.com/news/show/30150.html (accessed on May 26, 2010); and Desmond King, *The Liberty of Strangers: Making the American Nation* (New York: Oxford University Press, 2005), 3–24, and 167–76.

5 David Tyack, *Turning Points in American Educational History*, David Tyack, ed. (Waltham, MA: Blaisdell Publishing, 1967), 228–9.

6 Julie Sugarman, "Recent Immigrant Children: A Profile of New Arrivals to US Schools," *Migration Policy Institute*, https://www.migrationpolicy.org/sites/default/files/publications/mpi-recent-immigrant-children-2023_final.pdf (October 23, 2023); Rong and Preissle, *Educating Immigrant Students in the 21st Century*, 19–20.

7 Oscar Handlin, "Education and the European Immigrant, 1820–1920," in *Immigrant America: European Ethnicity in the United States*, Timothy Walch, ed. (New York: Garland Publishing, Inc., 1994), 7–12.

8 Elwood P. Cubberley, *Public Education in the United States: A Study and Interpretation of American Educational History* (New York: Houghton Mifflin, 1919), 337–8.

9 Karen Humes and Jesse McKinnon, "The Asian and Pacific Islander Population in the United States: Population Characteristics," *Current Population Reports*, US Census Bureau, Department of Commerce, Economics and Statistics Administration (March 1999); Kelly Simpson, "Chinese-Americans: Remembering a Golden Legacy," PBS, https://www.pbssocal.org/history-society/chinese-americans-remembering-a-golden-legacy (accessed on January 24, 2012).

10 "Asian Americans Then and Now: Linking Past to Present," Asia Society, https://asiasociety.org/education/asian-americans-then-and-now (accessed on December 28, 2023).

11 Meyer Weinberg, *Asian-American Education: Historical Background and Current Realities* (Mahwah, NJ: Lawrence Erlbaum Associates, 1997), 22–4; and Don T. Nakanishi, "Growth and Diversity: The Education of Asian/Pacific Americans," in *The Asian American Educational Experience: A Source Book for Teachers and Students*, Don T. Nakanishi and Tina Yamano Nishida, eds (New York: Routledge, 1995), xiii.

12 *Lau v. Nichols*, 414 US 563 (1974), at http://supct.law.cornell.edu/supct/html/historics/USSC_ CR_0414_0563_ZO.html (accessed on May 15, 2010). See also Weinberg, *Asian-American Education*, 24–8.

13 William J. Galush, "What Should Janek Learn? Staffing and Curriculum in Polish American Parochial Schools, 1870–1940," *History of Education Quarterly*, vol. 40, no. 4 (Winter 2000): 395–400.

14 Ibid., 417.

15 Timothy Walch, "The Ethnic Dimension in American Catholic Parochial Education," in *Immigrant America: European Ethnicity in the United States*, Timothy Walch, ed. (New York: Garland Publishing, Inc., 1994), 142; and Mark M. Krug, *The Melting of the Ethnics: Education of the Immigrants, 1880–1914* (Bloomington, IN: Phi Delta Kappa Educational Foundation, 1976), 6–7., 49–51.

16 Krug, *The Melting of the Ethnics*, 23–5.

17 Ibid.

18 Walch, "The Ethnic Dimension in American Catholic Parochial Education," 142–6.

19 See, for example, Colin Greer, *The Great School Legend: A Revisionist Interpretation of American Public Education* (New York: Basic Books, 1972), and Michael Katz, *Class, Bureaucracy, and Schools: The Illusion of Educational Change* (New York: Praeger, 1971).

20 Salvatore J. LaGumina, "American Education and the Italian Immigrant Experience," *American Education and the European Immigrant: 1840–1940*, 61–72; and Krug, *The Melting of the Ethnics*, 25–8, 51–4.

21 Diana Roy and Claire Klobucista, "What Is Temporary Protected Status?" *Council on Foreign Relations*, https://www.cfr.org/backgrounder/what-temporary-protected-status (accessed on April 19, 2024); Diana Roy and Amelia Cheatham, "Central American's Turbulent Northern Triangle," *Council on Foreign Relations*, at https://www.cfr.org/backgrounder/central-americas-turbulent-northern-triangle (accessed on April 18, 2024).

22 Rong and Preissle, *Educating Immigrant Students in the 21st Century*, 216–17.

23 Allison O'Connor, Jeanne Batalova, and Jessica Bolter, "Central American Immigrants in the United States," *Migration Policy Institute*, https://www.migrationpolicy.org/article/central-american-immigrants-united-states-2017 (accessed on April 19, 2024).

24 Congressional Research Service, "The Trump Administration's 'Zero Tolerance' Immigration Enforcement Policy," (CRS Report Prepared for Members and Committees of Congress, Updated February 2, 2021), https://sgp.fas.org/crs/homesec/R45266.pdf

25 US Department of Justice and US Department of Education, "Dear Colleague" letter: School Enrollment Procedures, at https://www2.ed.gov/about/offices/list/ocr/letters/colleague-201405.pdf (May 8, 2014).

26 Ibid., 3.

27 Rong and Preissle, *Educating Immigrant Students in the 21st Century*, 8.

28 Wayne E. Wright, *Foundations for Teaching English Language Learners: Research, Theory, Policy, and Practice* (Philadelphia, PA: Caslon, 2019), 68–72.

29 James Crawford, *Educating English Learners: Language Diversity in the Classroom*, 5th edn (Los Angeles, CA: Bilingual Education Services, Inc., 2004), 107–8; Sandra Del Valle, *Language Rights and the Law in the United States: Finding Our Voices* (Bristol: Multilingual Matters, 2003), 227–8.

30 Ibid., 111–13; Ibid., 236–42.

31 Crawford, *Educating English Learners*, 116–18.

32 Del Valle, *Language Rights and the Law in the United States*, 245–7.

33 Corey Mitchell, "'English-Only' Laws in Education on Verge of Extinction," *Education Week*, https://www.edweek.org/teaching-learning/english-only-laws-in-education-on-verge-of-extinction/2019/10 (October 23, 2019); New America, "English Learners/State Legislation," https://www.newamerica.org/education-policy/topics/english-learners/state-legislation/ (accessed on April 23, 2024); Crawford, *Educating English Learners*, 127–8; and Eugene E. García, *Teaching and Learning in Two Languages: Bilingualism and Schooling in the United States* (New York: Teachers College Press, 2005), 160–1.

34 Rachel Levinson-Waldman, "The Abolish ICE Movement Explained," *Brennan Center for Justice*, https://www.brennancenter.org/our-work/analysis-opinion/abolish-ice-movement-explained (July 30, 2018).

35 Esther Yu-Hsi Lee, "ICE Agents Are Arresting Teens on Their Way to School," *Foster US & Global Immigration Services*, https://www.fosterglobal.com/blog/ice-agents-are-arresting-teens-on-their-way-to-school/ (accessed on April 26, 2024); Trevor Hughes, "Immigration Agents Accused of Targeting Parents Taking Their Kids to School," *USA Today*, at https://www.usatoday.com/story/news/nation/2020/02/27/ice-criticized-detaining-parents-school-trump-enforcement-push/4891529002/ (February 27, 2020).

36 Claire Klobucista, Amelia Cheatham, and Diana Roy, "The US Immigration Debate," *Council on Foreign Relations*, https://www.cfr.org/backgrounder/us-immigration-debate-0 (accessed on April 26, 2024); American Immigration Council, "The Dream Act: An Overview," at https://www.americanimmigrationcouncil.org/research/dream-act-overview (March 16, 2021).

37 "Important Update on Deferred Action for Childhood Arrivals," *US Citizenship and Immigration Services*, at https://www.uscis.gov/newsroom/alerts/important-update-on-deferred-action-for-childhood-arrivals#:~:text=Currently%20valid%20grants%20of%20DACA,appropriate%20time%20to%20seek%20renewal. (accessed on April 26, 2024).

38 Klobucista, Cheatham, and Roy, "The US Immigration Debate."

39 Nathan Layne, Gram Slattery, and Tim Reid, "Trump Calls Migrants 'Animals,' Intensifying Focus on Illegal Immigration," *Reuters*, https://www.reuters.com/world/us/trump-expected-highlight-murder-michigan-woman-immigration-speech-2024-04-02/ (April 3, 2024); Josh Boak, "AP Fact Check: Trump Plays on Immigration Myths," *PBS News Hour*, https://www.pbs.org/newshour/politics/ap-fact-check-trump-plays-on-immigration-myths (February 8, 2019).

40 H. Kenny Nienhusser and Toko Oshio, "Awakened Hatred and Heightened Fears: 'The Trump Effect' on the Everyday Lives of Mixed-Status Families," *Cultural Studies↔Critical Methodologies*, vol. 19, no. 3 (December 2018): 173–83; Carolina

Valdivia, Marisol Clark-Ibáñez Carolina, Lucas Schacht, Juan Duran, and Sussana Mendoza, "Heightened Uncertainty and Determination: The 'Trump Effect' and College Aspirations for Undocumented Students," *Journal of College Access*, vol. 6, no. 2 (September 2021): 28–43; Olga R. Rodriguez et al., "Trump Won't Bean Immigration Arrests at School. Some Families Are Now Weighing School Attendance, AP," https://apnews.com/article/trump-immigration-ice-raids-school-2d899678264f44fe1021847ee385fd15 (accessed on January 22, 2025).

41 Victor Nava, "Texas Gov. Abbott Vows More Migrants to NYC and Other Cities Until Biden 'Secures the Border,'" *New York Post*, at https://nypost.com/2023/11/29/news/texas-gov-abbott-vows-more-migrants-to-nyc-and-other-cities-until-biden-secures-border/# (November 29, 2023).

42 Sofia Ferreira Santos, "What Is the 1978 Law That Trump Used to Deport Migrants?" *BBC*, at https://www.bbc.com/news/articles/cy871w21d3vo (May 13, 2025).

43 National Center for Education Statistics, Racial/Ethnic Enrollment in Public School, *Condition of Education*, US Department of Education, Institute of Education Sciences (accessed on February 29, 2024, at https://nces.ed.gov/programs/coe/indicator/cge).

44 Sugarman, "Recent Immigrant Children: A Profile of New Arrivals to US Schools," 7–8.

45 Estimating the undocumented population is challenging, given many within this group do not report their status on the US census or through other means. The Migration Policy Institute has developed sophisticated methods to estimate the size of this population.

46 Ibid., 9–14.

47 Robert Crosnoe and Ruth N. López Turley, "K-12 Educational Outcomes of Immigrant Youth," *Future Child*, vol. 21, no. 1 (Spring 2011): 120–52; Margarita Pivovarova and Jeanne M. Powers, "Generational Status, Immigrant Concentration and Academic Achievement: Comparing First and Second-Generation Immigrants with Third-Plus Generation Students," *Large-Scale Assessment in Education*, vol. 7, no. 7 (2019): 1–18.

48 Rong and Preissle, *Educating Immigrant Students in the 21st Century*, 13; 248–9.

49 Jeanne M. Powers and Margarita Pivovarova, "Analyzing the Achievement and Isolation of Immigrant and US-Born Students: Insights from PISA 2012," *Educational Policy*, vol. 31, no. 6 (2017): 830–57.

50 Crosnoe and López Turley, "K-12 Educational Outcomes of Immigrant Youth," 136; Pivovarova and Powers, "Generational Status, Immigrant Concentration and Academic Achievement: Comparing First and Second-Generation Immigrants with Third-Plus Generation Students," 5; Powers and Pivovarova, "Analyzing the Achievement and Isolation of Immigrant and US-Born Students: Insights from PISA 2012," 834.

51 Crosnoe and López Turley, "K-12 Educational Outcomes of Immigrant Youth," 129; Rong and Preissle, *Educating Immigrant Students in the 21st Century*, 109–16.

52 Powers and Pivovarova, "Analyzing the Achievement and Isolation of Immigrant and US-Born Students: Insights from PISA 2012," 844–6.

53 US Department of Justice Civil Rights Division and US Department of Education Office for Civil Rights, "Protecting Access to Education for Migratory Children: A Resource for Families and Educators," accessed at https://www2.ed.gov/about/offices/list/ocr/docs/ocr-factsheet-migratory-children-202306.pdf (June 2023).

54 Alexandra Filindra, David Blanding, and Cynthia Garcia Coll, "The Power of Context: State-Level Policies and Politics and the Educational Performance of the Children of Immigrants in the United States," *Harvard Educational Review*, vol. 81, no. 3 (Fall 2011): 407–38; Justin Giovannelli and Rachel Schwab, "States Expand Access to Affordable Private Coverage for Immigrant Populations," *To the Point* blog, Commonwealth Fund, https://doi.org/10.26099/7vqm-g291 (accessed on February 8, 2024).

55 "States Offering Driver's Licenses to Immigrants," *National Conference of State Legislatures*, at https://www.ncsl.org/immigration/states-offering-drivers-licenses-to-immigrants (accessed on May 30, 2024).

56 "Portal to the States," *Higher Ed Immigration Portal*, at https://www.higheredimmigrationportal.org/states/ (accessed on May 29, 2024); "Basic Facts About In-State Tuition for Undocumented Immigrant Students," *National Immigration Law Center*, at https://www.nilc.org/issues/education/basic-facts-instate/ (accessed on April 22, 2025).

57 Ibid.

58 Filindra et al., "The Power."

59 Rong and Preissle, *Educating Immigrant Students in the 21st Century*, 87.

60 National Center for Education Statistics, English Learners in Public Schools, *Condition of Education*, US Department of Education, Institute of Education Sciences, at https://nces.ed.gov/programs/coe/indicator/cgf (accessed on May 20, 2024).

61 Claudio Sanchez, "English Language Learners: How Your State Is Doing," *NPR*, https://www.npr.org/sections/ed/2017/02/23/512451228/5-million-english-language-learners-a-vast-pool-of-talent-at-risk (accessed on February 23, 2017).

62 Beth Clark-Gareca, Deborah Short, Marguerite Lukes, and Mary Sharp-Ross, "Long-Term English Learners: Current Research, Policy, and Practice," *TESOL Journal*, vol. 11, no. 1 (March 2020): 1–15.

63 Mark Murphy and Angela Johnson, "Dual Identification? The Effects of English Learner (EL) Status on Subsequent Special Education (SPED) Placement in an Equity-Focused District," *Educational Evaluation and Policy Analysis*, vol. 45, no. 2 (June 2023): 311–35.

64 US Department of Education Office of Civil Rights, "Profile of English Learner Students in U.S. Public Schools During the 2020–21 School Year," https://www2.ed.gov/about/offices/list/ocr/docs/crdc-el-students-snapshot.pdf (accessed on March, 2024); Sanchez, "English Language Learners: How Your State Is Doing."

65 Sanchez, "English Language Learners: How Your State Is Doing."

66 US Department of Education Office of Postsecondary Education, "Teacher Shortage Areas Nationwide Listing 1990–1991 through 2020–21," at https://www2.ed.gov/about/offices/list/ope/pol/tsa.html (accessed on June 5, 2024).

67 Kat Devlin, "Most European Students Are Learning a Foreign Language in School While Americans Lag," *Pew Research Center*, https://www.pewresearch.org/short-read/2018/08/06/most-european-students-are-learning-a-foreign-language-in-school-while-americans-lag/ (August 6, 2018).

68 Virginia Gonzalez, "Assessment of Bilingual/multilingual Pre-k–grade 12 Students: A Critical Discussion of Past, Present, and Future Issues," *Theory into Practice*, vol. 51, no. 4 (2012): 290–6.

69 Crosnoe and López Turley, "K-12 Educational Outcomes of Immigrant Youth," 129; Wright, *Foundations for Teaching English Language Learners*, 428–48.

70 National Center for Education Statistics, English Learners in Public Schools, *Condition of Education*, US Department of Education, Institute of Education Sciences, at https://nces.ed.gov/programs/coe/indicator/cgf (accessed on May 20, 2024).

71 Ofelia García, Susana Ibarra Johnson, Kate Seltzer, and Guadalupe Valdés, *The Translanguaging Classroom: Leveraging Student Bilingualism for Learning* (Philadelphia, PA: Caslon, 2017).

72 Candace R. Black, Arthur Chou, and Charlotte R. Hancock, "The 2018–2019 National Seal of Biliteracy Report," https://sealofbiliteracy.org/doc/2020-National-Seal-of-Biliteracy-Report-Final.pdf (accessed on December 27, 2020).

73 Kristin J. Davin and Amy J. Heineke, "The Seal of Biliteracy: Variations in Policy and Outcomes," *Foreign Language Annals*, vol. 50, no. 3 (Fall 2017): 486–99.

74 International Schools Network, at https://www.internationalsnetwork.org (accessed on April 23, 2025).

6

Gender, Sexuality, and Education

Chapter contents

Chapter objectives

- To explain how gender and sexual identities are contextually defined and subject to change over time.
- To discuss the progress and challenges surrounding gender and sexual identity bias in education.
- To delineate the historical efforts to overcome inequalities in education based on gender and sexual identity.
- To analyze how gender continues to shape the status of the teaching profession.
- To explore how major theories of knowing, learning, and thinking reflect prevailing societal attitudes toward individuals of various gender and sexual identities.
- To clarify how children learn culturally constructed gender identities and gender roles.
- To develop better understanding of gender equality and conditions in educational institutions that perpetuate biases toward individuals' gender and/or sexual identities.
- To analyze societal constructions of femininity/masculinity and how these affect the educational achievement of individuals with various gender and sexual identities.
- To analyze reform efforts intended to eradicate gender and sexual identity bias in education.

Opening questions

1. In what way are concepts of gender and sexual identity culturally defined, and what social forces lead to such definitional changes?
2. What historical developments have most affected individuals with various gender and/or sexual identities and why?

3. How has the teaching profession been shaped by gender and sexual identity?
4. How do gender and sexual identity continue to affect theories of learning and knowing?
5. How do gender and sexual identity influence the socialization of the young?
6. How do educational institutions at the elementary and secondary levels reflect gender and sexual identity bias?
7. What efforts are being made to transform schools into inclusive spaces for all gender and sexual identities, and how successful are these efforts?

The issue

One of the human relations that has historically been characterized by mystery and misunderstanding is the relationship among individuals with different gender identities. Art and literature are devoted to it; powerful religions contain ideals and prescriptions regarding it; and major social institutions such as families have been organized around it. Just as race, ethnicity, and class invariably influence people's lives, so do **gender** as well as **sexual identity**. Educational institutions shape gender relations and are shaped by them. Images of what is appropriate for individuals of various gender identities have long impacted admissions, educational opportunities, curricular as well as extracurricular activities, and more. Educators and students, furthermore, may consciously or unconsciously perpetuate **gender stereotypes** while also striving to create more equitable gender relations.

Much has changed in recent times in regard to gender, and some might argue that it has ceased to be a problem in education; after all, dramatic improvements have been made in girls' and women's access to schools and educational programs, and such blatant practices as routinely scheduling girls in home economics and boys in shop classes have been reduced or eradicated. Much has been done to encourage females, especially females with intersecting identities, in STEM and other traditionally male disciplines. In higher education, women have surpassed men in college admission and graduation rates. In addition, there is increased consciousness of the fact that gender is not binary, but instead individuals may have identities not simply captured by "man" or "woman."

However, such improvements do not mean **gender bias** has disappeared in education; rather, it has become more subtle and informal. For example, better educational opportunity has not necessarily meant that females reap the same occupational benefits as males. Although there have been improvements, the so-called glass ceiling continues to keep women underrepresented in the higher echelons of power and influence. In other words, it is not so much the formal obstacles to education that are of primary concern today but more subtle and informal obstacles that demarcate as effectively as the old ones did. While much has been done to improve gender equity and inclusion, all students need education that is appropriate for them, and the quest for equal educational opportunity, as far as gender is concerned, remains uncompleted.[1] In addition, nonbinary individuals continue to be stigmatized, victimized, and overlooked, and inequities still exist, especially for individuals who suffer from intersecting forms of oppression such as sexism and racism.

The meaning of the term gender arises from cultural conventions and institutional arrangements, and it differs from **sex** which has been defined as "[a] multidimensional construct based on a cluster of anatomical and physiological traits."[2]

Sex and gender have often been treated as binary and even interchangeable constructs, determined at birth. The way people think about sexual orientation is also frequently based upon binaries, assuming a unity of sex and gender. The reason may be that sexual identity is typically based upon the sex/gender of the preferred partner relative to one's own, as in same-sex/gender (i.e., **gay** or **lesbian**), opposite sex/gender (i.e., **straight**), both-sexes/genders (i.e., **bisexual**) type of thinking. These binary conceptualizations, however, do not do justice to people's reality which is much more complex. For example, not all sex traits necessarily correspond to the same sex, or a person's gender identity may be different from their sex and may not fit into simple male/female constructs.[3]

Understanding such complexity, this chapter strives to be inclusive, acknowledging the diversity surrounding gender and sexual identities. However, particularly in the historical treatment of the topic, due to the predominance of gender binaries and **heteronormativity** in historical records, we had trouble at times finding resources that acknowledged, much less attended to, queer, trans, or nonbinary identities. That said, the main purpose of the chapter is to understand how gender, as a sociocultural term based on ideas, concepts, or abstractions of what it means to be feminine, masculine, or nonbinary, as well as sexual orientation impact educational opportunities.

There is a long history of debate over gender relations and the conditions that prevent **cisgender**, heterosexual females as well as sexual and gender minority populations such as **lesbian, gay, bisexual, transgender, queer, individuals**

(LGBTQ+) from having the same rights, educational opportunities, and control over their lives and bodies as cisgender, heterosexual males tend to have. Instead, minoritized individuals continue to experience inequitable treatment, discrimination, and even violence in multiple realms of their lives, including education. The problem is compounded for individuals with intersecting identities who may belong to the LGBTQ+ community and, for example, identify as a member of a minoritized racial or ethnic group. The debate has shifted over time from an emphasis on the more blatant to the more subtle forms of discrimination involving socialization patterns and deeply internalized assumptions about gender and sexuality.

Suggested Activity: When people discuss parental involvement in school and other issues relating to the care of their children, does the conversation typically involve diverse gender identities equally? Or are they focused primarily on mothers? How do you explain your observations?

Historical background

Historically speaking, male dominance has been a feature of many cultures. Attempted rationalizations for this include differences between males' and females' brain size, chromosomes and hormones, spinal curvature, physical strength, genitalia and reproductive systems, but none satisfactorily explain the extent of gender-based social and cultural distinctions made over the course of history. Clearly, women's inferior status did not evolve around physical or biological differences but around cultural ideals of womanhood.[4] For many women, male dominance has intersected with other forms of oppression such as those based upon race, social class, sexual identity, or disability.

The colonial period

Experiences of women in colonial America varied widely, depending upon race, ethnic, and social group as well as the particular colony. While the sex/gender system of white women on the North American continent was steeped in the European attitudes of the first settler colonialists, there were indigenous people in the Western Hemisphere who had cultivated different systems. The gender system of the Iroquois, for example, showed signs of relative sexual equality.

Iroquois women were involved in governance, able to vote, shape religious activities, and play significant roles in daily activities, to name a few examples of the power they held. Significantly, they were treated with respect. White women, however, suffered significant gender inequities despite their importance for domestic economic production and in social life. While men's work was located outdoors or related to external business pursuits, women's was in child care, household industries, and community functions such as caring for the sick and taking in orphans. Although white women were put into inferior positions in the power hierarchy, they met important social and economic needs crucial to society.[5]

Suggested Activity: Interview several family members or friends, and ask them to define or describe their understanding of "womanhood" and "manhood" today. Do their views differ from one another? how do they compare to definitions that prevailed in earlier times? and what challenges become obvious when such binary concepts are used?

White women also played an important educational role. In early colonial times, the family served as the basic educational institution, because formal schooling was not readily available in many communities. Few overt gender distinctions occurred in the earliest years, but by age 5 or 6, gender came into sharper focus in chores and work assignments. Boys dominated apprenticeship opportunities, although some girls were apprenticed too. Most literate parents promoted education for both male and female children for practical reasons and for religious purposes such as Bible reading. Over time, schools increasingly complemented family-based education. The number and types of schools grew until, by the early 1700s, there were at least four basic school types, including dame schools, reading and writing schools, Latin grammar schools, and colleges. Most teachers at the time identified as male, but dame schools were usually taught by women and concentrated on the rudiments for small boys and girls. The reading and writing schools, adapted along the lines of the petty schools of England, provided a more thorough grounding in the three R's (reading, writing, arithmetic). Some women taught in these schools, and a fair number of girls attended as well, but as age increased and school type changed, males became dominant, both as teachers and as students. This was true in the Latin grammar schools, which provided secondary education and preparation for higher education, but it was particularly true at the college level with male domains concentrating on classical studies in the liberal arts as preparation for the professions and for leadership positions in society.[6]

From roughly 1750 to 1820, some fundamental changes occurred. In 1776, the Declaration of Independence proclaimed that "all men are created equal," and Abigail Adams asked her husband John about the exclusion of women from this statement. Others also advocated for change. In the eighteenth century, Benjamin Franklin thought females should be educated not only in basic literacy but also in foreign languages, business management, and accounting, and he professed respect for women's abilities in philosophical and scientific matters as well. Benjamin Rush urged that women should not only be educated in child rearing and home economics. Rather, they should learn about bookkeeping so that they could assist their husbands in taking care of their property, and learn such subjects as the English language and history to prepare their sons for political responsibilities. These points of view were echoed by De Witt Clinton and Charles Burroughs in the nineteenth century.[7] Although few advocates saw women taking on equal roles with men, they did reflect a slowly developing view that the better education of females was indispensable to the survival of organized society and cultural life.

Suggested Activity: Look up a source of correspondence between Abigail Adams and her husband John Adams or read biographical treatments of the Adamses. What were their views on the education of females and the status of women?

While the position of white women during colonial times was shaped by patriarchy and sexism, women of color endured racism in addition to these other forms of oppression. African women were brought to the colonies and enslaved, forced to perform hard labor which included the reproduction of the labor force. Slave owners appropriated the reproductive lives of female slaves and claimed their children as property.[8] Both slavery and marriage based on patriarchal norms curtailed the freedom of Black women.[9]

It has been argued that the role of Black women in white society was ambiguous. Beginning in the era of slavery, Black women nursed and raised white children, cared for white people when they were sick and took care of their homes, thereby acquiring intimate knowledge of white culture that prepared them as interpreters and intermediaries of the white culture in the Black home. At the same time, Black women also fought, alongside Black men, to sustain Black families and communities.[10] Regarding Black families in particular, scholarship indicates the crucial significance of kinship. From the beginning of slavery, African-Americans extended the bonds of kinship beyond individual farms and plantations and even beyond blood relationships, seeking to unite families torn apart by slavery, addressing each other as brothers and sisters, and seeing familial and communal relations as one.[11]

As far as education for Black people is concerned, it was what has been called a "**fugitive project**," one that was outlawed and seen as entailing criminal behavior in the South, and regarded with suspicion in the North.[12] Violation of anti-literacy laws and teaching enslaved persons to read and write was punishable, including punishment of death. Therefore, enslaved persons had to resort to extreme measures to be educated, and they did so, given the widely held belief in the importance of education.

One such example was the ascendance of underground schools. Susie King Taylor, who published a Civil War memoir, describes how she gained literacy. She recalls how she and her brother were sent to a friend of her grandmother's, a free woman, to learn to read and write. The children's books were wrapped in paper so they would not be discovered by the police or by white people. The teacher's kitchen served as the schoolroom for twenty-five to thirty children. Neighbors assumed the children were learning trades, which was customary. After the lessons, the children would leave as they had come, one by one.[13]

The cult of "true womanhood" and the idea of education as "race uplift"

The decades from 1820 to 1860 witnessed upheavals that fundamentally altered American society. Sometimes called the Era of the Common Man, this period generated moral crusades to extend democratic citizenship rights, abolish slavery, provide humane treatment of people with intellectual disabilities, soften the impact of industrialization, and spread the development of public common schools. Major changes occurred in patterns of living and in the roles that men, women, and children of all racial and ethnic backgrounds occupied. Public elementary and secondary schools were established across the country during the nineteenth century, and women made advances in many spheres of life, often including education, while also experiencing blatant sexism and a distinctly inferior status.

The Industrial Revolution spread the factory system, and the economic role of most men was transformed from independent farmer or artisan to factory laborer working for someone else. Many products formerly handcrafted on farms or in small shops were now machine made in mass-production factories more cheaply than those made by hand. At the same time, industrialization also displaced many women from the traditional household or domestic economy, and they entered the industrial labor force in growing numbers as well. Children, too, were hired out to factories to supplement meager family incomes. Important aspects of industrialization were based on the cheap labor supply of the lower classes, and among the cheapest were the women and children. For example, Samuel Slater, a nineteenth-century Rhode Island industrialist, recruited whole families to work in his textile factories. One man entered a contract with Slater for weekly wages on the following basis: $5.00 for himself, $2.33 for his sister, $2.00 for a 16-year-old son, $1.50 for a 13-year-old son, $1.25 for a 12-year-old daughter, and $.75 for an 8-year-old daughter.[14]

During this time period, many Black people, as well as some whites, fought to abolish slavery. Free Black men were mainly restricted to menial labor and Black women to service as domestic workers. Education, though often prohibited, was seen by the Black community as a way to improve the conditions of their race, or "**race uplift**." After the end of the Civil War, this role was ascribed to Black women, in particular.[15]

The image of uplifting the race contrasted with a new image emerging for white women during the early to middle decades of the nineteenth century, sometimes referred to as the **cult of true womanhood**. As reflected in images presented in books, popular religious literature, and women's magazines from 1820 to 1860, a new abstraction of womanhood—based on a view of woman as domestic, submissive, pliable, and pious—was lifted to such heights that "if anyone, male or female, dared to tamper with the complex of virtues which made up True Womanhood, he was damned immediately as an enemy of God, of civilization, and of the Republic"; moreover, the greatest responsibility for upholding the image belonged to the female, "to uphold the pillars of the temple with her frail white hand,"[16] a role clearly excluding women whose hands were not white.

In fact, the philosophy of "true womanhood" shaped mostly the education of upper- and middle-class white women as good wives and mothers, and literacy was seen as important for such things as reading the Bible. Black women's lives in contrast, never characterized by submissiveness and fragility, became shaped by the educational philosophy of "racial uplift," as mentioned above.

The Black community expected women, in particular, to use education as a tool for the improvement of their race, in economic, educational, and social matters. However, this occurred within a difficult context as many whites perceived the education of Black people as a threat, and that often included the education of free Black people. Nevertheless, Black women felt the call to teach and, for example, devoted themselves to helping former slaves transition to freedom after emancipation. Notably, Black women in the South provided impressive labor to uplift their communities, aiding the sick, caring for orphaned children, and teaching in large numbers in the schools for Black children established after the Civil War. Yet while public schools for Black children were coeducational, Black men greatly outnumbered Black women in higher education, and Black women encountered both racism and sexism, including sexism displayed by a number of Black men who subscribed to the belief dominating white society, namely that women are subordinate to men.[17]

> **Suggested Activity:** Study images of women in the popular media today, particularly in magazines, television, movies, and on the internet. To what extent are women still portrayed as "soothers," "tamers," and "superior moral forces"? How are present-day images of femininity constructed, in what ways do they differ by race and ethnicity, and how have they changed from older images? If so, what role has education played in those changes?

Women in the common school movement

The common school movement was supported by large numbers of women. Although the aim of providing tax-supported schools to every child fell short of the mark (such as Black children being excluded in the slaveholding South), the movement provided many children throughout the nation with a chance to attend school. Men filled leadership roles in the movement, but great numbers of women were active on its behalf. People in the movement were convinced that the solutions to major social problems ultimately rested on education.[18]

A reflection of the "true womanhood" image found in the movement was the belief that female teachers would provide a superior morality, better social harmony, and a more civilizing kind of influence, a view that has also been called **sentimental womanhood**. This challenges the assumption that women's new status was due solely to economic change; rather, sentimental womanhood was anchored in traditional assumptions that man was governed by the head

Figure 6.1 Banner with the motto of the National Association of Colored Women's Clubs, 1910.

and woman by the heart, a concept that neatly fit emerging economic beliefs that men were naturally competitive, rational, and unemotional in the pursuit of economic gain, while women were inherently maternal, affectionate, and moral in pursuit of cultural and social uplift. It was thus but a small step for adherents of this view of womanhood to conclude that the answer to the social stresses of industrialization was the maternal instinct. If the essence of motherhood was teaching, then society would be more effectively served if women's maternal influence dominated the schoolroom.[19]

Be that as it may, economic factors still influenced women's entry into the teaching profession. Many men left teaching because they could ill afford to ignore the economic opportunities opening to many of them in the expanding industrial markets of the day. Furthermore, women entered teaching because of their need for paid work as much as "maternal instinct." Teaching was one of the few professions open to women at the time. Whether it was the cult of true womanhood, the quest for racial uplift, economic necessity, or free choice that led them to it, the fact remains that an increasing number of women became teachers. Where teaching was once mostly a job for men, by the mid-nineteenth century, women were openly recruited to teach in the new common schools. The belief that women were better at working with children was shared by reformer Horace Mann, who was pleased to report in 1843 that over a five-year period, male teachers in Massachusetts had increased by only 131, while women teachers increased by 691. He also noted that the average monthly pay for men was $32.22, and for women, $12.78. Throughout the 1840s and 1850s, female teachers were paid about one-third of what male teachers were paid; nevertheless, females continued to enter the profession in growing numbers.[20]

Teaching was also one of the few professions open to people of color. Before the Civil War, most Black people who possessed any formal education entered the teaching profession, and that was true for both men and women.[21] However, over the course of the nineteenth century, additional professional opportunities became available to Black men, and Black women played significant roles in the education of Black people, opening schools across the country. Among them were Mary Peake, who established the first school for Black freedmen near Hampton, Virginia in 1861 and Milla Granson from Natchez, Mississippi, who taught Black people in the 1860s. Similarly, there were exemplary Black women in the northern part of the country who contributed greatly to education. Fanny Jackson Coppin, for example, became the first Black woman to lead an institution of higher learning in the United States by assuming the position as principal of the Institute for Colored Youth in 1869. Coppin exemplified the "racial uplift" philosophy described above, as well as a commitment to self-help. She combined her leadership in education with engagement in social movements. For example, she began offering classes in trades to working adults, and she specifically supported women who had migrated north, only to find limited employment opportunities, and offered housing and nurse's training to indigent women.[22]

One of the white pioneers of female education in the nineteenth century was Emma Hart Willard, who devised a plan for a secondary school that led to the founding in 1821 of the **Troy Female Seminary** in Troy, New York. Willard sought financial support from the New York legislature on the grounds that women deserved education as much as men, but an education designed specifically for their needs. Mirroring the notion of sentimental womanhood, Willard proclaimed that appropriate female education would enhance the prosperity of a nation dependent on the character of its citizens, the formation of which rested on mothers. How much better mothers could perform this vital task, she argued, if they were properly educated. The New York legislature rebuffed her request, but by 1850, the diligent Willard garnered sufficient private support to found Troy Female Seminary and to establish its good academic reputation in quick order. She also believed that women would make good teachers for the common schools because nature had designed them with the capacities of persuasion, softness, and patience to care for children. If properly trained, they would educate children better than men and more cheaply too. Furthermore, it would free up men otherwise engaged in teaching to go out and create new wealth for the nation in the many business and industrial occupations for which, she believed, women were not naturally suited.[23]

Other advocates of women's role in the new schools included Catherine Beecher and Mary Lyon. Beecher, who founded **Hartford Female Seminary** in 1823, a private girls' school in Connecticut, was a strong advocate of public schooling, **coeducation**, and teacher preparation. She also founded an organization called the National Board of Popular Education that, among other things, helped place young women in teaching positions in the public common schools. Beecher, too, was a believer in the socially redemptive power of women, that it was to mothers and teachers that society should look for those who could most effectively mold the character of each rising generation.[24]

Mary Lyon founded a school for women that was an equivalent in scholarly effort and liberal education to men's colleges when she opened **Mount Holyoke Female Seminary** (later Mount Holyoke College) in 1837. Her plans for the institution included an evangelical religious emphasis and a strong academic reputation, with a primary objective of preparing young women to be teachers. Like Willard and Beecher, Lyon spread the view of womanhood devoted to social and moral redemption, but she also believed that teaching was a sacred activity and that teachers should be paid no more than ministers or missionaries. Indeed, she gave half of her own salary to mission work, and she argued that the true rewards of teaching were spiritual, not material.[25] For all her earnest idealism, however, Lyon's views on teacher pay may have contributed to the poor economic status of the teaching profession.

By 1890, the work of Willard, Beecher, Lyon, and others led to women holding a predominant numerical role in the teaching profession at the elementary level. Women's numbers in high school teaching increased as well. Public high schools grew rapidly after the 1870s, and like the common school, they embraced coeducation and admitted girls as well as boys on a tax-supported tuition-free basis. Eventually, women occupied roughly two out of every three teaching positions by the early 1900s. The greater number of women in the teaching profession helped open the doors of the colleges and universities, which by the early twentieth century surpassed the normal schools in the preparation of teachers. Oberlin College was the first to admit women on a coeducational basis as early as 1833, but after 1865, there was a vigorous growth of private women's colleges, such as Vassar (1865), Smith (1875), Wellesley (1875), and Bryn Mawr (1885), to name a few. These institutions rejected domestic studies for women and promoted a rigorous academic education on par with men's colleges. In addition, most of the new public colleges and state universities that opened in the late nineteenth and early twentieth centuries also admitted women students.[26]

It may be reasonably argued that entry into the teaching profession helped women gain a foothold in other learned professions. In effect, teaching aided women in achieving new levels of occupational status. And yet, progress was slow, especially for women of color. In 1920, for example, only one half of a percent of Black doctors in the United States were women.[27]

Perhaps one of the more significant developments from 1870 to 1900 was the increasing attendance of girls in the American high school, an institution that changed from a relatively elite institution to an extension of common schooling as it displaced the academies and seminaries of the early nineteenth century. By 1900, girls represented 59 percent of all secondary school enrollments, by which time the public high school was also the dominant American secondary school. Despite some efforts to stem the tide of coeducation, girls and boys studied many of the same subjects together, and this higher level of curricular equality allowed many girls to develop a new sense of their abilities to compete with boys intellectually. Such experiences were important to the rising generations of women involved in reforms for the rights of women.[28]

One of the outgrowths of women's participation in the public school movement was their acquisition of knowledge and skills about the inner workings of social institutions. From 1860 to 1920, there was a growing conviction among women that they should enjoy all the rights of citizenship and become involved in all the proper spheres of organized society. Not to be discounted was the surge of women into the labor market, for while they were economically exploited, they also gained experience with independence and self-sufficiency outside the traditional bounds of home and marriage. Salary discrepancies were stark, however. For example, in 1860, women textile workers only earned about $3.00 for a seventy-five-hour week, as opposed to about $5.00 for men. By 1900, the average female tobacco worker in Pittsburgh still only earned about $5.00 per week as compared to $10.00 for men, and male bakers earned up to $100.00 per month, while women bread packagers earned only about $22.00 per month. (By way of comparison, a subsistence wage for an individual was figured at $7.00 per week in 1906.) Of course, women were not alone in being wage exploited, for most men did not earn much more than women, and children earned far less. Labor unions were not well organized at the time, and employers were able to take advantage of their employees.[29]

> **For Further Reflection:** What appears a relic of "the olden days" continues to this day, albeit to a lesser degree. Discrimination still exists in wage or salary discrepancies where women earn less than men. Why does this inequity continue? What needs to happen, in your opinion, in order for women to gain equal pay? How is education connected to this issue?

Black women had worked in tobacco and textile factories in the South since slavery but were kept out of other types of factory employment until the First World War. Prior to 1910, most Black women labored on farms, as domestic servants, or as laundresses.[30] There were exceptions, however. One of them consisted of a small number of Black women entering the medical profession in the second part of the nineteenth century. Finding themselves at the intersection of both sexism and racism intent on keeping them out of the profession, they nevertheless persevered and provided essential services, especially to the Black community.[31]

Once again, a new interpretation of the cult of true womanhood came into being, this time based on helping people learn to manage their lives better and to adjust to the demands of industrialized society. Perhaps the best known of these "housekeepers of society" was **Jane Addams**, who founded **Hull House**, a social settlement house in the slums of Chicago. The Hull House program was designed to help poor immigrants ease their way into the American social and industrial mainstream by teaching them home economy, sanitation, and child care, among other things.

Another reformer was Crystal Eastman (1881–1928), a pacifist working in the settlement houses of New York. She was a leading advocate of voting rights for women and one of the founders of the American Civil Liberties Union. Another influential figure was Charlotte Perkins Gilman (1860–1935), who advocated that the motherly instinct of love and service should be directed outward to large-scale social problems rather than focused inward on the home. Still others were Susan B. Anthony (1820–1906), a teacher who became an acknowledged leader in the **temperance movement** (control or prohibition of alcoholic beverages) and in the **women's suffrage movement** (right to vote for women); and Carrie Chapman Catt (1859–1947), an Iowa school superintendent who became prominent in the women's suffrage movement.[32]

These and other women were so successful that by 1920, the Eighteenth Amendment prohibiting the manufacture and sale of alcoholic beverages and the Nineteenth Amendment giving women the right to vote were added to the US Constitution. Notwithstanding these steps forward for women, the First World War put the country through a strenuous test, and afterward there was a strong desire to return to normalcy and a resultant faltering of the women's movement. For example, Carrie Catt tried to use the **League of Women Voters** to get women more effectively involved in exercising their newly won right to vote, but she found that women did not vote any more intelligently than men. Crystal Eastman agitated for a home- and school-based education that freed children from gender stereotyping, but to no avail. [33]

As far as the intersections of race and gender are concerned, women's and Black people's voting rights were related in complicated ways, as were racism and sexism. Many Northerners who worked for women's suffrage had also worked for the abolition of slavery, but coalitions of advocates for both women's and Black people's voting rights did not endure. In 1860, the Fifteenth Amendment to the Constitution granted all men, regardless of race, the right to vote, but not women. While Black women suffragists such as Sojourner Truth and Mary Ann Shadd Cary were disappointed that women were left out, some white women suffragists were especially upset because not only were they left out, but men of color had now attained a right that white women did not have.[34]

Especially once whites in the South reversed the progress that had been made during the period of Reconstruction, coalitions for Black and women's voting rights faltered. Influential figures such as Elizabeth Cady Stanton and Susan B. Anthony, for example, distanced themselves from the Black suffrage issue, abandoning the Equal Rights Association in 1869 to form the National Woman Suffrage Association. Some white suffragists worried that their support

Figure 6.2 Poster advocating for women's suffrage, 1910.

of Black women's right to vote would weaken their own chances of obtaining suffrage. Black women suffragists were often denied admission to "mainstream" conventions and other political events and even harassed, and therefore, they established their own organizations. However, members of the Black community, primarily in the South, held that there were more pressing problems: increasing disenfranchisement of Black male voters as well as mounting violence against all people of color. Nevertheless, at the end of the nineteenth century, Black women did create women's clubs for "social uplift" and, in 1896, formed the **National Association of Colored Women (NACW)**. Mary Church Terrell was the first president of NACW which supported education, temperance, health, prison reform, and other civic matters of great concern to Black people, and by the early twentieth century, tens of thousands of women were engaged in the pursuits of women's clubs run by women of color.[35]

> **Suggested Activity:** Read historical accounts of women's participation in such movements as the abolition of slavery and temperance. What roles did they play in these organizations and how did their participation mark a major change in the social and political fabric at the time?

Women's changing status

While discriminatory practices against women continued into the twentieth century, their struggles for equality continued as well. Black women, for example, continued to face sexual exploitation even after the abolition of slavery, supported by several myths, such as Black women lacking morals and therefore not deserving the respect of white women.[36]

Concerning white womanhood, in the 1920s, the image emerged of women as frivolous flappers. The idea was anchored in the materialism unleashed after the lean times of the First World War and was not stifled until the Great Depression of the 1930s. These myths defied reality, of course, as most women worked as hard as ever in the home or in the paid labor force. Women workers dealt with the Depression very much the same as men: they endured deprivation and took whatever work became available. Labor unions gained some recognition during Roosevelt's New Deal administration, but women were still paid less than men. In some cases, women could hardly get any paying jobs because of the persisting view that their role was homemaking, while men's was breadwinning. Generally, in schools the issue of girls and boys being educated in the values of shared power was ignored.

Among the notable female leaders of the Depression and Second World War eras was Eleanor Roosevelt (1884–1962), who urged women to work for social change but also believed that women should place family before career. Intellectuals such as anthropologist Margaret Mead (1901–78) researched how cultural and educational practices brought about inequalities between males and females, but progress in transmitting such views to the wider society was slow.

The Second World War took white women out of the home and into the labor force as never before, but (as after the preceding war) there was a desire to return to domesticity and material consumption afterwards. Women, as the chief purchasers of household goods and services, again became targets of the hard sell, and the sexually alluring temptress image was marketed more vigorously than ever. In the 1950s, a new woman as sex symbol image, typified by such public personas as Marilyn Monroe, became firmly implanted. By the 1960s, the nation's former inhibitions against pornography slowly gave way, and by the 1970s, X-rated movies and pornographic magazines became common.

For Further Reflection: Does the use of women as sex objects sell products? What "educational effect" does this have on children and young adults, and how does it impact the status of women? How does the image of woman as sex object in advertising affect children's thinking about femininity and masculinity? For example, does the Barbie doll phenomenon have anything to do with how girls come to view themselves? What do you think about the critique of sexism inherent in the 2023 Barbie movie?

The sex symbol image did not go unchallenged, however, and numerous studies found that the professional ranks did not admit enough women, graduate schools did not encourage women to apply, and the public schools "programmed" girls to accept traditional roles. Feminist activists urged a more concerted effort, and the **National Organization of Women (NOW)** was formed in 1966 to promote initiatives such as equal employment, equalization of social security benefits, and equal educational opportunity. NOW challenged existing inequities, although it mostly represented white women's concerns. At any rate, rapid change remained elusive. Conditions led to what was loosely termed the **women's liberation movement**, which helped focus public attention on the general status of females in society and on the specific issues of sexism and gender bias in schools and in educational materials.

While the media may have exaggerated the impact of such developments, there were some concrete results: for one thing, the closing decades of the twentieth century saw a vigorous scrutiny of education concerning how male and female roles were presented. Hundreds of studies examined curriculum materials, school rules and regulations, and the organizational and employment structures of school systems. The extent of actual improvement might be questioned, but the fact remains that from the 1960s on, increasing public attention was turned to the issue of gender bias in American society.[37]

Along with an increasing attention to sexism, the second half of the twentieth century also saw the articulation by women of color as to how sexism and racism intersected in general, and how white women did not understand this intersectionality, in particular. White feminists, for example, steeped in Eurocentric thinking and presuming to speak on behalf of all women, tended to ignore or tokenize the experiences of women of color. To illustrate the point, Audre Lorde wrote an open letter to Mary Daly, inviting her to " ... a joint clarification of some of the differences which lie between us as a black and a white woman."[38]

Based upon their feelings of alienation from white feminist organizations, as well as from Black male dominated political organizations like the Black Panther Party (BPP), Black women founded their own organization, the **National Black Feminist Organization (NBFO)**, in 1973. One of its chapters wrote the **Combahee River Collective (CRC)** Statement which would become one of the most significant Black feminist documents.[39] The document makes clear that Black feminists aimed to " ... struggle together with Black men against racism, while we also struggle with Black men about sexism."[40]

Contemporary conditions

In order to understand how people come to possess viewpoints on gender and sexual identity, especially those that fuel discriminatory laws, policies, norms, and practices, it is necessary to examine several influences. If gender bias permeates institutions and social values, it must have avenues of expression by which the young are initiated into its beliefs. These include traditions about gender differences, the innumerable influences impinging on children as they grow up, and the schooling experience itself.

Notions about whether and how males and females differ have undergone significant changes. For centuries, the thinking about sex and gender was binary, and the predominant belief was that there were two sexes that were fundamentally different in educational potential. Beginning in the second half of the twentieth century, however, as women gained more participation and power in social institutions, and dichotomous thinking about sex and gender began to be questioned, such assumptions have come under intense scrutiny.

Gendered approaches to thinking and knowing

The early 1980s saw the publication of important studies on **women's ways of knowing** and moral reasoning that were previously missing from educational theory and practice. Traditional educational institutions were mostly designed for males, and when female learners were included, they were expected to fit into existing institutional frameworks. The new studies attempted to understand female perspectives and to incorporate them into educational institutions in ways to serve all students better. However, it is more difficult to make historic institutions gender inclusive than it is simply to admit females into them, and it is even more complex to break out of dichotomous thinking about gender.

Human intelligence has always been a domain of interest to educators and psychologists alike. By the 1970s, studies indicated that girls in their early years were generally more precocious than boys, learning to talk and to discern differences in objects at an earlier age. It was suggested that this precociousness might be due to myelinization (maturation of the myelin sheath that speeds nerve impulses), which occurs earlier in girls than in boys. Boys, however, caught up later, and while girls excelled in such things as reading and writing by first grade, boys excelled in numbers, spatial concepts, and similar areas.

In addition, as development continued, girls showed fewer extremes on the intelligence continuum than boys. By adolescence, males appeared to be more analytical and logical and tended to take more intellectual risks, while females appeared to be more attuned to emotion, more holistic in decision-making, and more intuitive and comparative in their approach to problems. Some researchers attributed the differences to hormones, and others suggested a difference in the use of right- and left-brain hemispheres by males and females, but overall whether the differences were due to socialization or to innate sex differences or some combination of the two was not clear because researchers could not determine where innate sex differences ended and socialization or acculturation began. A tentative conclusion was that, since girls and boys faced different cultural expectations in learning how to behave as adults, each apparently developed mental attributes necessary to meet those expectations.[41]

Current research has evolved and debunked, for example, the myth of the "math brain" which implied cognitive biological differences between women and men in their abilities to perform well in math. Continuing gender gaps in STEM fields are explained by stereotypical thinking of STEM fields as masculine, male-dominated cultures that do not support girls and women, a scarcity of female role models, and math anxiety among females stemming from how girls are treated in school.

Yet the situation is complicated, as the gendered math gap in elementary school, for example, is only evident between boys and girls in higher-income and predominantly white schools, while girls score higher than boys in lower-income, predominantly Black schools, indicating that social class and race mitigate gender gaps.[42] Similarly, based upon research in Western countries, the gap in reading motivation among elementary students may indicate that boys tend to value reading less than girls. However, recent research also reminds us that boys are not a homogeneous group, and that the gender gap in reading attitudes may have been oversimplified.[43]

Ways of knowing

Researchers examined different conceptions of knowledge and learning, seeking to understand how gender-related socialization led to gender-specific approaches in education. While it was important to comprehend that males and females might differ, it was just as important to study how approaches to learning and knowing were sanctioned and rewarded by society, and what approaches were not. For example, as women gained full access to higher education, they frequently felt alienated, had difficulty asserting themselves with authority, and were not always fully respected for their research and scholarship. Although women made progress, they often encountered difficulties because of male-oriented academic conventions built into educational institutions and processes, including how human learning and knowing were evaluated. It seemed that such gendered frameworks did not value modes of thought found among women.

One of the pioneering researchers on gender issues was Mary Belenky, widely recognized for her work on women's ways of knowing. A metaphor women often use to capture their intellectual development is voice (such as "finding your voice"), which differs from the visual metaphors males tend to use, such as "seeing the light" when something becomes clear. Visual imagery implies seeing an object to properly know it, while speaking and listening imply face-to-face engagement between knower and object. Belenky and her associates found that women's ways of knowing include a variety of approaches and concluded that educational institutions need to accommodate female ways of learning and knowing and to accept female students as knowers with functioning minds that bring prior knowledge and experience to the educational environment.

Traditional higher education institutions used a doubting model of teaching that challenged students' prior beliefs, but many women students have been socialized into self-doubt and find the doubting model of teaching unhelpful. The authors argue that many older women students use "maternal thinking" based on individualized responses in rearing children, a mode of thought that differs from the replication and universal application model valued in academia. In addition, some women respond better to evaluation standards that are set collaboratively by students and teachers rather than by traditional academic authority. They prefer a "housewifery" model where people work and produce according to their own rhythms. Thus, women may benefit from a "connected" model where teachers act as "midwives" helping students "give birth" to ideas instead of the traditional "banking model" where teachers "deposit" knowledge and ideas into students' minds, from which students may later "draw."[44]

For Further Reflection: Do individuals of different gender identities truly differ in their ways of knowing and, if so, what are the ramifications for educational institutions? More specifically, think about your own recent class assignments and exercises. Were there differences in how individuals of various gender identities in your class approached certain discussion questions? Did they use different ways of knowing in order to solve problems and make sense of material?

Ways of moral reasoning

Another pioneer is **Carol Gilligan**, who addressed the role of gender in moral reasoning. She maintains that psychological theorists long misunderstood how women think about moral issues, going back at least to Sigmund Freud who cast women as emotional and presumably less able to develop a strong sense of justice. **Jean Piaget** and **Lawrence Kohlberg**, two prominent developmental psychologists, continued that tradition in the twentieth century by implying that women's sense of justice is compromised. They believed their theories were based on universal standards; however, Gilligan maintains that their theories represent male conceptions of human developmental stages.

For example, Kohlberg's "universal" stage theory was developed solely from male samples, which ignores the early childhood experiences of girls encouraged to embrace relationships and fear separation because they are of the same gender as their typical primary caregiver, the mother. Boys, being of a different gender from their mothers, are reared to embrace individuation and separation and may feel threatened by the level of intimacy girls come to prefer.

According to the theory, these experiences may lead to significant differences between men and women, shaping not only the play of children but also the problem-solving strategies and moral reasoning of adults. Thus, women tend to be concerned about human relationships and connections that lead to different choices, while men are more concerned with individual achievement, autonomy, and justice. The assumption that female constructions of moral problems are inferior to male constructions has led stage theorists such as Kohlberg to conclude that women will have difficulty reaching the highest stage of moral development where people are concerned about rights, responsibilities, and individualism rather than care, connection, and relationships. Instead, Gilligan maintains that psychological theories should account for the developmental experiences of both genders, and psychological understanding of humanity would thereby be enriched.[45]

Gilligan's work is a powerful reminder that gender equality does not mean exact sameness. Both theory and practice should reflect the differences between genders and how people approach things and choose courses of action. Gender differences should not be interpreted as deficiencies but as assets, each with its own merits.

For Further Reflection: A spontaneous reaction to gender stereotyping may be: "How terrible! Surely such behavior disappeared a long time ago. Women today are just as autonomous as men!" Have gender expectations become more open minded and balanced? Are male and female roles now rewarded equally? Compare predominantly female professions with predominantly male professions on such things as pay, status, and public esteem. What do your comparisons show, and how do you explain the results?

Suggested Activity: Daily routines are often powerful indicators of social reality. Study some behaviors of friends and acquaintances that continue to be associated with particular genders, and explain why those differences persist. Do people consider women or men to be better equipped to do certain things? Why?

Justice and caring: A philosophical dichotomy?

Morality has a long tradition as a quest for justice, expressed in principles of what is good, right, and virtuous. Along similar lines, the search for truth, including moral truth, rests on the supposedly masculine foundations of reason, neutrality, and detachment. Feminists have questioned these assumptions, particularly the view that they are the only philosophically defensible ways of getting close to moral knowledge or truth; instead, feminists claim that the good may be defended just as well in terms of relationships, and that moral truth may be pursued from the vantage point of personal experience.

However, caution needs to be exercised when approaching the good and right from the standpoint of gender, because it seems simplistic to claim that men always think in principled, rationally detached fashion or that women always view the world through the lens of relationships and care. Such thinking is untenable because it assumes that caring men and principled women are contradictions in terms, and it locks moral thought into narrowly defined gender categories. In addition, of course, it presupposes that gender is binary.

Nel Noddings, who has been instrumental in developing an **ethic of care** in educational theory, maintains that care and justice are not mutually exclusive and may be applied at different points in a moral undertaking. Justice is an invaluable ethical goal when developing educational policy, and care needs to be a central goal when implementing policy. An example would be a justice-based policy to eliminate academic tracking, a practice that is often discriminatory and fraught with social class implications. If justice demands the abolition of tracking, an ethic of care also demands that educators avoid forcing all students into a one-size-fits-all curriculum that ignores individual talents, needs, and interests.[46]

However, justice and caring are not always easily compatible, as any teacher knows who has struggled with assigning grades. Grades are supposed to be just (or fair), accurately reflecting academic achievement or progress. At the same time, grading should also be used to motivate the student, a concern steeped in care. Because justice and care may sometimes conflict does not mean that they are inherently different or that one is superior to the other.

Kenneth Strike argues that the tension between justice and care is rooted in the moral pluralism (or conflict in moral values) that is simply a part of contemporary society. In order to make the best choices when faced with difficult moral questions, one has to consider individual cases, seek reflective equilibrium between conflicting values, and settle on a reasonable course of action, such as a reasonable balance of justice and care.[47]

It is clear that moral life is complex and that one is unlikely to achieve good moral reasoning by a simplistic "either justice or care" type of thinking. The point is that various ways of moral reasoning are significant resources in ethical decision-making, and when used effectively should help inform educational theories and scholarly discourse to include all of humanity rather than one portion thereof.

> **Suggested Activity:** Interview a teacher, counselor, or administrator about situations in which the ethic of care may have conflicted with the ethic of justice. How did the educator approach the dilemma? Share your findings with others in class.

Gender and sex-role identities

Despite the growing acknowledgment that gender is not a binary concept, many children continue to be molded by socially defined gender roles, a process that begins long before they enter school. Clothing may be chosen on the basis of gender, like blue for boys and pink for girls; adults may react differently and give boys rougher treatment and girls more gentle handling; and toys are often viewed as gender specific with girls being encouraged to play with dolls and boys with trucks. A visit to any mainstream toy store demonstrates that while exceptions exist, many toys, games, and play devices continue to be designed along gender lines. If these differences were purely based upon individual preferences, they would hardly matter, but since gendered socialization closely ties in with inequalities resulting from it, the topic is of concern for parents and educators alike who are seeking to transform education to make it equitable and eradicate gender bias. In addition, gender matters where it intersects with other forms of oppression such as racism, resulting, for example, in what has been called "double jeopardy" for females of color.[48]

> **Suggested Activity:** Visit a toy store and consider how toys influence the formation of gender identities. Note details of what you observe, considering the types of toys, their colors and functions, and the gender messages they convey. Does playing with these toys socialize and perpetuate gender stereotypes in children? Why or why not?

Figure 6.3 Toy store aisles reveal gendering of toys.

Gender and mental health

Over the past few decades, schools have increased their attention to the mental and emotional well-being of students as diagnoses of mental health disorders among youth have risen. Although the COVID-19 pandemic intensified this rise, the trend began long before the pandemic. For example, between 2009 and 2019, the rate of high school students reporting persistent feelings of sadness or loneliness rose from 26.1 to 36.7 percent. Between 2016 and 2020, the number of children ages 3–17 diagnosed with depression rose 27 percent and anxiety 29 percent.[49]

Rates of various mental health disorders vary by sex and gender. For example, adolescent girls have higher rates of suicidal ideation and attempts than adolescent boys; however, adolescent boys are more likely to die by suicide. As will be discussed further in this chapter, adolescent girls are more likely to suffer from low self-esteem and eating disorders than boys are.[50] At the same time—while girls and women may be more likely to suffer from eating disorders such as anorexia or bulimia—males are more prone to "bigorexia," a body disorder involving obsessive increase of muscle mass. Furthermore, boys are often socialized to develop "**heroic intelligence**" focused on risk-taking rather than "**health intelligence**" focused on physical and emotional health. Gender norms make it easier for girls to express a need for help while boys often feel pressure to hide their vulnerabilities.[51]

One way in which social media influences the mental health of adolescent boys is through targeting and manipulation by extremist groups. The past decade has seen a rise in white supremacist groups using social media to recruit emotionally vulnerable young-adult white men. These groups often exploit their targets' low self-confidence and loneliness to manipulate them to feel victimized, emasculated, and loyal to the white supremacist group. This loyalty is then converted into a desire to commit acts of domestic terrorism. This disturbing trend has led to calls for more government oversight of how social media platforms regulate their content.[52]

Because many studies are pointing to social media as one factor contributing to the rise in depression and loneliness among youth, the US Surgeon General recently issued an advisory warning the public about the risks of social media. Surgeon General advisories are rare, reserved only for urgent public health issues, and they can shift social norms and behaviors. For example, the advisory on the harms of cigarettes initiated efforts that ultimately transformed perceptions and rates of cigarette smoking.[53]

The surgeon general's warning on the impacts of social media on youth mental health cited research showing that youth who spend more hours on social media have higher rates of depressive symptoms, low self-esteem, poor sleep, and experiences of cyberbullying. These associations were higher for girls than for boys. These are only correlations and therefore do not prove social media is *causing* these problems; however, some experimental studies have shown that reducing time on social media improves well-being. The Surgeon General advisory also points out the potential benefits of social media, such as finding support networks and identity-affirming content, particularly for youth of color and LGBTQ+ youth.[54]

Intersectional perspectives on gender in schools

Research with an intersectional perspective unearthed ways in which gender and race or ethnicity work against boys and young men of color. For example, during high school and college, significant gaps exist between Black/Latinx males and females with Black and Latinx men taking fewer AP courses,[55] or completing high school and especially college degrees.[56] It has been argued that one important reason for the gap in performance relates to such cultural factors as a misalignment between what students learn at home, and what they are expected to do in school. Therefore, they need to become either "cultural mainstreamers" or "cultural straddlers," and for reasons unknown, girls may be more likely to do so.[57]

However, it may be simplistic to generalize about *all* boys in this context, given that a number of them do indeed comply with dominant cultural expectations related to schooling, and are academically successful. One suggestion is to expand the discourse and acknowledge the diverse ways in which boys and young men of color navigate expectations of homes, schools, as well as ideologies of manhood.[58]

The emerging field of Black girlhood studies has also illuminated some of the ways in which Black girls' schooling experiences are influenced by cultural, structural, and interpersonal forces. One review of seventy-five research studies found that these forces yield inequitable access to high-quality STEM classes and affirming curriculum, as well as surveilled for adherence to white-female notions of femininity. This surveillance would often take the form of adultification and criminalization, ultimately dehumanizing Black girls and denying them access to joy and hope in schools. The review called for improving teacher preparation, strengthening recruitment and retention of Black women educators, and creating spaces in schools for Black girls to share their experiences and critique policies.[59]

Reflection question: To what extent does sexism negatively impact everyone, irrespective of gender identity?

LGBTQ+ students

Gender is a social and cultural construction, and notions of male, female, and other identities are defined by human beings in particular social and cultural contexts. When those contexts change, gender definitions are subject to change as well. For example, binary conceptions of gender, as in "man" and "woman," that have long been the dominant form of categorization, are too narrow to capture existing identities, and are increasingly substituted with a broader, more encompassing nonbinary nomenclature.

Not only do social and cultural conventions vary considerably when it comes to gender, but notions of sexual identity, a concept related to gender, do as well. What is declared "normal" depends on the historical time period, who defines the term, dominant religious and ideological beliefs, and so forth. Consequently, in the United States, beliefs about sexuality, including **heterosexuality** and lesbian, gay, bisexual, transgender, queer or questioning plus (LGBTQ+) identities, have varied by time and setting.

Homosexuality, for instance, has been seen as a sin, a crime, an illness, or simply as one of many possible sexual identities. Much was accomplished by the civil rights movement of the 1950s and 1960s, but where social justice concerns equal rights for LGBTQ+ persons, there are still significant challenges to be met. This fact is illustrated by developments spurred by the second Trump administration, for example, President Trump's January 20, 2025, executive order declaring that the United States recognizes only two sexes and genders fixed at birth.[60] Members of the LGBTQ+ community continue to face violence and harassment which, in the case of students, can impact academic achievement and other school-related factors.

Over the last few decades, cultural norms and, subsequently, how individuals choose to identify in terms of gender and sexual identity, have become more representative of a wide range of identities. For instance, identity labels might include distinctions between cisgender and **transgender**, or **monosexual** and **plurisexual**, individuals. Younger generations, in particular, continue to challenge binary thinking and instead capture gender and sexual identities, as well as sexual desire, using a much more expansive lexicon.[61] An implication for societal institutions such as schools is the need to revise some of their practices, for example, binary bathroom configurations.[62]

One theory that has shaped discussions about gender and sexuality is **queer theory**, which defines gender as "performances," and gender norms being repeated, embodied, and performed through language and actions. Those performances are often based on compulsive heterosexuality enforced by society through rewards for appropriate gender-related, heterosexual behaviors and through punishments for deviations from heteronormative sexual behavior. Examples in schools include assumptions that everyone is heterosexual (married characters in stories presumed to be male and female and little girls presumed to like playing princesses attracted to princes, for example). Heteronormativity is also found when parents are assumed to be a man and a woman, thus negating the fact that some children have LGBTQ+ parents, or when members of the LGBTQ+ community face discrimination in their personal and professional lives because of their sexual identities.[63]

Discrimination of LGBTQ+ students in and outside of schools takes many forms, including bullying, which a disproportionate number of LGBTQ+ youth experience. LGBTQ+ students have a right to safe, affirming, and supportive school environments. Schools need to develop effective strategies to deal with bullying, and to address bullying victimization to prevent adverse physical and mental health outcomes for LGBTQ+ youth. School health professionals, among others, need to be better prepared for these tasks. Importantly, any effort to respond to bullying has to recognize intersectionality among LGBTQ+ students and the fact that those with multiple marginalized identities may be most at-risk of targeted bullying victimization. There is also a need for clear and consistent reporting protocols, anti-bullying policies and for the school leadership to publicly address LGBTQ+ bullying, thereby conveying its importance to the broader community. All these efforts go hand in hand with the goal of building and maintaining a school culture of inclusivity.[64]

LGBTQ+ students themselves are actively forming alliances and advocating for equity. National organizations supporting this work include the Gay, Lesbian and Straight Education Network (GLSEN) and the Gay and Lesbian Alliance against Defamation (GLAAD). As powerfully expressed by scholar Michelle Fine, "(...) young people do not simply internalize rejection, betrayal, or social violence. Instead, they seem to draw strength while living in the borderlands, leaning on activist legacies, turning to social media, and joining with activist friends to challenge heteronormativity, gender binaries, poverty and racism, and to suture solidarities among movements that have long been divided."[65]

LGBTQ+ youth are significantly overrepresented among the unhoused youth population. Being unhoused is not always simply the result of parents who are rejecting their children once they disclose an LGBTQ+ identity. Instead, unhoused LGBTQ+ youth often have experienced a list of intersecting factors, some of which may be familial abuse, relegation to state custody systems, or drug use. In addition to the family, other social institutions like schools may also fail LGBTQ+ youth in that they police and punish rather than adequately support, and allow bullying as well as the continuing existence of unsafe spaces, for example. Structural racism intersects with oppressive practices regarding gender expression and sexuality for youth of color, and Black and Brown LGBTQ+ youth living in poverty tend to face the most punishing conditions.[66]

Given this context, LGBTQ+ youth are at relatively high risk of compromised mental health, experiencing what has been called **minority stress**. The minority stress model captures how stressors such as anti-LGBTQ+ stigma, prejudice, and discrimination cause hostile and stressful environments that undermine the mental health of individuals.[67]

Transgender and nonbinary students may be particularly harmed. Recent waves of anti-transgender legislation, including bills that propose to deny transgender individuals access to suitable bathroom facilities, sports, and healthcare or the right to have legal documents reflect their self-determined gender, illustrate the challenges.

Consider These Statistics: The Trevor Project's 2023 US National Survey on the Mental Health of LGBTQ Young People found that 41 percent of LGBTQ young people seriously considered attempting suicide in the past year, and young people who are transgender, nonbinary, and/or people of color reported higher rates than their peers. Fewer than 40 percent of LGBTQ young people found their home to be LGBTQ affirming. Roughly half of transgender and nonbinary young people found their school to be gender-affirming, and those who did reported lower rates of attempting suicide. A majority of LGBTQ young people reported being verbally harassed at school because people thought they were LGBTQ.[68]

Recommendations to improve the situation include for law and policy makers at the federal, state, and local levels to put measures in place that reduce structural barriers for these students, allow for gender self-determination, and assure their full access to sports, appropriate facilities, and healthcare. Furthermore, there is a need to develop curricula in cooperation with the trans community that include gender and sexuality, provide professional development for educators so they acquire trans-competent knowledge, reduce systems of sex and gender recording, and strengthen support networks in schools for transgender youth. The latter include gender and sexuality alliances, peer-to-peer support networks, and trans-competent and supportive adults.[69]

Despite the challenges they face, however, transgender students have also been found to possess significant coping strategies and resilience. They develop strategies to connect with their peers as well as school staff, making sure there are individuals who support them in important ways. Some find ways to thrive, even under difficult circumstances, displaying confidence and pride in their identities.[70]

In conclusion, educators have a significant impact on LGBTQ+ students' experiences in schools, and they function **in loco parentis** (in the place of a parent). Therefore, significant preparation in teacher education as well as professional development programs is needed so that educators are well equipped for creating a positive school climate that fosters learning for all students.[71]

Gender and elementary school

There have always been education critics, some of them alleging that schools contribute to various social ills rather than solve them. Such is the case with gender, particularly in the late twentieth and early twenty-first centuries when schools have been scrutinized as never before in regard to gender discrimination in curriculum materials, teaching practices, and educational policies.

The single most influential school is probably the elementary school, because it touches virtually everyone and may even surpass family influence for some children. In many families, caregivers work outside the home, and this means a large number of children are in school longer, particularly where after-school care is available. Elementary school spans those crucial years when children's basic moral values are learned and when gender identities that become significant in adulthood are formed. Elementary school teaches the basic knowledge most people carry with them the rest of their lives. In many respects, then, the elementary school is still the *common* school, coming closest of all other school levels to serving the American ideal of equal educational opportunity.

Definitions of gender roles

Despite the elementary school's historic role as a unifying and equalizing institution, it is by no means immune to gender bias. In the 1970s, critics charged that gender bias permeated the elementary school, not only in curriculum, but in **sex-segregated** activities, such as boys grouped for contact team sports, and girls grouped for home-oriented play activities. More subtle differentiations were found in separate boy and girl seating arrangements and lineups for marching to lunch or recess. Similarly, men occupied school leadership positions, while women occupied the lower ranks. In effect, children only had to observe school surroundings and role models to learn the gender stereotypes of the larger society.[72]

Since those days, curriculum materials have generally become more gender sensitive and inclusive, and yet they do remain gendered. Not only official written curricula but also the **hidden curriculum** (messages conveyed by teachers, staff, and peers in subtle and often subconscious ways) continue to be shaped by cultural definitions of femininity and masculinity. One can easily see how gender matters in school through an analysis of factors that are often taken for granted, for example, the fact that males are dominant among top administrators and coaches. Furthermore, curriculum reforms have tended to be additive, meaning that females and historically marginalized groups have been added to school curricula but without the disruption of patterns of dominance among these groups.[73]

> **Suggested Activity:** Form a research team with a few classmates and compare recently published elementary curriculum materials with sources published prior to 2000. Examine both sets for gender stereotyping. What do you find? Have changes been made? Discuss your findings in class. What are the implications of your research?

Male elementary school teachers

Pre-school and elementary school gender equity is not merely an issue of materials or curriculum but also of staffing. Children learn much about the relationships between gender and work through exposure to adult role models, of which teachers are among the more prevalent for children on a daily basis. Teaching tends to be a challenging profession regardless of gender identity, given the combination of great responsibilities and poor salaries, for example.

> **Cross-reference:** For more information on gender in the teaching profession, see Chapter 1: The Teaching Profession

The problem is compounded for men who have long been discouraged from pursuing a teaching career at the pre-school and elementary levels because of traditional gender bias, such as the belief that women are more naturally capable than men of nurturing young children.

That there has been a shortage of male teachers can be verified by the historical record. It needs pointing out, however, that male percentages have fluctuated over time, due to various developments. For example, in the 1879–80 school year, the percentage of male teachers in public elementary and secondary school stood at 42.8 percent, but in 1919–20, the male teacher percentage was a mere 14.1 percent (probably due to the effects of the First World War).[74]

Most recently, in the school year 2020–1, 11 percent of all elementary school teachers identified as male and 89 percent as female. However, male teachers have historically had a stronger numerical presence at the secondary level; nevertheless, in the school year 2020–1, only 36 percent identified as male, and 64 percent as female at the secondary level.[75]

In order to increase the recruitment and retention of male teachers, the barriers that deter them from entering the profession need to be addressed. Teacher education programs are called upon to play a role in the process and ensure that male preservice teachers are well supported and able to thrive while preparing to teach at the elementary and middle school levels.[76]

Gender and secondary school

Studies conducted in the 1970s and 1980s generally found that harmful stereotyping occurred at the secondary level with gender-differentiated curricula and the channeling of female and male students into different experiences. More recent studies show a marked decrease in such overt gender discrimination, but gender equity still remains a goal to be achieved. Just as significantly, the discourse about gender and sexual identity has become much more nuanced and inclusive over the last few decades, gradually overcoming simplistic and binary thinking, as discussed previously in this chapter.

Peer culture and gender roles

Gender-related behavior in schools is shaped by adults, but also by peer culture.[77] Student peer groups not only influence one another and construct powerful peer cultures that shape, and limit behavior, but they also mediate images related to gender identity, including masculinity and femininity. Those conceptions are not static, however.

A British study explored adolescents' perspectives on gender diversity, generating findings that support research conducted elsewhere. Although schools often continue to reinforce binary thinking about gender, for example, through binary bathroom designations, attitudes of many young people are changing rather significantly and moving toward embracing gender diversity, equality, and the rights of gender and sexual minorities. In fact, it may sometimes be the adults who are challenged to keep up with young people's changing mindsets.[78]

One aspect where **peer culture** proves to be very powerful spans notions of bodies, sexuality, and beauty. Peer opinions matter for most students, and as children develop and encounter sexuality and eroticism, they also face peer pressures and feelings of shame related to gender roles and sexual identities. Closely related are cultural images of bodies and beauty. Many adolescent girls fall victim to **eating disorders**, reinforced by media images and adolescent peer perceptions that beauty is equated with thinness. Research has shown that dissatisfaction with body image is more common among females and is positively correlated with Body Mass Index (BMI) as a predictor of eating disorders.[79]

Though much of the research and attention around eating disorders has focused on girls, cultural body images and peer-reinforced standards of appearance affect boys too. Athletes and members of racial, ethnic, as well as sexual and gender minorities are at increased risk of developing eating disorders. Those disorders differ from prevalent disorders in females, however, with boys engaging in muscularity-oriented disordered eating, and the use of steroids to bulk up for competitive athletics and to enhance muscular physical appearance. Despite the negative health implications, the guidelines for how to best manage eating disorders in adolescent boys and young men remain underdeveloped.[80]

For Further Reflection: Based on your own experience, describe how virtual and physical peer groups shape identities. Can you think of instances in your own life where the peer group shaped your gender identity and how you thought of yourself as a woman, man, or nonbinary person?

Classrooms and courses

Although gender relations are rooted in traditions, they are not static. Evidence suggests that students today are much more likely than previous generations to perceive individuals of all gender identities as equally capable rather than seeing male achievement as the standard. Another change is that girls today tend to perceive future careers as higher priorities than previous generations. Girls no longer worry that academic achievement is "unfeminine," and, for example, are more willing than boys to reveal academic successes to their friends.[81]

As far as academics and gender is concerned, the picture is complex. On the one hand, female students continue to outperform male students; for example, female high school graduates have long earned more credits in academic courses and a higher overall grade point average (GPA) than their male counterparts.[82] On the other hand, boys tend to outperform girls in mathematics and science. For example, while math scores recently declined for both male and female fourth-graders, boys not only continue to outperform girls in math but the gender gap even widened.[83] As far as other indicators of academic achievement are concerned, the number of girls who take the Advanced Placement (AP) Test in mathematics each year has risen over the last few decades but boys continue to outperform girls. In general, the gender gap in STEM (science, technology,

Figure 6.4 A pair of Calvert County, Maryland students test their tool to launch a projectile, 2025.

engineering, math) fields is still stark and continues into college and beyond, perpetuating the underrepresentation of females in STEM careers.[84]

Many factors contribute to these persistent gaps, among them gender stereotypes, with STEM professions often being seen and portrayed as "masculine." STEM fields continue to be characterized by male-dominated cultures. In addition, there is a lack of female role models in STEM fields, as well as few women scientists and engineers depicted in books, media, and popular culture. This is particularly true for STEM women of color. Yet another factor is the so-called confidence gap, referring to many girls losing confidence in math as early as elementary school. Contributing to this phenomenon is the insidious myth of men being more likely than women to have a "math brain" when, in fact, no research shows innate cognitive biological differences between women and men when it comes to their ability to do math.[85]

Extracurricular activities

The importance of extracurricular activities has long been recognized for children's and adolescents' development, academic performance, and other factors related to well-being as well as future opportunities and attainment. Students involved in sports, music, school governance, clubs, and other activities tend to do better in school and have better college prospects than those not involved. They also tend to engage to a lesser degree in substance use. Extracurricular activities, especially those that are school-based and thus supported by the schools, have the potential to equalize educational opportunities.

However, one concern is that extracurricular activities can also exacerbate inequalities, for example, when programs are being squeezed out of schools into the private sector where they become "pay-to-play" activities some parents and caretakers may not be able to afford. In addition to the "class gap," with participation higher among middle- and upper-class children, there is also a race/ethnicity gap. In part due to Title XI's requirement that schools provide equal opportunities for girls and boys, the gender gap has been shrinking over time. However, concerning race and ethnicity, non-Hispanic Black youth have lower rates of participation in activities that fall outside of sports, such as Model UN, Beta Club, or Student Government, which matters because these types of activities are important for school success and college expectations.[86]

As far as gender is concerned, girls have long participated more in non-sport extracurricular activities but are now also participating more than boys in school-based activities across domains, meaning both sport and non-sport activities. Boys, however, continue to participate more in only sport activities, despite the fact that this gap has decreased over time. In fact, boys are now more likely than girls not to participate in any extracurricular activities. In conclusion, while gaps continue to exist, in particular social class gaps, girls have made great progress and are actually doing at least as well as boys in terms of to their participation in extra-curricular activities.[87]

Career choices

Gender is highly influential when it comes to making career choices which are directly related to the underrepresentation of women in many high-paying and prestigious occupations. Men, in comparison, are underrepresented in prosocial occupations such as teaching and those in the healthcare field. One national study found that men tend to be more interested in working with things (as engineers, for example) while women tend to be interested in working with people (as teachers and caregivers, for example). Vocational interests, however, can change, which means that schools and other educational institutions have opportunities to develop programs, policies, and practices that reduce stereotypical thinking about occupations.[88]

As it is, the upper echelons within professions often continue to be dominated by men, and while women's numbers have increased and continue to grow, gaps remain. Despite the increasing significance of the STEM disciplines for the nation's economy and growth, for instance, women still lag behind. They earn fewer computer and information science degrees, and are underrepresented in computer technology-related professions. In 2022, for example, only 23 percent of Computer and Information Sciences bachelor's degrees were received by women, and in 2023, women accounted for only 27 percent of the workforce in professional computing occupations. Factoring in race and ethnicity, only 3 percent of the computing workforce in 2023 consisted of Black or African American women, and only 2 percent were Hispanic or Latinx women.[89]

The income gap between men and women has narrowed significantly over the long run for workers across age groups, and it is relatively narrow among young workers. However, in recent years, not much has changed otherwise. Women across age groups still earn less than men: in 2022, women's earnings were on average 83 percent of men's earnings. The gap between men and women is most pronounced among Asians and whites. Pay gaps vary significantly by state: for example, in 2022, in Utah, women's average earnings were 73.1 percent of men's, while in Rhode Island, women earned 99.6 percent of what men earned.[90]

The underrepresentation of women in high-paying positions and their overrepresentation in low-paying positions account in part for the persisting gender wage gap; another reason may be differential treatment of women in comparison to men by their employers, as well as women feeling more pressure to take on family caretaking obligations which may reduce women's earnings.[91]

Given the **gender stratification** in both educational institutions and the workplace, it is crucial for schools to prepare individuals of all gender identities equally well in a wide range of competencies, and ready them for successful futures. However, schools may be able to influence students' career choices, but they cannot alone resolve culture scripting or eliminate gendered stereotypes and gender-related biases about careers and professions that continue to be ingrained in the larger society.

Sex-based harassment

Although it has long been a factor in schools, workplaces, and other realms of life, it is not always exactly clear what sex-based harassment is. Helpful definitions of sex-based harassment are needed for courts, policy makers, and educators to deal with it effectively. **Title IX**, a federal law passed in 1972 that outlaws sex-based discrimination in educational settings that are supported by federal funds, defines sex-based harassment as including sexual harassment and sexual violence. Sexual harassment, consists of " … unwelcome sexual advances, requests for sexual favors, and other verbal, nonverbal, or physical conduct of a sexual nature." Sexual violence " … refers to physical sexual acts perpetrated against a person's will or where a person is incapable of giving consent." Included are " … rape, sexual assault, sexual battery, sexual abuse, and sexual coercion." Gender-based harassment, furthermore, is defined as "unwelcome conduct on a student's gender or gender identity or harassing conduct based on a student's failure to conform to gender stereotypes." Sex-based harassment may be perpetrated by school employees as well as other students or third parties, and it may affect any student, regardless of gender or sexual identity, disability status, race, national origin, or age, and it also includes sex-based harassment by members of the same sex.[92]

Sex-based harassment may lead to the creation of a hostile environment for students and can have profound effects on their lives. Sexual harassment may push students to study less, curtail participation, cut classes, or avoid school altogether in order to avoid or escape such harassment.[93]

Sex-based harassment may not only affect a student's grades and self-esteem, but it may also result in serious complaints and even lawsuits for school systems. An example of court decisions involving sexually related cases was ***Franklin v. Gwinnett County Public Schools*** **(1992)**, in which student Christine Franklin reported sexual advances from a teacher on school grounds, but she was instructed by school administrators not to tell anyone. She sued for compensatory damages under Title IX of the Education Amendments of 1972 (now known as the Patsy T. Mink Equal Opportunity in Education Act). The case was appealed to the US Supreme Court, which ruled that the school had discriminated against Franklin by not dealing with her complaint. It is the first case of its kind where compensatory damages were awarded.[94]

However, in ***Gebser v. Lago Vista Independent School District*** **(1998)**, the Supreme Court ruled in favor of the school administration on the grounds that the administration had no actual knowledge of the student-teacher sexual relationship. These two cases illustrate the extent to which school personnel are legally responsible for adult-to-student sexual harassment.[95] As for student-to-student sexual harassment, the Supreme Court ruled in ***Davis v. Monroe County Board of Education*** **(1999)** that schools are liable if they are aware of the sexual harassment but do not stop it.[96] Court involvement is only one way to deal with sexual harassment. Ideally, it should be handled at the school level, and there need to be effective ways to prevent all types of sex-based harassment in schools, given that physical safety and psychological well-being in schools are central goals.

How schools are required to deal with sex-based harassment is an inherently political issue. The first Trump administration, for example, put rules in place in 2020 that allowed for sexual harassment to be labeled as less credible than other forms of misconduct, and permitted schools to conduct fewer investigations into sexual harassment claims.

Subsequently, the Biden administration strengthened protections against sex-based harassment and clarified protections of LGBTQ+ as well as pregnant and parenting students. For example, schools began to be required to respond with more care to a greater number of sex-based harassment incidents, using the same standards as are in place for racial as well as disability-based harassment. It became obligatory that schools address off-campus harassment as well as complaints by individuals who are no longer in school, and take "prompt and effective action" and offer supportive measures, such as counseling, to reporting students. Specifically concerning LGBTQ+ students, Title IX rules explicitly defined discrimination to " … include discrimination based on sexual orientation, gender identity, sex characteristics [including intersex traits], and sex stereotypes." Transgender individuals, for example, had to be permitted " … to participate in classes and activities, use bathrooms and locker rooms, and dress and groom themselves consistent with their gender identity." In regard to pregnant and parenting students, many do not know that they have rights which need to be affirmed. They may not be excluded from participation in school activities, including physical activities; they must be permitted leaves of absence as well as reasonable accommodations, and provided clean, non-bathroom lactation spaces.[97]

The second Trump administration, however, has been working to turn the tide again, re-interpreting Title IX and weakening many of its protections. Among the recent developments are the US Department of Education's commitment to enforcing the 2020 Title IX regulations that were enacted during President Trump's first term. Critics are concerned that one of the implications is an enforcement of protections in schools and on campuses on the basis of biological sex, restricted to "male" and "female."[98]

Single-sex education

Championed as a device to achieve gender equity and attacked as an anachronism standing in the way of equal educational opportunities, **single-sex education** is a controversial issue. Advocates of single-sex education argue that public as well as private schools ought to provide students, in particular girls, with separate and safe learning environments. If boys dominate the classroom and receive more of the teacher's attention, the argument goes, schools ought to provide opportunities for girls to excel in their own ways. Single-sex education is seen not only as a remedy for problems faced by girls but for boys as well, especially when boys are assumed to be disadvantaged or discriminated against. Critics of single-sex education argue that such practices are forms of segregation and that students of diverse gender identities will never learn to get along in life if they do not learn to do so in school.

The research is equally conflicted about what environment is best for students, single-sex or coed, and what role the teacher's gender plays in providing the best education. Under such conditions, it is usually possible to find evidence supporting most ideological positions held on the issue.[99]

A recent and extensive review of research in twelve countries focused on elementary and secondary schools found that there is no unequivocal relationship between academic achievement and single-sex classes; rather, the results are mixed. Claims that single-sex education alone positively influences post-secondary plans and career readiness are also unsubstantiated at this time.[100]

At the K-12 level, single-sex education is an umbrella term for diverse approaches, including both single-sex classrooms and single-sex schools, which makes simple generalizations about this approach to education difficult. Widely accepted evidence that single-sex education works better than coeducation is scarce, and single-sex education in and of itself does not ensure good education (another term subject to variable meanings). Research provides positive results for some students in some settings, but long-term results are even less certain. Furthermore, single-sex education does not mean the absence of gender bias because gender stereotypes can be perpetuated almost anywhere, including in single-sex and coeducational settings.[101]

Summary and conclusions

It is difficult to bring about immediate changes in institutions such as schools because the redirection of an institution (let alone a whole society) seldom proceeds in full-scale fashion. Progress has been made, but bias related to gender and sexual identity has not disappeared. Although biological sex is one factor related to gender, it is not the same as gender, and gender as well as sexual identities are complex in and of themselves. Perceptions and definitions have long been steeped in sociocultural conventions and institutional arrangements, and they are ever-changing. For example, women's subordinate status did not arise from biology so much as from social and cultural ideas of womanhood or manhood, and what it meant to be feminine or masculine. Along the same lines, binary conceptions of gender have long been questioned as it has become clear that individuals do not necessarily fall squarely within the categories of "male" or "female."

Concerted efforts for social, political, and economic equity have mostly occurred in recent times. However, back in the late eighteenth century, female education gained attention as indispensable to the new republic. During nineteenth-century industrialization, the education of girls was expanded, as was the role of women in social reform and in education, particularly as teachers in the new public common schools. By the end of the century, public schools embraced coeducation from elementary through high school, and by the early twentieth century, female students outnumbered male students in the schools.

The conviction that females should have citizenship rights and societal access on par with males gained ground over time, and by the end of the twentieth century, females actually gained numerical dominance in schools from kindergarten to higher education. Female participation in the labor market also greatly expanded, although still hampered by pay and job discrimination. Nevertheless, by the twenty-first century, more women participated in greater numbers in almost all social institutions and at all levels than ever before. In education, females were gaining academic standing equal to that of males, with greater recognition of women's ways of learning and knowing.

As barriers to gender equity in education were reduced, attention was also directed to boys, with growing recognition that gender bias affected both girls and boys. However, female achievement in math and science still lagged behind that of males, just as achievement of males lagged behind that of females in verbal and written achievement. For all the changes, gender inequities lingered in institutional structures, professional practices, and behavioral patterns. Some critics pushed single-sex schooling as a remedy to gender problems in education. Others countered that sex segregation did not address the sources of most gender problems, particularly sociocultural forces that transmit gender messages, often without people being aware of it.

At the high school level, females are still less likely than males to pursue such fields as math, science, and technology, and males continue to be underrepresented in the performing arts and literary activities. In higher education, males still outnumber females in certain fields and in the higher ranks of the professoriate and administration. In careers, males continue to be over-represented in many of the higher-paying fields such as STEM. The issue of sexual harassment, while much more prominent in public awareness, has not disappeared from either schools or workplaces.

Narrow images of masculinity and femininity also play roles in defining sexuality and sexual identities. The ways these issues are viewed have changed as well, but sexual identities defying heterosexual norms often continue to meet hostile prejudice in social institutions, including schools. Students facing such treatment often suffer from isolation and stigmatization and are even subjected to overt violence, while a cloak of silence remains in many schools concerning issues of sexuality.

It is evident that individuals, in whatever way they will come to identity, are socialized into gender roles virtually from the moment of birth, and as they mature the roles are reinforced by many forces such as families, communities, and other societal and institutional settings, including schools. Although human beings of any gender and sexual identity possess so many characteristics in common, differences continue to matter in countries around the globe.

There is a continuing need to examine and correct the root causes for gender and sexuality related bias, particularly the educational roots. Regardless of identity, all persons possess equal rights and should have equal opportunities and the best education possible.

Vocabulary

Addams, Jane
bisexual
coeducation
Combahee River Collective (CRC)
cult of true womanhood
Davis v. Monroe County Board of Education (1999)
eating disorders
ethics of care
Franklin v. Gwinnett County Public Schools (1992)
fugitive project
Gebser v. Lago Vista Independent School District (1998),
gay
gender
gender bias
gender stereotypes
gender stratification

Gilligan, Carol
Hartford Female Seminary
health intelligence
heroic intelligence
heteronormativity
heterosexuality
hidden curriculum
homosexuality
Hull house
in loco parentis
Kohlberg, Lawrence
League of Women Voters
lesbian
lesbian, gay, bisexual, transgender, queer or questioning plus (LGBTQ+)
minority stress
monosexual
Mount Holyoke Female Seminary
National Association of Colored Women (NACW)
National Black Feminist Organization (NBFO)
National Organization of Women (NOW)
Noddings, Nel
queer theory
peer culture
Piaget, Jean
plurisexual
race uplift
sentimental womanhood
sex
sexual identity
sex-segregated
single-sex education
straight
temperance movement
Title IX
transgender
Troy Female Seminary
women's liberation movement
women's suffrage movement
women's ways of knowing

Notes

1 Jenny Shaw, *Education, Gender and Anxiety* (London: Taylor and Francis, 1995), 1–3.
2 National Academies, *Measuring Sex, Gender Identity, and Sexual Orientation* (Washington, DC: National Academies Press, 2022), 3, https://nap.nationalacademies.org/read/26424/chapter/1 (accessed on February 14, 2024).
3 Ibid., vii–viii.
4 Mary P. Ryan, *Womanhood in America: From Colonial Times to the Present*, 2nd edn (New York: New Viewpoints, A Division of Franklin Watts, 1979).
5 Ibid., x–xvii, 10, 14–16, 28–9.
6 See Lawrence A. Cremin, *American Education: The Colonial Experience, 1607–1783* (New York: Harper and Row, 1970).
7 June Sochen, *Movers and Shakers: American Women Thinkers and Activists, 1900–1970* (New York: Quadrangle/New York Times Book, 1973), 1; and Merle Curti, *The Social Ideas of American Educators* (Totawa, NJ: Littlefield, Adams, 1968), 176.
8 Jennifer L. Morgan, *Laboring Women. Reproduction and Gender in New World Slavery* (Philadelphia: University of Pennsylvania Press, 2004), 1.
9 Catherine Adams and Elizabeth H. Peck, *Love of Freedom: Black Women in Colonial and Revolutionary New England* (New York: Oxford University Press, 2010), 3.
10 Gerda Lerner, *Black Women in White America: A Documentary History* (New York: Random House, 1972), xxiii.
11 Ira Berlin, Steven F. Miller, and Leslie S. Rowland, "Afro-American Families in the Transition from Slavery to Freedom. 89–121," in *Black Women in United States History*, Darlene Clark Hine, ed. (Brooklyn, NY: Carlson Publishing Inc., 1990), 89.
12 Jarvis R. Givens, *Fugitive Pedagogy: Carter G. Woodson and the Art of Black Teaching* (Cambridge, MA: Harvard University Press, 2021), 10.
13 Susie King Taylor, *Reminiscences of My Life in Camp* (Boston, MA: Published by the Author, 1902), 5.
14 Ryan, *Womanhood in America,* 53–4, and 82–5; and Lawrence Cremin, *American Education: The National Experience, 1783–1876* (New York: Harper and Row, 1980), 348–50.
15 Linda M. Perkins, "The Impact of the 'Cult of True Womanhood' on the Education of Black Women," in *Black Women in the United States History*, vol. 3, Darlene Clark Hine, ed. (Brooklyn, NY: Carlson Publishing Inc., 1990), 1065–70.
16 Barbara Welter, "The Cult of True Womanhood," *American Quarterly*, vol. 18, no. 2 part 1 (Summer, 1966): 152–3.

17 Perkins, "The Impact of the 'Cult of True Womanhood' on the Education of Black Women," 1066–72.

18 Eleanor Wolf Thompson, *Education for Ladies, 1830–1860: Ideas on Education in Magazines for Women* (Morningside Heights, NY: King's Crown Press, 1947), 73–90.

19 Phillida Bunkle, "Sentimental Womanhood and Domestic Education, 1830–1870," *History of Education Quarterly*, vol. 14, no. 1 (Spring 1974): 3–30.

20 Michael Apple, "Teaching and 'Women's Work': A Comparative Historical and Ideological Analysis," in *Expressions of Power in Education: Studies of Class, Gender and Race*, Center for Cross-cultural Education Lecture Series, vol. 3, Edgar B. Gumbert, ed. (Atlanta, GA: Center for Cross-Cultural Education, 1984), 35, 38; and Robert E. Potter, *The Stream of American Education* (New York: American Book Company, 1967), 238–9.

21 Bettina Aptheker, "Quest for Dignity: Black Women in the Professions, 1865–1900," in *Black Women in the United States History*, vol. 1, Darlene Clark Hine, ed. (Brooklyn, NY: Carlson Publishing Inc., 1990), 28.

22 Constance E. Cunningham, "Sin of Omission: Black Women in Nineteenth Century American History," in *Black Women in the United States History*, vol. 1, Darlene Clark Hine, ed. (Brooklyn, NY: Carlson Publishing Inc., 1990), 283–4.

23 Emma Hart Willard, "A Plan for Improving Female Education," in *Pioneers of Women's Education in the United States: Emma Willard, Catherine Beecher, Mary Lyon*, Willystine Goodsell, ed. (1931, reprint, New York: AMS Press, 1970), 58, 62, and 72.

24 Catherine Beecher, "Suggestions Respecting Improvements in Education," in *Pioneers of Women's Education*, 147; and Bunkle, "Sentimental Womanhood and Domestic Education, 1830–1870," 20.

25 Mary Lyon, "New England Female Seminary for Teachers," in *Pioneers of Women's Education*, 254; and Bunkle, "Sentimental Womanhood and Domestic Education, 1830– 1870," 21–2.

26 Lynn D. Gordon, *Gender and Higher Education in the Progressive Era* (New Haven, CT: Yale University Press, 1990), 13–51.

27 Aptheker, "Quest for Dignity: Black Women in the Professions, 1865-1900," 29.

28 John L. Rury, *Education and Women's Work: Female Schooling and the Division of Labor in Urban America, 1870–1930* (Albany: State University of New York Press, 1991), 17–18, 35–48.

29 Ibid., 83, 120–4.

30 Lerner, *Black Women in White America*, 238.

31 Darlene Clark Hine, "Co-Laborers in the Work of the Lord: Nineteenth-Century Black Women Physicians," in *Black Women in the United States History*, vol. 2, Darlene Clark Hine, ed. (Brooklyn, NY: Carlson Publishing Inc., 1990), 637–55.

32 Rury, *Education and Women's Work*, 135–44.

33 Ibid.

34 Adele Logan Alexander, "How I Discovered My Grandmother … and the Truth About Black Women and the Suffrage Movement," in *Black Women in the United States History*, vol. 1, Darlene Clark Hine, ed. (Brooklyn, NY: Carlson Publishing Inc., 1990), 18–20.

35 Ibid.

36 Lerner, *Black Women in White America*, 163–4.

37 Judith Stacey et al., eds, *And Jill Came Tumbling After: Sexism in American Education* (New York: Dell Publishing, 1974).

38 Audre Lorde, "An Open Letter to Mary Daly," in *This Bridge Called My Back: Writings by Radical Women of Color*, Cherríe Morraga and Gloria Anzaldúa, eds (New York: Kitchen Table: Women of Color Press, 1981), 94.

39 Duchess Harris, *Black Feminist Politics from Kennedy to Obama* (New York: Palgrave Macmillan, 2009), xiii.

40 Combahee River Collective, *The Combahee River Collective Statement* (1977), https://www.blackpast.org/african-american-history/combahee-river-collective-statement-1977/ (accessed on October 25, 2024).

41 Jack Fincher, *Human Intelligence* (New York: G. P. Putnam's Sons, 1976).

42 American Association of University Women (AAUW), *The STEM Gap: Women and Girls in Science, Technology, Engineering and Mathematics* (Washington, DC: AAUW), https://www.aauw.org/resources/research/the-stem-gap/ (accessed on March 27, 2024).

43 Laura Scholes, "Differences in Attitudes Towards Reading and Other School-Related Activities Among Boys and Girls," *Journal of Research in Reading*, vol. 42, no. 3–4 (2019): 485–503, https://doi.org/10.1111/1467-9817.12279

44 Mary Field Belenky et al., *Women's Ways of Knowing: The Development of Self, Voice, and Mind* (New York: Basic Books, 1986).

45 Carol Gilligan, *In a Different Voice: Psychological Theory and Women's Development* (Cambridge, MA: Harvard University Press, 1982).

46 Nel Noddings, *Caring: A Feminine Approach to Ethics and Moral Education* (Berkeley: University of California Press, 1984); Nel Noddings, *The Challenge to Care in Schools: An Alternative Approach to Education* (New York: Teachers College Press, 1992); and Nel Noddings, "Introduction," in *Justice and Caring: The Search for Common Ground in Education*, Michael Katz, Nel Noddings, and Kenneth Strike, eds (New York: Teachers College Press, 1999), 1–2.

47 Kenneth Strike, "Justice, Caring, and Universality: In Defense of Moral Pluralism," in *Justice and Caring*, 21–6.

48 Terms coined by Frances Beal in a feminist pamphlet in 1969; see Cierra Kaler-Jones, "'I Rewrote Their Story and You Can, Too:' Black Girls' Artistic Freedom

Dreams to Create New Worlds," *Frontiers in Education*, vol. 7 (2022): 983496, doi: 10.3389/feduc.2022.9834963

49 Mark D. Weist, Sharon A. Hoover, Brian P. Daly, Kathy H. Short, and Eric J. Bruns, "Propelling the Global Advancement of School Mental Health," *Clinical Child and Family Psychology Review*, vol. 26, no. 4 (2023): 851–64.

50 Linda Dil, Saskia Mérelle, Nick Lommerse, Jaap Peen, Pety So, Rien Van, Jeroen Zoeteman, and Jack Dekker, "Gender-Specific Pathways in Mental Health Crisis in Adolescents, from Consultation to (in) Voluntary Admission: A Retrospective Study," *BMC Psychiatry*, vol. 24, no. 1 (2024): 235.

51 Warren Farrell and John Gray, *The Boy Crisis* (Dallas, TX: BenBella Books, 2018).

52 Eleanor Boatman, "The Kids Are Alt-Right: How Media and the Law Enable White Supremacist Groups to Recruit and Radicalize Emotionally Vulnerable Individuals," *Law Journal for Social Justice*, vol. 12 (Fall 2019): 2–61.

53 Remy Tumin, "A Half-Century of Surgeon General Warnings," *New York Times* (May 23, 2023).

54 "Social Media and Youth Mental Health: The U.S. Surgeon General's Advisory," 2023, https://www.hhs.gov/sites/default/files/sg-youth-mental-health-social-media-advisory.pdf on (accessed on November 7, 2024).

55 Danny Lackey and Kendra Lowery, "Where Are the African American Males? Enrollment Criteria and the Placement of African American Males in Advanced Placement Courses," *Urban Education*, vol. 58, no. 10 (2023): 2628–57.

56 National Center for Education Statistics, *Table 104.10. Rates of High School Completion and Bachelor's Degree Attainment Among Persons Age 25 and Over, by Race/Ethnicity and Sex: Selected Years, 1910 Through 2022*, https://nces.ed.gov/programs/digest/d22/tables/dt22_104.10.asp (accessed on July 4, 2024); National Center for Education Statistics, *Fast Facts: Degrees Conferred by Race/Ethnicity and Sex, 2020–2021*, https://nces.ed.gov/fastfacts/display.asp?id=72 (accessed on July 4, 2024).

57 Prudence L. Carter, *Keepin' It Real: School Success Beyond Black and White* (New York: Oxford University Press, 2005).

58 Suneal Kolluri, "'Chill Dudes' and 'Academic-Type Students': Relational Masculinity and Straddling Culture at an Urban High School," *American Journal of Education*, vol. 129, no. 3 (2023): 355–81.

59 Danielle Apugo, Andrene J. Castro, and Sharyn A. Dougherty, "Taught in the Matrix: A Review of Black Girls' Experiences in U.S. Schools," *Review of Educational Research*, vol. 93, no. 4 (August 2023): 559–93.

60 The White House, "Defending Women from Gender Ideology Extremism and Restoring Biological Truth to the Federal Government," https://www.whitehouse.gov/presidential-actions/2025/01/defending-women-from-gender-ideology-extremism-and-restoring-biological-truth-to-the-federal-government/ (January 20, 2025).

61 Phillip L. Hammack, Sam D. Hughes, Julianne M. Atwood, Elliot M. Cohen, and Richard C. Clark, "Gender and Sexual Identity in Adolescence: A Mixed-Methods Study of Labeling in Diverse Community Setting," *Journal of Adolescent Research*, vol. 37, no. 2 (2022): 167–220.

62 Carolyn M. Porta, Amy L. Gower, Christopher J. Mehus, Xiaohui Yu, Elizabeth M. Saewyc, and Marla E. Eisenberg, "Kicked Out": LGBTQ Youths' Bathroom Experiences and Preferences," *Journal of Adolescence*, vol. 56 (2017): 107–12.

63 Mindy Blaise, *Playing It Straight: Uncovering Gender Discourses in the Early Childhood Classroom* (New York: Routledge, 2005), 22; William J. Letts IV and James T. Sears, eds, *Queering Elementary Education: Advancing the Dialogue About Sexualities and Schooling* (Lanham, MD: Rowman and Littlefield Publishers, 1999), 165–204, and 207–56; and Madiha Didi Khayatt, *Lesbian Teachers: An Invisible Presence* (Albany: State University of New York Press, 1992).

64 Sari L. Reisner et al., "Addressing LGBTQ Student Bullying in Massachusetts Schools: Perspectives of LGBTQ Students and School Health Professionals," *Prevention Science*, vol. 21 (2020): 408–21.

65 Michelle Fine, *Just Research in Contentious Times: Widening the Methodological Imagination* (New York: Teachers College Press, 2018), 106.

66 Brandon Andrew Robinson, *Coming out to the Streets: LGBTQ Youth Experiencing Homelessness* (Oakland: University of California Press, 2020), 5; The Trevor Project, 2023 U.S. National Survey on the Mental Health of LGBTQ Young People, https://www.thetrevorproject.org/survey-2023/ (accessed on April 28, 2024).

67 Ilian H. Meyer, "Prejudice, Social Stress, and Mental Health in Lesbian, Gay, and Bisexual Populations: Conceptual Issues and Research Evidence," *Psychological Bulletin*, vol. 129, no. 5 (2003): 674–97, https://doi.org/10.1037/0033-2909.129.5.674; Jeremy T. Goldbach and Jeremy J. Gibbs, "A Developmentally Informed Adaptation of Minority Stress for Sexual Minority Adolescents," *Journal of Adolescence*, vol. 55 (2017): 36–50, https://doi.org/10.1016/j.adolescence.2016.12.007

68 The Trevor Project, 2023 U.S. National Survey on the Mental Health of LGBTQ Young People.

69 Elizabeth J. Meyer, Bethy Leonardi, Harper B. Keenan, *Transgender Students and Policy in K-12 Public Schools: Acknowledging Historical Harms and Taking Steps Toward a Promising Future* (Boulder, CO: National Education Policy Center (NEPC), 2022), https://files-eric-ed-gov.proxy.library.vcu.edu/fulltext/ED620507.pdf

70 Michelle M. Johns et al., "Minority Stress, Coping and Transgender Youth in Schools: Results from the Resilience and Transgender Youth Study," *Journal of School Health*, vol. 91, no. 11 (2021): 883–93.

71 Melissa Doellman, "A Call to Action: The Importance of School Climate, Professional Development, and Teacher Education Programs in Fostering LGBT Supportive Educators," in *Queering Classrooms: Personal Narratives and Educational Practices to Support LGBTQ Youth in Schools*, Erin A. Mikulec and Paul Chamness Miller, eds (Charlotte, NC: Information Age Publishing, 2017), 184.

72 Betty Levy and Judith Stacey, "Sexism in the Elementary School: A Backward and Forward Look," *Phi Delta Kappan*, vol. 50, no. 2 (October 1973): 105–9.

73 Nancy Lesko and Stephanie D. McCall, "Curriculum and Gender" (Routledge Resources Online, 2022), https://www.taylorfrancis.com/entries/10.4324/9781138609877-REE127-1/curriculum-gender-nancy-lesko-stephanie-mccall?context=rroe

74 NCES, "Table 32. Historical Summary of Public Elementary and Secondary School Statistics, 1869–70 Through 2005–06," *Digest of Education Statistics* (2008), https://nces.ed.gov/programs/digest/d08/tables/dt08_032.asp (accessed on May 6, 2024).

75 NCES, Figure 1. Percentage distribution of teachers in public elementary and secondary schools, by institutional level and sex: School year 2020-1, https://nces.ed.gov/programs/coe/indicator/clr/public-school-teachers (accessed on August 23, 2024). Note: source does not provide nonbinary data.

76 Katie D. Lewis and Nicole Hesson, "The Unicorn Teacher: Males in Early Elementary and Middle Level Education," *Teacher Educators' Journal*, vol. 17 (2024): 49–75.

77 For more detail on understanding peer influence in general, see Brett Laursen and Vennstra René, "Toward Understanding the Functions of Peer Influence: A Summary and Synthesis of Recent Empirical Research," *Journal of Research on Adolescence*, vol. 31 (2021): 889–907, https://doi.org/10.1111/jora.12606 (accessed on February 10, 2024).

78 Sara Bragg, Emma Renold, Jessica Ringrose, and Carolyn Jackson, "'More than Boy, Girl, Male, Female': Exploring Young People's Views on Gender Diversity Within and Beyond School Contexts," *Sex Education*, vol. 18, no. 4 (2018): 420–34, https://doi.org/10.1080/14681811.2018.1439373

79 Candy Laurine Suarez-Albor, Maura Galletta, and Edna Margarita Gómez-Bustamante, "Factors Associated with Eating Disorders in Adolescents: a Systematic Review," *Acta Biomiomedica*, vol. 93, no. 3 (2022): e2022253, doi:10.23750/abm.v93i3.13140 (accessed on September 29, 2024).

80 Jason M. Nagata, Kyle T. Ganson, and Stuart B. Murray, "Eating Disorders in Adolescent Boys and Young Men: An Update," *Current Opinions in Pediatrics*, vol. 32, no. 3 (2020): 476.

81 Ellen Rydell Altermatt and Jackson Kai Painter, "I Did Well. Should I Tell? Gender Differences in Children's Academic Success Disclosures," *Sex Roles*, vol. 74 (2016): 46–61.

82 National Center for Educational Statistics (NCES), *The Nation's Report Card. 2019 NAEP High School Transcript Study (HSTS) Results.* Coursetaking (accessed on October 5, 2024)

83 National Center for Educational Statistics (NCES), *The Nation's Report Card.* 2022 NAEP Mathematics Assessment Highlights. Figure: Changes in Fourth-grade NAEP Mathematics scores between 2019 and 2022, by gender, https://www.nationsreportcard.gov/highlights/mathematics/2022/ (accessed on May 10, 2024).

84 Kadir Bahar, "Girls Still Fall Behind in Top Scores for AP Math Exams," *The Conversation* (2022), https://theconversation.com/girls-still-fall-behind-boys-in-top-scores-for-ap-math-exams-174192 (accessed on May 10, 2024).

85 American Association of University Women (AAUW), *The STEM GAP* (accessed on July 10, 2024).

86 Ann Meier, Benjamin Swartz Hartmann, and Ryan Larson, "A Quarter Century of Participation in School-Based Extracurricular Activities: Inequalities by Race, Class, Gender and Age?" *Journal of Youth and Adolescence*, vol. 47, no. 6 (2018): 1299–316, doi:10.1007/s10964-018-0838-1

87 Ibid.

88 Kevin A. Hoff, Kenneth E. Granillo-Velasquez, Alexis Hanna, Mike Morris, Hannah S. Nelson, and Frederick L. Oswald, "Interested and Employed? A National Study of Gender Differences in Basic Interests and Employment," *Journal of Vocational Behavior*, vol. 146 (February 2024): 103942, https://doi.org/10.1016/j.jvb.2023.103942 (accessed on August 10, 2024).

89 The National Center for Women and Information Technology (NCWIT), "By the Numbers," https://wpassets.ncwit.org/wp-content/uploads/2024/05/03092125/NCWIT_4-24_BTN_FullSize.pdf (accessed on August 10, 2024).

90 US Bureau of Labor Statistics, Table 3: Median Usual Weekly Earnings of Full-Time Wage and Salary Workers, by State, 2022 Annual Averages, https://www.bls.gov/opub/reports/womens-earnings/2022/ (accessed on October 9, 2024).

91 Carolina Aragão. Pew Research Center, "Gender Pay Gap in U.S. hasn't Changed Much in Two Decades," https://www.pewresearch.org/short-reads/2023/03/01/gender-pay-gap-facts/ (accessed on September 10, 2024).

92 US Department of Education, "Sex-Based Harassment," https://www.ed.gov/laws-and-policy/civil-rights-laws/protecting-students/sex-based-harassment#:~:text=Title%20IX%20also%20prohibits%20gender,other%20students%2C%20and%20third%20parties (accessed on November 10, 2024).

93 AAUW, *Harassment-free Hallways: How to Stop Harassment in Schools* (Washington, DC: American Association of University Women Educational Foundation, 2004), 8.

94 Christine FRANKLIN, Petitioner, v. GWINNETT COUNTY PUBLIC SCHOOLS and William Prescott. | Supreme Court | US Law | LII / Legal Information Institute (cornell.edu) (accessed on November 10, 2024).

95 Gebser v. Lago Vista Independent School Dist., 524 U.S. 274 (1998), https://supreme.justia.com/cases/federal/us/524/274/ (accessed on November 10, 2024).
96 Davis v. Monroe County Bd. Of Ed., 526 U.S. 629 (1999), https://supreme.justia.com/cases/federal/us/526/629/ (accessed on November 10, 2024).
97 National Women's Law Center, "Summary of Changes to the Title IX Rules," June 2024 *Fact Sheet*, https://nwlc.org/wp-content/uploads/2024/06/Biden-Title-IX-Rule-Fact-Sheet-6.12.24-vF.pdf (accessed on November 10, 2024).
98 Inside Higher Ed, "Department of Education Reverts to Trump's Title IX Rule," https://www.insidehighered.com/news/government/politics-elections/2025/02/03/department-education-reverts-trumps-title-ix-rule (February 3, 2025).
99 Michael Gurian and Kathy Stevens, "Foreword," in *Debating Single-Sex Education*, Frances R. Spielhagen, ed. (Lanham, MD: Rowman and Littlefield Education, 2008), 1.
100 Daniel B. Robinson, Jennifer Mitton, Greg Hadley, and Meagan Kettley, "Single-Sex Education in the 21st Century: A 20-Year Scoping Review of the Literature," *Teaching and Teacher Education*, vol. 106 (2021), https://doi.org/10.1016/j.tate.2021.103462 (accessed on October 14, 2024).
101 AAUW, *Separated by Sex: A Critical Look at Single-Sex Education for Girls* (Washington, DC: American Association of University Women Educational Foundation, 1998), 2–3.

7

Education of People with Disabilities

Chapter contents

Chapter objectives

Readers should:

- Become aware of issues connected with the education of students with disabilities.
- Appreciate the ethical, social, political, and economic complexities of inclusion.
- Understand the history and present-day issues of education of people with disabilities.
- Become informed about the legal bases of inclusion, such as relevant laws and court decisions.
- Understand major findings on the effectiveness of inclusion, particularly those concerning teacher, student, and parental responses.
- Develop a better understanding of the issues involved in the education of people with disabilities.

Opening questions

1. What role does the education of people with disabilities play in the daily life of a classroom teacher?

2. What are the issues that raise particular concern among educators regarding inclusion?
3. How can we learn from the history of educating students with disabilities in order to understand current questions about mainstreaming and inclusion?
4. What do we need to know about the legal basis as well as current research findings on the effectiveness of inclusion in order to begin our preparation for the classroom?
5. How do inclusion and the education of people with disabilities tie into larger philosophical concerns about equal opportunities for all students?
6. What do educators need to understand about the impacts of labels and language decisions on students and families?
7. How can the use of accommodations, modifications, and universal design for learning principles help support the education of students with disabilities?
8. How do general education and special education teachers collaborate?

The issue

In early times, children with disabilities, particularly the more severe kinds, seldom survived infancy, and those who did usually faced uncertain futures. In some historical eras, people with disabilities might be considered deficient in rationality, while in others they might be viewed as "touched" by divine intervention, perhaps possessing special powers or serving as warnings to others about divine retribution. In some cultures, disabilities might be perceived as sources of evil, while in others they might be treated with pity and charity.[1] In short, history reveals a variety of ways people in the more distant past viewed and dealt with disabilities.

From about 1820 to 1860, important American reform movements were set in motion that met with varying degrees of success (the abolition of slavery, prison reform, state hospitals for mental illness, and state systems of public schools). One such movement concerned the education of people with disabilities, but at that time, policy decisions were made to educate them separately from other children. In some cases, this meant isolated residential institutions; in others, it meant separate day schools or at least separate classes in regular schools, due not only to traditional prejudices but also to well-intentioned beliefs that the needs of people with disabilities could best be met in separate facilities.

However, institutions often became places of permanent abode, particularly for individuals with severe disabilities. Many institutions suffered from inadequate funding, which meant ineffective care and education, a problem also experienced by separate day schools and separate classrooms in regular schools. Some locales were unable or simply refused to educate children with special needs, particularly those with severe disabilities. By the mid-twentieth century, the perception was growing that such separation was, like racial segregation, not only morally unfair and undemocratic but unconstitutional as well. Separate education isolated children from interaction with the larger society, which did little to foster greater independence. Critics pointed out that, while some needed long-term support, other children with special needs could become independent. In addition, researchers were finding that many disabilities once considered educationally hopeless could be ameliorated with better, more appropriate educational intervention.

Mainstreaming and ***inclusion*** are late twentieth-century terms applied to integrating students with disabilities into regular schools and classrooms. The terms represent general concepts rather than specific teaching techniques or curricular programs, and they are outgrowths of the larger movement to reduce or abolish separate education for children with special needs. Despite the fact that mainstreaming was designed primarily for students with the least severe disabilities and inclusion was intended to take in students with moderate to severe disabilities, the two concepts are similar. Both are grounded in civil rights, embrace the placement of students with disabilities in general education settings, and share similar aspects of implementation. The essential idea is the integration of students with disabilities into regular schools and classrooms, with any exceptions carefully considered according to individual need and context.

It is sometimes easy to assume that earlier times were backward while the present is enlightened. Progress has been made, of course, but change rarely occurs without controversy and uncertainty. Today, many school systems across the United States have become inclusive settings in which students, both those with and without disabilities, are educated together as much as possible in common environments. At the same time, problems and issues remain that educators, students, parents, and citizens must face in the process.

> **For Further Reflection:** How may we create a society that allows all people, including those with disabilities, to lead fulfilling, active lives?

Historical background

If the United States had its revolution in the late eighteenth century, it experienced another "revolution" in the early nineteenth century through energetic institution building. As Alexis de Tocqueville observed upon his visit to the United States in 1831, Americans from all walks of life constantly formed associations, "to give entertainments, to found seminaries, to build inns, to construct churches, to diffuse books, to send missionaries to the antipodes; they found in this manner hospitals, prisons, and schools."[2] To de Tocqueville, it seemed that whenever Americans encountered a problem, they founded an institution to deal with it. This tendency was readily apparent in how Americans approached education, including the education of people with disabilities. At that time, the special needs most often recognized were those readily observed according to physical conditions and outward behavior, such as sight, hearing, and mental disabilities.

Education and hearing disabilities

A pioneer in American education for people with hearing disabilities was Thomas Hopkins Gallaudet, a young minister who attempted to teach 9-year-old Alice Cogswell, a neighbor's child who was deaf. He turned this interest into his life's work. Gallaudet went to France to study under Abbé Roche-Ambroise Cucurron Sicard, head of the Institution Nationale des Sourds-Muets (National Institution for Deaf-Mutes), where he became an advocate of **sign language** as the most appropriate mode of education for people with hearing disabilities. In the meantime, Dr. Mason Fitch Cogswell (the father of Alice) secured an act of incorporation from the Connecticut legislature in 1817 to establish an asylum for the education of deaf persons.[3]

Before returning to the United States, Gallaudet convinced Laurent Clerc, a student of Sicard and also a prominent teacher at France's National Institution, to come with him. Clerc had participated in developing a system of writing, hand signs, and grammatical rules that later influenced the development of American Sign Language (ASL). He lost his hearing in infancy, but when he became a student at the National Institution at age 12, he progressed rapidly. Sicard soon made him an assistant and eventually a teacher. Clerc became a major advocate of sign language and of the idea of a **deaf community**, with students taught by instructors who were also deaf.[4] In the United States, both Gallaudet and Clerc wanted the Connecticut Asylum (later renamed the American School for the Deaf) to become a model school for the education of people with hearing impairments.[5]

Gallaudet's son Edward was instrumental in securing an act of Congress in 1864 to establish a college for students with hearing disabilities in Washington, D.C. That institution, today called Gallaudet University, was the first higher education institution in the world designed specifically for students with hearing disabilities, and it enhanced the growth of the notion of a deaf community.[6]

Sign language approach

Under the Gallaudet-Clerc approach, sign language became a part of the culture and community of many deaf Americans. Where the larger society saw deafness as an affliction, many people in the deaf community came to view themselves as a linguistic minority, a viewpoint enhanced by sign language and by residential schools providing the means and the nurturing environment where students could share cultural outlooks and values. To this day, the idea of a deaf culture and community endures: In autumn 2006, students and faculty at Gallaudet University were able to force that institution's governing board to rescind its decision to hire a new president because, among other things, the candidate was deemed not "adequately committed to American Sign Language."[7]

Oralist approach

The **oralist approach** or speech approach, which emphasized the senses of touch and sight to help students learn how to speak, also had its own tradition going back at least to sixteenth-century Spain. It was boosted by Édouard Séguin, a prominent French physician-educator, who emigrated in 1848. Although Séguin's area of expertise was intellectual disabilities, he was sympathetic to oralism because it emphasized the senses of touch and sight to help students learn to speak. At least one residential school, the Virginia School for the Deaf and Blind, emphasized speech to help its students earn a living. The school opened in 1839, with Joseph D. Tyler, who was himself deaf, as its first principal.[8]

The most famous oralist in the United States, by far, however, was Alexander Graham Bell, who was born in Scotland and immigrated to the United States in 1871. He is known worldwide for inventing the telephone, but what is less known about him is his interest in hearing and speech that led to it. Bell's grandfather and father were well-known teachers of elocution, and his mother had a hearing disability, as did his wife, Mabel Hubbard. His mother inspired him to employ teaching techniques that used music and dancing to show the rhythms of speech.

In 1872, Bell founded a school for the deaf in Boston that soon became a part of Boston University, where he was the professor of vocal physiology. He attempted to build a "phono-autograph" to enable deaf students to observe the vibrations of spoken words on an electrified membrane that moved a mechanical lever. The device failed, but from it Bell would invent the telephone in 1876.[9]

Bell not only believed that some forms of deafness were hereditary, but he also alienated the deaf community with his view that couples with congenital deafness should not have children. Bell's belief that sign language was inferior to speech was also criticized, but his influence boosted oralism. By the time he died in 1922, most American schools for the deaf taught at least some speech, even though the deaf community continued to question Bell's views.[10]

An example of an oralist school began in 1864 as a small private school in Chelmsford, Massachusetts. Although founded by Harriet Rogers, the school carried a name that would now be considered offensive, namely the Clarke Institution for Deaf Mutes, because wealthy industrialist John Clarke made a substantial donation. The school also secured state funding and allied itself closely with the public schools, admitted children as early as age 5, and lengthened the period of instruction to ten years. The Clarke School (as it came to be called) reflected middle-class standards and projected a familial, surrogate mother image to its students, rather than the more impersonal learning environment the large residential sign language schools had cultivated. Although the Clarke School promoted oralism as a competitor to sign language, oralism never achieved the long-term dominance that sign language did.[11]

For Further Reflection: Do debates such as the one between advocates of sign language and advocates of oralism advance or hinder the cause of education?

Education and visual disabilities

American education for people with visual disabilities followed a pattern similar to that for hearing disabilities. When Bostonian John Fisher was a medical student in Paris in the 1820s, he became familiar with the work of Valentin Haüy. Haüy developed a system of teaching that used the sense of touch, including reading by means of raised letters. He also taught vocational skills related to touch, such as basket weaving. Impressed by Haüy's work, Fisher returned to Boston determined to establish an American institution along similar lines. Equipped with data from a survey on the number of people with sight disabilities who needed education, Fisher and his supporters obtained an act of incorporation to establish the New England Asylum for the Blind in 1829, although the school did not actually begin operation until 1832. Other states soon followed: New York in 1832, Pennsylvania in 1833, Ohio in 1837, Tennessee in 1838, and Virginia in 1839. By 1890, there were eighteen state schools for students with visual disabilities, but none had quite the impact of the Massachusetts institution founded by Fisher and brought to prominence by Samuel Gridley Howe.[12]

Samuel Gridley Howe

Howe, a physician and passionate social activist, assumed active leadership in 1832 of what would be called the Perkins Institute and Massachusetts School for the Blind. Howe modeled his curriculum after the common schools, but he also included vocational training in music and handicrafts. Music, in particular, offered his students occupational opportunities, several becoming church organists. The school band also became popular, and students helped raise funds for the school through concerts.[13]

Reading through the sense of touch

Students learned to read with plaster-cast letters and raised-print reading materials, and Howe taught writing through two approaches: writing with pencils on grooved paper and writing with letters pricked into paper. He taught geography using maps with raised borders and physical features, and he taught arithmetic on boards with raised figures and letters. By 1836, he had students who were able to study French, higher mathematics, and natural philosophy. He also taught traditional handicrafts such as mat, basket, and mattress making. Always short of funds, the school maintained a department where student-made items were on sale to the public.[14]

Perhaps the single most important technical development fostered by Howe was his raised-letter printing method. Apparently unaware at the time of the work of Louis Braille in France, Howe developed a phonetic alphabet employing both stenographic symbols and the common alphabet. He set up a press that produced raised-letter reading materials that were cheaper and smaller in size than European braille. In the late 1830s, he published raised-letter editions of the Old and New Testaments as well as numerous raised-letter textbooks. Inadequate funds hampered Howe's publishing efforts, but his operation printed more reading material for blind people than any other school in the English-speaking world at that time.[15]

Figure 7.1 Braille.

For Further Reflection: Why did American educators rely so heavily on European models for educating people with disabilities?

Suggested Activity: Explore the biographical materials on Samuel Gridley Howe, and present an oral report (individual or small group) to the class on why he was such a dominant figure in the education of people with disabilities in the United States in his day.

Education and intellectual disabilities

Reforms in the education of people with visual and hearing disabilities helped direct attention to the education of people with intellectual disabilities. In 1839, a child with both visual and intellectual disabilities was brought to Howe for instruction at the Perkins Institute. Howe was convinced that this child could be educated, and he improvised an instructional approach. He intended it to become part of the institute's program, but nothing came of it at first. In 1846, the governor of Massachusetts established a commission to investigate the condition of individuals with intellectual disabilities in the state, and he appointed Howe as the chair. The commissioners shared a belief that intellectual disabilities might be caused by the sins of the parents, but they also believed it could be alleviated by humane care and education; consequently, the commission succeeded in getting the Massachusetts legislature to fund a school for children with intellectual disabilities.[16]

In 1850, the then-called "Massachusetts School for Idiotic and Feeble-Minded Children" (see the grey call-out box below on the evolution away from terms like "idiotic" and "feeble-minded") became the first state-financed public school for the education of students with such learning difficulties in the United States. It was to move from the Perkins Institute into its own quarters in 1856, and it served as a model for other states to open their own schools, including Rhode Island in 1850, New York in 1851, Pennsylvania in 1852, Ohio in 1857, and Kentucky in 1860. By 1888, at least eleven states were operating schools for children with intellectual disabilities.[17]

Language Choices and Impacts (Part I)

Many people do not know the origins of the terms "idiot," "imbecile," and "moron," and their usage has greatly changed over time. Some now use these terms broadly in informal conversations, often not referring to people with disabilities. However, as the poet Maya Angelou wrote, "do the best you can until you know better. Then when you know better, do better." Educators with knowledge of the disturbing origin of these terms can help educate others, potentially reducing the harm that can come from their usage.

Édouard Onesimus Séguin

The education of people with mental disabilities was influenced significantly by Édouard Onesimus Séguin.[18] Séguin studied medicine under Jean Marc Gaspard Itard, a physician at France's National Institution who gained recognition for his educational work with a "feral" or abandoned boy who exhibited characteristics of intellectual disabilities, the so-called Wild Boy of Aveyron.[19]

Itard and the Wild Boy of Aveyron

Jean Marc Gaspard Itard was a physician at France's Institution Nationale des Sourds-Muets (National Institution for Deaf-Mutes) who strongly believed that a cure could be found for deafness. Although he never achieved such a cure, his name is recognized today in medical circles for his invention of the eustachian catheter (sometimes called Itard's catheter) and his work in identifying Tourette's syndrome, among other accomplishments. Itard gained fame, however, for his educational work with the "Wild Boy of Aveyron," an abandoned boy found in a remote rural area of France in 1799. Itard was influenced by individuals at that time who taught that people could be changed if environmental conditions were altered and proper education used. They emphasized the role of sense experience in learning and argued that learning best occurred from interactions with natural environmental surroundings. Some of them developed this into a sensationalist learning theory, or learning through the five senses from one's experiences of natural conditions and from social interactions. Some also believed that human progress would be advanced with greater attention to the natural developmental processes of childhood. Living in an intellectual environment in which these ideas had currency, Itard thought the "wild boy" was a promising example to demonstrate what could be done with proper environment and instruction. In 1800, he began working with the boy, who was about 10 or 11 years old at the time; the boy appeared to be congenitally deaf and mute, and some observers believed he also had intellectual disabilities. Itard thought the boy's intellectual disabilities stemmed primarily from his previous isolation from human nurture and socialization. He named him Victor, because he hoped to show the victory of education over what was then called "idiocy." A woman named Madame Guerin took care of Victor in her home while Itard worked with him in a variety of carefully planned educational activities organized around socialization, sensory stimulation, concept formation, speech development, and transfer of training. Itard worked with Victor from 1800 to 1804, and Victor learned to discriminate objects and conditions through touch, taste, smell, sight, and hearing, but he never learned to speak beyond simple sounds and gestures. Victor also learned social skills, and he developed emotional attachments to both Itard and Madame Guerin, but Itard concluded that his work with Victor was a failure and that disabilities such as Victor's could not be cured. Despite Itard's pessimism, his work proved to be an important foundation for later advances, and today he is considered to be one of the key founders of special education.

Sources: Jean Marc Gaspard Itard, *The Wild Boy of Aveyron*, George and Muriel Humphrey, trans. (New York: Appleton-Century-Croft, 1962); Harlan L. Lane, *The Wild Boy of Aveyron* (Cambridge: Harvard University Press, 1976).

At the National Institution, Séguin was an apt student of both education and medicine. He was also influenced by the belief that people had a right to education regardless of their station in life. Under Itard's guidance, Séguin specialized in the education of individuals with intellectual disabilities, and from his study and subsequent professional practice, he developed what he called the **physiological method** of motor and physical sensory training, language and speech training, and socialization. Working at the Hospice des Incurables at Bicêtre, Séguin taught students to use language, to count, and to develop memory. He advocated separating individuals with intellectual disabilities from persons with a mental illness because he believed that intellectual disabilities were not caused by disease or sin but rather by **developmentally delayed** growth of the brain, a condition he thought could be ameliorated by education. By the time he immigrated to the United States in 1848, Séguin had an international reputation and had influenced the thinking of Howe and other American educators.[20]

Howe persuaded Séguin to come to his Massachusetts school to use the physiological method of teaching. These two strong personalities clashed, however, and after only three months, Séguin resigned and left Massachusetts. Despite Séguin's reputation, Howe grumpily wrote a friend that "'I have found out that in the matter of idiocy they do not know so much in England as they do in France, & in France not half so much as they & the rest of the world think they do.'"[21]

Undeterred, Séguin continued teaching his approach to other educators in Pennsylvania and New York. In 1866, he published his most important book, *Idiocy and Its Treatment by the Physiological Method.* Although he carefully noted that science had yet to determine the cause of "idiocy," Séguin defined it as "a specific infirmity of the cranio-spinal axis, produced by deficiency of nutrition *in utero* and in *neonati*."[22] He also described ways to manage institutions, select and train teachers, and investigate mental disabilities with both a medical and educational rationale. His neurological investigations helped advance the scientific study of mental disorders, and in his later years, he researched fever as a causal factor of mental disabilities. Séguin was steadfast in his commitment to education as a human right and a means of social reform, and while he never held a permanent school post, he made significant contributions through his publications, his teaching, and his advising of fellow educators. Today, he is generally credited with being a leading founder of special education in the United States.[23]

For Further Reflection: Why was Séguin's view that some disabilities were due to delayed development rather than mysterious forces a major contribution to educational theory?

The era of special education

Generally speaking, by the close of the nineteenth century much of the education of people with disabilities took place in separate institutions, which most people at the time thought was the best approach. Indeed, it has also been suggested that the way special education institutions developed served to separate them from general education, and the preponderance of the **medical model of disability** helped keep special education a separate field within education.

> **Suggested Activity:** Investigate what is meant by "the medical model" in special education. How has it helped or hindered the development of the education of people with disabilities?

Origins of separate special education

The Enlightenment's belief in progress and romanticism's distrust of tradition and its love of institution building all had impacts. In addition, the Industrial Revolution also generated large-scale system building in the form of factories and the beginning of industrial corporations. The resulting growth in communication and transportation technology brought forth telegraphs, highways, canals, streetcars, and railroad systems, and by the late nineteenth century, telephone and electrical power systems.

A note of caution is needed about the complexity of historical events, however. While statewide systems of public schools also developed during the time, they were accompanied by another set of institutions that was neither orderly nor particularly systematic. These were the hospitals for individuals with mental illnesses, almshouses for individuals living in extreme poverty, orphanages, and residential educational institutions for those with disabilities, and they developed not as systems but as single institutions. Each institution stood alone with its own board of directors, and while a number of such institutions received public funding, philanthropy and voluntarism were also significant sources of income. Thus, institutions for people with special needs developed separately from public school systems, and each institution established its own traditions that, once in place, proved difficult to change.

For example, when Cogswell and Gallaudet opened their school for deaf students in 1817, they followed a model of organization called corporate voluntarism, that is, a group of citizens simply formed a legal corporation to establish an entity, in this case a school for children with hearing disabilities.

Over time, such institutions appeared across the country, and schools for students with disabilities continued to be seen as separate institutions rather than integral parts of public school systems. They were usually built in remote rural areas, even as society was becoming more industrialized and urban, and they had names that rang of separate status: asylum, training school, and even colony.[24]

It has been argued that two trends in the last few centuries were largely responsible for the separate schools, one intellectual (the **medicalized theory of deviance**) and the other social (demographic and socioeconomic changes).

Eighteenth-century scholars, influenced by ideas of the so-called Age of Reason, came to see what was called "deviance" not as willful behavior to be controlled by coercion but as unintentional behavior requiring treatment and/or therapy. This intellectual shift led to the medicalized theory of deviance, which had a profound impact on how we educate children with special needs. In the nineteenth century, this view helped promote "child-saving institutions" for pupils with blindness, deafness, and some types of mental disability. By the twentieth century, there was a greater sense of responsibility for low-achieving pupils, with **learning difficulties** also coming under the sway of the medicalization trend. The demographic and socioeconomic trends included population growth and new ways of earning a living through wage labor and manufacturing in densely populated urban areas, which increased the number and diversity of children entering the school systems and a rise in public expectations that everyone should be educated, including individuals with disabilities. These two trends provided fertile ground for the growth of special education, although still separated from regular education.[25]

Motivations behind separate special education ranged from the humanitarian to the economic and political. A plethora of **labels,** now deemed derogatory and therefore inappropriate, such as "backwardness," "incorrigibility," and "mental retardation," emerged. Some educators maintained that placement in regular classrooms had a negative effect on students with disabilities, while others argued that the classification and segregation of students by disability was desirable for both humanitarian and economic reasons.

Although the change from an older "deviance as willful behavior" to "deviance as a neurological condition" produced a new consciousness of **disabilities as treatable conditions,** reformers still maintained that social control was needed, and education was the best way to provide it. Educators were not alone in promoting educational therapy for so-called deviant behavior; they were joined by penologists and criminologists as well. Similarly, not only did physicians spread the medicalized view of deviance, but psychiatrists, psychologists, and educators did as well. It was only a matter of time before such views found their way into the schools, and the early decades of the twentieth century witnessed the appearance of guidance counselors, school psychologists, and special education professionals who brought with them such techniques as group counseling, testing, and behavior modification techniques. As the century progressed, definitions of childhood disabilities expanded to include "intellectual disability," "emotional disturbance," and "learning disabilities."[26]

Advent of psychological testing

By the early twentieth century, the new discipline of psychology was seeking to establish its scientific reputation, and it hoped to discover the inner workings of the mind and to develop better treatments for mental disabilities. However, psychology faced the entrenched position of medicine as the "healing" profession with an established track record in special education (physicians such as Itard, Séguin, and Howe). Since psychologists sought to establish their area of specialization as legitimate, they went about doing so (though never so securely as physicians) through **mental measurement** or **psychological testing**.

Pioneers included Wilhelm Wundt in Germany; Sir Francis Galton in Britain; Alfred Binet in France; and James McKeen Cattell, G. Stanley Hall, Lewis Madison Terman, and Henry Herbert Goddard in the United States. Cattell was an early advocate of mental measurement, but existing techniques measured physiological responses to stimuli by way of blood pressure and breathing rate. Called brass instrument psychology because of its mechanical apparatuses, this form of measurement was cumbersome. Hall favored child study through clinical observation, but two of his students, Lewis Terman and Henry Goddard, became avid leaders in the testing movement. In France, Alfred Binet and Theodore Simon developed an **intelligence scale** to measure varying levels of what was then-called "idiocy" in 1904, and by 1908, they had also developed a battery of tests for "normal" children. Cheap and easily administered, the new tests quickly replaced mechanical measurement. Binet wanted his tests used on an individual and small-scale basis, but many other psychologists wanted large quantities of data to lend scientific objectivity to their efforts.[27]

> **For Further Reflection:** How have testing and mental measurement affected the education of people with disabilities?

Mental measurement and special education

Before psychology and mental measurement became prominent in special education, however, they were pulled in some now-discredited directions by other developments. In the late nineteenth and early twentieth centuries, the United States was experiencing a major population increase from immigration, and many of the newcomers had difficulty adjusting to urban crowding and industrial work. The sheer numbers threatened to overwhelm existing educational institutions. For example, New York City saw a 60 percent increase in school enrollments from 1890 to 1914, which drastically strained school facilities, personnel, instructional materials, and funding. To some critics, the newcomers were "strangers" who were culturally different and who posed threats to "the body politic."[28]

For Cross-Reference: See the section on social Darwinism in Chapter 3, Social Class and Education, pp. 123–4, for additional background information.

Under the influence of social Darwinism and its doctrine of survival of the fittest, a new theory emerged called ***eugenics***, a term coined by British psychologist Sir Francis Galton in the 1880s. It combined Mendelian genetics and social Darwinism into a system promoting the mentally healthy, or "the fit," and segregating or sometimes even sterilizing the "unfit." Not only did eugenicists adopt the medical metaphors of disease, germ, and infection, but also some psychologists who saw themselves as scientific experts believed they could "doctor" society and prevent "social infections" from spreading through the body politic. Just as society quarantined people with infectious diseases, eugenicists urged, it must also quarantine the "misfits" from infecting society with the "germ" of deviancy. Society must be "disinfected" through institutionalization and even sterilization.

For example, Walter Fernald of the Massachusetts Institute for the Feebleminded was concerned that "feebleminded" females could spread the "contagion" if they were allowed to procreate, while educational psychologist E. L. Thorndike held that children with certain kinds of disabilities should be put in separate schools described as educational hospitals. Advocates saw the new intelligence tests as the way to discover who should be segregated because, they claimed, the test results were scientific and objective. They seemed to ignore evidence that tests were not always trustworthy, and they optimistically

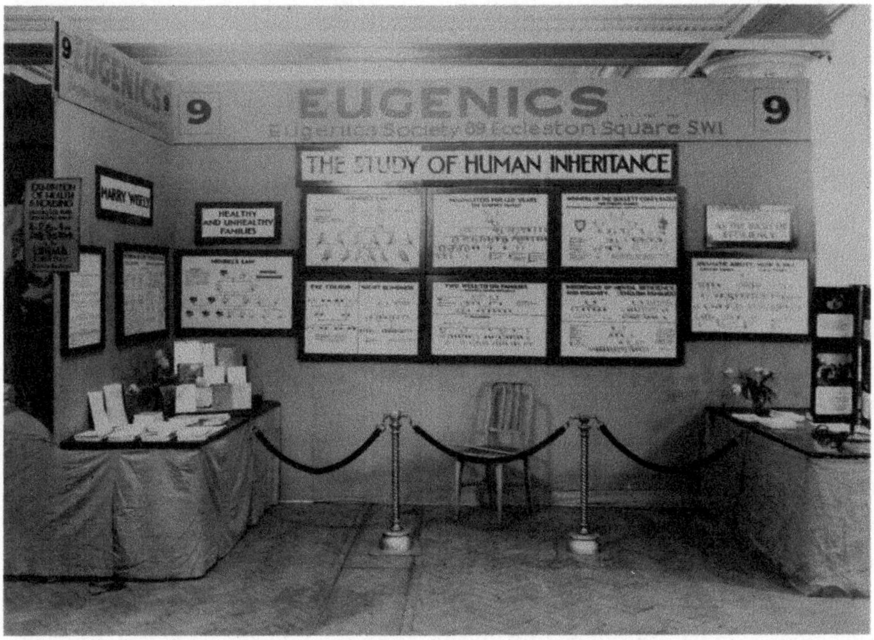

Figure 7.2 Eugenics Society exhibit, 1930s.

believed the Binet scale was akin to a fine surgical instrument, if administered and interpreted by trained professionals such as themselves.[29]

One leading American advocate of mental measurement was Henry Goddard. First a teacher and then a principal, Goddard was influenced by the writings of G. Stanley Hall. He completed his PhD in 1899 at Clark University (where Hall was president) and became a zealous disciple of scientific psychology. He took a position at the so-called Training School for Feebleminded Girls and Boys at Vineland, New Jersey, where he translated the Binet-Simon scale into English and promoted its widespread use. After Lewis Terman of Stanford University revised the Binet-Simon scale in 1916, millions of people were tested with the new Stanford-Binet IQ test over the next several decades, and Goddard was one of its leading advocates.[30]

Suggested Activity: Individually or in a small group, read up on social Darwinism and eugenics. How did they affect the education of people with disabilities? Do remnants of these outlooks still exist, and do they still impact the education of people with disabilities? If so, how and to what effect?

Goddard understood that people with mental disabilities were a diverse group, and he wanted a better classification system. Some people were born with mental disabilities, while others acquired them by illness or trauma, and traditional classifications were too inexact. Persons with serious mental disabilities were the easiest to classify, while the most difficult were persons who seemed "normal" in appearance and behavior but were unable to learn elementary material. The latter individuals tantalized Goddard because he believed they could be educated within certain limits. At first, he thought mental disabilities were largely due to environmental conditions, but under the sway of eugenics he turned to inner conditions as the probable causes. Using the Binet-Simon scale as a departure point, Goddard compared the test taker's chronological age with the scale's "mental age" and came up with the following classification system: an "idiot" tested below the mental age of 3, an "imbecile" with a mental age of 3–7, and a *moron* (Goddard's own invented term for a person with arrested mental development) with a mental age of 8–12 years.[31]

In 1907, Goddard accepted that "feeblemindedness" was educational and psychological in nature, but by the time he wrote *The Kallikak Family: A Study in the Heredity of Feeble-Mindedness* (1912) and *Feeble-Mindedness: Its Causes and Consequences* (1914), he thought eugenics offered the best explanation for inner causal factors. In *The Kallikak Family*, he traced the offspring of Martin Kallikak, who "dallied" with a "lowly barmaid" but married a "wholesome Quaker woman." According to Goddard, the Kallikak descendants of the barmaid were individuals with disabilities, while descendants of the Quaker wife were not. He associated mental disability with criminality, alcoholism, prostitution, poverty, and truancy. For *The Kallikak Family*, Goddard conducted case studies of 327 families he classified as "feebleminded," and he concluded that more than 70 percent of it could be attributed to heredity. He strongly recommended that people with such hereditary disabilities should be prevented from reproducing, perhaps by sterilization but certainly by being "colonized" in separate institutions guided "by high eugenic ideals." He thought such measures would diminish the condition, but he also recognized that those who acquired mental disabilities from accidental trauma or disease could not possibly transmit their condition through reproduction. Although he made important contributions, Goddard interjected personal biases into purportedly objective findings and offered simplistic explanations for complex sociocultural conditions.[32]

Despite their grave inherent flaws, social Darwinism and eugenics influenced attitudes, public policies, and educational practices in ways that prolonged the separation of people with disabilities from the larger society. Eventually,

Figure 7.3 Plaque preserving memory of 1907 Indiana Eugenics Law.

however, it became increasingly clear that those most often separated into special institutions or programs were disproportionately poor, as well as individuals from racial and culturally minoritized communities. The drive to identify, test, label, and segregate people with disabilities, while it may sometimes have had humanitarian impulses to help and to educate behind it, was flawed by misrepresentations of Darwinian natural selection and the unfounded claims of eugenics, as well as motivations reflecting class, race, and anti-immigrant biases.[33]

> **For Further Reflection:** How have so-called scientific and objective claims often negatively impacted the development of educational theory and practice? Are similar claims still being made today, and if so, what impact do they have?

Separate special education

Eventually, separate special education institutions attracted a growing number of critics. If people with disabilities were placed in institutions that segregated them from the larger society, they were denied sufficient opportunities to learn from and interact with that society; likewise, the larger society was cut off from the understandings and interactions to be gained from direct contact with those who were institutionalized. Actually, Samuel Howe made this point back in 1849 when he realized that the segregation of blind children in separate institutions had some deleterious effects, but his complaint gained little public notice.[34]

Gradually, criticism of separate institutions gained a wider audience as more people came to believe that, while some forms of disability were so severe that institutionalization might be a reasonable choice, children with less severe conditions would have greater opportunities and lead happier lives as part of the larger society if given the chance.

Learning disabilities

As Séguin understood back in the nineteenth century, some students were easily identified as needing special education, but many others with learning difficulties had no apparent abnormalities. Nevertheless, the specific classification called **learning disabilities** did not emerge until the 1930s, when researchers concluded that not all learning disorders could be attributed to intellectual disabilities, particularly disorders in the development of language, speech, reading, and other communication skills. By 1967, Samuel A. Kirk and a group of like-minded colleagues were using the term *learning disability* to designate "a retardation, disorder, or delayed development" in speech, language, reading, writing, arithmetic, or other school subjects, "a psychological handicap" related to "cerebral dysfunction and/or emotional or behavioral disturbances."[35]

Although some researchers believed all learning disabilities were due to brain injury of one kind or another, Kirk maintained that learning disabilities had various origins, some due to brain injury but others to psychological disorders affecting such things as language processing. At a meeting in Chicago in 1968, Kirk chaired the National Advisory Committee on Handicapped Children, which developed a definition of learning disability as "a disorder in one or more of the basic psychological processes," such as "listening, thinking, talking, reading, writing, spelling, or arithmetic." The disorders included "perceptual handicaps, brain injury, minimal brain dysfunction, dyslexia, developmental aphasia, etc.,"[36] a list that excluded the traditionally recognized disabilities of blindness, deafness, mental retardation, and emotional disturbance. The committee hoped its general definition would clarify understanding and lead to better school programs for students with disabilities.

What appeared to be a promising development soon encountered opposition, however. Some critics accused the learning disabilities movement of inventing a disease that had no discernible physical or biochemical characteristics, and others dismissed it as being pushed by professionally self-interested medical, psychological, educational, and pharmaceutical interests. Still others claimed that learning disabilities were a new label for middle-class children with academic difficulties, while lower-class children with the same difficulties continued to be labeled mentally retarded or emotionally disturbed. Some critics argued that greater attention was needed on effective teaching, not new labels to classify and separate students. Within the field of learning disabilities itself, there was criticism of overzealous advocates who failed to understand the history of the problem and too quickly discarded educational techniques still useful with some children.[37] Despite the critics, the learning disabilities idea gained acceptance and became an established view in education.

In the 1950s, the education of people with disabilities seemed securely divided into several options: there were still separate institutions for the blind and deaf, most of which had reasonably strong educational programs. Institutions for those with mental disabilities were facing increasing criticism, particularly those providing only custodial and protective services. A number of states also had other specialized institutions, such as those for children with disabilities such as epilepsy and for incarcerated youngsters. The variety of institutions and disabilities, the levels of severity, the range of ages, and the diversity of institutions (ranging from schools to hospitals to custodial and even correctional institutions) made standardization and systematization virtually impossible.[38]

By the 1960s, the education of people with disabilities was ready for major reform. One development, the idea of **normalization**, came in response to the issue of labeling people with disabilities as deviant. It originated in Europe and was popularized in the United States by people such as Wolf Wolfensberger, who noted how persons can be perceived as deviant if they differ significantly from those considered normal, particularly if the differences are viewed negatively. Various definitions of "deviancy" have emerged from different historical and cultural contexts, and societies have differed in how they treat people with disabilities, ranging from destroying "deviant" persons to segregating them to attempting to reverse or cure their perceived conditions.

The idea of normalization was intended to help people with mental disabilities achieve a life as close to what was considered normal as possible. Normalization also addressed how labels and stereotypes influenced behavior, as when pupils considered to have mental disabilities were placed in separate special education classrooms, they usually did not perform as well as when placed in general education classrooms. In short, normalization meant the physical and social integration of persons with disabilities into the general population, with both physical integration (including accessibility to service facilities) and social integration (inclusion in regular childcare and general education classrooms as much as possible).[39]

Mainstreaming and inclusion

There was growing pressure to desegregate special education students and include them in regular schools and classrooms where possible. The 1970s witnessed efforts to abolish traditional labels such as "mentally retarded" and "emotionally disturbed" on the grounds that they were simplistic, negative stereotypes. Many critics of old-style special education argued that labels and the separation into special classes or schools actually made education more difficult to achieve.[40]

> **For Further Reflection:** How can schools ensure equal educational opportunity while simultaneously meeting individual needs? Does equality mean sameness?

Legal bases

The US Constitution enunciates a legal view of equality under the **equal protection of the laws** that is as significant in education as in other aspects of life. In the past, persons with disabilities were often denied equal protection of the laws not only by being sequestered in separate institutions or classrooms but sometimes by not receiving any educational services at all. When the mainstreaming movement gained traction in the mid-1970s, it was estimated that children with disabilities comprised between 10 and 13 percent of the total school population.[41] The argument was that equal educational opportunity was needed for this significant minority, and mainstreaming came about through a combination of efforts by advocates and the application of "the equal protection of the laws" clause in the Constitution.

Court decisions

Perhaps the landmark decision on equal protection of the laws was *Brown v. Board of Education* (1954), in which the US Supreme Court declared racially segregated public schools in violation of the Constitution. While race was central in that case, the court's decision articulated a broad principle that would eventually be applied to the education of children with disabilities. Under the US Constitution, the power to establish public schools is an implied state power delegated under the Tenth Amendment, and the equal protection of the laws provided by the Constitution's Fourteenth Amendment is also a responsibility of the states. In the *Brown* ruling, the Supreme Court affirmed state responsibility for both education and equal protection of the laws: If a state provides public schools for its citizens, then it cannot deny them equal access to those schools in the absence of compelling reasons, and race is not a compelling reason.[42]

Over subsequent years, the principle of equal access was broadened by the courts to include other circumstances, including physical, mental, emotional, and learning disabilities. For example, a Pennsylvania district court in *Pennsylvania Association for Retarded Children (PARC) v. Commonwealth of Pennsylvania* (1972) ruled that Pennsylvania, having undertaken to provide a free public education to all of its children, "including its mentally retarded children," must not deny to "any mentally retarded child access to a free public program of education and training." In short, an intellectual disability was not a compelling reason. Shortly thereafter, in *Mills v. Board of Education* (1972), a Washington, D.C., district court held that publicly supported education could not be denied to "exceptional children." This interpretation was broadened in *Maryland Association for Retarded Children v. State of Maryland* (1974), when the circuit court declared that the public schools must include "children with handicaps, and particularly mentally retarded children."[43] These rulings illustrate the evolving legal right of equal access to public schools.

Legislation

The inclusion of students with disabilities in public schools and classrooms was not generated solely by judicial decisions, however. Parents of children with disabilities, with the help and support of special education professionals and other interested citizens, played central roles not only in moving the action to the courts but also to state legislatures and the US Congress, which passed laws requiring better and more equitable educational opportunities for children with disabilities.

By far the most important legislative act to show the changing climate of public opinion was the **Education for All Handicapped Children Act (Public Law 94–142)**, passed by Congress and signed into law by President Gerald Ford on November 29, 1975. It defined children with disabilities as the "mentally retarded, hard of hearing, deaf, orthopedically impaired, other health impaired, speech impaired, visually handicapped, seriously emotionally disturbed, or children with specific learning disabilities" who needed "special education and related services."[44]

When Congress passed P.L. 94–142, the intent was to mainstream at least the "mildly educationally handicapped" into general education classrooms. Placement was to be determined by the needs of the pupil, such as academic remediation, social skills development, auditory training, perceptual and motor exercises, speech correction, occupational therapy, physical therapy, and so forth. Each placement had to be accompanied by an **individualized education program (IEP)**, a key feature that has been maintained through all subsequent revisions of the law. The IEP is an educational plan limited to a student's unique requirements. It must also be mutually agreeable to the school administrator, the teacher, the parent or guardian, and the student (where appropriate). The IEP must include an assessment of the student's performance, a statement of annual goals, and a statement of expected duration. It may also involve related services such as transportation and corrective and supportive services like speech pathology and physical and occupational therapy.[45]

Other significant features of the law were the requirement that local school systems receiving federal funds must establish **free appropriate public education** for all applicable children between the ages of 3 and 21, or between 5 and 18 under some state laws and court orders.[46] Still another was the requirement of the **least restrictive environment (LRE)**, intended to avoid the problem of indiscriminate placement. To bolster these features, federal regulations accompanying the law required that "to the maximum extent appropriate, handicapped children in public or private institutions or other care facilities, … [shall be] educated with children who are not handicapped." Special classes, separate schools, or other means of separating children with disabilities from regular educational environments were allowable "only when the nature or severity of the handicap is such that education in regular classes with the use of supplementary aids and services cannot be achieved satisfactorily."[47]

Since the passage of P.L. 94–142, the law has been revised numerous times in both terminology and provisions. In October 1990, Congress broadened the act's provisions and changed its title to **Individuals with Disabilities Education Act (IDEA)** in P.L. 101–476. The term *handicapped* was replaced with "individuals with disabilities" as a more appropriate descriptor. The law has since been amended several times, the latest version being P.L 108–446, the Individuals with Disabilities Education Improvement Act of 2004. It is important to note that in all its different versions, some key ingredients were maintained, including "free appropriate public education," "individualized education program," and "least restrictive environment."[48]

By the mid-1990s, approximately 70 percent of all students with disabilities were placed for at least a portion of each day in general education classrooms. There was a decrease in the number of pupils in separate schools, a slight increase in separate classrooms in regular schools, and an increase in the overall number of students identified as having learning disabilities during the same period. In general, placement of students with disabilities varied across the fifty states: some states placed the majority of students with learning disabilities in general education classrooms, while others continued to place some in either separate classrooms or schools. Still, the majority of students considered as having a disability were being included in general classrooms and schools.[49]

Contemporary conditions

Where inclusion was once an issue in debates about the education of students with disabilities, by the twenty-first century, a central topic seemed to be not whether inclusion was a good idea but how best to conduct it in general education environments. The 1997 revision of the IDEA signaled that schools must ensure that all students receive a quality education, with special and general educators collaborating on such matters as student instruction, assessment, and evaluation. The scope was extended in the No Child Left Behind (NCLB) legislation in 2001, which required all school districts to set proficiency goals and test all their students on an annual basis, creating new pressures for the schools to improve student outcomes.[50]

Under the 2015 Every Student Succeeds Act (ESSA), states must hold all students to "challenging academic standards," except those with the most significant cognitive disabilities, for whom aligned "alternate achievement standards" can be used. These students can also be awarded an alternate diploma upon graduation, as long as the diploma is standards-based and aligned with the state requirements for the regular high school diploma. States must also report their test results both as a whole and disaggregated by group, one group being children with disabilities. Assessments must be designed using universal design for learning (UDL) principles, described below.

By the 2022–3 school year, the total number of children 3–21 years old in federally supported programs for disabilities was 7.5 million. This was an increase of almost one million when compared to the 2007–8 school year. There were programs for specific learning disabilities, speech or language impairments, intellectual disabilities, emotional disturbance, hearing impairments, visual

Table 7.1 Relative Prevalence of Types of Disabilities: School Year 2022–3

Disability Type	Percent
Specific learning disability[51]	32
Speech or language impairment	19
Other health impairment[52]	15
Autism	13
Developmental delay	7
Intellectual disability	6
Emotional disturbance	4
Multiple disabilities	2
Hearing impairment	1

Source: National Center for Education Statistics (NCES). "Students with Disabilities." *Condition of Education*. US Department of Education, Institute of Education Sciences. Accessed https://nces.ed.gov/programs/coe/indicator/cgg on June 6, 2025.

impairments, multiple disabilities, deaf-blindness, autism, traumatic brain injury, developmental disabilities, and other health impairments (such as heart conditions, tuberculosis, rheumatic fever, nephritis, asthma, sickle cell anemia, hemophilia, epilepsy, lead poisoning, leukemia, and diabetes).

Attention deficit hyperactivity disorder (ADHD) is not considered a learning disability but can still fall under the category "other health impairments," depending on the degree to which it impacts major life functions such as learning. Table 7.1 shows the prevalence of each type of disability in US schools.

Today, the vast majority of students with disabilities are educated in general public education settings. For example, in fall 2022, approximately 95 percent of school-aged students with disabilities were served in general education public schools, with only 2 percent in separate schools for students with disabilities, 2 percent parentally placed in general education private schools, and less than 1 percent in separate residential facilities, homes, or hospitals, or correctional facilities. The percentage of students with disabilities spending 80 percent or more of their day in general education classrooms increased from 61 to 67 percent between fall 2012 and fall 2022.[53]

For Further Reflection: Compare the rates of inclusion in general education today, described in the above section, with what you learned about how students with disabilities were served in the first half of the twentieth century. How would you explain this dramatic change in inclusion rates to a peer unfamiliar with this history?

Another central topic of the twenty-first century has been shifting mindsets and redesigning institutions to eliminate **ableism**. Ableism is a set of beliefs or practices that discriminate against or devalue people with disabilities. This can take many forms, such as making jokes at the expense of people with disabilities, failing to ensure accessibility, questioning if someone "actually" has a disability, and treating people with disabilities as if they have deficits or inferior abilities that need to be "fixed." The origins of ableism likely stem from the medical model of disability and eugenics-era ideas that able-bodied people are superior.

Disability studies is an academic discipline that has emerged over the past few decades to develop an understanding of the **social model of disability** and increase access to civil rights and quality of life. The social model of disability conceives of disabilities not as biological deficiencies but rather as individual differences that are only perceived as disabilities because of biases entrenched in society.

Language Choices and Impacts (Part II)

All languages are continually evolving, and with that come changes to which terms are considered respectful and which are considered offensive. The 1980s saw advocacy from the disability rights movement for **person-first language**. This meant, for example, using the term "a person with autism" rather than "an autistic" or "an autistic person." Proponents of person-first language argued that this language choice emphasized individuals' humanity and the fact that they are more than their disability. More recently, some within the deaf and autism communities have started to prefer **identity-first language** because they view deaf culture or autism as a central part of their identity and take pride in it. Many parents of children with autism, however, still prefer person-first language.[54]

The bottom line is that it is important to ask individuals how they choose to identify and which terms they prefer. When working with young children, educators should follow cues from their parents. Although some can feel paralyzed by a fear of saying the wrong thing, as long as one is genuinely trying to be respectful and honor the wishes of the individual, they will generally find that the occasional misstep followed by an apology is interpreted as an honest mistake rather than intentional harm. It is also important to be flexible and prepared for language conventions to continue to evolve. Some can find it frustrating to be told that a term that was once preferred is now considered offensive, but the more one can accept that language inevitably evolves, the easier it will be to modify one's language choices as the times change.

Why inclusion? Some ethical considerations

Inclusion is an educational movement that seeks, among other things, to break down segregation based on disabilities and to promote the idea that all persons should have equal access to education and other personal and social opportunities. In this sense, the ideal of inclusion belongs within the American tradition of equal rights, a tradition that also values education as a common good. At the same time, while we affirm our moral and political equality, everyday experience tells us that people differ in intellectual capacity, creativity, and physical ability, for example, and disagreements often arise over the best ways to meet those differences.

The idea of inclusion can be supported by two historic ethical ideas: **respect for persons** and **equal educational opportunity**. Part of the reason inclusion came about may be due to their role in a slowly developing realization that class, race, ethnicity, gender, disability, and other such identity markers are insufficient reasons to deny respect for persons and equal educational opportunity; instead, they support helping people participate in personal and social life.

There are many sources for respect for persons and equal educational opportunity, but for present purposes, two philosophical viewpoints will serve to illustrate evolving outlooks about the human condition, one historical and the other contemporary.

Respect for persons

One of the more influential views on respect for persons may be found in the ethical writings of Immanuel Kant, a teacher and philosopher in Germany during the late eighteenth century. Kant argued that every human is equal in their humanity and each is a personality of absolute worth; thus, every child needs to develop their full potential, and education is a necessary ingredient in making that happen. He believed that the highest educational objectives should involve learning to live according to universal principles of right and good, which requires discipline, culture, discretion, and moral training. Such an education should reflect the ethical principle of respect for persons; that is, we should always treat other persons as ends and never as mere means to ends.[55]

Kant lived at a time when serfdom was only a memory, but slavery was still in existence and even growing in such places as the United States. Kant was a teacher and scholar, not a revolutionary, but the quality of his thought and the influence of his writings helped spread his ideas. Of course, respect for persons long pre-dated Kant and his era, but his particular formulation helped stimulate new levels of thought about the ethical treatment of others, just as it continues to impact ethical thought today.

Conflicts often arise over how people differ, and pertinent ethical concerns Kant helped elevate include "What is right and good?" and "What is fair and just?" In a society with democratic goals, questions about rightness and fairness soon lead to the question, "How do we provide equal respect and equal opportunities for all persons, regardless of their differences?" It could be argued that at every historic juncture when education became available to more people (whether involving class, race, ethnicity, gender, or disabilities), ethical concerns about rightness, fairness, and justice were significant elements.

> **For Further Reflection:** Kant argued that we should "treat other persons as ends and never as mere means to ends" in education. Think of a current educational practice or policy you're familiar with. How well does it align with Kant's principle of respect for persons? In your analysis, consider both how this practice might support students as "ends in themselves" and ways it might risk treating them as "means to ends."

Equal educational opportunity

An influential present-day view on equal opportunity is provided by American philosopher John Rawls, who critiqued how some people are born advantaged while others are born disadvantaged, circumstances that impact their life chances from birth (or some could become disadvantaged from catastrophic events or disease, for example). He sought to develop a better concept of **distributive justice**, and his general concept in its simplest form is that all social values (such as liberty, opportunity, wealth, and the social supports of self-respect) should be distributed equally unless an unequal distribution of one or more such values is to everyone's advantage. Two refinements form what Rawls calls the **difference principle**: any privileges or benefits attached to offices and positions must be open to all under fair equality of opportunity, and any resulting inequalities must provide the greatest benefit to the least advantaged members of society.[56]

At first glance, this may appear extreme, but there is ample evidence that liberty, opportunity, wealth, and position are currently distributed unequally to the most advantaged members of society, which almost guarantees that their advantages will continue or possibly compound. Under such unequal distributions, most disadvantaged persons will probably never realize any equal rights to basic liberties.

Rawls's views encompass any disadvantaged individuals or groups, not just those with disabilities, but his recommendations reflect some existing policies and programs for people with disabilities that are widely evident, such as barrier-free access to public facilities to benefit people with physical disabilities or special services in the schools to benefit students with learning disabilities. Such measures are examples of unequal distributions that benefit disadvantaged people along the lines Rawls recommends.

Critics may object that if unequal distribution is made only to benefit the least advantaged, over time it will raise them to the most advantaged status, and the formerly advantaged will be reduced to the least advantaged status; this would churn society and probably produce social anxieties leading to violent upheavals. This may be true; however, when the rich get richer and the poor get poorer, violent upheavals also sometimes occur, as witnessed by historic revolutions. Moreover, Rawls argues against precipitous, all-at-once redistributions and recommends carefully planned and executed programs designed to improve the long-term prospects of the least advantaged, an approach that does not require the destitution of any other group. Rawls also recommends redistributions to benefit everyone, such as the preservation of important gains made in society and civilization, the development of better means of production, and better investments in education and learning.[57]

The difference principle and education

According to Rawls, it is difficult for education to redress injustice immediately because it is far better at improving people's long-term prospects, including those of the least favored. Some critics might insist that educational resources should be distributed unequally in favor of those with high ability and intelligence. Rawls thinks this is permissible, but only if it serves to improve the long-term prospects of the least favored. Education is often touted for its economic benefits, but for Rawls it is far more important in helping people enjoy and participate in their society and helping them develop a secure sense of self-respect, both of which also involve moral ideals, a sense of right and justice, and respect for others. Self-respect is a primary good because without it, people are plagued by self-doubt and a lack of will to strive. Thus, a society committed to democratic equality of opportunity will cultivate social conditions that promote self-respect among all its members, and it will seek to prevent the undermining of the social supports of self-respect almost at any cost.[58]

For Further Reflection: Consider a specific example from your own educational experience or observation where resources were distributed unequally (such as special education services, gifted programs, or remedial support). To what extent did this distribution align with Rawls's difference principle? Consider both the immediate impacts and long-term effects on students' self-respect, social participation, and life prospects.

Conflict, language, labels, and ethical consequences

History is full of examples of opposed points of view struggling against each other. Philosopher John Dewey made the resolution of such opposing ideas (he called them dualisms) an important part of his philosophy. He particularly noted the harm done to education when controversial issues split people into contending camps over the differences between such things as what kinds of knowledge should be taught and what societal interests should be served. He also decried the harmful effects of the division of society into "more or less rigidly marked-off classes and groups" and the resulting "social ruptures of continuity" brought on when contentious dualisms remain unresolved.[59]

The education community has experienced some ruptures over contending views about separate special education and inclusion. As inclusion became a public issue, there were criticisms about how societal divisions along the lines of race and social class, for example, seemed to have undue influence on special education placements. There was also considerable debate about whether separate special education was right or whether it unfairly segregated students on the basis of disabilities. It is impossible to ascertain how fluctuations and misuse of language contributed to all of this, but a good case can be made that it did contribute to some extent.

In 1974, mainstreaming was described by one of its advocates as providing "high quality special education" to exceptional children in regular grades for as much of the school day as possible. In 2008, a US Department of Education document also referred to a particular new instructional approach in inclusive settings as "high-quality."[60]

Descriptors such as "high-quality" are abundant, but there can be much disagreement over what is high quality. Along the same vein, an evolving nomenclature may make it difficult to follow and participate in debates about how best to educate diverse learners. Traditionally, what was called special education was for children with mental, emotional, and physical disabilities, but the addition of learning disabilities broadened the meaning considerably. The term *learning disabilities* proved helpful in many ways, but it also helped increase disagreement and debate. In the past, the term *exceptional* was used, and sometimes still is, to refer to persons with disabilities who need special education services, but it has also been used to refer to students labeled "gifted and talented."

Other potentially confusing and ableist terms are *regular, normal,* and *general* when they are applied to curriculum programs apparently designed for persons who are not deemed special, exceptional, or as having disabilities. As can be seen, various descriptive terms and labels historically connected to inclusion help illustrate how words, terms, and labels can contribute to confusing language that often reinforces prejudices against those with disabilities.

Such is an issue not only in the American context but in other countries as well. For example, a critique of terms used in inclusive schooling in England found that inclusion, inclusive education, and inclusive schools had very loose meanings, while terms such as *special educational needs* suggested attributes specific to the learner unless given precise definition.[61]

The sorting or separating of children in schools has a fairly long history, and schools have been called "sorting machines,"[62] although not just because of special education classifications. At the same time, educators need to take stock of student differences and provide appropriate educational experiences that accommodate or develop those differences, which may sometimes necessitate separate individual and small group instruction. One way in which such separations can go wrong is when they become long-lasting, because—as experience seems to show—this tends to sharpen perceived differences, promote self-fulfilling prophecies, and encourage the students caught up in it (and sometimes their teachers) to think of individuals in terms of group labels, all of which can give the "special" (and also "gifted") pupils a limited (or exaggerated) sense of their own capacities, thereby affecting their efforts to develop healthy self-respect and respect for others.[63]

Part of the problem students with disabilities face, particularly those who do not receive the services they need, can stem not only from inadequate resource allocations but also from inadequate assessment and description of individual needs, an issue that better identification, assessment, and placement seek to address.[64] This underlines the ethical duty for educators to show respect for persons, individually and collectively, by delivering competent educational services that extend equal educational opportunities to every student.

For Further Reflection: Parents and caregivers sometimes avoid referring their children for special education services because they fear the effect that a label will have on their child. What can be done about this?

What are some examples of the ways in which stigmas around disabilities have changed in recent years? You might consider examples from popular culture, such as protagonists with disabilities in shows, films, or books being depicted in humanizing ways. (For instance, the protagonist in the *Percy Jackson* young adult book series by Rick Riordan has attention deficit hyperactivity disorder, or ADHD.)

Inclusion and special education services

As applied in education, the term *inclusion* refers to students with disabilities having access to the standard curriculum in general education classrooms; however, the manner in which inclusion is accomplished varies from one state or locale to another. In some instances, pull-in programs are used where students receive all education services in the general education classroom, such as when a speech pathologist comes to the general education classroom to work with an individual student. Another version of inclusion is co-teaching, meaning special education teachers coming to general education classrooms to work with students who have special needs. There are also pull-out programs in which students leave regular classrooms to go to resource rooms, partially self-contained classes, or self-contained special classes to receive special services.[65]

Some leading aspects of inclusive education

Inclusive education is backed by legal and policy requirements that differ from most traditional forms of education. The following provides selected terms with brief descriptions.

- **Evidence-Based Practices:** Use of teaching interventions/strategies shown to be effective by rigorous and systematic research, which may differ from those in general education and which typically focus on individuals as much or more than groups, such as seeking skill mastery rather than in-depth understanding.
- **Family Involvement:** Expectation that each child's parent/guardian will be involved in the child's education to a greater extent than for children without disabilities, including membership on the child's individualized education program (IEP) team and also partnership in planning and decision-making, with rights to challenge IEPs for their child and for services not typically offered to students without disabilities.
- **Free Appropriate Public Education (FAPE):** Right to appropriate educational services at no cost to the student, parent, or guardian.
- **Frequent Monitoring of Progress:** Frequent, systematic assessments/evaluations of how students with disabilities respond to plans/practices used to develop student skills and comprehension, and the linkage of instruction with such assessments.
- **Individualized Education Program (IEP).** For individuals with disabilities ages 3–21, to ensure appropriate educational services designed by an IEP team for each individual student, composed of the student's parent/guardian, general and special education teachers, other individuals with expertise relevant to the student's situation, and, where appropriate, the student with the disability.
- **Individualized Family Service Plan (IFSP).** For infants and toddlers with disabilities through age 2, to ensure early identification, assessment, and provision of appropriate services according to a plan developed by a multidisciplinary team (with parental participation and informed consent for implementation) to support the child's transition to preschool or other educational services.
- **Least Restrictive Environment (LRE):** Right to be educated with nondisabled peers to the maximum extent possible, with separation from general education classrooms only when the kind or severity of a disability requires it (including services general education classrooms cannot provide, such as skills and comprehensions best learned in community settings and on-the-job sites).

- **Related Services:** Additional services to help students with disabilities in general education schools, such as paraprofessionals for individualized assistance; multidisciplinary teams for family therapy, occupational therapy, and physical therapy; and other professional services (school nurses, social workers).
- **Systematic Identification Procedures:** To improve identification of individuals needing special education services, determination of appropriate services, and avoidance of over-identifications due to ethnic, cultural, and linguistic factors, or underidentifications associated with gifts and talents. Designed to enhance expertise of general educators to ensure a student's difficulties are not caused by regular interventions/strategies that fail to produce desired performance and behavioral outcomes.

Sources: Diane P. Bryant et al., *Teaching Students with Special Needs in Inclusive Classrooms* (Boston: Pearson, 2008), 23–31, 183; and US Department of Education, "Building the Legacy: IDEA 2004," at http://idea.ed.gov/explore/view/p (accessed on August 24, 2010).

Suggested Activity: Conduct an interview with parents of students with or without disabilities. Analyze their perceptions of inclusion and its effect on their children. What do your results show?

Curriculum, instruction, and universal design for learning

Various curricular and instructional approaches have been developed to achieve a more inclusive education. One of them is **assistive technology**, which seeks to enable students to achieve in ways that might otherwise be difficult or impossible through technology that helps reduce obstacles. This includes traditional devices such as walkers and wheelchairs, but it also encompasses new technologies such as computer hardware, software, and related technological developments.[66] For example, students with sight impairments may be provided with assistive technology to enhance their audio and tactile capacities through the use of computer hardware and software capable of transmitting screen text to a board that raises and lowers pins to produce text in braille. More recently, AI-driven accessibility tools offer such things as AI-enhanced screen readers and real-time automatic speech recognition (ASR) captioning.

Another is **response to intervention (RTI)**, which is a three-tier model requiring research-validated instructional interventions in core subjects (such

Figure 7.4 Assistive keyboard with large print, bright yellow keys, and joystick.

as reading) in general education classrooms. RTI starts with careful screening to identify those with learning disabilities who need special interventions. Interventions must be research-backed and provided for a specific period of time, and as student progress is made, the intervention must intensify to improve the student's achievement. In addition, progress monitoring must occur along the way to evaluate student advancement and response to instruction in order to determine next steps. About 80–85 percent of students fall into Tier 1 (universal), which means they perform near or above grade level when receiving high-quality instruction. About 10–15 percent of students fall into Tier 2 (targeted instruction), meaning they can perform at grade level when provided research-based small group instruction. They can then return to Tier 1. Tier 3 (intensive intervention) is required for the approximately 5 percent of students who need more intensive, smaller group or individual instruction. RTI can also help with the identification of students with specific learning disabilities.[67]

Accommodations and modifications

Teachers can support students with disabilities in many ways, including accommodations and curriculum modifications. **Accommodations** are changes that allow a student to access the curriculum or demonstrate learning in different ways without substantially changing the instructional level or content. Examples include reading directions aloud to a student, giving extended time on assignments, providing study aids, or reducing the number of questions on an assessment while keeping the same amount of content assessed.

Modifications, on the other hand, do substantially change the curriculum and thus need to be considered carefully to ensure students with disabilities are supported to meet the same standards as other students. An example would be having students with disabilities do a reading comprehension assignment that requires them only to locate definitions in a passage, while the rest of the class answers higher-order thinking questions that promote their analytical skills. Such modifications risk denying students with disabilities practice with high-level skills they will need in the future.

For Further Reflection*:* Imagine you are teaching a sixth-grade class to write an essay with a clear organizational structure. What are some accommodations you could include that would support students with learning disabilities to succeed in this task?

Universal design

The universal design concept probably originated in architectural and engineering efforts to design structures that benefit the widest possible range of users and usages. Common examples include buildings with electronic door openers, ramps, and elevators. These are considered universal because they not only increase accessibility to individuals using wheelchairs or other assistive technologies but also to parents with strollers, bicycle riders, and others. In other words, they universally increase accessibility. In regard to the use of universal design in higher education, federal legislation defines it as "a scientifically valid framework" to guide educational practice in ways that not only provide flexibility in how information is presented, how students acquire knowledge and skills, and how students are engaged in the process but also reduce instructional barriers, provide appropriate accommodations, and support high achievement expectations for all students, including those with disabilities and those with limited English proficiency. It also must use curricula specifically designed to meet the needs of as many users as possible.[68]

Universal design for learning

Probably the most general educational development that encompasses the efforts described in the preceding section is **universal design for learning (UDL)**. It is based on curriculum and instruction that employ multiple ways of presenting subject matter in formats that recognize sensory and cognitive differences among learners. Often, UDL involves teachers offering students multiple means of representation, engagement, and expression. For example:

- providing multiple means of representation through presenting the same content through a reading, a video, a short lecture, and/or a podcast
- providing multiple means of engagement by allowing students to choose between a menu of activities that all reinforce the same content or allowing them to incorporate their own interests or background experiences into the lesson (e.g., allowing them to share with a peer what this topic reminds them of)
- providing multiple means of expression by allowing students to choose among several assessment options, such as creating a presentation, writing a paper, or performing a play to demonstrate their understanding of the content

The idea is that this flexibility and adaptability to each student's needs and interests will benefit all students, not just those with disabilities. This can also allow students with disabilities to feel more included in the classroom than when they are the only ones receiving a given accommodation. With the UDL approach, curriculum content can be provided in a variety of formats so that students are able to work individually or in small groups and configurations that include both students with disabilities and those without.[69]

In effect, UDL attempts to address the long-standing problem of a traditional, one-size-fits-all curriculum that is unable to accommodate many individual learning preferences. UDL takes its descriptor "universal" from its intention to benefit all students and to harm no one, but the term *universal* should not be taken to mean a final and complete educational design that applies to everyone perfectly. There is no such universal curriculum or instructional strategy, and the variety of individual differences (learning preferences, backgrounds, interests, or abilities) means that diversity rather than homogeneity is typical of both individuals and groups.[70] However, individual differences do not make separate species, and members of the human race share far more in common than not. Moreover, the moral/ethical and political concepts of human equality and equal educational opportunity are central values in any democratic society.

Who needs to learn? Universal design for learning and assistive technologies

The goal of UDL is to reach all learners, but some groups are especially underserved. Lack of access to technology often correlates not only with disabilities but also with socioeconomic status, ethnicity, language, educational level, and age. Digital access is important today because so much information and so many services are now readily available through digital resources. Some groups particularly need attention:

- Low-Income Learners. They often have less access to computers, the internet, and family and immediate community resources that provide technology-based learning at home. An example includes extending the hours of use of networked computers in schools, libraries, and community centers.
- English Learners. English predominates as the language of instruction in most schools and on most websites. The acquisition of essential knowledge and skills needed today is hampered when English is not one's first language. Properly designed translation technology helps reduce language barriers and offers help with English and unfamiliar vocabulary or syntax through translation and other assistive technologies.
- Learners with Disabilities. Many learners with physical and sensory disabilities need assistive technologies to achieve along with their peers. Examples include electronic mobility switches and alternative keyboards for students with physical disabilities; computer screen enlargers, text-to-speech devices, and screen readers for individuals with visual disabilities; electronic sign-language dictionaries and signing avatars for learners with hearing disabilities; and calculators and spellcheckers for individuals with learning disabilities. Many UDL digital resources are possible through assistive technologies.
- Pre-K Learners. Learning gaps in literacy begin in early childhood and become increasingly difficult to surmount over time. Early intervention is crucial for underserved children to keep pace with their peers, especially to augment the linguistic, visual, and symbolic worlds they experience. One example is technology-based resources that target school readiness skills.
- Adult Workforce. Many working people are underproductive and face limited job opportunities because of insufficient skill development. They may also lack the time or opportunity for the sustained learning that skill development requires. Technological avenues such as online courses expand worker opportunities for when and where they may learn. Not only do individual workers benefit from increased worker productivity, but companies and agencies do as well.

- Seniors. Many older adults develop visual, hearing, motor, and cognitive disabilities as they age, just as they also have special strengths of accumulated wisdom and experience. Improving their strengths through lifelong learning opportunities requires careful design and the use of assistive technologies so that the disabilities of aging do not become obstacles to continued learning, independence, and social life.

Source: USDOE, "Who Needs to Learn?" at http://www.ed.gov/technology/netp-2010/ who-needs-to-learn (accessed on September 13, 2010).

Suggested Activity: Interview an experienced classroom teacher about the inclusion of students with disabilities in the general education classroom. Seek insight on the strategies used, enablers and barriers encountered in the process, and successes and failures.

Teacher roles and responsibilities

School personnel are key to the success of inclusion. Obviously, inclusive education has its best effects if certain essential conditions are met: educators must be well prepared and committed to inclusion; they must be provided with adequate materials, support services, and equipment; appropriate physical accommodations must be made; and sufficient funding and active family involvement must also be present. In regard to the latter, families of students with disabilities not only need to be involved in their children's schooling, but they also may need support themselves. To improve the chances of successful inclusion, then, educators need to be cooperative, empathetic, and respectful of parents while providing the leadership necessary to meet the needs of all their students.[71]

It should be noted, however, that general education teachers have not always received the training, assistance, or information needed to implement inclusion effectively. Past research indicates that most teachers supported the idea of inclusion, but a sizable portion felt most comfortable working with students with less severe disabilities. Many teachers believed they did not have the necessary background training or essential resources; the more severe the disability, the less confident they felt. Research also indicates that as teachers gained experience with students with disabilities, they usually moved beyond their initial concerns and came to appreciate how special services aided their work, not only with students with disabilities but also with students who needed but did not qualify for special services. Similarly, parents—whether of children with or without disabilities—became more accepting of inclusion once they became familiar with how it worked and what effects it had.[72]

Comprehensive staff development programs, flexible time for school personnel to meet and plan together, and supplemental support are important. Well-prepared teachers report positive outcomes for students, an enhanced sense of professional competence, and a new pattern of collegial cooperation. Teamwork is seen as the key strategy if inclusive education is to work for all children, regardless of disability. A first step toward successful teamwork is the building of trust, because collaborative efforts among school personnel are essential for successful inclusion programs in schools.[73]

The general education teacher's role has changed in today's inclusive classrooms. Prior to inclusion, regular classroom teachers typically identified the students they thought had special needs and referred them for separate special education provisions. In inclusive classrooms, however, the general education teacher is usually expected to provide educational services for almost all students, aided by special education teachers and support specialists who may co-teach, collaborate, and/or provide consultative support. As a result of inclusion, the general education teacher has had to learn new skills, such as serving on IEP committees, interacting with parents of children with special needs, providing greater individualization of instruction, applying a greater variety of instructional techniques, and using more diverse applications of new technology.[74]

For Further Reflection: In what ways do you think the expanded role of general education teachers serves both students with and without disabilities?

Co-teaching models

Co-teaching is a type of collaborative teaching in which two teachers share instructional responsibility in the classroom. Typically, teachers use one or more of six approaches, depending on the lesson type, objectives, student needs, and teachers' styles:

1. One Teach, One Observe—the second teacher observes and collects data on students while the first teaches the class.

2. One Teach, One Assist—the second teacher circulates and assists individual students while the first leads the lesson.
3. Parallel Teaching—the class is divided into two groups, and both groups are taught simultaneously.
4. Station Teaching—students rotate through different stations, two of which are led by the two teachers, and the remainder of which consist of independent work.
5. Alternative Teaching—one teacher works with a small group needing specialized attention, while the other teacher leads instruction for the rest of the class.
6. Team Teaching—both teachers are instructing at the same time, similar to a tag team approach.

Inclusion and its impact on teacher education

Debate about inclusion is not confined to the United States, because it has shaped educational policies and practices internationally. Consequently, a growing body of research is investigating the changes occurring in different countries' teacher preparation programs, often engaging in international comparisons.[75]

Pressures for change

In the United States, the inclusion movement has clearly impacted the preparation of teachers, but much more needs to be done. Pressures for change are contained in IDEA, NCLB, and ESSA, but there are also those who have been pushing change for years. A persistent teacher education challenge has been the need for interdisciplinary and interdepartmental cooperation, especially between special and general education. Collaboration is an essential ingredient in schools that successfully implement inclusion. Many teacher education reformers maintain that such collaboration should be first rooted in the preparatory programs in the colleges and universities.[76]

Research on teacher education indicates that to improve teacher candidates' knowledge about students with disabilities and inclusive education, preparation programs must include coursework and related learning activities on collaboration and cooperative participation that cut across education departments and programs. These activities could involve team-teaching experiences that cross majors, co-teaching experiences within majors that combine contributions from both general and special education, and field experiences for all candidates that emphasize cross-major collaborations. It would also be beneficial if teacher education faculty outside special education increased their knowledge and experience concerning special education services and collaboration. A general need is for more resources, funding, and time allocations for teacher education faculty to provide their students with better preparation for inclusive classrooms and schools.[77]

Some teacher education reformers want to go beyond programmatic changes. One view is that both inclusion and curriculum detracking help call into question all policies and practices that sort, rank, and label learners. Divisive they may be, but they continue to be entrenched in many ways. To help counteract harmful practices, teacher preparation programs need to help candidates question the assumptions behind differentiations of learners that undermine respect for persons and equal educational opportunities for all.[78]

Some possible directions

Promising approaches include the following: providing future teachers with the tools for observing learners in open-minded ways, engaging them in critical inquiry into traditional and current standards, and ensuring that they have experiences critiquing and developing curricular and pedagogical strategies that promote equality of educational opportunity by meeting diverse student needs.[79]

The first component, tools for understanding learners, is based on the idea that teachers need to assess students in ways that emphasize student potential as starting points for teaching and learning strategies directed toward growth in learning. The goal is to enable future teachers to recognize the potentials and complexities of students, not to prejudge and categorize them by such things as test scores interpreted on the basis of some "normalized" statistical curve. Instead, teacher candidates need to become professionals who approach their work by recognizing student strengths to learn and then developing teaching and learning practices that build on those strengths to help students further expand their potential. Such an orientation is part of a "capacity-oriented" framework for effective inclusion practices.[80]

Suggested Activity: Independently or with your peers, create an observation protocol of ten items that would foster preservice teachers' abilities to notice individual learner needs in *open-minded and non-judgmental ways.* For example, one item might be, "What strategies does the learner you are observing use to decode words as they are reading?" rather than "Does the learner have challenges decoding words while reading, and, if so, what are they?"

The second orientation is critical inquiry into the standards against which students are measured. Teachers today face a dilemma: Under ESSA, they must respond to diverse learning preferences, but they must also help all students meet the standards. To address this quandary, teacher candidates must learn not simply to align their teaching with prescribed standards but also to carefully analyze the standards for the kinds of knowledge, learning preferences, and ways of knowing that are most valued within the standards. Such inquiry helps teacher candidates reflect thoughtfully on how the standards can be used to expand their curricular, pedagogical, and assessment practices and help them create more effective learning environments for their students.[81]

Finally, it is important for teacher candidates to understand the relationship between schooling and inequality, just as they also need to know how to develop relationships with families and communities to better comprehend the cultural competency and knowledge expectations of the local communities surrounding the schools in which they teach. In other words, prospective teachers need to develop cultural understandings that help them develop relevant instructional plans for their students that do not rely on stereotypes. Advocates maintain that such approaches are necessary if teacher education is to prepare the kinds of teachers needed by schools in the present and foreseeable future.[82]

Although there have been efforts to prepare both general and special educators to meet the needs of diverse learners, some critics might argue that the inclusion movement has not impacted teacher education strongly enough. There is still insufficient attention to cross-program and cross-departmental collaboration, and much remains to be done concerning entrenched attitudes and cultural assumptions regarding the inclusion of diverse learners. Maybe the difficulties are simply due to stubborn biases and fear of change, but perhaps it is more likely that fundamental changes to long-established attitudes and cultural assumptions simply take patience and persistence.

For Further Reflection: What do you think explains the persistence of difficulties in preparing both general and special educators to meet the needs of diverse learners?

Student outcomes

Effective inclusive schools are characterized by an emphasis on the learning of all students, and an essential benchmark of success is when students with disabilities in general classrooms progress as much or more than they would in separate settings. Inclusive education is not problem free, but it is possible for important academic, behavioral, and social benefits to be gained by all students (and their teachers) if effective teaching and learning strategies are used. Not only is it possible for students with disabilities to learn new skills and experience new interactions and friendships but also for general education students who may experience positive outcomes in classrooms where students with disabilities are their classmates.[83]

Positive student outcomes are not easy to achieve. For example, consider 10-year-old fourth grader Don, who was identified as "profoundly learning disabled." He lacked the fine motor skills necessary for writing and experienced difficulty reading and understanding text. In addition, he was frequently absent due to severe bouts of asthma. While Don was usually working with a learning disabilities specialist outside the general science classroom, his teachers made arrangements to include him in a special program of study. Soon, positive learning outcomes could be observed. When the class examined what objects sink or float, he was actively engaged in problem-solving, constructed a diver system more quickly than some of his peers, and triumphantly shared his learning. In addition, he was able to write about, revise, and elaborate on his thinking with minimal adult assistance.

Still, challenges became obvious. One was that Don struggled socially, especially in a small group activity where his contributions were either ignored or rebuffed. While such occurrences might have gone undetected by the general education teacher busy with twenty-eight students, if a specialist shadowing Don had been present, such events might have been noticed, and assistance immediately given. In addition, this specialist could have assisted the general education teacher in modeling group interactions that allow all students to equally participate, such as taking turns.[84]

Don's case illustrates what has been emphasized before: the inclusion of students with disabilities in general education settings has much to offer and can be highly successful, although inclusion is not without its challenges. Certain conditions must be met to make inclusion work for all concerned, both academically and socially, and close collaboration among educators is one essential prerequisite if the goal is to achieve optimal learning outcomes for students like Don and his classmates.

Suggested Activity: Interview a student or former student (with or without disabilities) about experiences of inclusion in his or her own education.

Summary and conclusions

The education of children with disabilities shows a long process of trial and error, proceeding from the more obvious disabilities (such as deafness or blindness) to less obvious ones (such as learning disabilities). Among the most striking historical changes was the move from viewing people with disabilities as uneducable, then to providing education in separate institutions and classrooms designed for specific disabilities, and finally to the inclusion of students on a large scale in ordinary educational institutions and processes among people not considered disabled. Today, the education of people with disabilities is still far from perfect, but progress has been made, and it seems unlikely that society will revert to prior levels of neglect.

Despite such progress, how we educate people with disabilities is still hampered by some seemingly intractable problems. One of them is a continuing tendency to categorize and classify people, which can define individuals according to disability rather than their other human qualities. At the same time, there are practical needs to be descriptive in order to provide services where needed. For good care and service, it is necessary to research, assess, and devise appropriate educational plans for specific needs and differences.

A person's right to an education, regardless of disability, has been guaranteed and protected by legislation and judicial decision. Parents of children with disabilities, interested citizens, educators, and other human service professionals, community leaders and lawmakers, and a host of other people all played significant roles in making this possible at both the state and national levels. The law requires that students with disabilities must have equal access to the schools, with due regard for individual needs and appropriate educational provisions. Equal educational opportunity is a historic ideal, but the inclusion of people with disabilities is a relatively recent addition to the debate, due in part to the realization that persons with disabilities could be educated far beyond most people's previous expectations but also to greater awareness of the ethical demands of fairness and democratic equity.

By the twenty-first century, inclusive education was widely recognized in the United States, with separate education reduced but not completely gone. Public schools were expected to take in all students and were held accountable to meet the demands of federal and state education laws in regard to inclusive education. While inclusive education seemed to be settled policy, there were still issues concerning funding and the better preparation of teachers, as well as the degree and exact form inclusive education should take.

Vocabulary

ableism
accommodations
assistive technology
attention deficit hyperactivity disorder (ADHD)
deaf community
developmentally delayed
difference principle
disabilities as treatable conditions disability studies
distributive justice
Education for All Handicapped Children Act (Public Law 94–142)
equal educational opportunity
equal protection of the laws
eugenics
free appropriate public education
identity-first language
inclusion
individualized education program (IEP)
Individuals with Disabilities Education Act (IDEA)
intelligence scale
labels
learning difficulties
learning disabilities
least restrictive environment (LRE)
mainstreaming
medical model of disability
medicalized theory of deviance
mental measurement
modifications
normalization
oralist approach
person-first language
physiological method
psychological testing
respect for persons
response to intervention (RTI)
sign language

social model of disability
universal design for learning (UDL)

Notes

1 Herbert C. Covey, *Social Perceptions of People with Disabilities in History* (Springfield, IL: Charles C. Thomas, 1998), 6–8.
2 Alexis de Tocqueville, *Democracy in America*, Richard D. Heffner, ed. (New York: Mentor Books, New American Library, 1956), 198.
3 Cathryn Carroll, "A Father, a Son, and a University: Thomas Hopkins Gallaudet," at http://clerccenter.gallaudet.edu/InfoToGo/751.html (accessed on August 18, 2010).
4 Philip L. Safford and Elizabeth J. Safford, *A History of Childhood and Disability* (New York: Teachers College Press, 1996), 3, 41–2.
5 Covey, *Social Perceptions of People with Disabilities in History,* 219–23; Safford and Safford, *A History of Childhood and Disability,* 40–1.
6 Margaret A. Winzer, *The History of Special Education: From Isolation to Integration* (Washington, DC: Gallaudet Press, 1993), 21–2, and 99 and Safford and Safford, *A History of Childhood and Disability*, 92–6.
7 Lubna Takruri, "Gallaudet Exposes Debate over Deafness," *The Associated Press*, at http://www.washingtonpost.com/wp-dyn/content/article/2006/10/30/AR2006103000087.html (October 30, 2006); Susan Kinzie, "New Gallaudet President Met with Protest," *The Washington Post*, A01, at http://www.washingtonpost.com/wp-dyn/content/article/2006/05/01/AR2006050100770.html (May 2, 2006); Susan Kinzie et al., "Gallaudet Board Ousts Fernandes," *The Washington Post*, A-1, at http://www.washingtonpost.com/wp-dyn/content/article/2006/10/29/AR2006102900533.html?nav=emailpage (October 30, 2006) and Sue Ann Pressly and Susan Kinzie, "Trustees Seek Student and Faculty Input Before Leadership Search," *The Washington Post* (November 12, 2006), C-06, at http://www.washingtonpost.com/wp-dyn/content/article/2006/11/11/AR2006111100781.html?nav=emailpage (all accessed on August 18, 2010).
8 Safford and Safford, *A History of Childhood and Disability,* 96–9.
9 Michael E. Gorman, "Alexander Graham Bell's Path to the Telephone," at http://www3.iath.virginia.edu/albell/homepage.html (accessed on August 18, 2010).
10 Safford and Safford, *A History of Childhood and Disability,* 100–1; Winzer, *The History of Special Education,* 53–5, 154–5, and 195–6.
11 Winzer, *The History of Special Education,* 126–9. See also, "About CLARKE: History," at http://www.clarkeschools.org/about/ welcome (accessed on August 18, 2010).

12 Winzer, *The History of Special Education*, 104, 109.

13 Harold Schwartz, *Samuel Gridley Howe: Social Reformer* (Cambridge, MA: Harvard University Press, 1956), 49–58. See also "History," Perkins School for the Blind, at http://www.perkins.org/about-us/history (accessed on August 18, 2010).

14 Schwartz, *Samuel Gridley Howe: Social Reformer*, 49–58.

15 Ibid., 59–61.

16 Samuel G. Howe et al., *On the Causes of Idiocy; Being the Supplement to a Report by Dr. S. G. Howe and the Other Commissioners Appointed by the Governor of Massachusetts to Inquire into the Condition of the Idiots of the Commonwealth, February 26, 1848* (reprint, New York: Arno Press, 1972), xv–xvi ff; Schwartz, *Samuel Gridley Howe: Social Reformer*, 140–2.

17 Schwartz, *Samuel Gridley Howe: Social Reformer*, 142–4; Winzer, *The History of Special Education*, 115.

18 The authors acknowledge indebtedness to Joy L. Johnson, "Edouard Seguin's Contributions in Education for Children with Mental Retardation," unpublished paper, Virginia Commonwealth University, 1998. For contemporaneous views of Séguin, see "In Memory of Edouard Seguin, M.D." (1880), at http://www.disabilitymuseum.org/lib/docs/1924.htm (accessed on August 18, 2010).

19 Jean-Marc Gaspard Itard, *The Wild Boy of Aveyron*, George and Muriel Humphrey, trans. (New York: Appleton-Century-Croft, 1962).

20 Mabel E. Talbot, *Édouard Seguin: A Study of an Educational Approach to the Treatment of Mentally Defective Children* (New York: Teachers College Press, 1964), 1–12.

21 As quoted in Schwartz, *Samuel Gridley Howe: Social Reformer*, 146.

22 As quoted in Talbot, *Édouard Seguin*, 69. Seguin developed a tripartite classification system of "idiot" (arrested development), "retarded" (delayed development), and "imbecile" (defects in social development).

23 Talbot, *Édouard Seguin*, 74–6, 78–80.

24 Winzer, *The History of Special Education*, 93–6.

25 Barry M. Franklin, *From Backwardness to "At-Risk": Childhood Learning Difficulties and the Contradictions of School Reform* (Albany: State University of New York Press, 1994), xii–xiii.

26 Ibid., 6, 11–12.

27 JoAnne Brown, *The Definition of a Profession: The Authority of Metaphor in the History of Intelligence Testing, 1890–1930* (Princeton, NJ: Princeton University Press, 1992), 35–40.

28 Ibid., 46–8.

29 Ibid., 80–3, 92–4. The authors also wish to acknowledge background material on eugenics from Stephen R. Hall, *Oscar McCulloch and Indiana Eugenics*, Thesis (PhD) (Richmond, VA: Virginia Commonwealth University, 1993). See also Richard Hofstadter, *Social Darwinism in American Thought* (1944,

reprint, Boston, MA: Beacon Press, 1992); and Herbert Spencer, "Progress: Its Law and Cause," at *Modern History Sourcebook*: "Herbert Spencer: Social Darwinism (1857)," at http://www.fordham.edu/halsall/mod/spencer-darwin.html (accessed on August 18, 2010).

30 Leila Zenderland, *Measuring Minds: Henry Herbert Goddard and the Origins of American Intelligence Testing* (New York: Cambridge University Press, 1998), 17–18, 20–3, 25–43. See also "Henry Herbert Goddard" (2003), at http://www.indiana.edu/~intell/goddard.shtml; and "Goddard and Eugenics," at http://www.vineland.org/history/trainingschool/history/eugenics.htm (both accessed on August 18, 2010).

31 Zenderland, *Measuring Minds*, 71–104.

32 Henry Herbert Goddard, *Feeble-Mindedness: Its Causes and Consequences* (reprint, New York: Arno Press, [1926] 1973), 566; *The Kallikak Family: A Study in the Heredity of Feeble-Mindedness* (New York: Arno Press, 1912), 105–7; and Zenderland, *Measuring Minds*, 353.

33 Steven Selden, *Inheriting Shame: The Story of Eugenics and Racism in America* (New York: Teachers College Press, 1999), 1–21 and Beth A. Ferri and David J. Connor, *Reading Resistance: Discourses of Exclusion in Desegregation & Inclusion Debates* (New York: Peter Wang, 2006), 26–39.

34 Schwartz, *Samuel Gridley Howe: Social Reformer*, 271–4.

35 Scott B. Sigmon, *Radical Analysis of Special Education: Focus on Historical Development and Learning Disabilities* (New York: Falmer Press, 1987), 12.

36 As quoted in Franklin, *From Backwardness to "At-Risk"*, 68. See also J. Lee Wiederholt, "Historical Perspectives on the Education of the Learning Disabled," in *The Second Review of Special Education*, Lester Mann and David A. Sabatino, eds (Philadelphia, PA: JSE Press, 1974), 142–3.

37 See, for example, Peter Schrag and Diane Divoky, *The Myth of the Hyperactive Child: And Other Means of Child Control* (New York: Pantheon, 1975), 30–1; Christine E. Sleeter, "Learning Disabilities: The Social Construction of a Special Education Group," in *Critical Voices on Special Education: Problems and Progress Concerning the Mildly Handicapped*, Scott B. Sigmon, ed. (Albany: State University of New York Press, 1990), 33; and William M. Cruickshank, *Disputable Decisions in Special Education* (Ann Arbor: The University of Michigan Press, 1986), 6.

38 Robert L. Osgood, *The History of Inclusion in the United States* (Washington, DC: Gallaudet University Press, 2005), 34–61.

39 Wolf Wolfensberger, *Normalization: The Principle of Normalization in Human Services* (Toronto: National Institute of Mental Retardation, 1972), 13, 25, 27, and 31. See also Osgood, *The History of Inclusion in the United States*, 94–5.

40 Sigmon, *Radical Analysis of Special Education*, 28, 30.

41 Alan Abeson, "Legal Forces and Pressures," in *Mainstreaming and the Minority Child*, Reginald L. Jones ed. (Minneapolis, MN: Leadership Training Institute/ Special Education, 1976), 15.

42 Brown v. Board of Education of Topeka (1954), 347 U.S. 383, at http://supct.law.cornell.edu/supct/search/display.html?terms=Brown%20v.%20Board%20of%20Education&url=/supct/html/historics/USSC_CR_0347_0483_ZO.html (accessed on August 18, 2010).

43 Abeson, "Legal Forces and Pressures," 18. For the full decisions, see also *Brown v. Board of Education*, 1954, 347 U.S. 483; *Pennsylvania Association for Retarded Children v. Commonwealth of Pennsylvania*, 343 F. Supp. 279; *Mills v. Board of Education of the District of Columbia*, 348 F. Supp. 866 (Dist. D. C. 1972); *Maryland Association for Retarded Children v. State of Maryland*, Equity No. 100-182-77676 (Circuit Court, Baltimore, Maryland, 1974).

44 US Congress, Public Law 94–142, "Education for All Handicapped Children," November 29, 1975 (sec. 4).

45 Ibid., 42, Section 4(a), 16–17.

46 Ibid., Section 3(c).

47 "Education of All Handicapped Children, Part II," *Federal Register*, vol. 42, no. 163 (Tuesday, August 23, 1977): 42497–. Italics added.

48 "Education of the Handicapped Act Amendments of 1990," in *United States Statutes at Large, 1990*, vol. 104, part 2 (Washington, DC: US Government Printing Office, 1991), 1103–51. For the "Individuals with Disabilities Education Act Amendments of 1991," see *United States Statutes at Large, 1991*, vol. 105 (Washington, DC: US Government Printing Office, 1992), 587–608. For the latest version of the law as of this writing, see P.L. 108–446, Individuals with Disabilities Education Improvement Act of 2004, at http://frwebgate.access.gpo.gov/cgi-bin/getdoc.cgi?dbname=108_cong_public_laws&docid=f:publ446.108 (accessed on July 7, 2010).

49 Tom E. C. Smith et al., *Teaching Students with Special Needs in Inclusive Settings*, 2nd edn (Boston, MA: Allyn & Bacon, 1998), 31.

50 Robert A. Gable and Jo M. Hendrickson, "Teaching All the Students: A Mandate for Educators," in *Successful Inclusive Teaching: Proven Ways to Detect and Correct Special Needs*, Joyce S. Choate, ed., 4th edn (Boston, MA: Pearson, 2004), 2–4.

51 Specific learning disabilities are disorders that affect one or more of the basic psychological processes involved in understanding language, for example, dyslexia.

52 Other health impairments include having limited strength or alertness due to an acute or chronic health problem, such as asthma, sickle cell anemia, hemophilia, leukemia, diabetes, or a heart condition.

53 National Center for Education Statistics (NCES), *Digest of Education Statistics, 2022*, at https://nces.ed.gov/programs/digest/d23/tables/dt23_204.30.asp?current=yes (accessed on March 11, 2025).

54 Shannon Woolridge, "Writing Respectfully: Person-First and Identity-First Language," National Institutes of Health (April 12, 2023).

55 Immanuel Kant, *Education*, Annette Churton, trans. (Ann Arbor: University of Michigan Press, 1960).

56 John Rawls, *A Theory of Justice*, rev. edn (Cambridge, MA: Belknap Press of Harvard University Press, 1999), 53–4 and *Political Liberalism* (New York: Columbia University Press, 1993), 291.

57 Rawls, *Political Liberalism*, 65–70, 252 specifically, and Chapters 4, 5, and 6 generally.

58 Ibid., 87, 92, 386–91, 452.

59 John Dewey, *Democracy and Education: An Introduction to the Philosophy of Education* (New York: The Macmillan, 1916), 340, 377.

60 For the 1974 mainstreaming reference, see J. W. Birch, *Mainstreaming: Educable Mentally Retarded Children in Regular Classes* (Reston, VA: The Council for Exceptional Children, 1974), 2; for the 2008 reference to RTI, see United States Department of Education (USDOE), Office of Special Education and Rehabilitation Services, "Coordinated Early Intervening Services (CEIS) Guidance," 6, at http://www2.ed.gov/policy/speced/guid/idea/ceis-guidance.pdf (accessed on September 23, 2010).

61 Alan Dyson and Alan Millward, *Schools and Special Needs: Issues of Innovation and Inclusion* (London: Paul Chapman Publishing, 2000), viii.

62 David L. Kirp, "The Great Sorting Machine," *Phi Delta Kappan*, vol. 8, no. 5 (April 1974): 522–4. See also Joel Spring, *The Sorting Machine Revisited: National Educational Policy Since 1945*, updated edn (New York: Longman, 1989).

63 Osgood, *The History of Inclusion in the United States*, 2–12.

64 Cathleen G. Spinelli, *Classroom Assessment for Students with Special Needs in Inclusive Settings* (Upper Saddle River, NJ: Pearson/Merrill/Prentice Hall, 2006).

65 Diane P. Bryant et al., *Teaching Students with Special Needs in Inclusive Classrooms* (Boston, MA: Pearson, 2008), 32–4.

66 "What Is Assistive Technology?" *The National Center on Accessible Information Technology in Education*, at http://www.washington.edu/accessit/articles?109 (accessed on September 14, 2010).

67 USDOE, "CEIS and Response to Intervention RTI," at http://www2.ed.gov/policy/speced/guid/idea/ceis_pg4.html (accessed on September 13, 2010); and Nicole Strangeman et al., "Response-to-Instruction and Universal Design for Learning: How Might They Intersect in the General Education Classroom?" LD OnLine, at http://www.ldonline.org/article/13002?theme=print (accessed on September 13, 2010);

Mark Batshaw, Nancy Roisen, Louis Pellegrino, Nancy Peterson, and Catherine Twomey, *Children with Disabilities* (Towson, MD: Brookes Publishing, 2019), 677.

68 "Universal Design for Learning," Title I, § 103, ¶ 24, of the Higher Education Opportunity Act (P.L. 110–315—August 14, 2008), 122 Stat. 3088, at http://frwebgate.access.gpo.gov/cgi-bin/getdoc.cgi?dbname=110_cong_public_laws&docid=f:publ315.110.pdf (accessed on September 13, 2010).

69 "What Is Universal Design for Learning?" Center for Applied Special Technology, at http://www.cast.org/research/udl/index.html (accessed on August 18, 2010); "What Is a Refreshable Braille Display?" Center for Universal Design in Education (CUDE), at http://www.washington.edu/doit/CUDE/articles?140 (accessed on September 14, 2010); and Bryant et al., *Teaching Students with Special Needs in Inclusive Classrooms*, 22, 204, 205.

70 "Universal Design … What It Is and What It Isn't," Trace Center, at http://trace.wisc.edu/docs/whats_ud/whats_ud.htm (accessed on September 14, 2010).

71 Joyce S. Choate and Dorothy C. Schween, "Special Needs of Diverse Learners," in *Successful Inclusive Teaching: Proven Ways to Detect and Correct Special Needs*, Joyce S. Choate, ed., 4th edn (Boston, MA: Pearson, Allyn and Bacon, 2004), chapter 2; Katie Blenk and Doris L. Fine, *Making School Inclusion Work* (Cambridge, MA: Brookline Books, 1995), 213; and Larry D. Bartlett et al., *Successful Inclusion for Educational Leaders* (Upper Saddle River, NJ: Pearson College Division, 2002), 27.

72 Peggy Dettmer et al., *Consultation, Collaboration, and Teamwork for Students with Special Needs* (Boston, MA: Pearson Education, 2005), 41, 220; Thomas E. Scruggs and Margo Mastropieri, "Teacher Perceptions of Mainstreaming/Inclusion, 1958–1995: A Research Synthesis," *Exceptional Children*, vol. 63, no. 1 (Fall 1996): 59–74; and National Center on Educational Restructuring and Inclusion (NCERI), *National Study of Inclusive Education*, 2nd edn (New York: CUNY, 1995), 14, 20.

73 National Center on Educational Restructuring and Inclusion (NCERI), *National Study of Inclusive Education*, 2; June E. Downing and Joanne Eichinger, "Educating Students with Diverse Strengths and Needs Together," in *Including Students with Severe and Multiple Disabilities in Typical Classrooms: Practical Strategies for Teachers*, June E. Downing, ed. (Baltimore, MD: P.H. Brookes Publishing, 2002), 11; and Pam Hunt and Lori Goetz, "Research on Inclusive Educational Programs, Practices, and Outcomes with Students with Severe Disabilities," *Journal of Special Education*, vol. 31, no. 1 (Spring 1997): 26.

74 Smith et al., *Teaching Students with Special Needs in Inclusive*, 29.

75 Chris Forlin et al., "Demographic Differences in Changing Pre-service Teachers' Attitudes, Sentiments and Concerns About Inclusive Education," *International Journal of Inclusive Education*, vol. 13, no. 2 (March 2009): 195–209.

76 Michael W. Harvey et al., "Pre-service Teacher Preparation for Inclusion: An Exploration of Higher Education Teacher-Training Institutions," *Remedial and Special Education*, vol. 31, no. 1 (January/February 2010): 24–33; Mary T. Brownell et al., "Critical Features of Special Education Teacher Preparation: A Comparison with General Teacher Education," *The Journal of Special Education*, vol. 38, no. 4 (February 2005): 242–52; Nancy Burstein et al., "Moving Toward Inclusive Practices," *Remedial and Special Education*, vol. 25, no. 2 (March/April 2004): 104–16.

77 Harvey et al., "Pre-service Teacher Preparation for Inclusion," 28–31.

78 Woo-Sik Jung, "Pre-service Teacher Training for Successful Inclusion," *Education*, vol. 128, no. 1 (Fall 2007): 106–13.

79 Thea Renda Abu El-Haj and Beth C. Rubin, "Realizing the Equity-Minded Aspirations of Detracking and Inclusion: Toward a Capacity-Oriented Framework for Teacher Education," *Curriculum Inquiry*, vol. 39, no. 3 (June 2009): 435–63.

80 Ibid., 453–4.

81 Ibid., 454–6.

82 Ibid., 456–8.

83 Dettmer et al., *Consultation, Collaboration, and Teamwork for Students with Special Needs,* 41; Hunt and Goetz, "Research on Inclusive Educational Programs, Practices, and Outcomes with Students with Severe Disabilities," 25–6; Jeanette Klingner and Sharon Vaughn, "Students' Perceptions of Instruction in Inclusion Classrooms: Implications for Students with Learning Disabilities," *Exceptional Children*, vol. 66, no. 1 (Fall 1999): 23; Dorothy K. Lipsky and Alan Gartner, *Inclusion and School Reform* (Baltimore, MD: Paul H. Brookes Publishing, 1997), 197; and Margaret Tomasik, "Effective Inclusion Activities for High School Students with Multiple Disabilities," *Journal of Visual Impairment & Blindness*, vol. 101, no. 10 (October 2007): 657–9.

84 Annemarie S. Palinscar et al., "Investigating the Engagement and Learning of Students with Learning Disabilities in Guided Inquiry Science Teaching," *Language, Speech, and Hearing Services in Schools*, vol. 31, no. 3 (July 2000): 240–51.

Index

Note: Page numbers in *Italics* refer to figures and tables.